Hospitality Human Resources Management and Supervision

Second Edition

PEARSON

Boston   Columbus   Indianapolis   New York   San Francisco   Upper Saddle River
Amsterdam   Cape Town   Dubai   London   Madrid   Milan   Munich   Paris   Montréal   Toronto
Delhi   Mexico City   São Paulo   Sydney   Hong Kong   Seoul   Singapore   Taipei   Tokyo

Pearson

Editorial Director: Vernon R. Anthony
Executive Acquisitions Editor: Alli Gentile
NRA Product Development: Randall Towns and
 Todd Schlender
Senior Managing Editor: JoEllen Gohr
Associate Managing Editor: Alexandrina B. Wolf
Senior Operations Supervisor: Pat Tonneman
Senior Operations Specialist: Deidra Skahill
Cover photo: Hemera/Thinkstock

Cover design: Karen Steinberg, Element LLC
Director of Marketing: David Gesell
Marketing Coordinator: Les Roberts
Full-Service Project Management: Barbara Hawk and
 Kevin J. Gray, Element LLC
Text and Cover Printer/Binder: LSC Communications
Text Font: Minion Pro, Myriad Pro Semicondensed

Photography Credits

Front matter: iHemera/Thinkstock; vii (left) Suhendri Utet/Dreamstime; (right) Meryll/Dreamstime; viii (top) Mtr/Dreamstime; (bottom) Stratum/Dreamstime; ix (bottom left) Aprescindere/Dreamstime; xv (bottom left) Petar Neychev/Dreamstime; 63, 97, 167, 233, 297, 329 Nikada/iStockPhoto

All other photographs owned or acquired by the National Restaurant Association Educational Foundation, NRAEF.

The information presented in this book is provided for informational purposes only and is not intended to provide legal advice or establish standards of reasonable behavior. Individuals who develop operational procedures are urged to obtain the advice and guidance of legal counsel. Although National Restaurant Association Solutions, LLC (NRA Solutions) endeavors to include accurate and current information compiled from sources believed to be reliable, NRA Solutions and its licensor, the National Restaurant Association Educational Foundation (NRAEF), distributors, and agents make no representations or warranties as to the accuracy, currency, or completeness of the information. No responsibility is assumed or implied by the NRAEF, NRA Solutions, distributors, or agents for any damage or loss resulting from inaccuracies or omissions or any actions taken or not taken based on the content of the publication.

Many of the designations by manufacturers and sellers to distinguish their products are claimed as trademarks. Where those designations appear in this book, and the publisher was aware of a trademark claim, the designations have been printed in initial caps or all caps.

6   17

ISBN-10:   0-13-217525-8
ISBN-13: 978-0-13-217525-8

ISBN-10:   0-13-272449-9
ISBN-13: 978-0-13-272449-4

Contents in Brief

Contents

About the National Restaurant Association and the National Restaurant Association Educational Foundation

Founded in 1919, the National Restaurant Association (NRA) is the leading business association for the restaurant and foodservice industry, which comprises 960,000 restaurant and foodservice outlets and a workforce of nearly 13 million employees. We represent the industry in Washington, DC, and advocate on its behalf. We operate the industry's largest trade show (NRA Show, restaurant.org/show); leading food safety training and certification program (ServSafe, servsafe.com); unique career-building high school program (the NRAEF's *ProStart*, prostart.restaurant.org); as well as the *Kids LiveWell* program (restaurant.org/kidslivewell) promoting healthful kids' menu options. For more information, visit www.restaurant.org and find us on Twitter *@WeRRestaurants*, *Facebook*, and *YouTube*.

With the first job experience of one in four U.S. adults occurring in a restaurant or foodservice operation, the industry is uniquely attractive among American industries for entry-level jobs, personal development and growth, employee and manager career paths, and ownership and wealth creation. That is why the National Restaurant Association Educational Foundation (nraef.org), the philanthropic foundation of the NRA, furthers the education of tomorrow's restaurant and foodservice industry professionals and plays a key role in promoting job and career opportunities in the industry by allocating millions of dollars a year toward industry scholarships and educational programs. The NRA works to ensure the most qualified and passionate people enter the industry so that we can better meet the needs of our members and the patrons and clients they serve.

What Is the ManageFirst Program?

The ManageFirst Program is a management training certificate program that exemplifies our commitment to developing materials by the industry, for the industry. The program's

EXAM TOPICS

ManageFirst Core Credential Topics

Hospitality and Restaurant Management
Controlling Foodservice Costs
Hospitality Human Resources Management and Supervision
ServSafe® Food Safety

ManageFirst Foundation Topics

Customer Service
Principles of Food and Beverage Management
Purchasing
Hospitality Accounting
Bar and Beverage Management
Nutrition
Hospitality and Restaurant Marketing
ServSafe Alcohol® Responsible Alcohol Service

most powerful strength is that it is based on a set of competencies defined by the restaurant and foodservice industry as critical for success. The program teaches the skills truly valued by industry professionals.

ManageFirst Program Components

The ManageFirst Program includes a set of books, exams, instructor resources, certificates, a new credential, and support activities and services. By participating in the program, you are demonstrating your commitment to becoming a highly qualified professional either preparing to begin or to advance your career in the restaurant, hospitality, and foodservice industry.

These books cover the range of topics listed in the chart above. You will find the essential content for the topic as defined by industry, as well as learning activities, assessments, case studies, suggested field projects, professional profiles, and testimonials. The exam can be administered either online or in a paper-and-pencil format (see inside front cover for a listing of ISBNs), and it will be proctored. Upon successfully passing the exam, you will be furnished with a customized certificate by the National Restaurant Association. The certificate is a lasting recognition of your accomplishment and a signal to the industry that you have mastered the competencies covered within the particular topic.

To earn this credential, you will be required to pass four core exams and one foundation exam (to be chosen from the remaining program topics) and to document your work experience in the restaurant and foodservice industry. Earning the ManageFirst credential is a significant accomplishment.

We applaud you as you either begin or advance your career in the restaurant, hospitality, and foodservice industry. Visit www.nraef.org to learn about additional career-building resources offered by the NRAEF, including scholarships for college students enrolled in relevant industry programs.

MANAGEFIRST PROGRAM ORDERING INFORMATION

Review copies or support materials

FACULTY FIELD SERVICES
Tel: 800.526.0485

Domestic orders and inquiries

PEARSON CUSTOMER SERVICE
Tel: 800.922.0579
http://www.pearsonhighered.com/

International orders and inquiries

U.S. EXPORT SALES OFFICE
Pearson Education International Customer Service Group
200 Old Tappan Road
Old Tappan, NJ 07675 USA
Tel: 201.767.5021
Fax: 201.767.5625

For corporate, government, and special sales (consultants, corporations, training centers, VARs, and corporate resellers) orders and inquiries

PEARSON CORPORATE SALES
Tel: 317.428.3411
Fax: 317.428.3343
Email: managefirst@prenhall.com

For additional information regarding other Pearson publications, instructor and student support materials, locating your sales representative, and much more, please visit www.pearsonhighered.com/managefirst.

Acknowledgements

The National Restaurant Association is grateful for the significant contributions made to this book by the following individuals.

Mike Amos
Perkins & Marie Callender's Inc.

Steve Belt
Monical's Pizza

Heather Kane Haberer
Carrols Restaurant Group

Erika Hoover
Monical's Pizza Corp.

Jared Kulka
Red Robin Gourmet Burgers

Tony C. Merritt
Carrols Restaurant Group

H. George Neil
Buffalo Wild Wings

Marci Noguiera
Sodexo—Education Division

Ryan Nowicki
Dave & Busters

Penny Ann Lord Prichard
Wake Tech/NC Community College

Michael Santos
Micatrotto Restaurant Group

Heather Thitoff
Cameron Mitchell Restaurants

Features of the ManageFirst books

We have designed the ManageFirst books to enhance your ability to learn and retain important information that is critical to this restaurant and foodservice industry function. Here are the key features you will find within this book.

BEGINNING EACH BOOK

Real Manager

This is your opportunity to meet a professional who is currently working in the field associated with the book's topic. This person's story will help you gain insight into the responsibilities related to his or her position, as well as the training and educational history linked to it. You will also see the daily and cumulative impact this position has on an operation, and receive advice from a person who has successfully met the challenges of being a manager.

BEGINNING EACH CHAPTER

Inside This Chapter

Chapter content is organized under these major headings.

Learning Objectives

Learning objectives identify what you should be able to do after completing each chapter. These objectives are linked to the required tasks a manager must be able to perform in relation to the function discussed in the book.

Case Study

Each chapter begins with a brief story about the kind of situations that a manager may encounter in the course of his or her work. The story is followed by one or two questions to prompt student discussions about the topics contained within the chapter.

Key Terms

These terms are important for thorough understanding of the chapter's content. They are highlighted throughout the chapter, where they are explicitly defined or their meaning is made clear within the paragraphs in which they appear.

THROUGHOUT EACH CHAPTER

Exhibits

Exhibits are placed throughout each chapter to visually reinforce the key concepts presented in the text. Types of exhibits include charts, tables, photographs, and illustrations.

Think About It …

These thought-provoking sidebars reveal supportive information about the section they appear beside.

AT THE END OF EACH CHAPTER

Application Exercises and Review Your Learning

These multiple-choice or open- or close-ended questions or problems are designed to test your knowledge of the concepts presented in the chapter. These questions have been aligned with the objectives and should provide you with an opportunity to practice or apply the content that supports these objectives. If you have difficulty answering the Review Your Learning questions, you should review the content further.

AT THE END OF THE BOOK

Field Project

This real-world project gives you the valuable opportunity to apply many of the concepts you will learn in a competency guide. You will interact with industry practitioners, enhance your knowledge, and research, apply, analyze, evaluate, and report on your findings. It will provide you with an in-depth "reality check" of the policies and practices of this management function.

Amy O'Neil

Chief Operating Officer

Phase*Next* Hospitality

REAL MANAGER

Philosophy: **What keeps me going is the people around me—both personally and professionally—and the desire to make a difference. There are so many great things about our industry—we have exceptional talent, our industry has depth as well as breadth. Getting to be a part of that in big and small ways makes me happy. One should never be bored working in our industry—there is so much to learn, to do, and simply enjoy. I'm proud to say that I'm part of the restaurant and foodservice industry.**

MY BACKGROUND

I was born and raised in Milwaukee, Wisconsin. I attended the University of Wisconsin–Madison, receiving my BA in 1993 with a double major in classics and ancient history. My father worked as an antitrust attorney and my mother was responsible for the administration of the Sunday school program at our church for 25 years. I'm the youngest of five children and have an identical twin. My twin sister, Sarah, is five minutes older than I am and lives in Chicago. It is uncanny how much alike we look.

Truly, my very first job was in the restaurant and foodservice business—working in a popcorn wagon during the summer at Milwaukee's Summerfest. That was the start of my engagement in the industry. (By the way, I'm still an expert popcorn maker today!) My first experience as a manager in our industry was at Caribou Coffee, when I became a store manager in 1994. Perhaps the *most* important lesson I learned there was about the dynamics of being promoted from among my peers and having to supervise colleagues who were previously at my same level. This situation occurs quite frequently in the restaurant and foodservice industry. New managers are often unprepared for these types of scenarios, and I've always talked about this experience with the people I've promoted internally.

MY CAREER PATH

In 2001, I made a 100 percent commitment to devote my career to the restaurant and foodservice business. It sounds funny today because I had already been in the industry for about eight years after graduating from college. But it was in 2001 that I really stopped "looking around." Prior to that, I continued to consider moving into different industries, second-guessing if I "really wanted to do this for the rest of my life."

I was passionate about the industry from the beginning. I enjoyed working with the public; it helped me get past being a bit shy. I especially enjoyed two aspects: (1) developing a team of people for restaurant openings, and (2) seeing that I could have an impact on people's career aspirations and job satisfaction. Having played sports when I was younger, it was an easy transition to view a profit & loss statement as my own scoreboard and measure my performance with it.

Something I always think about: **In my career, as critical as performance is, I've also learned the importance of patience. It takes time for a good culture and solid operations to take hold. Impatience can have its own consequences. I was taught to try and be "patient with people, while being impatient for results."**

When I first started at Caribou Coffee in 1993, I was approached about going into management. I was very conflicted because that was not how I saw my career developing. At the time, I was 23 years old and had plans to go to graduate school. So this was all about recalibrating my perceptions—both about myself and about the industry. I finally decided to pursue management. Since then I've mostly been in line management/operating roles. At Caribou Coffee, I was a store manager, district manager, director of operations, vice president of operations, and senior vice president of operations. I'm now co-founder and chief operating officer of Phase*Next* Hospitality.

As an operator, I think the human resources partners I have worked with know that I highly value the HR function, and believe that it is a strong part of the value equation for business. Specifically, I became passionate about working in partnership with human resources when I had to terminate a manager for the first time. I felt terrible about it—really. He was such a nice guy, and he had been part of helping the company grow. I was very respectful of the contributions he had made, but I also realized that he just didn't have the skill set for the position. I believe employers should handle people—even during termination, regardless of why they are being terminated—with respect, professionalism, and class. How you hire people and how you handle departures says a lot about both your organization and the leader you are.

Remember: **It's important to "own" and value your people and their inherent diversity—employees, customers, coworkers. Value the unique contributions of each person.**

Most of us wake up every day willing to go to work, wanting today to be a good day. We cannot know the internal unspoken struggles each of us face, but we *can* have an impact on the environment we create. Set the temperature around you—create an upbeat, positive environment that people want to be a part of and involve them in the creation of that culture. Very adept leaders can help people bring their best to the workplace. They create an environment that people *want* to be a part of, one in which people can thrive.

WHAT DOES THE FUTURE HOLD?

I believe the human resources function is undervalued in most organizations. After all, our greatest value is our people. Human resources is more than just the "policy department." Human resources, at its best, is the partner in the business that supports all other functions by staying focused on people as the most valuable business asset. I see this function as increasingly gaining in importance and value now and in the future.

MY ADVICE TO YOU

My advice to you is to always be a student, always keep learning. I always had an "annual commitment" process when I was at Caribou. Every year I would ask myself two questions: First, am I learning new things, growing my knowledge and experience base? Second, can I see the road ahead even if the outline of it is vague? If the answer to both questions was yes, then I stayed for another year. In 2008, when I came to the conclusion that a future assignment wasn't going to help me expand my knowledge, I decided to leave. It was hard to say goodbye, but I knew I couldn't stay because I needed to be learning new things to be happy professionally.

So what have I learned lately? Two things that are interrelated. First, it's good to have a dream and to talk about it. I'm always amazed at the number of people who want to help others realize their dreams and aspirations. I think the universe really does often conspire in our favor.

When I was a kid, I always wanted to be a restaurateur; I used to have fantasies about owning my own restaurant but I never talked about it. I loved it when my grandparents would take us to this fine-dining restaurant in Milwaukee called the Boulevard Inn. To me, it evoked the same ethos and elegance as Cary Grant or Grace Kelly. It's funny because for a long while I was part of the coffee/foodservice segment—actually, from the time I got out of college until I was almost 40 years old. Eventually, I found my way back to my childhood aspiration. The point is that dreaming about future goals is the first step in making them real.

The related point that I've relearned is that the things that "got you here, will not necessarily get you there." That is to say that as a person grows in a career, areas that the person typically has relied on as strengths and key to his or her current success don't always ensure the person's future success. I do believe that self-knowledge is critical and that understanding what you are really, really good at is key. As a co-owner and franchisee, over the last few years I've found myself having to work in areas that are not necessarily my strengths. We have to be excited, though, by the new challenges and learning that come with additional responsibilities and change; our success often is directionally aligned with our ability to be flexible and learn new things.

1

Restaurant and Foodservice Operations Are Labor-Intensive

INSIDE THIS CHAPTER

- Management of Human Resources Is Important
- Managers Facilitate Their Employees' Work
- Diversity in Restaurant and Foodservice Operations
- Ethical Concerns

CHAPTER LEARNING OBJECTIVES

After completing this chapter, you should be able to:

- Explain management activities and how evolving employee expectations can influence managers as they facilitate the work of their employees.

- Describe strategies for facilitating the work of employees.

- Explain how skills, abilities, leadership style, and corporate culture impact a manager's human resources activities.

- Identify the benefits of and procedures for promoting employee diversity within restaurant and foodservice operations.

- Explain the importance of ethical decision making; the role of codes of ethics in restaurant and foodservice operations; and tasks involved in developing, implementing, and enforcing codes of ethics.

KEY TERMS

CASE STUDY

"You've got to do something, Jeremy," said Zelly, the area manager for Nick and Nan's Restaurants.

"Well, I suppose I do," replied Jeremy, the general manager at one of the units.

"However," Jeremy continued, "when I talked to the kitchen manager about his high employee turnover rate compared to other departments, he was quick to point out that the kitchen is a hot, humid, noisy, and extremely busy place to work. He says more kitchen employees leave because of the working conditions. He thinks that more employees and an air-conditioning system will reduce his turnover."

"The kitchen employee turnover rates are much higher than those of other departments in our other restaurants. I think the problem is the manager," Zelly replied.

1. What do you think about the kitchen manager's analysis of the situation?

2. What are some points Jeremy should make in his next meeting with the kitchen manager?

MANAGEMENT OF HUMAN RESOURCES IS IMPORTANT

Restaurant and foodservice managers must successfully complete several important activities, and they are evaluated on their ability to do so. Restaurant and foodservice operations are labor-intensive; technology and equipment have not eliminated the need for employees to produce and deliver products and services to customers. Managers must spend a significant amount of their time planning and facilitating the work of their employees.

Managers Must Manage

While managers must be concerned about supervision of staff, other activities are also important. *Exhibit 1.1* reviews tasks that indicate the management context within which supervisory activities occur. In addition, there are employee-related aspects to all of the basic management activities.

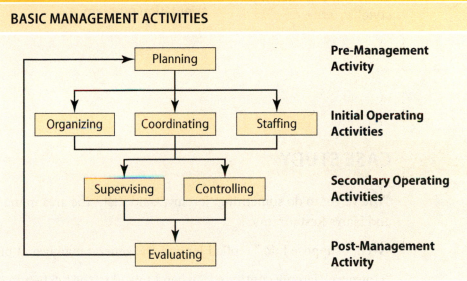

Exhibit 1.1

BASIC MANAGEMENT ACTIVITIES

Each of the basic management activities noted in *Exhibit 1.1* involves distinct tasks:

- Planning involves defining goals, establishing strategies to achieve them, and designing ways to get work done. Managers develop strategic plans to help their organization remain competitive and profitable. They also interact with their employees to plan professional development goals and to develop policies and procedures that guide employees' work.

- Organizing involves determining how and by whom work tasks will be done. Managers have formal **authority**, the power to direct the work of employees. They develop organizational charts that show how authority and communication flow down, up, and across the operation.

Manager's Memo

When managers undertake coordinating activities, they should remember that responsibility cannot be delegated. Responsibility is the obligation to do the work and achieve the goals and objectives associated with a specific position.

For example, if a manager delegates a task to an employee, the power to perform the work must also be given to that staff member. However, if the work is not done correctly, the manager cannot blame the failure on the employee. First, the manager should have been confident that the employee could complete the assignment and had the time, tools, and other resources required. The manager should also have checked with the employee as the work was being done to ensure that no corrective actions were needed to remain on schedule.

Coordinating involves arranging group efforts in an orderly manner. Managers coordinate when they analyze the **span of control**, which considers how many employees can be supervised by one person.

Exhibit 1.2

- **Staffing** is finding the right people for the job. It involves recruiting applicants, selecting employees, making job offers, and helping new staff members feel comfortable in their positions. Staffing activities are more successful when managers use current **job descriptions** that indicate the tasks a person in a position must be able to perform. **Job specifications** are also helpful. They tell the personal requirements necessary for someone to successfully complete the tasks of a position.

- **Supervising**, also referred to as directing, involves planning for and facilitating the work of employees (*Exhibit 1.2*). A good manager involves employees when making plans that will impact them, and uses different leadership styles based on the individual worker.

- **Controlling** involves keeping the establishment on track to achieve goals. It requires a significant amount of planning to set performance standards and determine whether they are attained. The best managers help employees establish goals, determine if they were attained, and provide assistance when necessary.

- **Evaluating** assesses the extent to which plans are attained, and can identify issues or problems. Therefore, the management process is cyclical. Evaluation will likely lead to issues to be addressed by additional planning. Managers evaluate employees and their work output. In the process, they make new plans based on observed results.

Managers Must Supervise

Since restaurant and foodservice operations are labor-intensive, the most important assets are the employees rather than the facility, equipment, or other items entered on a balance sheet. A balance sheet is the accounting tool that summarizes what an establishment owns, owes, and is worth. Without dedicated employees who know their jobs, no operation could survive, let alone grow, expand, and be profitable.

Consequently, managers typically spend more time on staff-related issues than on any other activity. They must have significant knowledge and skills to recruit, train, supervise, and develop employees.

Manager's Memo

It would be convenient to do one management activity at a time. Ideally, a manager could spend time planning (for example, developing a budget). Then, the manager might spend time organizing procedures and coordinating work between departments. The ideal workday could continue with specific times set aside for supervisory duties, activities for controlling labor costs, and evaluating progress toward plans that have been made.

In fact, the manager's work is much more complicated. In the real world, the manager must do many things at the same time. For example, he or she might be planning how to best use organizational resources, but be interrupted to supervise work. Then the manager might begin thinking about how to coordinate activities between departments when inventory control issues arise. An interview, a performance review, and a strategic planning meeting could occur in quick succession. Managers must attend to tasks as they present themselves.

Exhibit 1.3

THE EMPLOYMENT CYCLE

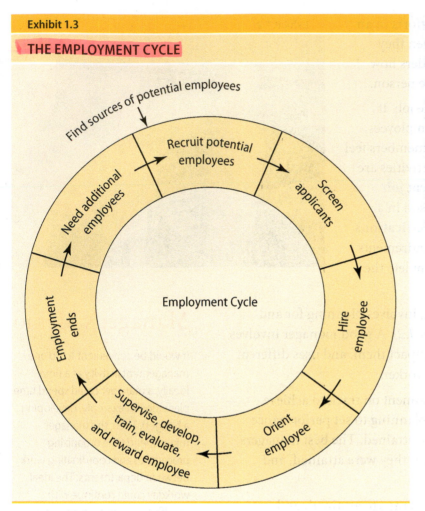

Managers must address challenges in a continuous cycle of employee-related responsibilities. The employment cycle is a series of repeating activities that managers and human resources professionals perform to ensure their operation is fully staffed and their employees are as productive as possible. This cycle incorporates activities that occur before, during, and after a person works for an operation. *Exhibit 1.3* highlights each step of the employment cycle.

- **Finding sources of potential employees:** Managers must develop a system for identifying groups of persons who might be interested in working at the operation. These persons can help spread the establishment's employment message, so it is important to maintain ongoing relationships with them. Educational institutions with hospitality-related programs are an obvious source of employees, as are the job fairs available in many communities.

- **Recruiting potential employees:** Once sources of potential employees have been identified, managers can promote their establishment's vacancies.

- **Screening applicants:** After applicants have been recruited, their knowledge, skills, and abilities must be evaluated to assess their fit for the job and the operation. It is important to develop and use practices for identifying the best applicants as well as ensuring equal opportunity for all candidates who will be considered.

- **Hiring employees:** After the best candidate has been identified, a job offer that specifies the terms of employment should be made. If the offer is accepted, many procedures must be followed to ensure that the new employee can legally work for the establishment, and that he or she receives the wages and benefits promised.

- **Orienting employees:** New employees typically require much information and assistance to learn their job and become comfortable at work. An **orientation program** is a formal plan for welcoming new employees and teaching them general information that all staff members must know. Orientation programs typically include procedures for processing hiring documents, such as tax and benefit enrollment forms.

- **Supervising employees:** Employee supervision is an ongoing activity to ensure that employees are productive, motivated, and supported in their work. Then the operation can run smoothly and customers will have the best possible experience. Supervisory responsibilities include training and developing employees as well as activities related to motivation, appraisal, discipline, and managing change.

- **Managing employee terminations:** When an employee leaves the operation, an exit interview should be conducted to learn the employee's views about the job even if the termination was not the employee's choice. Collecting and analyzing information from exit interviews may help continuously improve the operation and retain employees.

These topics will be covered in detail in later chapters.

Changing Employee Expectations

Persons of all ages enjoy stimulating careers in the restaurant and foodservice industry. Employees differ from each other because of their life experiences, which are impacted by when they grew up and entered the workforce. Managers know that these differences should be considered in managing staff. *Exhibit 1.4* provides an overview of the generations in today's workforce.

Exhibit 1.4

GENERATIONS IN TODAY'S WORKFORCE

Generation	Dates of Birth	Age of Members (2012)	
		Oldest	Youngest
Baby Boomers	1946–1964	66	48
Generation X	1965–1978	47	34
Millennials	1979–1994	33	18

Note: *Birth years vary slightly in the literature. An earlier generation, Traditionalists, born between 1922 and 1945, is omitted from this discussion because the youngest members are now at retirement age. Millennial is also called "Echo Boomer" and "Generation Y." Some writers are now beginning to discuss "Generation 5," 16- to 18-year-old employees.*

Exhibit 1.4 provides useful information for managers. Baby Boomers and many Generation X employees occupy a large number of senior management positions in restaurant and foodservice organizations. Younger Generation X employees and some older Millennial staff members are now advancing to middle-management positions, and other Millennial employees are now assuming early management positions.

Manager's Memo

The employee-related responsibilities just discussed include important behind-the-scenes activities. For example, policies must be in place so that all employees are consistently treated the same way. Salary, wage, and benefits programs must be established within the boundaries of numerous legal regulations.

Managers must understand and implement the various legislative, executive, regulatory, and judicial requirements concerning fair employment practices and other employee-related issues. While these requirements can be complicated, they benefit the operation and its employees, and someone within the establishment must be knowledgeable about them.

Managers must develop compensation and performance appraisal systems, as well as general training programs related to safety and customer service for employees in all departments. These efforts serve as additional examples of support activities that managers perform as they plan and meet their daily operating goals.

Exhibit 1.5

Managers can make mistakes when they generalize about persons based on nationality, ethnicity, and other factors. When considering age, managers should be cautious not to suggest sweeping generalizations that apply to all persons of a given age group, especially those 40 and over who are afforded unique legal protections. However, there may be advantages to managers changing, when possible, the ways they interact with employees of different ages to recognize factors that are important to them (*Exhibit 1.5*). It is also important to note that some states may have laws that protect younger workers.

Is adjusting one's leadership style based on employee age a good idea? This might be easy to do when all or most employees belong to the same workforce generation, and this might be the case in many operations. However, it is more difficult to implement when there are many employees of differing ages.

Employees may have different perceptions about work, its meaning, and their interest in it based on their age and other factors. Supervisory training sessions can address these topics, and managers can analyze whether generational differences may be a cause of problems that are occurring. For example, if there is high turnover in a department with mostly young persons that is supervised by an older employee, this may be a factor. **Turnover** is the replacement of employees when other employees leave.

Managers gain several benefits from learning about the workforce generations and their differences:

- Labor-intensive industries will continue to need employees, regardless of their age, to staff the many positions.
- The range of differences between generations can be wide.
- Differing values, experiences, lifestyles, and attitudes toward the future and life in general can create significant misunderstandings and frustrations.
- Those who better understand and appreciate each generation may gain ideas about how to effectively facilitate the work of different-aged staff members.

It is difficult for some managers to interact with different generations. Doing so can challenge their own beliefs and values, force them to think about change and conflict, and require them to modify their communication skills.

Manager's Memo

There are many different opinions about how people should be supervised. Some say everyone should be treated the same. Others say it is important to at least consider generational differences.

While different generations may appreciate different leadership strategies, there are also some best practices that typically work well with all staff members in any organization at any time:

- Explain that what employees do really matters.
- Tell employees the truth.
- Explain to staff members why they are being asked to do something.
- Learn the employee's language.
- Provide rewarding opportunities.
- Praise staff members in public.
- Make the workplace fun.
- Model the desired behavior.

MANAGERS FACILITATE THEIR EMPLOYEES' WORK

The term *facilitate* means to make something easier. Managers facilitate their employees' work when they help them get ready to do it and when they address challenges as the work is done. In order to facilitate, managers require the necessary skills. In addition, the establishment's culture must support employees and encourage different leadership approaches.

Leadership Behaviors

The best managers do not spend their time "bossing around" their employees. Instead, they are leaders who recognize and appreciate the work of their staff members. These managers see their role as one that involves selecting and preparing the best employees for the tasks to be done. They also recognize the importance of providing information, necessary tools and equipment, and the necessary time for employees to do their work so they can meet required quality and quantity standards. When these tasks have been done, managers can allow employees to do what they are capable of doing, while always being available to provide direction and answer questions.

These leadership factors can motivate employees to do their best:

- **Provide direction:** Leaders communicate clearly and ensure that their employees know what is expected. One way to do this is to discuss roles and responsibilities with employees. Managers should confirm that broad assignments, such as "help other employees help the customers," are understood.

- **Lead consistently:** It is important to maintain the operation's standards, and managers do this by holding themselves and others accountable for their actions. Effective managers treat all employees the same; there are no favorites.

Exhibit 1.6

- **Influence others:** Gaining cooperation through caring acts, using persuasion to convince employees of appropriate behavior, and offering constructive feedback are excellent ways to influence others (*Exhibit 1.6*). The best managers also build consensus using a give-and-take approach, and they encourage superior performance by relating their employees' actions to the organization's **vision**. A vision is an idea about what the organization would be like if it were ideal.

- **Foster teamwork:** Effective managers create functional work teams that build members' skills. They also establish cross-functional teams to monitor, standardize, and improve work processes across an organization. Assigning problems to specially selected groups of employees is one way to begin developing these teams.

- **Motivate others:** The importance of communication cannot be overstated. Leaders give pep talks, ask their employees for advice, and praise their work. They also keep employees informed and provide them with a sense of belonging by allowing them to solve problems and contribute ideas.

- **Coach and develop employees:** Leaders use coaching strategies to inform employees about better ways to perform a task. Coaching is the process of using positive reinforcement such as praise to encourage proper work practices, and guidance to correct problems if a task is being performed improperly. Managers also offer insights to high-potential workers and ensure that all employees have a development plan in which they are actively engaged.

- **Champion change:** Anticipating the need for change, supporting it, and looking for better ways to do things are strategies that managers can use in the ever-changing restaurant and foodservice industry. Managers should also understand the link between change and learning, and discuss the benefits of new processes and procedures to help facilitate the work of their employees.

Supervision Skills and Abilities

In addition to the behaviors discussed in the last section, successful managers have typically developed several important skills and abilities. *Exhibit 1.7* identifies some of them.

Exhibit 1.7

ESSENTIAL LEADERSHIP SKILLS AND ABILITIES FOR MANAGERS

Interpersonal Skills	Employee Development
• Listens well. • Respects others. • Supports own company values. • Has a sense of self-worth, responsibility, and accountability. • Values trust and human dignity. • Encourages employees to adopt the company's vision. • Keeps calm in a crisis.	• Takes responsibility for developing future leaders. • Enables employees to realize their full potential. • Teaches and mentors employees who desire this assistance. • Removes obstacles that prevent employees from doing their jobs. • Encourages taking risks. • Makes a meaningful difference in employees' lives.

Managers should have the knowledge and skills to do some, if not all, of the technical aspects of the work done by those they supervise. They must also be confident in their abilities and be concerned about those they supervise. Effective managers provide information to employees to help them participate in decision making, and they help employees develop an attitude of responsibility for their work.

The best managers also exhibit several other traits that set them apart:

- **They can manage within financial constraints.** Financial concerns and cost minimization efforts are of heightened importance today. Managers must be able to develop, control, and evaluate budgets with increasing financial limitations. They must be comfortable with their financial management responsibilities, know the financial basics, and recognize that their establishment cannot be successful unless budget goals are consistently attained. Labor costs are the largest or second-largest category of expenses (after food) in almost every operation, and employee-related decisions frequently have important financial impacts.

- **They can implement quality management processes.** The term **quality** relates to a philosophy that drives almost everything done by the best operations. It is the consistent production and delivery of products and services according to expected standards. Quality intersects customer satisfaction, costs, employee-related concerns, and even the meaning of hospitality professionalism. The extent to which quality work processes are developed and quality results are measured is a very important factor in the facilitation of employee work efforts.

- **They can view problems as opportunities.** Once problems are discovered, understanding them is often relatively easy. For example, budget numbers alert leaders with financial knowledge to problems, and employees are often quick to alert supervisors to problems. Other problems, such as what is causing high food costs, are more difficult to define. Historically, managers were problem solvers. In addition to routine decision making, they fixed problems and then moved on to others. Problems were often identified very narrowly and were resolved that way. Today, problems are viewed as challenges and opportunities to move closer toward ideal quality goals. Leaders recognize that numerous procedures make up processes that comprise systems, such as those for cost control. Therefore, decision making must address big picture issues that may extend beyond a specific defect.

Factors That Impact Human Resources Activities

Two very important factors impact how managers perform many of their human resources duties. These factors are leadership styles and corporate culture.

RESTAURANT TECHNOLOGY

There are many ways that managers can use technology for finding potential employees and to plan and supervise the work of employees. For example, technology can assist with recruitment, such as when social media sites are used to promote job openings. Computerized selection tests can be used to provide information about job applicants, and computer-based training programs are available. Also, employee scheduling can be computerized, with the resulting schedules provided to employees over the Web.

Payroll calculations and human resources records are increasingly handled electronically. Webcasts are used for meetings attended by persons at different locations. As these systems become more common, managers will be able to use the time historically spent for office work to interact with employees and customers.

LEADERSHIP STYLES

Managers must use the appropriate skills as they help their employees work. They must combine their own knowledge, skills, attitudes, and abilities with those of their employees to accomplish assignments. They know that leadership is an art that involves common sense and the ability to interact with their staff. At the same time, it is a discipline that applies proven management principles and procedures.

Supervisors can use four basic styles of leadership. These styles are identified in *Exhibit 1.8*.

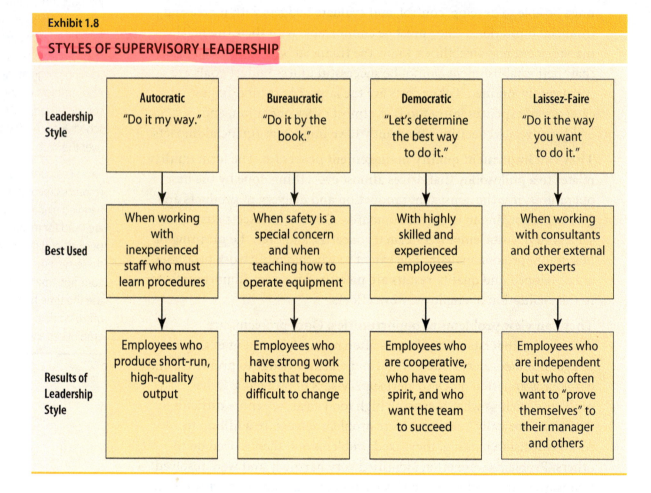

Exhibit 1.8

STYLES OF SUPERVISORY LEADERSHIP

	Autocratic	Bureaucratic	Democratic	Laissez-Faire
Leadership Style	"Do it my way."	"Do it by the book."	"Let's determine the best way to do it."	"Do it the way you want to do it."
Best Used	When working with inexperienced staff who must learn procedures	When safety is a special concern and when teaching how to operate equipment	With highly skilled and experienced employees	When working with consultants and other external experts
Results of Leadership Style	Employees who produce short-run, high-quality output	Employees who have strong work habits that become difficult to change	Employees who are cooperative, who have team spirit, and who want the team to succeed	Employees who are independent but who often want to "prove themselves" to their manager and others

The leadership styles shown in *Exhibit 1.8* are appropriate for different situations:

- The **autocratic** leadership style is generally the best approach for managing inexperienced employees who must learn proper procedures. It may also be useful when there is an emergency or little time to perform a task, such as when a large group of diners arrives earlier than expected. When this style is used, the manager generally makes decisions and resolves problems without input from employees. An autocratic leadership approach can yield employees who produce short-run, high-quality output. However, it is not likely to yield team players, and it can cause resentment between the manager and employees.

- A **bureaucratic** leadership style relies on rules, regulations, policies, and procedures. It may be effective when new equipment or procedures are being implemented and when there are safety concerns. However, the style does not help motivate employees, and it can create strong employee resistance when future changes are required.

- The **democratic** leadership style is most effective when used with highly skilled and experienced employees. It is a leadership approach that encourages employees to participate in the decision-making process. The appropriate use of this style leads to cooperation and group spirit because the manager is focused on staff members while the work is being done.

- The **laissez-faire** leadership style removes the manager from the decision-making process. When this style is used, the manager does not direct work but instead delegates most decisions. This leadership style is best used with very highly skilled, experienced, and educated employees or when working with outside experts including consultants.

Ideally, the manager would consider the situation, including the employees involved and the context, and then use a leadership style that is likely to be most helpful. In fact, most managers use one style in all situations with every employee, perhaps without even being aware of it. One reason may be that the style best fits their personality and beliefs about how employees should be managed. They may also be unaware of the advantages to using different styles in different situations.

There are generally two groups of employees in an operation: those who may be interested in a restaurant and foodservice career and those who are not. Effective mangers might use an autocratic leadership style with both groups as new employees learn their job. Then, depending on each staff member's personality and abilities, a democratic or laissez-faire approach might be best for long-term staff members. An autocratic or bureaucratic approach might be best for those less interested in a long-term relationship with the establishment.

CORPORATE CULTURE

The best organizations are thought of as **employers of choice** within their communities. An employer of choice is one that is a desired place of employment because employees are treated with dignity and respect. These operations create a work environment that attracts and retains the highest quality employees. Managers in these establishments emphasize careers rather than jobs, and their supervisory strategies maximize employee retention.

Manager's Memo

Effective entry-level staff members are often promoted to supervisory positions. However, the work done by supervisors is usually different from that performed by entry-level employees. For example, a dish washer may be very good at the physical tasks of the job. But the same employee may not immediately be good at scheduling employees, handling complaints, or doing other tasks that a supervisor must perform.

How does a new supervisor learn to do these management-related activities? It should be obvious that training is required. The manager making the promotion should recognize his or her responsibility to help the new supervisor become successful by providing the necessary training. If this occurs, a good employee can become a good supervisor. If proper training does not occur, the good staff member will become an ineffective supervisor, and the responsibility for problems that arise rests with the manager.

Manager's Memo

Managers in many operations indicate that they have high turnover rates. There are three basic strategies for addressing labor shortages. Managers can increase productivity levels of existing employees. They can also recruit from nontraditional labor markets, such as "empty nesters" seeking employment after their children leave home and older persons seeking employment during traditional retirement years. Finally, managers can increase efforts to retain existing employees.

There are many low- and no-cost ways to encourage employee retention. Many center on treating staff members with dignity and respect. Employers of choice use these strategies, and they can be adopted by all establishments that want to minimize cycles of recruitment to termination.

Organizations cannot become employers of choice until top-level leaders, managers, supervisors, and others become committed to treating staff members with respect. They do so as they recruit the very best applicants, prepare them for success, and provide an environment in which they can find pride and enjoyment in what they do.

Many operations incur employee turnover rates that are higher than ideal. Reasons may include the nature of the labor market, such as the number of organizations in the area who compete for the same employees. Additional reasons include an inability to match the establishment's and the employees' needs, and ineffective employer retention practices. In fact, some employees "leave their manager" rather than their organization when they resign. This occurs when they encounter ongoing negative interpersonal relationships with those who supervise them. It is always best to evaluate employee turnover rates in different departments separately. Significantly higher rates in some departments may suggest supervisory issues rather than other causes.

Employee retention can be a **competitive advantage**, or a strategy, tactic, or process that is not offered by a competitor. This term is often used in marketing to mean a popular product or service that is not available elsewhere at the same quality and price. However, it can also relate to advantages that managers offer to employees that are not available anywhere else.

Traditionally, many employees have thought that most jobs were equal. Therefore, compensation, even if only a few dollars more, was most important. However, employees often have vast networks of families and friends, and they tell their contacts about work experiences. Employees in employer-of-choice establishments talk about their considerate, professional employers. The recruitment task is then made much easier, and employees stay longer, so recruitment tasks are reduced. This occurs because the organization stands out from others competing for the same employees.

Talented staff members are an operation's most important asset. Employee retention practices must be carefully planned to begin when new employees are hired. These concerns should also be factored into the ways things are done within the establishment. As this occurs, a proper emphasis on employees will become ingrained in the organization's **corporate culture**, which is the shared beliefs, experiences, and standards that characterize a company. This strategy is much better than taking action only when a staff member expresses the intent to leave. Retention should be an ongoing priority strategy and not a series of unplanned and often relatively ineffective actions.

Managers should consider how they can develop and maintain an organizational culture that encourages associates to stay. Exit interviews of departing employees might indicate, for example, that many employees leave because of lack of development opportunities, better opportunities elsewhere, or because they are not treated well.

When asked about the most important factors that influence job satisfaction, many staff members at various operations indicate that a lack of challenge and recognition, inadequate work–life flexibility, and limited advancement opportunities encourage them to look elsewhere.

Studies across different industries and organizations typically suggest similar factors that help retain employees. For example, *Exhibit 1.9* shows the results of one recent study that involved 400 human resources executives from 40 different countries.[1]

Exhibit 1.9

IMPORTANT CONCERNS IN EMPLOYEE RETENTION DECISIONS

Factors That Help Retain Employees	Percentage of Respondents
The job routinely provides new or challenging responsibilities.	50%
The company provides clear career growth opportunities.	45
The job offers compensation and benefits equal to or greater than industry or local norms.	42
Company values are aligned with personal values.	38
The company has a track record of transforming itself and continuing its market success.	30
The job provides an ability to balance work and life demands.	28
The company's reputation is one of manager and employee cooperation.	26
The job offers the opportunity to build specific skills.	15
The job allows an employee to work with a specific manager or set of peers.	12
The company offers educational opportunities for employees.	11

Note that in *Exhibit 1.9* almost all of the retention factors relate directly to leadership and supervision and that, compensation is ranked third. Another way to view the information is to consider that, within reason, compensation paid by a competitor is not an overriding factor contributing to employee turnover if staff members think other benefits at their present employer are satisfactory. By

[1]IBM Global Business Services, *Unlocking the DNA of the Adaptable Workforce: The Global Human Capital Study*. 2008.

Manager's Memo

Some managers believe that the level of compensation is the most important factor in determining whether an associate remains with the operation. However, it is more correct to say that fair compensation is a basic foundation necessary to attract and retain associates.

Do all employees know the true value of their total compensation package including benefits? Taken in total, the value of wages and benefits paid is often much more than many people realize, especially those who think of compensation as just "take-home pay."

Managers should not create false hopes of unreasonable wage or benefit increases when they recruit employees or conduct employee performance appraisals. They should also ensure compensation equity by using external compensation surveys and internal guides based on employees' qualifications and performance.

THINK ABOUT IT . . .

If you had a job with characteristics like those in *Exhibit 1.9,* would you leave for an establishment paying 50 cents more per hour with a bad reputation as an employer? Why or why not?

contrast, compensation paid by a competitor is more likely to be viewed as a reason to leave if other reasons to remain are viewed as unsatisfactory.

Several recommendations to become an employer of choice can be made:

- Select the right people. Match the establishment's expectations with those of potential employees.
- Provide training and professional development opportunities for managers to constantly improve their supervisory skills.
- Understand the factors that encourage employees to remain with the organization. If possible, conduct employee surveys, listen during performance appraisal sessions, and use effective exit interviews.
- Do not take employees at high organizational levels for granted. Staff members throughout the establishment may have concerns about staying versus leaving.

DIVERSITY IN RESTAURANT AND FOODSERVICE OPERATIONS

Providing a welcoming environment is a good way to encourage employees to do their best. It is part of a manager's commitment that he or she values the quality of their work, desires the work environment to be hospitable, and recognizes the benefits of diversity. The concept of **diversity** encompasses an understanding that each employee is unique, and this fosters an environment of acceptance and respect for this uniqueness. This welcoming philosophy should also extend to customers and vendors.

Creating an environment in which all people are valued has benefits beyond fulfilling legal obligations. Encouraging and honoring differences can mean a larger and higher-quality labor pool, a more enjoyable and productive environment, improved public relations, and ultimately, more customers. It is also the right thing to do in a social environment that increasingly recognizes the importance of protecting people from discriminatory treatment and honoring individual differences.

Benefits of Diversity

A diverse workforce means that employees with different cultural and socioeconomic backgrounds will consider the same situations and challenges from different viewpoints. These diverse views can lead to a more productive work environment and better creative problem solving, an especially valuable benefit in the fast-paced environment of most restaurant and foodservice operations.

PROMOTES POSITIVE WORKPLACE

Employees with different cultural and socioeconomic backgrounds can contribute their talents and be recognized for making a difference. In addition, all employees can learn from one another and appreciate the value that rich dimensions of diversity bring to their work interactions. Sometimes this learning translates into helping with the dietary requirements of some guests. Sometimes it means recognizing different ways of celebrating religious beliefs. Sometimes it just means learning about the lives of coworkers so that everyone enjoys and respects each other more fully. All of these benefits contribute to creating a positive workplace (*Exhibit 1.10*).

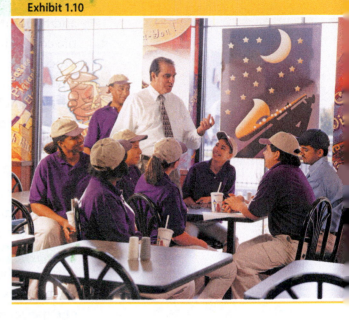

Exhibit 1.10

ATTRACTS MORE CUSTOMERS

Recruiting and hiring people from a range of areas including the local community will help ensure that the operation's staff mirrors the community. This practice often builds new business from customers who feel more comfortable visiting establishments where the staff is drawn from their community, or who want to support diverse businesses. Another benefit is publicity about the operation if, for example, there are newspaper articles about the operation's efforts to recruit a diverse workforce.

INCREASES LABOR POOL

When managers encourage diversity and demonstrate that value by hiring a diverse staff, more people will likely seek employment in such a positive environment. When there are persons of many backgrounds working in and patronizing the establishment, a person who identifies with those backgrounds may feel more comfortable. Many potential employees will recognize diversity and may feel better about seeking employment. For these reasons, promoting an environment in which diversity is encouraged and honored helps potential job seekers view the operation as a good place of employment.

With a wider range of potential employees to consider, the labor pool increases, and the chances of finding good employees increase dramatically as well. Given the frequent challenge of finding qualified employees and the high rate of turnover in the industry, any activity that improves the quality of the labor pool is worth pursuing.

IMPROVES LEGAL PROTECTION

Promoting diversity helps fulfill legal requirements and allows managers to better defend against any claims of illegal discrimination. **Discrimination** is the act of treating persons unequally for reasons that do not relate to their abilities, including race, color, religion, gender, national origin, age, and mental or physical abilities. Establishments that provide a welcoming environment and honor differences are less likely to have employees who feel mistreated and file complaints. If complaints do occur, having antidiscrimination policies, processes, and practices in place can provide a strong defense. The work environment should be one in which all employees feel comfortable to do their job without being mocked, criticized, or mistreated on the basis of differences from other employees.

Stereotypes and Prejudices

Restaurant and foodservice operations employ many diverse groups of persons, and it can be easy to get caught in an atmosphere in which differences are stereotyped. Stereotypes are beliefs about particular groups that assume all members of that group are the same. They often can alter a person's behaviors toward a group and negatively impact that group. Stereotypes are often not based on actual experience, and it can take a lot of experience to alter them. For example, people who think that members of a certain group are always late or are not trustworthy are caught in stereotypes. In fact, those who are inappropriately labeled and those who stereotype are both hurt by stereotyping. Those who believe in stereotypes will be cheated out of genuine relationships because of their clouded judgment.

Stereotypes produce prejudice, or bias, which is a general attitude toward a person, group, or organization based on judgments unrelated to abilities or reality. Some persons are brought up in an environment in which they learn to like certain people and groups and dislike others. Sometimes the prejudice comes from their own experience, and sometimes it comes from the lessons taught by family members and other adult role models.

Managers should develop an establishment culture that helps break down stereotypes. This is important in building a team that works well together, where everyone understands and values the strengths that individuals bring to the team. Prejudice and stereotypes must be exposed for the problems they are. If this is not done, employees may learn it is acceptable to treat each other as less than equals and colleagues. A culture of distrust and frustration may be created, making teamwork almost impossible.

If employees do not feel trusted or welcome, they will not work hard, their productivity will fall, and their willingness to help each other will diminish dramatically. The result will be a poorly functioning operation in which food will not be prepared well, service will often be unacceptable, and customers will be unhappy. *Exhibit 1.11* summarizes the negative effects of prejudice and the positive effects of diversity.

THINK ABOUT IT . . .

Has anyone ever done something that made you suspect prejudice against you? How did it make you feel? How does that experience affect your views about prejudice among employees who must work together?

Exhibit 1.11

PREJUDICE VERSUS DIVERSITY

Effects of Prejudice	Effects of Diversity
Limits the labor pool	Increases the labor pool
Increases turnover; lowers morale	Promotes the operation as a viable employer
Stifles new ideas, talents, and perspectives	Encourages new ideas, talents, and perspectives
Increases conflict and misunderstanding	Encourages appreciation of other cultures
Decreases productivity	Creates a positive work environment
Decreases profitability	Builds business with new customers
Decreases customer service	Creates an environment where a diverse group of customers is comfortable
Increases likelihood of discrimination claims and litigation	Fulfills regulatory guidelines

Promoting Diversity

Building a work environment in which people are honored for their contributions makes a real difference in an operation. It is important for employees to know that they are not being judged by factors, such as race and gender, or by other factors, including membership in a group or being the same as or different from the manager or other employees. To promote a culture of mutual respect it is necessary to break down stereotypes and manage activities that impact diversity.

RECRUITING FOR DIVERSITY

Recruiting a diverse workforce is an active process. It demonstrates the manager's commitment to honor differences and encourage diversity while trying to find the best qualified persons regardless of race, color, national origin, or other differences. One recruiting goal should be to employ a diverse workforce, regardless of the diversity of the local community and the customer base. Sometimes accomplishing this takes a very active recruiting effort. Information about recruiting is presented in chapter 2.

INCREASING CROSS-CULTURAL INTERACTION

Encouraging meaningful communication among employees from diverse cultures and socioeconomic backgrounds helps break down stereotypes and prejudices and improves the workplace environment. One way to do this is to establish policies and procedures based on a mission that supports diversity and discourages prejudice and makes it clear that all employees are valued and treated equally. Aggressive recruiting practices that seek out people of both genders from various cultural backgrounds, religions, mental and physical conditions, races, colors, and national origins help convey the message that these differences are valued.

However, merely employing a diverse staff will not foster positive cross-cultural interaction. Managers can do several things to help employees of all cultures feel comfortable in the operation. One is to model the behavior expected from employees. If managers tease, tell jokes, or do other things that suggest they tolerate or even encourage stereotyping, they are sending the message that these behaviors are acceptable. In contrast, demonstrating how to encourage and honor diversity helps establish a hospitable and welcoming environment for all employees.

Other positive activities involve communication. The presence of many languages promotes an enriching environment that enables everyone to learn other languages. Learning at least a few key words of employees' native languages will help them feel welcome and more comfortable. Using posters and charts with the languages spoken by staff also improves communication. Offering training in applicable languages ensures that important knowledge and skills are learned. Multilingual materials illustrate that diversity is valued in the operation.

Since language competencies may vary among employees, providing educational opportunities for those who want to learn English and improve their reading and writing skills can affect how well the employees interact. However, sometimes employees are embarrassed to admit they have literacy problems. Try to arrange for classes or tutors to work with these employees in private locations or at times when other employees are engaged in other tasks.

EDUCATING EMPLOYEES AND SETTING EXPECTATIONS

Part of promoting diversity is educating employees about the value of tolerance, acceptance, understanding, and teamwork as well as the inappropriateness of prejudice. Employees must be educated about behaviors that are not acceptable in the workplace. Managers must set the expectation that hostility, prejudicial treatment, and stereotyping have no place in the operation.

Holding diversity training sessions helps employees overcome their misconceptions and learn about other cultures, especially if the training is enrichment rather than punishment for violating diversity policies. Managers may conduct ongoing diversity training by learning and sharing facts about the customs, languages, and habits of different employees' cultures. This strategy allows them to demonstrate that differences are interesting and not something to be hidden, feared, or ashamed of.

The federal government's Equal Employment Opportunity Commission (EEOC) requires companies to post a notice about laws prohibiting discrimination. Some managers hold periodic meetings or training events about diversity and acceptance. Common topics include avoiding and managing sexual harassment and racial or religious discrimination. **Sexual harassment** relates to unwelcome sexual advances, sexual favor requests, and other verbal or physical conduct that is sexual in nature and may create an offensive, intimidating, or hostile work environment.

ADDRESSING ISSUES AND ACCOUNTABILITY

Managers should actively look for signs of improper behavior leading to a hostile, offensive, or intimidating environment, such as inappropriate joking, teasing, comments, or name-calling or the posting of improper cartoons, posters, or notes posted in common areas. It is important to stop this behavior as soon as it is noticed, and not wait until someone complains. Employees should be encouraged to present their concerns, and they should never be punished for doing so.

Consistently follow the establishment's guidelines and policies for investigating and managing these issues in a fair and reasonable manner. Hold employees accountable for their behavior. A consistent record of addressing these issues shows that managers really do mean what they say and want the work environment to be tolerant.

Sometimes, intervening places managers in the middle of a conflict. It is helpful then to focus on the issue and not on the personalities of those involved. Focus on correcting and reshaping employees' behavior, and remember that some people mean well but may not understand how their behavior discourages a welcoming environment. Others may know what should ideally be done but not what is and is not tolerated in the establishment.

When managers intervene to correct a behavior, their actions can have a tremendous impact on the entire workforce. Other employees will learn that the establishment is serious about the need for a welcoming environment, and they will act accordingly.

THINK ABOUT IT . . .

Managers should emphasize diversity and encourage acceptance. Some consider it as a factor in employee performance evaluation, asking whether a supervisor manages all employees in the same way. Do you agree with this approach?

ETHICAL CONCERNS

The concept of **ethics** relates to rules or principles that help define what is right and what is wrong. However, the definitions of right and wrong vary based on the person who is deciding. An individual's ethical behavior is influenced by many factors including his or her cultural background, religious beliefs, personal code of conduct, and personal experiences.

Society, through its laws, does not take a position on whether something is right or wrong until it is determined to be illegal. Then, something that is illegal is also judged to be unethical. However, something can be legal (no laws have been broken) but still be unethical. For example, a vendor can give tickets to sporting events to purchasers who buy from the vendor, with the hope that doing so will influence their purchasing decisions. In determining what is ethical, managers can follow the guidance of their own manager and their professional peers. A code of ethics is a written set of guidelines to indicate the preferred behavior of an establishment's employees. They are developed by their organizations and their industry and are important concerns as decisions are made and evaluated.

Consider a manager determining which employee should attend a professional association meeting out-of-town. The establishment may have a policy relating to factors such as length of employment and ability to improve work as a result of attendance. If so, these factors will help narrow the list of employees eligible to attend. However, two staff members with equal qualifications might remain. One is the personal favorite of the manager, who dislikes the second candidate. Which employee should be selected?

The manager must consider several factors, all of which are important, as this seemingly small decision is made. Many relate to employee morale and post-decision supervisory concerns. **Morale** refers to the feelings employees have about their employer, their workplace, and other aspects of the operation. The ethical aspects of favoritism are also present. What should the manager do? Perhaps more information is needed, but all managers have experiences with decision making that test their ethical beliefs.

People should always make ethical decisions in their personal lives. However, managers must also make ethical judgments as they make decisions that affect their organization. Professional managers consistently practice ethical behavior and avoid unethical behavior.

The corporate culture of an operation may or may not support and reward its members for making ethical decisions. For example, concerns about the environment are an important ethical issue in the culture of some organizations, and their codes of ethics require managers to consider the environmental impacts of their decision making. Other organizations may not share this concern. Since the culture of the organization affects how managers make decisions, the culture also impacts the organization's ethical aspects of a manager's responsibilities.

Ethical Decisions and Actions

Managers should lead by example. They should always be honest; they should not mislead or deceive others, and they should always do what is right. Here are some basic principles managers should follow:

- **Trustworthiness:** Supply accurate information, and make corrections when information is incorrect.
- **Loyalty to organization:** Avoid conflicts of interest, and do not disclose confidential information.
- **Fairness:** Treat individuals equally and always appreciate diversity.
- **Concern and respect:** Be considerate of persons affected by the decisions that are made.
- **Commitment to excellence:** Always do the best job possible.
- **Reputation and morale:** Work to enhance the establishment's reputation and to improve employee morale.
- **Accountability:** Accept responsibility for decisions after they are made.

To determine whether a proposed decision or action is based on sound ethics, a manager should ask the following questions:

- Is the action or behavior legal?
- Will the action or behavior hurt anyone?
- Does the action or behavior best represent the core values of the operation?
- Does the action or behavior make anyone uncomfortable?
- Does the action or behavior show respect for others, and is it fair?
- Would I be comfortable sharing my decision with my manager, family, or friends?
- What would others say and think if the decision were posted on the establishment's bulletin board or reported in the property's newsletter?

Effective managers know they are role models, and many employees naturally expect their manager to set an example. Those who consistently see a manager applying professional leadership skills are more likely to want to behave in a similar manner. When this occurs, the manager's ethical behavior also helps build trust between the manager and the staff members.

THINK ABOUT IT . . .

A manager requests a sample of steaks from a vendor. The vendor provides them, along with "a few more for you to barbeque at home." Should the manager accept the samples? Explain.

Exhibit 1.12

Purchasers must closely follow their employer's code of ethics at all times. For example, kickbacks are a serious ethical transgression.

Manager's Memo

A code of ethics may address general beliefs that, in turn, drive more specific concerns:

- Importance of the facility's customers
- Respect for individual staff members
- Need for honesty
- Compliance with all laws all the time
- Avoidance of conflicts of interest
- Confidentiality of proprietary information
- Reporting of financial operating results honestly

To avoid unnecessary details, supporting codes of ethics might be developed for specific functions. Examples include purchasing codes of ethics and ethical codes relating to financial management.

Code of Ethics

As previously mentioned, many establishments create a written code of ethics designed to remove much of the guesswork about what is right or wrong behavior. A code of ethics is a formal statement developed by an operation that explains how its employees should relate to each other and to the persons and groups with whom they interact. The code of ethics acts as a safety check for evaluating decisions before implementing them. As such, their intention is to provide a framework for decision making rather than to specify exactly what should or should not be done in a specific situation (see *Exhibit 1.12*).

Codes of ethics are developed for several reasons:

- To identify a foundation of acceptable behavior
- To promote standards to guide decision making
- To provide a benchmark for evaluating decisions
- To support the obligations that decision makers have to their company, operation, customers, society, and the law

Upholding a code of ethics can be directly related to the company's bottom line and profits, and it can help avoid fraud and theft. Ethical behavior encourages repeat business and a loyal customer base. Managers should also be concerned about complying with the code of ethics because of the impact some decisions may have on the health and safety of others. For example, most operations have policies about discard times for food and a requirement that employees always wash their hands before preparing food. An establishment's code of ethics might reinforce these rules by addressing the need to never take "shortcuts" relating to food safety.

The most effective codes of ethics emphasize the ethical commitment of the operation and how it intends to interact with others. The best codes are developed specifically for the organization and incorporate input from the employees who will be expected to follow them. This frequently includes staff members at all organizational levels. Additionally, input should be solicited from investors (if applicable), vendors, and perhaps even community organizations. Those who assist in the development of an ethics code should understand the establishment's mission, and they should be concerned about its commitment to a positive professional and community image.

The establishment's corporate culture will drive the concerns that are emphasized in the code of ethics. For example, consider an organization that is concerned about employees, providing great value to customers, and doing its fair share to save the environment. These topics will be included in the organization's code of ethics. Day-to-day activities can then be planned that will be in concert with the code of ethics. If there is an emphasis on respecting employees, managers will plan training programs for supervisors, and career development programs can be planned for all employees who want to participate. Also, effective performance appraisal procedures will be in place with an emphasis on helping employees reach their full potential.

The support of top-level leadership is of obvious importance as codes of ethics are developed. Codes should be reviewed by legal counsel, and formal approval from the highest levels in the establishment will be required.

Managers should consider whether the code of ethics will be an internal document or whether it should be made public. Increasingly, for example, organizations publicize their codes of ethics on their Web sites and through other advertising media. They want the public to know about their concerns and how the operation is attempting to address them.

One common way to develop a code of ethics is to consider the categories of concerns that should be addressed. For example, a manager might determine that the code should consider several topics:

- Overview: purpose and goals of the ethics code
- Responsibilities to customers
- Responsibilities to employees
- Responsibilities to the community and society
- Responsibilities to vendors and other external organizations
- Employees' responsibilities to the employer
- Employees' responsibilities to other employees
- Matters relating to violations of the code of ethics

Examples of concerns that might be addressed could include how employees will be treated and how interactions with vendors should take place.

The strategies used to implement and educate staff members about a code of ethics are also important. For example, a display of the code in the manager's office and as an introduction for an employee handbook will do little good unless the code is incorporated into the organization's culture.

In many companies, employment is dependent on the prospective employee reading the code of ethics and signing an agreement saying that he or she agrees to abide by the company or operation's code of ethics (*Exhibit 1.13*). Then the employee is asked to sign another agreement if any changes are made. Implementation

Exhibit 1.13

strategies in other companies may include roll-out meetings and use of the organization's Intranet that is available to all employees. After reading and discussing the code, employees may be asked to interpret the code of ethics by role-playing situations that involve the code. Including discussions about the code of ethics in employee orientation programs and in the employee handbook are other possibilities. Before-shift line-up meetings, training programs, and coaching activities provide other opportunities to ensure that staff members know about the code of ethics.

Any enforcement actions that are applicable if the code is violated should be addressed with employees. Remember, a code of ethics should be a permanent policy. All staff members should be held accountable for the behavior described in the code of ethics.

A code of ethics is easier to implement and enforce when policies and procedures are developed to indicate what managers and employees should do on the job. Then supervisors and managers can use a progressive system to help employees comply with the policies. For example, if a supervisor allows working conditions to become less than ideal, the manager can coach him or her. This can be followed by more formalized discussions, training, and warnings about taking corrective actions. In this way, the code of ethics will drive how things are done in the organization.

Those who comply with the code's policies and procedures should be recognized and rewarded for doing so. The ways to do so can range from a sincere thank-you to special considerations during performance appraisal sessions that affect promotions and compensation.

Codes of ethics may need to be changed, just as most other planning and managing tools must change. Anything that affects the corporate culture is likely to affect the code of ethics, which is driven by it. Changes in top-level management, laws and regulations, and strategies to improve profitability are examples of factors that may require the need for updating the code of ethics.

SUMMARY

1. **Explain management activities and how evolving employee expectations can influence managers as they facilitate the work of their employees.**

    Management activities include planning, organizing, coordinating, staffing, supervising, controlling, and evaluating. While all of these activities are involved in managing the work of employees, staffing and supervising directly focus on this area.

    Managers must assist with activities in the employment cycle that begin with finding, recruiting, and screening applicants. The cycle continues with hiring, orienting, and supervising new employees. It concludes with activities relating to employee terminations and then begins again.

Three generations of employees comprise the majority of today's workforce: Baby Boomers, Generation X, and Millennials. While some basic supervisory strategies are useful with employees of all ages, strategies will ideally be changed to address the concerns of employees in specific age groups.

2. **Describe strategies for facilitating the work of employees.**

Effective managers provide direction, lead consistently, influence others, and foster teamwork. In addition, they can motivate employees, coach and develop them, and champion change.

3. **Explain how skills, abilities, leadership style, and corporate culture impact a manager's human resources activities.**

Managers manage within financial restraints, implement quality management processes, and make effective decisions to turn problems into opportunities. They can use several different leadership styles including autocratic, bureaucratic, democratic, and laissez-faire. Ideally, they will modify their leadership style based on the needs of specific employees.

The organization's corporate culture impacts how managers supervise. Operations that are thought of as employers of choice work hard to treat employees with respect. Supervisory strategies can be an important employee retention factor.

4. **Identify the benefits of and procedures for promoting employee diversity within restaurant and foodservice operations.**

Benefits of diversity include a more positive workplace, the ability to attract more customers and employees, and improved legal protection. Managers must work to reduce the impact of prejudice and stereotypes that hinder team development. They can promote diversity by using appropriate recruiting strategies, increasing cross-cultural interactions, educating employees and setting expectations, and addressing accountability.

5. **Explain the importance of ethical decision making; the role of codes of ethics in restaurant and foodservice operations; and tasks involved in developing, implementing, and enforcing codes of ethics.**

Ethical principles help define what is right and wrong. Managers should be honest, should not mislead others, and should always do what is right. They should use a questioning approach to determine whether a decision is based on sound ethics.

Written codes of ethics, driven by corporate culture and implemented with policies and procedures, provide a foundation for employee behavior. These codes also guide decision making, facilitate decision evaluation, and support the obligation managers have to the corporation, operation, customers, society, and the law. Input from all employee levels is helpful as codes are developed, and the support of top-level leadership is required. Education and enforcement are critical.

APPLICATION EXERCISE

Think about one or two of the very best and very worst supervisors for whom you have ever worked. (If you have never worked, think about your best or worst teacher.) Complete the following information about them.

Type of Supervisor	Reasons for Selecting This Person (Actions)	Two Leadership Principles Used/Not Used
Best supervisor		
Worst supervisor		

If time permits, your instructor may ask students to volunteer examples.

1. What did your best and worst teachers do to make you rate them as you do?

2. What are examples of how their actions might relate to the activities of the best and worst supervisors in the workplace? (For example, perhaps your best teacher seemed to be genuinely concerned that you learn. One's best supervisor might be the person who was genuinely concerned about employees being successful. Likewise, your worst teacher may have complained about your performance in front of your classmates.)

3. How would an employee like to be "bawled out" in front of other employees?

REVIEW YOUR LEARNING

Select the best answer for each question.

1. **What management activity involves determining how and by whom work activities will be done?**
   A. Directing
   B. Evaluating
   C. Organizing
   D. Controlling

2. **A job specification contains**
   A. personal requirements for completing position tasks.
   B. tasks of a position that staff members must perform.
   C. guidelines for relating to various persons on the job.
   D. professional development goals for a position.

3. **A code of ethics is easier to implement and enforce when what tools are implemented?**
   A. Job descriptions
   B. Business plans
   C. Policies
   D. Budgets

4. **What is one way to begin developing teams?**
   A. Assign problems to specially selected groups of employees.
   B. Pay employees based on the performance of their departmental teams.
   C. Pay employees more if other employees say the person is a high performer.
   D. Indicate that supervisors receive better employee support when teams are used.

5. **What is a vision?**

    A. A plan for the next five years

    B. A strategy to attain an objective

    C. A plan for the next calendar year

    D. An idea about an ideal organization

6. **What is the correct definition of quality products?**

    A. High-end products that typically cost more

    B. The best products at the least expensive price

    C. Products that meet the establishment's standards

    D. The greatest output for the least time investment

7. **Which leadership style uses the "do it my way" approach?**

    A. Bureaucratic

    B. Laissez-faire

    C. Democratic

    D. Autocratic

8. **Which item is a component of an organization's corporate culture?**

    A. Budget

    B. Beliefs

    C. Profits

    D. Costs

9. **Treating persons unequally for reasons unrelated to their legal rights or abilities is called**

    A. discrimination.

    B. stereotyping.

    C. harassment.

    D. prejudice.

10. **Which question can help determine whether an action is based on sound ethics?**

    A. Would others take this action?

    B. Is the action worth taking a risk?

    C. Would my family care about my action?

    D. What is the level of risk involved in the action?

2

Recruiting and Selecting the Best Employees

INSIDE THIS CHAPTER

- Position Analysis: Describing Job Tasks
- Job Descriptions: Important Recruitment Tools
- Employee Recruitment Procedures
- Employee Screening and Selection
- The Job Offer

CHAPTER LEARNING OBJECTIVES

After completing this chapter, you should be able to:

- Describe the four tasks in the position analysis process.

- Explain the uses of job descriptions and how they should be developed.

- Review basic employee recruitment procedures.

- List and explain the tools that can help screen job applicants to determine which should receive job offers.

- Review details about job offers made to candidates who meet job requirements.

KEY TERMS

CASE STUDY

"You know why employee turnover is so high?" asked DeShawna. "I'm just a server who worked my way up to dining-room manager. But I know something about this restaurant!"

DeShawna was talking to Demarco, the kitchen manager and another long-time employee.

Demarco replied, "I've seen so many employees come and go that I figured it was how organizations operated."

"I don't think so," said DeShawna. "My sister works in a department store, and they don't just hire the first person who shows up. There are a lot of activities and paperwork required before someone is employed. And most people stay a long time. We're lucky to have employees stay a few months!"

1. What are some basic things that managers of department stores, restaurant or foodservice operations, and other businesses might do when employees must be hired?

2. Do you think that procedures for employee recruitment and selection at a department store would differ greatly from those at a restaurant or foodservice establishment? Why or why not?

POSITION ANALYSIS: DESCRIBING JOB TASKS

Managers have many responsibilities as they recruit, screen, and select the best employees for their operation. Actually, this work begins long before they announce position vacancies. They must develop important recruitment and selection tools that can be used to find the best talent.

Position analysis refers to the process used to identify each task an employee must do and explain how it should be done. Tasks are duties or activities that are part of a position. For example, one task in a dish washer's job is to wash dishes. However, they also need to know how to operate a complex dish machine and may need to know how to replenish servers' stations and buffet lines. Once developed, a position analysis provides information for the job description needed for employee recruitment.

Another benefit of a position analysis is that it explains how tasks should be done. This description is useful for training new employees, coaching existing staff members, and developing training programs for all staff members in the same position.

There are four basic steps in the position analysis process:

1. Develop a task list.

2. Decide how to break down each task into small activities.

3. Determine performance standards.

4. Develop a job description that includes the job's most important tasks.

A task list specifies all tasks that are part of a job and focuses on the activities an employee must be able to do. For example, a cook must know how to operate food-production equipment. A bartender must know how to prepare drinks. Managers can use these procedures to develop a task list:

THINK ABOUT IT . . .

What are some advantages to employees doing the same tasks in the same correct way? Do you think a position analysis is worth the time and effort required to do it? Why or why not?

Exhibit 2.1

- Ask supervisors and experienced workers in a position questions such as "What do you do in a normal work shift from start to finish?"

- Observe employees as they work and compare what they actually do with what they say they do. (See *Exhibit 2.1*.)

- Review written information about a position, such as existing job descriptions and training materials.

- Talk to managers in similar operations.

- Review available industry resources.

After reviewing the information with a team of supervisors and employees, a manager can develop a list of the tasks that make up a job. Similar tasks can be combined, and factors such as differences between work shifts or production volumes can be identified. Then managers will know the scope of training requirements for new employees. They will also have benchmarks for evaluating performance: is the employee doing the work required by the position?

A **task breakdown** is the second part of a position analysis. It tells exactly how each task in the task list should be done. For example, a bus person must know how to properly clear dining-room tables. Developing the task breakdown for this activity may be simple because the manager can probably use available training materials and will have knowledge about the procedure.

Task breakdowns have several benefits:

- They tell the correct way to perform a task to best ensure performance standards are met.

- Trainees benefit from having copies of task breakdowns that can be reviewed as needed, including during training.

- Trainees can practice each step and then compare what they did to the steps in the task breakdown.

Managers can develop task breakdowns by performing a series of actions:

- Watch an experienced staff member perform a task.

- Record each activity or step in sequence.

- Ask the staff member to review the information to confirm its accuracy.

- Share the information with other experienced staff members and their managers.

- Make changes as needed so everyone agrees with the procedure.

- Review the information obtained with the employee's manager and the employee.

- Confirm the final task breakdown by observing an experienced person who performs the task using the identified procedure.

Part A of *Exhibit 2.2* shows a task list for a food server in a full-service restaurant or foodservice operation. Part B shows a task breakdown for one of the tasks: checking customer identification.

THINK ABOUT IT . . .

A standardized recipe is a task breakdown. A cook must know how to prepare menu items, and standardized recipes explain every detail.

How can this idea be used to support the need for standardized recipes?

Exhibit 2.2

SAMPLE TASK LIST AND TASK BREAKDOWN FOR SERVER

Part A: Task List for Server

1. Sets up server workstations.
2. Collects and polishes flatware and glassware.
3. Sets all tables.
4. Welcomes customers.
5. Provides information about available food and beverage products.
6. Checks customers' identification if alcoholic beverages are ordered.
7. Records customers' orders.
8. Serves customers promptly and professionally.
9. Prepares guest check, collects payments, and records payment according to required procedures.
10. Clears tables.
11. Completes assigned tasks on dining-room cleanup schedule.

Part B: Task Breakdown for Task Six: Checking Customer Identification

- Politely ask customer for ID.
- Verify ID.
- If accepted, serve requested drink.
- If unsure, ask for second ID, compare customer's signature to ID signature, and/or ask questions ID owner can answer. If accepted, serve requested drink.
- If ID is not accepted, refuse service.

Determining performance standards is the third part of the position analysis process. **Performance standards** specify the required *quality* and *quantity* outputs that define the correct way to perform a task. Proper performance must be clearly defined so employees know what is expected and managers know when performance is acceptable.

An example of outputs might be for a cook to prepare so many meals per hour (quantity), produced according to an establishment's standardized recipe with less than 1 percent of the items returned by customers (quality). If a cook is asked to prepare 25 servings of a menu item, he or she would use the applicable recipe to do so. Since the recipe specifies the procedures to be used, it helps control the time needed to produce the required quantity of portions.

Performance standards should be reasonable. They should be challenging but achievable and tied to the procedures identified by the task breakdowns. Employees should also have the tools and equipment needed to work correctly.

Performance standards must be specific so that they can be measured. Compare these statements: "The cook will know how to prepare twice-baked potatoes" or "The cook will be able to prepare twice-baked potatoes according to the standardized recipe." The second standard is better because it can be objectively measured.

The fourth step in the position analysis process is to develop a job description. It indicates the tasks a person working in a position must be able to perform, along with other important information.

JOB DESCRIPTIONS: IMPORTANT RECRUITMENT TOOLS

Current and accurate job descriptions inform job applicants about what they would do if they worked in the position. This information will impact their interest in the job, so managers must develop it carefully.

Uses of Job Descriptions

Job descriptions provide many benefits to the managers who use them. Each relates to a clear understanding about what the job involves.

RECRUITING AND SCREENING

Clear and complete job descriptions are useful for recruiting and screening possible new employees. Job applicants want to know what they would do in a position. After job tasks have been developed during the position analysis process, managers can determine the requirements typically necessary for an employee to do the tasks. Therefore, the job description provides a foundation for evaluating applicants and developing interview questions and screening practices that are in compliance with legal requirements.

HIRING, ORIENTATION, TRAINING, AND DEVELOPMENT

The job description provides direction for hiring and orientation programs, and it identifies the types of training needed to perform the tasks. In addition, clear job descriptions make it easier to learn what must be done to prepare employees for other positions.

PERFORMANCE EVALUATION PROGRAMS

A job description provides basic information and expectations useful for creating performance evaluation programs. This includes establishing goals for the employee based on duties and focusing on areas where improvements are needed.

SALARY ADMINISTRATION

Job descriptions can provide the basis for structuring compensation or salary ranges. They provide a starting point for pooling jobs into classifications that drive pay differences. For example, all culinary positions would be in a culinary class. Executive positions, such as chef, would be paid more than entry- or mid-level positions, such as prep cook and baker. While large operations may have compensation specialists to study pay structures, managers in small establishments can use job descriptions informally to help determine if salaries are competitive.

SAFETY AND SECURITY

Job descriptions can formally define responsibilities for ensuring safety and security and preventing injuries. For example, a manager's position might include duties for ensuring security while closing, such as making sure exterior doors are locked and the alarm is set.

UNION AND LEGAL CONCERNS

Job descriptions are often carefully studied when misunderstandings occur between a union employee and supervisors or when there are union grievances. In addition, job descriptions clarify the responsibilities a person is expected to undertake, which may be a factor during contract negotiations. The more accurate job descriptions are the more protection an operation has against employee claims that may arise from performance disputes. These claims could be raised internally to HR or a union representative or taken externally to a legal agency.

Procedures for Developing Job Descriptions

Information from a task list developed during position analysis is used to develop a job description. A well-written job description provides the information needed to understand the job. It should be gender neutral and give potential applicants a good idea about the job's responsibilities.

OPEN FOR BUSINESS

RESTAURANT TECHNOLOGY

The Occupational Information Network (O*NET) offers a Web site geared toward schools, employers, students, and job seekers. The site provides lists of job titles and tasks and the knowledge, skills, and abilities needed for various jobs. This information can be used by managers developing job descriptions, and it can be used by others interested in learning what persons in specific positions do.

For example, entering "restaurant manager" will yield information about tasks, tools, technology, knowledge, skills, abilities, work contacts, and job zones. Other information about the job relates to education, interests, work styles and values, related occupations, and wage and employment trends.

The first task in developing a job description is to decide what information it should contain. Managers will already know the required information if a standard format or template is used, and it is a good idea to do so. If job descriptions are being developed for the first time, determine whether a standardized format already exists for use in the establishment or if managers wish to develop one. Alternatively, an online source can be consulted, and the samples obtained could be reviewed, revised, and agreed on. Enter "job description template" into a search engine.

It is important that all job description information comply with the **Americans with Disabilities Act (ADA)** and any other legal requirements. The ADA protects qualified individuals with disabilities from discrimination in the job application and hiring process as well as other terms, conditions, and privileges of employment. It covers employers with 15 or more employees as well as employment agencies and labor organizations. It encourages equal employment opportunities for all.

A good job description contains several components. Each is identified by a numbered box on the sample job description in *Exhibit 2.3*.

1. **Job identification information:** Includes the job title and other identifying information used by the operation. Examples include job grades, which are categories of jobs that fit into a defined wage or salary range, and job class, which is a cluster of jobs requiring the same basic knowledge or skills.

2. **Position manager:** Indicates the position to which an employee in the position reports, and sometimes information about other work relationships. For example, a cook may be supervised by the executive chef but work very closely with other cooks, the dish washer, dining-room staff, and the *sous chef* (assistant to the chef).

3. **Job summary:** Short paragraph that explains the core duties of a position to provide an overall view of what the job involves.

4. **Duties:** The major or essential duties of the job, or what a person in this position does. Duties often start with action verbs that identify something observable, such as *cook*, *serve*, or *prepare*. In some cases, teamwork goals and general duties related to safety and sanitation are included because they are so important.

5. **Position requirements:** These indicate the prior experience, industry knowledge, education, or skills a person should bring to the job or the mental, emotional, or physical skills associated with the position. This information will yield the "job specifications" part of job descriptions.

Manager's Memo

An effectively written job description defines a job. However, excessive information makes it lengthy and difficult to keep updated.

Some information is very important but not normally included in a job description. Examples include operating policies and procedures on such topics as promptness, food safety, dress code, and cleanliness. These are often addressed in employee handbooks, policy statements, operating and performance standards, checklists, and training documents.

Since most of this information applies to many or all employees, putting it in every job description would not be useful. Instead, this information is often covered by tasks that reference general policies, such as "Follows all policies and procedures as stated in the Employee Handbook."

Exhibit 2.3

SAMPLE JOB DESCRIPTION FOR SERVER

Position Title: Server

Job Title: Server	**Type of position:**	**Hours:** 40–50/week
Job Setting: Dining room — 6	☒ Full-time	
Reports to: Dining room manager — 2	☐ Part-time	☐ Exempt
Level/Grade: C3	☐ Contractor	☒ Nonexempt
	☐ Intern	

1

Job Summary — 3

Takes and serves customers' orders and presents guest checks. Presents professional and friendly image to customers at all times. Maintains side stands and prepares tables for service. Communicates and works effectively with other waitstaff and kitchen staff.

Duties — 4

- Learns and explains menu items
- Welcomes customers in a hospitable manner
- Provides information about beverages and food items promptly and positively
- Records orders
- Checks customers' identification to make sure they can legally consume alcohol
- Serves tables promptly and professionally
- Maintains high service standards of the restaurant
- Sets up side stands

- Collects and polishes flatware and glassware for tables
- Sets all tables with linens, plates, glasses, flatware, and accessories according to dining room standards
- Prepares tables for service at the beginning of each shift
- Maintains personal hygiene
- Works effectively with other waitstaff and kitchen staff
- Uses professional practices in all situations
- Performs other tasks as assigned

5

Position Requirements

- Two years of waiting on tables in à la carte settings or two years of banquet/catering waiting experience
- Experience with customer service
- Knowledge of dining room procedures and practices

- High school diploma
- Over twenty-one years old
- College education a plus

7

Publication Information

[signature] Aug. 23   _[signature]_ Date: 08-23-12

Human Resources Manager   Executive Chef, Director of Food and Beverages, General Manager

Some organizations include other information in a job description:

6 **Job setting:** Includes a physical description of the primary locations of the job, such as the kitchen or dining room. This section also includes a description of conditions in the work environment, such as a hot and noisy kitchen.

7 **Publication information:** Identifies who wrote the description or is responsible for its content, and the date it was approved or published.

Avoiding Discrimination in Job Descriptions

Writing a job description takes care. Job descriptions must focus on the required job duties, identify the essential functions of the position, and describe them in clear and neutral language.

Essential functions are the key duties an individual must be able to perform with or without reasonable accommodation. For example, the job description for a sauté cook might include several essential functions:

- Identifies and prepares selected cuts of meat, poultry, shellfish, fish, or vegetables for sautéing
- Sautés items and prepares appropriate sauces
- Plates sautéed items with appropriate garnishes
- Maintains a well-organized and sanitary workstation

To comply with the spirit and intent of the ADA, managers may be asked to clarify what is involved in specific duties and whether there are alternate ways to accomplish them. These alternate ways are known as **reasonable accommodations**. Reasonable accommodations include adjustments or modifications to facilities, job duties, equipment, policies, or practices provided by the employer to enable people with disabilities to perform the essential functions of the job. Reasonable accommodations enable a person with a disability to have equal employment opportunities (see *Exhibit 2.4*). Employers are not required to lower quality, service, or production standards. The accommodation should assist the individual in achieving these standards. Employers are best served when they focus on essential functions and minor duties of the position, and not dictate the method of completing a particular task when more than one acceptable method exists.

An employer does not need to accommodate a qualified person with a disability if doing so would cause an **undue hardship**. Undue hardship is an action causing significant difficulty or expense when considered in light of factors such as an employer's size, financial resources, and the nature and structure of its operation.

Exhibit 2.4

Magnifying tools or increased lighting may be a reasonable accommodation for an employee who is visually impaired.

The clearer the job description, the easier it will be to address accommodation issues and determine whether accommodation is possible. For example, if a person is not able to hold a knife, that person cannot be a butcher. There is no way to accommodate for the lack of that motor skill. However, if a bus person is not able to carry heavy trays, multiple clearing trips or the use of a cart may be possible.

Finally, employers must be very cautious if including position requirements in a job description that are based on religion, gender, age, and national origin. The **bona fide occupational qualifications (BFOQs)** rule allows for very narrow exceptions here. BFOQs are employment practices that would constitute discrimination toward certain individuals, but because they are related to an essential job function and reasonably necessary for the normal operation of the business they are permissible. For example, gender cannot be specified as a requirement unless it is necessary to perform job functions, such as specifying a female for a women's restroom attendant position.

Revising, Approving, and Maintaining Job Descriptions

Reviewing a written job description against current job duties can often be an eye-opening experience. This is especially true if the document has not been updated for a long time. There are several reasons job descriptions may change:

- Responsibilities or reporting structures evolve.
- **Job specifications** indicate the personal requirements such as skills and abilities that are required to successfully perform tasks in a position. These specifications may change to accommodate new regulations.
- Technology or new equipment affects the job.
- New menu items or operating procedures affect responsibilities or job requirements.
- New union contracts change responsibilities within positions.

Periodically reviewing and updating job descriptions is important. Typically, job descriptions are reviewed when employee performance evaluations are conducted. Policies require managers to review the job description at that time and make suggestions for changes, if necessary.

It may be helpful for an attorney to review job descriptions for legal compliance. Also, human resources personnel in organizations that employ them can provide advice. Based on these reviews, some revisions may be necessary before the job descriptions are finalized and approved. Recall that publication information is a final element in the job description shown in *Exhibit 2.3*.

Manager's Memo

When an establishment offers employment to a candidate who has disclosed a disability, health records or a physical examination are typically requested. When limitations are identified, requirements to accommodate the employee will be known and the manager can determine if the accommodations are reasonable. For example, hiring a person with limited vision might necessitate increasing the lighting in the employee's work area. To avoid discrimination, requests for health records or examinations should be made with or after an offer of employment.

According to the U.S. Equal Employment Opportunity Commission, reasonable accommodation includes:

- Making existing facilities readily accessible to and usable by persons with disabilities
- Restructuring jobs, modifying work schedules, or reassigning to a vacant position
- Acquiring or modifying equipment or devices; adjusting or modifying examinations, training materials, or policies; and providing qualified readers or interpreters

EMPLOYEE RECRUITMENT PROCEDURES

Recruiting and screening are two important tasks for finding new employees. Recruiting is a series of activities designed to influence the largest number of qualified persons to apply for a job. Screening is the process of reviewing the skills, experience, attitudes, and backgrounds of applicants to make a selection.

Recruitment Overview

In small operations, recruiting and screening are often done by the general manager, dining-room manager, or chef, depending on the position. In large organizations, human resources staff complete some of these tasks. Recruitment tasks range from considering the number of new employees needed in each position to deciding how, when, and where to encourage good applicants to seek employment with the establishment. Specific actions include:

- Deciding what vacancies exist based on future staffing levels
- Determining the skills and background new employees will need
- Clarifying what the establishment can offer to potential employees
- Identifying sources of applicants
- Effectively communicating vacancies to build a talent pool of qualified people

While communicating vacancies may be the most visible activity, the recruiting process actually starts when the manager identifies the need for additional employees. Ongoing recruitment occurs as part of the employment cycle when current employees leave. Also, some operations, such as those with seasonal employment, must recruit more employees as the volume of anticipated business increases.

Forecasting Staff Needs

The timing of recruiting efforts can have a huge impact on an operation's ability to hire and train new employees to be ready for work at the right time. Managers or human resources professionals normally analyze past staffing needs to forecast when additional employees must be hired. The analysis often involves examining information about the operation, similar operations, and the local labor market, including:

- **Last year's revenue and staffing patterns**: How much business did the operation do and how many employees in each position were needed? Comparing the number and cost of the staff, including overtime and any labor shortages, can help provide an estimate of how many new employees will be needed.

- **History of turnover:** Determine how often positions must be filled and at what times of year. This will indicate the seasonality of recruiting and suggest when new employees should be recruited so they can be trained.

The employee turnover rate, generally calculated on an annual basis, is easy to calculate:

Turnover rate ↘

16	÷	97	=	16.5%
Number of employees who terminate		**Average number of employees in workforce**		**Employee turnover rate**

Note that to find the average number of employees in the workforce, add the number of employees at the beginning of the year (January 1) and the number of employees at the end of the year (December 31). Then, divide that sum by two. It is best to calculate turnover rates on a by-department basis to determine whether some work areas have more employees who leave voluntarily. If so, the reasons should be investigated.

- **Current and seasonal staffing schedules:** Identify the periods of peak and low staff demand. In some locations, staff requirements vary dramatically between seasons. This information is critical to helping managers know whether to hire seasonal, part-time, or permanent full-time staff. Examining new assumptions about how business volume may change also provides information about when to hire additional staff to accommodate expected growth.

- **Staffing patterns and guidelines for similar establishments:** It is helpful to compare staffing patterns with those of other operations. To do so, managers use resources such as the National Restaurant Association or state and local restaurant associations. They also network with other local restaurant and foodservice professionals to learn how they handle staffing needs.

- **Local labor market realities:** Recognize the skill sets of those who can be recruited locally and learn who is competing for new employees. Knowing this information may dramatically change how new employees are recruited.

After staffing needs are identified, a recruiting plan can be developed. Part of this plan includes determining the skills and abilities desired in new employees and the advantages and compensation that can be offered.

Almost every operation has several sources of potential employees. They include the establishment's present employees as well as external alternatives.

Manager's Memo

The value of employee referrals is that current employees have a sense of how potential employees will fit into the corporate culture. Employees also serve as filters or prescreeners since they are not likely to suggest people they do not want to work with.

An important factor in the success of internal recruiting is to create and maintain the kind of relation-ship with employees that encourages them to help. If they like working in the operation, they are more likely to want friends and family members to work there as well.

Also, use every opportunity to remind employees about the employee referral program, including any incentives. Be sure to publicly and privately thank employees who make recommendations.

Internal Recruiting

Internal sources of potential employees include persons referred by employees and the employees themselves. Even customers may have suggestions about potential employees. A big advantage of internal recruiting sources is that job applicants are more familiar with the operation.

Managers typically use several internal recruiting methods including a policy of informing current employees of vacancies before searching outside the operation. Many establishments have employee referral programs that offer a bonus or reward for employees who refer candidates. Sometimes the bonus is paid when the individual is hired, sometimes after a trial employment period.

Current employees tend to recommend others like themselves, and this may affect diversity plans. Therefore, exclusive use of internal recruiting may limit employment opportunities to certain groups of people. This can result in claims of discrimination. However, if employees know that a diverse staff is desired, they can help in this effort.

The most common way to alert current employees about job openings is through regular employee communication methods such as crew meetings, company newsletters, and postings on bulletin boards. Operations with intranets post information there, and notices can also be placed in paycheck envelopes.

When current employees are promoted into open positions, recruitment time and costs are reduced. This practice, called promoting from within, offers many benefits. It rewards employees for good performance, motivates others to improve performance, and encourages all employees to consider long-term opportunities at the establishment. While the practice creates another vacancy, often it is for a less specialized position that can be filled more easily with an external hire.

Potential problems can occur if a manager advertises internally for a position but then does not seriously consider the internal applicants. If this occurs, employees will likely be suspicious of any further internal promotions. Employees also may lose faith in the system and may stop applying or encouraging people outside the operation to apply.

External Recruiting

There are a variety of external sources where managers can find new employees. The range and number of sources depend in large part on the establishment's location. *Exhibit 2.5* lists common sources.

Exhibit 2.5

COMMON EXTERNAL SOURCES OF POTENTIAL EMPLOYEES

- **Culinary schools**
- **Other schools, especially those with culinary programs:**
  - High schools
  - Colleges and universities
  - Vocational and technical training centers
  - Proprietary schools
- **Student organizations**
- **Federal, state, and local government agencies and programs, such as:**
  - Employment agencies and programs
  - Work-release and other programs for persons in jail, on parole, or on probation
  - Departments of labor
  - Social service departments
- **Business organizations**
- **State and local chambers of commerce**
- **Community organizations and clubs, such as:**
  - Youth groups
  - Career and vocational centers
  - Women's centers
  - Men's centers
  - Senior citizen centers
  - Student organizations
- **Private employment agencies**
- **Temporary employment agencies**
- **Welcome organizations**
- **Former employees**
- **Past applicants**
- **Health clubs, YMCAs, YWCAs, and exercise facilities**

- **Local sports teams**
- **Not-for-profit social service organizations, such as:**
  - Literacy-related organizations
  - Job placement centers in human service organizations
  - Employment programs for disabled or emotionally challenged individuals
- **Churches, synagogues, mosques, and other religious institutions**
- **Local hospitality-oriented professional organizations, such as:**
  - Local chapters of the National Restaurant Association
  - Local hospitality and lodging associations
  - Les Amis du Vin
  - Les Dames d'Escoffier
  - Local chapters of the American Culinary Federation
  - The Federation of Dining Room Professionals
  - La Chaîne des Rôtisseurs
- **Unions**
- **Competitors, other foodservice operations, and other businesses**
- **Internet-based job databases and services, including:**
  - Company Web sites
  - Professional or business organization Web sites
  - Privately owned Web sites such as Monster.com and CareerBuilder.com
- **Suppliers and salespeople**

Recruiting should be targeted to find the best applicants possible regardless of race, gender, national origin, age, religion, or other nonessential traits. To ensure the operation gives everyone a fair chance at employment, target external sources that encourage a diverse labor pool. For example, in addition to advertising in the local newspaper, advertise in a local foreign language newspaper or through a social service organization that works with people who have disabilities to help them find employment opportunities.

There are several popular external recruitment methods:

- **Networking:** Networking is the practice of building and maintaining ongoing communication with individuals who can provide potential assistance. These persons are sometimes but not necessarily in the restaurant and foodservice industry. For example, managers may network with other business leaders in community groups. Good networking produces referrals and word-of-mouth advertising. The keys to successful networking include making contacts with people in the industry and nurturing the professional relationships formed with them. Regular communication is important to do this.

- **Sponsoring school, community, and professional programs:** Possibilities vary widely depending on the type of organization. Managers can sponsor a meeting for a professional or community organization, or they can offer an internship program or sponsor a joint school–industry program.

- **Marketing to professional and community organizations:** Ongoing general marketing to professional and community organizations increases the establishment's name recognition as a place to visit and a place to work. Regular communication is important. Some operations develop electronic newsletters or their own email lists targeted for customers and others in the community. Others send information through their chamber of commerce or distribute a hard-copy newsletter. A chamber of commerce is a voluntary group of business leaders and others who promote businesses within a community. Convention and Visitor Bureaus are also popular employers in areas that attract tourists and meeting attendees.

Exhibit 2.6

- **Advertising through traditional media:** Job openings can be advertised through traditional media such as radio, television, newspapers, and magazines. Advertisements in local newspapers and other publications are commonly used by some operations.

- **Advertising through other media:** Signs and postings in and around the establishment (*Exhibit 2.6*), on public bulletin boards, and on Web sites are ways to advertise job openings. Public bulletin boards include those found in stores, coffee shops, and laundry facilities. The use of social media including Facebook and Twitter for recruitment purposes is an increasingly popular way to reach out to job applicants.

- **Participating in career development events:** Career development events, such as job fairs, provide an easy way to meet many potential employees in a short time. At a typical job fair, employers set up tables and job seekers visit to learn about opportunities. These events may be organized by colleges. Sometimes they are arranged by chambers of commerce, departments of labor, and other agencies. Managers who participate demonstrate the establishment's commitment to hire local people. Also, networking allows them to learn what is happening in the local labor market, what new developments may affect the operation, and what strategies have helped others recruit new employees.

- **Holding open houses and giving tours:** These recruiting alternatives can showcase the operation as a good place to work and to patronize. An open house is a designated time for people to visit the establishment. Food, beverages, and tours are often provided. The event allows visitors an opportunity to meet the staff, admire the establishment's products and atmosphere, and mix with others. These events build good public relations, often lead to temporary increases in business, and cement the relationship with people or organizations that visit the business. Distributing materials about the operation can complement goodwill-building events with some recruiting activities.

Managers will gain experience using one or more recruiting methods and use the sources that are best for their establishment. Their recruiting efforts will yield employment applications that provide information helpful during the screening process.

Effective Communication Is Important

It is important to effectively communicate information about job openings to remain in compliance with equal employment opportunity regulations. The information can be provided orally or in writing, but both types must be geared to potential applicants so they can decide whether the job sounds right for them.

A good job notice includes all important information. The exact requirements depend on whether it is intended for internal or external sources:

- **Job or position title:** The title should describe the position, such as line cook or server. Some titles create confusion, such as "sanitation engineer" for a dish washer. Use gender-neutral language when possible.

- **Desired qualifications or skills:** This helps potential employees self-screen for the position. As with the job description, be sure to address essential functions, minor functions, and when applicable, BFOQs.

RESTAURANT TECHNOLOGY

Technology offers many options for posting job notices and advertisements. If the establishment has a Web site, job openings should be posted on it. Employment Web sites sponsored by various organizations offer a variety of recruiting services. Many professional, business, and community organizations provide Web sites on which those they serve can post openings. In addition, college placement offices and chambers of commerce often allow the posting of job notices on their Web sites.

For a fee, Web sites that specialize in connecting employers and job seekers are available, such as Monster.com and CareerBuilder.com. Sites like these often provide sophisticated tools for recruiting, including resume searches and networking features.

Increasingly, social media including Twitter and Facebook are great places to announce position vacancies. One reason is that many of the target groups of potential employees routinely use these communication tools.

- **Company name:** This is important when advertising to external sources. Including the logo, when possible, continues promotion of the establishment. However, some companies use blind ads that omit the name to ensure privacy. For example, a company may not want to be observed advertising for a position that is currently filled by a person who must be replaced.

- **Benefits:** Including information about health insurance, for example, can encourage more applications. In addition, consider including information about other attractive benefits, such as formal training and flexible scheduling.

- **Work location:** This is especially important when there are multiple units in the company. For internal postings, include the department, region, or other location information as appropriate.

- **Ways to respond:** Should applicants apply in person or send in a resume or application? If in person, include the time and date to apply, the information to bring, and the establishment's address. If applicants should apply another way, tell them what information is needed and include the email, Web site, mailing address, or fax number.

Avoiding Discrimination in Recruitment

Asking people to apply in person is a legitimate way to screen. However, this practice cannot be used to avoid considering anyone based on race, age, disability, national origin, gender, religion, or any legally protected traits. This practice may expose the operation to discrimination claims.

Job notice information must be written in a way that provides clear information about the job and avoids discriminatory language. The Equal Employment Opportunity Commission (EEOC) and other government agencies enforce laws that ensure everyone gets a fair chance at any job opening. This means job notices or advertisements cannot be written in any way that discourages certain groups of people from applying.

A statement that identifies the operation as an equal opportunity employer will help encourage a diverse range of applicants. Consider adding a descriptive statement such as "Maynard's Chop House encourages all applicants for this position without regard to race, religion, gender, national origin, age, sexual orientation, disability, or other traits." If the establishment's vision or mission statement emphasizes a commitment to diversity, this statement helps reinforce it. Of course, merely including an EEO statement in a position notice does not make an operation an equal employment opportunity employer. All applicants and employees must be treated fairly.

Here are some guidelines for avoiding discriminatory language in job postings and advertisements:

- Avoid gender-specific titles and other language. Use gender-neutral or gender-inclusive language. For example, use a term such as *server*.

- Avoid references to groups that imply age, race, or other traits that do not relate to essential functions and, when applicable, BFOQs. For example, instead of advertising a position that is "good for homemakers," or "retirees," or "students," advertise the work hours or job seasonality.

- Focus on the actual skills, knowledge, and abilities needed for the job. Instead of advertising a position as "a man's job," state the actual requirement, such as "must be able to lift 50 pounds."

As with job descriptions, accurately describing duties provides honest information and encourages the broadest range of qualified applicants. Including this information also helps protect the operation from discrimination claims.

Evaluating Recruitment Methods

It is important to assess the effectiveness of recruiting activities. An effective evaluation identifies which activities have been most useful. Signs on doors and tabletops at many establishments may encourage the right applicants for counter and kitchen help. In fine-dining operations, networking may produce the best candidates for kitchen employees. Internal recruiting might produce the best source for table service staff.

The method and depth of assessment can vary. In small operations, managers often consider informally which activities have produced the right kinds of applicants. Typically, they are aware of the best recruiting methods for particular positions. Their assessment may be based on intuition and some evidence from observation. This assessment is used to decide which recruiting activities to continue.

Large organizations may evaluate their recruiting activities more thoroughly. For example, they may compare the direct and indirect recruiting costs with the number and sometimes quality of applicants produced. Some factors, such as the loss of productivity during a vacancy and the length of time a new employee will stay with the establishment, may not be measureable. It takes significant work to determine actual expenses, but considering the full costs of an activity against the number and quality of applicants it produced enables an operation to improve its recruiting efforts.

EMPLOYEE SCREENING AND SELECTION

Hiring the right people makes a dramatic difference in the success of an operation. Screening is the process used to ensure that the best candidates are chosen for vacant positions. The strategies used are very important in reducing turnover and its negative impact on profits, employee morale, and customer service. Screening procedures also help protect the establishment if it must defend itself against a discrimination or wrongful termination lawsuit. Hiring the best people is the starting point for making the operation a place where both customers and employees want to be.

In large operations, human resources professionals conduct several activities in the screening process. A manager and perhaps other employees may be involved in some steps. In small companies, the general manager conducts all the screening activities or delegates some steps to the manager of the position being filled. Everyone involved in screening must know all required procedures and ensure that all legal requirements are followed consistently.

Screening Process Overview

Screening involves a range of tools and techniques including application forms, interviews, tests, and background or reference checks (*Exhibit 2.7*). The forms and procedures used should be standardized to collect all appropriate and legally allowable information in the same way from every applicant. This ensures that everyone is treated equally.

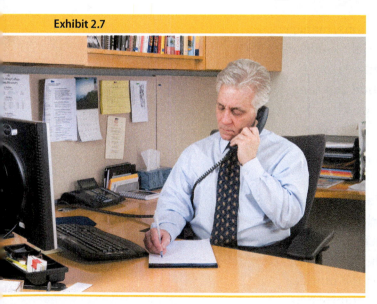

Exhibit 2.7

Not all operations use the same tools and techniques in the same order, but a planned process is required. For example, in a small establishment, an application form and a screening interview may be completed at the same time when someone applies for an entry-level job and the manager is available. This can be an efficient way for managers to obtain information quickly and determine whether the person should complete the next steps.

Other screening procedures may occur in different sequences depending on the operation, the urgency, and the type of position. Managerial candidates may complete applications and participate in screening interviews, testing procedures, and a job interview before reference and background checks are completed. **Background checks** are screening tools used to verify information provided by the applicant, learn more about the applicant's character, and possibly uncover information the applicant has withheld. These generally are done last because of the need for confidentiality during screening and hiring. When hiring is urgent, a job offer may be made contingent on the results of reference checks or other factors. A **job offer** is a formal invitation to become an employee of an establishment on a certain date to perform a described range of duties for a specific salary or wage including identified benefits. If serious issues arise after a contingent job offer is made, the offer may be withdrawn.

Background checks and other procedures such as medical and drug tests are expensive and time-consuming. Operations that use them should develop a policy about their use. For example, information from all selection tools might need to be available before a job offer is made. Alternatively, if a contingency offer is made and later information contradicts what was supplied by the applicant, the manager might then withdraw the offer or terminate the employee.

The goal of every screening process is to find the best-qualified person regardless of age, race, or other traits and to give each person a fair chance to be considered. This requires making judgments, which should be done very carefully and not arbitrarily. Discriminatory practices that adversely affect any protected class of people or that deny any individual an equal chance for consideration should never be used. All applicable laws must be followed consistently.

The best job candidates will be those who can perform the tasks of the open position with or without reasonable accommodation. These tasks are identified in a current and accurate job description. All tools and techniques used in screening should be designed to focus on essential skills of the job and the person's ability to perform them. It is important to have a clear and comprehensive knowledge of the job description. Managers must also understand the actual skills connected to the job description and the realistic range of skills required to perform the job. Doing so allows managers to clearly identify the criteria for selecting finalist candidates.

It is always important to be careful what is said, how things are said, and when things are said throughout the screening process. Avoid personal judgments and be open to how an applicant's skills and experience have been acquired. Consider alternative ways that a person might perform a job's essential functions, and do not allow others to offer inappropriate personal judgments of applicants.

Application Forms

Job applicants typically complete and submit an application form as a first step. It may be accompanied by a cover letter and resume. A **cover letter** is used to express interest in a position and offer to provide additional information, and a **résumé** provides an overview of an applicant's background. *Exhibit 2.8* shows a sample application form.

Exhibit 2.8

SAMPLE HOURLY EMPLOYEE APPLICATION

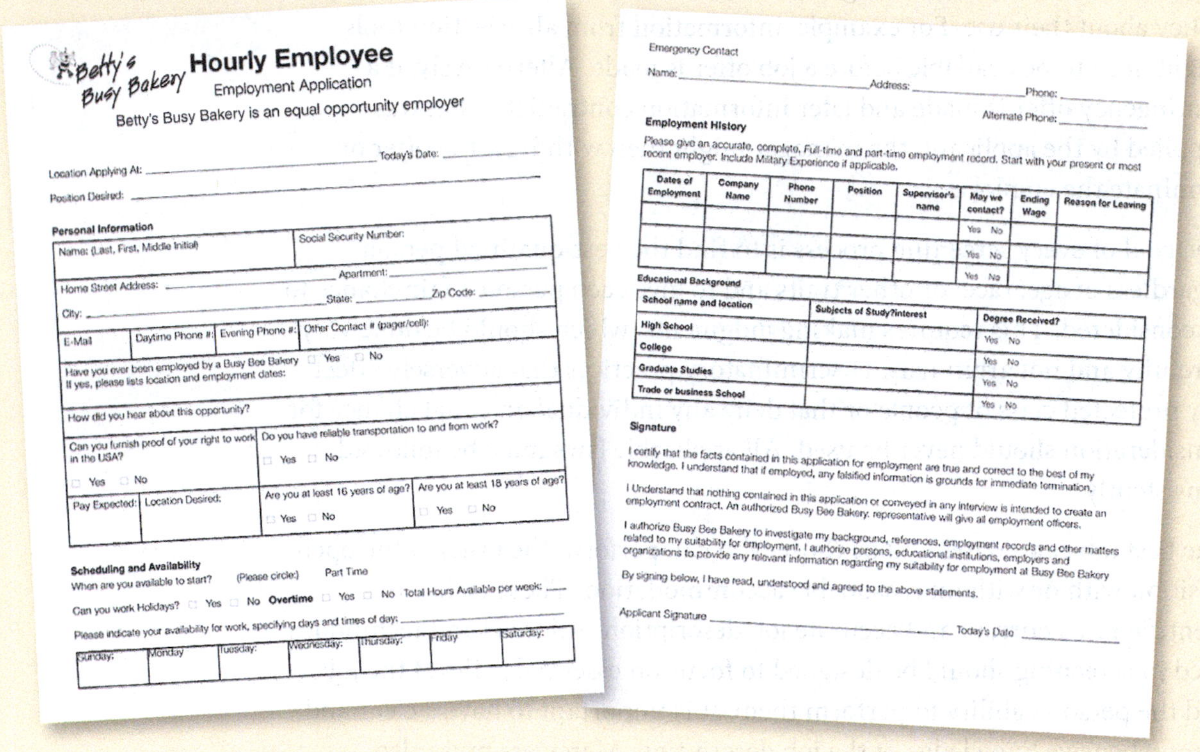

Betty's Busy Bakery

Hourly Employee

Employment Application

Betty's Busy Bakery is an equal opportunity employer

Location Applying At: ____ Today's Date: ____

Position Desired: ____

Personal Information

Name: (Last, First, Middle Initial)		Social Security Number:	
Home Street Address: ____ Apartment: ____			
City: ____ State: ____ Zip Code: ____			
E-Mail	Daytime Phone #:	Evening Phone #:	Other Contact # (pager/cell):
Have you ever been employed by a Busy Bee Bakery ☐ Yes ☐ No If yes, please lists location and employment dates:			
How did you hear about this opportunity?			
Can you furnish proof of your right to work in the USA? ☐ Yes ☐ No		Do you have reliable transportation to and from work? ☐ Yes ☐ No	
Pay Expected:	Location Desired:	Are you at least 16 years of age? ☐ Yes ☐ No	Are you at least 18 years of age? ☐ Yes ☐ No

Scheduling and Availability

When are you available to start? (Please circle:) Part Time

Can you work Holidays? ☐ Yes ☐ No **Overtime** ☐ Yes ☐ No Total Hours Available per week: ____

Please indicate your availability for work, specifying days and times of day: ____

Sunday:	Monday	Tuesday:	Wednesday:	Thursday:	Friday	Saturday:

Emergency Contact

Name: ____ Address: ____ Phone: ____

Alternate Phone: ____

Employment History

Please give an accurate, complete, Full-time and part-time employment record. Start with your present or most recent employer. Include Military Experience if applicable.

Dates of Employment	Company Name	Phone Number	Position	Supervisor's name	May we contact?	Ending Wage	Reason for Leaving
					Yes No		
					Yes No		
					Yes No		

Educational Background

School name and location	Subjects of Study?interest	Degree Received?
High School		Yes No
College		Yes No
Graduate Studies		Yes No
Trade or business School		Yes No

Signature

I certify that the facts contained in this application for employment are true and correct to the best of my knowledge. I understand that if employed, any falsified information is grounds for immediate termination.

I Understand that nothing contained in this application or conveyed in any interview is intended to create an employment contract. An authorized Busy Bee Bakery. representative will give all employment officers.

I authorize Busy Bee Bakery to investigate my background, references, employment records and other matters related to my suitability for employment. I authorize persons, educational institutions, employers and organizations to provide any relevant information regarding my suitability for employment at Busy Bee Bakery

By signing below, I have read, understood and agreed to the above statements.

Applicant Signature ____ Today's Date ____

Reviewing the application form, cover letter, and résumé is the first step in the screening process. A careful review of these documents allows the manager to learn about the applicant's work history, background, and skill level. It also helps identify the experience and information the individual can bring to the operation.

A standard application form approved by a qualified attorney should be required for all individuals to ensure the same information is received from each. Some operations use one form for entry-level positions and a different form for supervisory or management positions. This equal treatment process protects the manager and the establishment from potential criticism, claims, or lawsuits about discriminatory screening practices.

Most application forms include important statements or notices that individuals must sign to help protect the operation (*Exhibit 2.9*). One statement explains that providing false information is grounds for dismissal. Another obtains the person's permission to check references and other background information.

Completed application forms should be kept on file for future vacancies. For example, a person might apply for a kitchen position but not be qualified, although he or she might be a good candidate for a server's position.

Employment Interviews

A review of application forms will likely suggest that some candidates should receive further consideration. These applicants should be requested to participate in one or more job interviews. For example, some operations conduct a screening interview that may be over the telephone and another in-person job interview. The first interviews may be conducted by human resources personnel in larger establishments and later and final interviews may be conducted by managers including, if policy allows it, the individual who will supervise the new employee. Sometimes these interviews are combined due to the lack of time or staff or the level of the position. Most often, these interviews are separate meetings conducted at different points.

Screening interviews are conducted early in the process to help determine whether the person meets basic requirements. They are also used to gather more applicant information, to build interest, and to set the tone for other steps in the hiring process.

Asking the right kinds of questions in employment interviews requires a clear and comprehensive knowledge of the job description. It also requires focusing on the job duties and using language that pertains to the job. Asking questions about a candidate's past behaviors as they relate to the job is useful. Focusing on the skills, knowledge, and abilities required for the job helps ensure that persons are evaluated based on their qualifications rather than arbitrary judgments.

Exhibit 2.10 on the next page reviews examples of topics that can be asked about during employment interviews. Other topics to avoid include personal finances, transportation (unless relevant to an essential job function), political memberships, child-care arrangements, and union membership. Asking these questions can leave the establishment vulnerable to discrimination charges because these discussions might suggest these areas are factors in the hiring decision.

Exhibit 2.9

Manager's Memo

All potential employees must prove their legal right to work in the United States. An employment eligibility verification process has been established for this purpose. If a job applicant is not eligible to work, there is no need to request or analyze other information.

Some managers address this concern first in the screening process. For example, the application form contains a question such as, "Are you eligible to work in the United States?" Applicants answering yes would, at that time, provide one of several identification documents approved by the federal government. There are numerous documents that might be used and an employer cannot specify which approved documents they will accept. Applicants providing acceptable identification verification would remain in the screening process. Others would not be allowed to continue.

Exhibit 2.10	

TOPICS FOR INTERVIEW QUESTIONS

Forbidden Topics	Acceptable Topics
Birthplace or birthplace of parents	Current place of residence and length of stay in that location.
Age	Proof of eligibility to work, which will require the person's age. This is important, for example, to confirm an applicant is old enough to serve alcohol or to operate some equipment items.
National origin or ancestry	Languages spoken and extent of skills are permissible, especially if they relate to languages in the establishment or among customers.
Religion or religious beliefs	This topic should not be discussed.
Gender	This topic should not be discussed unless gender is a BFOQ.
Marital status	This topic is not relevant to hiring.
Parental status	These topics are not relevant to hiring and should be avoided. After explaining the hours and functions of the job, the applicant can be asked whether he or she can fulfill the job obligations.
Sexual orientation	This topic should not be discussed.
Disability or disabling conditions	Employers may not ask job applicants about the existence, nature, or severity of a disability. Applicants may be asked about their ability to perform specific job functions.
Criminal record	When asking criminal record questions, limit inquiries to records for which exclusion would be job related for the position in question, and consistent with business necessity. A company cannot refuse to hire a person based only on criminal record unless it can provide a business justification. If a company makes a tentative job offer and then rescinds the offer based on a criminal background check, the applicant must be notified in writing.
Height, weight, or other physical characteristics	These may be asked only if they are directly relevant to the job; for example, an interviewer can ask whether a person can carry heavy pots if this ability is essential to doing the job.

Managers have the right to ask about a person's ability to perform the job, such as required job hours and expectations for coming to work on time and in all kinds of weather. Instead of asking about transportation or child care, a better question would be, "Is there anything I should know about your ability to be here on time and work the full shift at all times of year and in all types of weather?" In short, ask questions that relate directly to the skills, knowledge, abilities, and requirements of the job for which the person is applying.

PLANNING AND CONDUCTING JOB INTERVIEWS

It is important to plan for interviews, and the clearer the manager is about what must be learned, the more successful they will be. Consider the interview's location, the time to be spent, how it will begin, what types of notes are needed, and what interview format will be used.

Use a standard list of questions such as those shown in *Exhibit 2.11* to avoid possible liability and ensure all desired information will be obtained. Use the same list for every candidate interviewed for the same position.

Exhibit 2.11

SAMPLE INTERVIEW QUESTIONS FOR PROFESSIONAL CANDIDATES

425 West 52nd Street
New York 10019

INTERVIEW SCHEDULE

BACKGROUND INFORMATION

- Tell me about your current job. What do you do? How do you like working there?
- What do you do best in that work environment?
- Tell me about yourself.
- Is there anything that will make it difficult for you to get to work on time? Is there anything that would prevent you from working shifts that may change from week to week?

JOB INTEREST AND EXPERIENCE

- What appeals to you about this job? Why are you interested in it?
- Why are you thinking about leaving your current job?
- What do you know about this company? What do you like about this company?
- What are the skills or strengths you can bring to our company?
- How would you do ? (? is relevant to the skills of the job for which the candidate is being considered)
- What are the most important qualities that you look for in a supervisor?
- Tell me about a decision-making or problem-solving situation you were in at work, how you handled it, and what you learned from it.

SELF-PERCEPTION

- How would your current team members or colleagues describe you as a coworker?
- What does your current supervisor think are your greatest strengths at work? What areas of growth would he or she say you need to focus on?
- Describe yourself as a worker.
- What do your close friends or associates think about your work and career?
- If you were to pick three words to be used to describe you at your retirement party from a career in the restaurant and foodservice industry, what would they be?

WORK ATTITUDE/PERSONALITY INFORMATION

- If you were to receive a package that you wanted sometime in this coming week, what would be in it and who would it be from?
- If you could call one famous person—historical or current—for advice about your career, who would the person be and what would you ask him or her?
- If you won the lottery tomorrow, what would you do with the money—where would you live, what would you do?
- What do you want to tell me about yourself that I have not asked?
- Tell me about one of the biggest mistakes that you ever made at work and what you learned from it.

GENERAL

- Any questions about the job?

Different types of questions and strategies can be used with two popular types of interviews: those used to gather background information, and those used to learn about an applicant's character or personality. Always use the same interview process and questions for each applicant being considered for the same job. Otherwise, the interview process will not be fair, and the establishment will be vulnerable to claims of discrimination.

Background interviews ask questions that focus directly on an applicant's work experience, previous employers, and job challenges. They are used to learn about past work situations and successes:

- How are you qualified for this job opening?
- What are your greatest strengths?
- What areas of your work skills do you want to improve?
- What do you expect from this job?
- What did you do on your last job, and what skills did you develop?
- What are you looking for in this job?
- How would your colleagues describe your work habits?

These examples suggest the range of questions that might be asked and may suggest follow-up questions. Give the applicant ample time to answer, show interest by nodding, and comment when appropriate. The goal is to put the applicant at ease so the information provided will enable the manager to make a judgment about this person for the job opening.

Character or personality interviews can be used when the person has the basic qualifications but the manager wants to learn whether he or she will work well in the pace and culture of the operation. In other words, the goal is to discover what the applicant is likely to do. The assumption is that the person has a work pattern and attitude that will be brought to the position. Here are several common questions:

- Why did you choose this career?
- How has your education helped you in previous jobs?
- How does this job fit into your long-range plans?
- How do you manage stress on the job?

The actual initial interview must be scheduled and conducted, and the interviewer will then benefit from the time spent on preparing for the interview. A structured interview process will help ensure that every applicant is asked the same questions and is given the same opportunities to learn everything necessary to help him or her make the employment decision.

Another aspect of the candidate interviewing process involves reviewing the job description with the applicant to determine whether reasonable

Manager's Memo

The interview process should also be used to provide job information to the applicant. Providing information about the position and the operation gives the applicant a realistic job preview. This will help the applicant understand if the establishment is one in which he or she wants to work and can be successful.

Managers can provide information in the form of brochures, sample menus, Web sites, and other documents. Providing a chance for the applicant to ask questions during the interview serves a similar purpose. Also, giving a tour as part of the screening and interview process can be very helpful.

accommodation is required. As discussed earlier, reasonable accommodation relates to a legal requirement that ensures persons receive accommodation for a disability as long as it does not cause undue hardship for the employer.

The best approach is to go through each task in the job description, since each will be an essential function. The candidate can indicate how they would perform the task and if they would need an accommodation to do so. The manager must know about reasonable accommodation and whether it can be provided without hardship in this specific instance. If it can be, there would not be a reason to exclude the candidate. He or she would then be encouraged to participate in the remaining steps in the process.

DETERMINING FINALIST CANDIDATES

After all interviews for a specific vacancy are completed, the best candidates should be determined based on an assessment of the applications and interviews. The manager can compare information from these sources with knowledge of the establishment's culture, possible fit of the candidate with current staff, and each applicant's abilities to perform the job's essential functions. The basic questions to be asked are "Who is the best candidate from those interviewed?" and "What makes this candidate stand out?"

Candidates who are finalists may be asked to continue with the screening process. This may involve applicant tests and should involve reference or background checks.

Applicant Tests

Managers may use different types of assessments to help determine an applicant's suitability for a job. Some, such as drug tests and physical examinations, are relatively common. Others are more often used by large operations to assess an applicant's personality, ability, aptitude, or skills. Testing is often done after job interviews suggest that the applicant may be offered the position.

To be fair to each individual and comply with the law, establishments that use tests should follow some guidelines:

- Give every applicant, or every applicant in a certain category, such as all managerial positions, the same test.
- Use a test that is culturally neutral so it does not negatively affect any classes of persons protected by law.
- Ask only about functions that relate to the specific duties or necessary skills to perform the job.
- Administer the test in a fair and consistent manner.
- Evaluate the test results against factors that apply to all applicants.

DRUG TESTS

Some operations routinely conduct drug tests as part of the hiring process or before a person begins work. When an operation uses drug testing for applicants or new hires, it must be equally and fairly implemented for all, not just for selected individuals. For example, if applicants for kitchen positions are tested, applicants for all other positions should also be tested. Singling out one job category for drug testing may be discriminatory and may encourage lawsuits. There may also be legal restrictions on drug testing under federal or state law, so it is important to understand the applicable laws before proceeding. Difficulties with drug testing may include inconsistent results from alternative testing systems, the possibility of false results, and the expenses that are incurred.

PHYSICAL EXAMS

All restaurant and foodservice employees work around food. Therefore, it is important to ensure that all employees meet all applicable health requirements of the job.

State and local health laws vary, so it is important to know and comply with all applicable laws regarding mandatory or voluntary employee testing. It is also important that workers with physical disabilities are not unfairly prevented from gaining employment if their disability does not negatively affect their job performance.

SKILL AND KNOWLEDGE TESTS

Skill tests range from simple keyboard tests for administrative staff to equipment operation, table setting, and food-preparation tests. Sometimes these tests involve real machines, dining-room tables, and food. At other times, they are organized as simulations.

Real testing situations provide a more thorough and authentic assessment. However, simulations, such as folding cloth napkins in the manager's office, can be done at any time and do not require an empty dining room or kitchen. These tests are often followed by discussion. Applicants can be asked why they did certain things, how well they think they did, and what they should have done differently. It is often possible to learn as much from this discussion as from observing and analyzing actual test results.

Reference and Background Checks

Reference checks can be another source of important information in the screening process. References provided on application forms may be personal or professional. Most managers are less interested in personal references. These do not relate to a candidate's work skills and experience, and they also may be more biased than professional references. Professional references are typically former managers or others who are familiar with the applicant's skills and abilities.

Company policies about reference checks should always be followed. These policies may address what types of references should be contacted, how they should be contacted, and the types of information that should be requested.

While application forms typically request reference names and contact information, some applicants do not fully complete the form. It is then necessary to request complete contact information. It will also be necessary to obtain permission from the applicant before references are contacted. If permission is not granted, this may impact the manager's interest in proceeding with the individual's application process.

After permission is received, the references may be contacted. The same questions should be asked of all references to obtain desired information and to ensure that all applicants are treated in the same manner.

Some applicants may not have many professional references, especially if they are early in their career or have just come back to the workforce. Then a wider range of references may be needed to learn about the applicant's background.

When a reference is called, listen for how the person talks about the applicant in addition to the content of the message. Pauses, choices of language, and the way the person responds to questions can sometimes provide good information.

The amount and quality of information received from reference checks is much less today than in previous years. Many references are reluctant to provide much information because they fear it will be misused or lead to the applicant being dismissed from consideration. This, in turn, can lead to lawsuits by applicants who allege that incorrect information, the reference's dislike for the applicant, or information not supported by facts resulted in the applicant not being offered a job.

Many references will provide little information besides acknowledging that the applicant was an employee from a specific start date to a specific end date. Managers must increasingly rely on other screening tools to obtain as much information as possible.

Numerous laws address the need for and procedures allowed in conducting background checks. These include the Family Educational Rights and Privacy Act of 1974, the Fair Credit and Reporting Act, and the ADA. Many laws set notice and consent requirements, limit the type or scope of information that can be gathered, and limit the employer's use of the information. While these checks can be done at almost any time in the screening process, they should

REAL MANAGER

RECRUITMENT PROCEDURES

I've always been a believer in a multidimensional recruiting process. At Phase*Next* Hospitality, even as small as we are, we do multiple rounds of interviews, testing, background checks, and drug screening as well as references checks. When I interview people, I like to invest time in getting to know them. If I'm going to be working alongside this person through thick and thin, I want to know who this person really is. How we onboard people has a direct impact on our culture; it messages to people how important we think they are.

Next in the process is testing, which can be a great tool when used correctly. We want to know how candidates stack up against a manager or leader profile so that we understand their abilities, and we make use of test results in assisting with individual development. The bottom line is that if a candidate doesn't possess the critical skills to execute in their position, he or she will not be successful.

Background checks and drug screening can be expensive, but given the locations in which we operate —airports and military installations—this is just a part of doing business. It's part of what we do and we believe that it ensures that we hire better, more successful people.

Reference checks always seem to be the last part of the process and more of an administrative matter. I disagree with that. Checking references provides a great opportunity to build your network and learn more about the candidate. Building and using your network comes in handy over time!

be done according to company policy and in full compliance with all applicable laws.

One important reason to conduct a background check is to prevent an accusation or lawsuit over **negligent hiring**: the failure to ensure, through background checks, that the applicant is a safe and competent person for the position. Many operations conduct careful background checks in some or all of the areas noted in *Exhibit 2.12*.

Exhibit 2.13

Exhibit 2.12	
EXAMPLES OF SEVERAL TYPES OF BACKGROUND CHECKS	
Area	**Common Methods**
Work experience	Conduct reference checks or request other documents such as pay stubs.
Education	Request school transcripts or copies of certificates. This can take several weeks.
Other preparation and background for the position	Request certificates, licenses, or other documents. These can vary greatly and could include, for example, photos of prepared food or letters of reference.
Criminal background	Hire a firm that conducts criminal background checks.
Driving record	Hire a firm that conducts background checks.
Credit record	Buy a credit report from a major consumer reporting agency. Be careful to comply with all federal and state restrictions for how to do this.
Drug use	Request that the employee take a drug test.

THE JOB OFFER

Review and analysis of information from all screening tools should provide the information needed to make a job offer. Job offers are typically made by managers of small operations (*Exhibit 2.13*) and human resources staff in large organizations.

Some managers conduct background checks, drug tests, or obtain other information after a job offer is made. They do so because they do not want to risk losing their best candidates while they wait for information.

When this approach is taken, a contingent job offer is made. This means the offer is based on the successful completion of any other screening activities and the receipt of no information that differs from information provided by the applicant. If a problem is discovered, the job offer is withdrawn. If no problem is identified, the candidate is informed and a start date is agreed on.

- The candidate should be contacted as soon as the decision is made. The actual job offer process depends on the establishment's policies and sometimes the type of position. Some operations use an initial telephone job offer followed by an employment letter; others use an employment letter or an employment contract. An **employment letter** conveys the job details and starting information to the potential employee. An **employment contract**, sometimes called an employment agreement, includes much of the same information. However, it is a legally binding agreement that includes additional terms of employment such as termination provisions. It may remove an employment at will relationship between the employer and employee. **Employment at will** relates to the idea that the employee or the employer can end the relationship at any time for any reason.

- A job offer should provide clear and detailed information so the candidate can make an informed decision:

  Position information: Job title, responsibilities, manager's name

  Compensation information: Salary in hourly or annual terms and timing of payments, such as weekly, biweekly, or monthly

  Applicable benefit information

  Logistical information: Examples include start date, contact person, work location, hours, scheduled shifts, and uniforms.

  Employment contingencies, if any

  Union information, if applicable: For example, is the operation a **union shop** in which all employees are required to join a union and pay dues as a condition of employment?

  At-will statement: If the operation is located in an employment-at-will state, the candidate should be told.

The candidate may want time to consider the job offer or negotiate elements such as the start date or salary. If agreement is reached that differs from the original offer, the final offer should be documented in another employment letter. If the candidate accepts the position orally, an employment letter noting this should be sent. Two copies of the final letter should be sent; the person should sign one copy and return it for the employee file that will be established.

The new employee generally begins work soon after accepting the job offer. When managers are hired from other operations, there may be a period of time between acceptance of the offer and the beginning of employment since a more lengthy notice may be given.

Manager's Memo

Candidates who are not offered a position should be notified in writing and thanked for their interest in the establishment. Wishing them well in their career is also appropriate. If some applicants' resumes and applications will be kept on file for other possible positions, this should be mentioned in the letter. In either case, a positive and encouraging letter contributes to a favorable image of the operation. This will make it easier to do further recruiting within the same population and area.

SUMMARY

1. **Describe the four tasks in the position analysis process.**

   A position analysis identifies each task of a position and explains how it should be done. A task list specifies all tasks of a job and focuses on the activities an employee must be able to do. A task breakdown tells how each task should be done. Performance standards specify the required quality and quantity outputs that define the correct way to perform a task. A job description indicates the tasks a person must be able to perform along with other important information.

2. **Explain the uses of job descriptions and how they should be developed.**

   Job descriptions are used to recruit and screen job applicants and as part of hiring, orientation, training, and development. They help in evaluating employees, making wage and salary decisions, and implementing safety and security concerns. They also impact union and legal concerns.

   The information to include in a job description should be determined, and the format to use for the document must be determined. Data from the position analysis undertaken for the position will be very useful in developing the job description.

   Good job descriptions identify the job, indicate the position's manager, and provide a job summary. They indicate the duties and job requirements. Job descriptions must comply with the Americans with Disabilities Act (ADA). This involves identifying the essential functions an employee in the position must be able to do, possibly with reasonable accommodation for a disability. Position requirements in rare circumstances may also include bona fide occupational qualifications (BFOQs).

   Early drafts of job descriptions must be revised, and then they must be approved according to company policy. They must also be updated as necessary.

3. **Review basic employee recruitment procedures.**

   Recruiting involves activities to encourage the largest number of qualified persons to apply for a job. Staffing needs are forecasted by reviewing last year's revenue and staffing patterns, turnover, and current and seasonal staffing schedules. Guidelines used by similar organizations and the realities of the local labor market may also be considered.

   Many companies have policies emphasizing internal recruiting. External recruiting methods include networking; interactions with school, community, and professional programs; and advertising through traditional and other media. Managers may also participate in career development events and offer open houses.

   Job notices must be written to provide clear information and avoid discriminatory language. The EEOC and other agencies require that everyone—regardless of race, age, gender, religion, national origin, color, or disability—receives a fair chance for any job opening.

   Recruitment methods should be evaluated. In small operations, managers can informally consider the best activities. Large operations may compare costs against applicants produced.

4. **List and explain the tools that can help screen job applicants to determine which should receive job offers.**

   Screening helps ensure that the best candidates are chosen for vacant positions. The goal is to find the best-qualified persons regardless of age, race, or other traits, and every applicant should be given a fair chance. Discriminatory practices should never be used. All screening should focus on the job's essential functions and the person's ability to perform them.

   Screening methods include application forms, interviews, and tests, including drug tests and physicals. Interviews should avoid topics that may imply discrimination. Reference and background checks may also be made.

5. **Review details about job offers made to candidates who meet job requirements.**

   A job offer is a formal invitation to become an employee on a certain date with specified duties and compensation. An initial telephone job offer may be followed by an employment letter, or an employment letter or contract may be sent. Job offers should provide clear and detailed information and may be contingent on completion of screening. Candidates not offered a position should be notified and thanked for their interest.

APPLICATION EXERCISE

Job descriptions are critical screening tools. Team up with another student and interview each other about a current or past job. If you are not participating in a class with other students, think about a present or past job.

Use the information to think about the job's essential functions. Then develop a draft of a job description using the format in the chapter or another template that you find on the Internet.

Share the draft with your student colleague or with your supervisor. Carefully review it, answer the following questions, and make any changes needed.

1. Would a new employee in the position do all of the work in the job description? Would he or she do any other important work not in the job description?

2. What type of reasonable accommodation might be made for one or two of the essential functions for a qualified individual with a disability without undue hardship to the employer?

3. Could any of the tasks be done by an employee without the job specifications listed?

REVIEW YOUR LEARNING

Select the best answer for each question.

1. **What position analysis document specifies all tasks that are part of a job?**

   A. Task list

   B. Task breakdown

   C. Task description

   D. Task specification

2. **What is the primary purpose of a position analysis?**

   A. It explains the need for changes in the organizational chart.

   B. It is used in performance evaluation discussions.

   C. It provides information for the job description.

   D. It provides justifications for wage increases.

3. **A job description that is in compliance with the ADA**

   A. specifies required quality outputs.

   B. focuses on the outcomes of duties.

   C. describes the correct way to perform duties.

   D. gives examples of persons suited for the job.

4. **An employer does not need to accommodate a person with disabilities if doing so would result in**

   A. job task revisions.

   B. an undue hardship.

   C. operating procedure changes.

   D. training material modification.

5. **Which term refers to the employment practices that would constitute discrimination toward certain individuals were they not related to an essential job function and reasonably necessary for the normal operation of the business?**

   A. Job specifications

   B. Performance standards

   C. Employment contingencies

   D. Bona fide occupational qualifications

6. **Placing notices about vacancies in employees' paycheck envelopes is an example of what type of recruiting?**

   A. External

   B. Internal

   C. Referral

   D. Traditional

7. **What is an advantage of internal recruiting?**

   A. No training time is required.

   B. Customers will know the employee.

   C. There is little training expense involved.

   D. Employees are familiar with the operation.

8. **If an operation uses drug testing with applicants for a dining-room position, who else must receive drug tests?**

   A. All existing employees except managers

   B. All applicants except managers

   C. Applicants in all job categories

   D. All existing employees

9. **One important reason to conduct a background check is to prevent an accusation about**

   A. negligent hiring.

   B. eligibility to work.

   C. ADA violation.

   D. EEOC violation.

10. **Which item refers to a legally binding agreement that includes terms of employment such as termination provisions?**

    A. Job offer

    B. At-will statement

    C. Employment letter

    D. Employment contract

FIELD PROJECT

Completion of the field project exercises in several chapters of this book will enable you and a team of your colleagues to develop a handbook of human resources management and supervision information. Divide into teams of three or four students and meet as a group to identify two different types of restaurant or foodservice operations you would like to study. For example, the team may decide that it wants to learn about a quick-service restaurant and a hotel food and beverage operation or a dietary service in a hospital or retirement center.

This chapter provides information about employee recruiting and selecting (screening) procedures. To learn more about these topics, you and your team members should do the following:

A. Develop a list of questions about the two primary topics in this chapter that you would like to ask managers at the two restaurant or foodservice operations you have identified. For example, recruiting questions might include:

- What role do job descriptions play in recruiting entry-level employees?
- How, if at all, do you use social media when recruiting new employees?

Sample selection (screening) questions could include:

- Who conducts applicant interviews in your operation and how important is the interview information you obtain in making a selection decision?

- What is your policy about drug testing for job applicants?

Note: *Save the questions you have developed. Later in this course, your team will conduct interviews with the managers of restaurant or foodservice operations selected by the team. These interviews will include the questions you have developed in this chapter, as well as questions from other chapters. You may want to use the interview form (template) in the Field Project Information Handbook at the end of this book, or develop an interview form of your own to list your interview questions. This form can then be used to record the managers' responses when you conduct your interview.*

B. Identify Internet resources that can provide additional information as your team studies recruitment and selection (screening). For example, enter the following terms into your favorite search engine:

- Recruiting entry-level employees
- Job applicant skill testing
- Job applicant interviews
- Elements in a job offer

Make a list of several suggestions for employee recruitment and selecting (screening) from each of at least four Internet resources. These suggestions can be recorded in Part II (Internet Resources) for chapter 2 in the Field Project Information Handbook at the end of this book.

3

Employee Orientation and Training

INSIDE THIS CHAPTER

- Employment and Payroll Documentation
- Hiring and Orientation Activities
- Orientation Programs
- Employee Training Programs

CHAPTER LEARNING OBJECTIVES

After completing this chapter, you should be able to:

- Review basic procedures that should be used for employment and payroll documentation.

- Explain basic procedures that should be included in hiring and orientation activities.

- Describe how to plan and evaluate orientation programs.

- Explain procedures for planning and delivering training programs.

KEY TERMS

CASE STUDY

"There is not much incentive to be a good employee around here," suggested Akusu, a server at Sand Dunes Restaurant.

"What do you mean?" asked Edison, another server.

Akusu replied, "I've been here a long time and do my work and never complain. I would think our manager would give me a little reward, even if it is just a thank-you. Instead, every time we get a new employee, I am asked to train that person. I have to do all of my beginning- and end-of-shift work, take the same number of tables, and also train. So I sometimes don't give the very best service. I feel bad, and I lose tips."

"That's true," said Edison, "but is there any other way to train a new employee?"

1. You are the manager of Sand Dunes Restaurant. Answer Edison's question.

2. Should Akusu tell the manager how she feels? Why or why not?

EMPLOYMENT AND PAYROLL DOCUMENTATION

At some point between the time a person accepts a position and the first days on the job, documents related to employment and payroll must be processed. The timing varies in different operations. Some documentation may be completed before the employee starts, some on the first day of work, and some during the first payroll period.

For example, before beginning work and being placed on the payroll, the employee must demonstrate that he or she is legally able to work in this country. This proof is documented on a **Form I-9**. Other documents, such as transcripts and benefit enrollment forms, can be processed when the employee begins work. The timing depends on an operation's hiring and orientation practices. Practices should accommodate payroll and benefit schedules, company policies, and legal requirements. The most important concern is that all necessary documents are completed and processed so there will be enough time to do several things:

- Meet all legal requirements.
- Ensure the employee will receive any benefits due on the first day of employment.
- Ensure that company policies are met, such as having emergency contact information or signed policy agreements on file.
- Enter employee payroll information before the first paycheck is due.

There are three major types of hiring-related documents: those for employment and payroll, and those for benefit enrollment. Managers or human resources professionals must provide some of these documents. The new employee must provide others. Examples are documents required by I-9 forms or needed to confirm job qualifications, such as a driver's license or sanitation certificate. Required forms may be available in hard copy or electronic versions. When an employee provides required hard copy documents that must be returned to the employee, the manager or human resources professional should make a copy for the new employee's personnel file, which is used to maintain all human resources–related records applicable to the employee.

Required Employment and Payroll Documents

The most critical documents to be completed or produced are those required by law and those that put an employee on the payroll. These documents are usually the first to be considered:

- **Form W-4**, **Employee's Withholding Allowance Certificate:** This federal tax form is provided by the employer. It is used for payroll and tax withholding purposes.

- **State and local tax forms:** The employer provides the necessary state and local tax forms for payroll and tax withholding.

- **Form I-9, Employment Eligibility Verification:** The employer provides this form, which requires each individual hired to show specific documents to prove his or her legal right to work in the United States. The employer must determine whether the employment eligibility and identity document(s) presented reasonably appear to be genuine and relate to the individual. Information from the approved document(s) must be recorded on Form I-9. *Exhibit 3.1* on the next page shows this form.

- **Other documents relating to the position:** Depending on the position, its requirements, company policies, or state and local regulations, the new employee may need to show or complete some other documents:

  - Sanitation certificate
  - Valid driver's license and proof of auto insurance
  - Responsible alcohol service certificate
  - Tip allocation agreement

- **Job eligibility documents, if applicable:** If a person is hired under a government program such as the Work Opportunity Tax Credit (WOTC) program, additional documents may be required.

- **Permission documents:** These forms give an employer permission to check references and background or perform drug testing if not already covered on the application form.

Additional documentation will be needed when hiring a minor or someone to prepare or serve alcoholic beverages. First, it is necessary to verify that the person is legally old enough to work in the position. Proof of age can be found on some of the other required documents. In addition, in most states, a person younger than eighteen must show written permission from a parent or legal guardian. Some locations may require a work permit instead, such as from a school district.

In addition, if the new hire did not complete a standard application form, this should be done before he or she begins work. This will ensure that all employees are treated equally. Additionally, some application forms provide a statement about grounds for dismissal.

Benefit Enrollment Documents

Typically, documents required to enroll an employee in health, life insurance, or other benefit plans are completed on or soon after the first day of work. Orientation programs may provide information about benefit choices. However, some establishments also send information to the new employee before he or she begins work. This allows the employee to review the choices and ask questions before completing the necessary paperwork.

Exhibit 3.1

FORM I-9

OMB No. 1615-0047; Expires 08/31/12

Department of Homeland Security
U.S. Citizenship and Immigration Services

**Form I-9, Employment
Eligibility Verification**

Read instructions carefully before completing this form. The instructions must be available during completion of this form.

ANTI-DISCRIMINATION NOTICE: It is illegal to discriminate against work-authorized individuals. Employers CANNOT specify which document(s) they will accept from an employee. The refusal to hire an individual because the documents have a future expiration date may also constitute illegal discrimination.

Section 1. Employee Information and Verification *(To be completed and signed by employee at the time employment begins.)*

Print Name: Last	First	Middle Initial	Maiden Name

Address *(Street Name and Number)*		Apt. #	Date of Birth *(month/day/year)*

City	State	Zip Code	Social Security #

I am aware that federal law provides for imprisonment and/or fines for false statements or use of false documents in connection with the completion of this form.

I attest, under penalty of perjury, that I am (check one of the following):

☐ A citizen of the United States

☐ A noncitizen national of the United States (see instructions)

☐ A lawful permanent resident (Alien #) _____

☐ An alien authorized to work (Alien # or Admission #) _____
     until (expiration date, if applicable - *month/day/year*)

Employee's Signature	Date *(month/day/year)*

Preparer and/or Translator Certification *(To be completed and signed if Section 1 is prepared by a person other than the employee.) I attest, under penalty of perjury, that I have assisted in the completion of this form and that to the best of my knowledge the information is true and correct.*

Preparer's/Translator's Signature	Print Name

Address *(Street Name and Number, City, State, Zip Code)*	Date *(month/day/year)*

Section 2. Employer Review and Verification *(To be completed and signed by employer. Examine one document from List A OR examine one document from List B and one from List C, as listed on the reverse of this form, and record the title, number, and expiration date, if any, of the document(s).)*

	List A	OR	List B	AND	List C
Document title:					
Issuing authority:					
Document #:					
Expiration Date *(if any)*:					
Document #:					
Expiration Date *(if any)*:					

CERTIFICATION: I attest, under penalty of perjury, that I have examined the document(s) presented by the above-named employee, that the above-listed document(s) appear to be genuine and to relate to the employee named, that the employee began employment on *(month/day/year)* _____ and that to the best of my knowledge the employee is authorized to work in the United States. **(State employment agencies may omit the date the employee began employment.)**

Signature of Employer or Authorized Representative	Print Name	Title

Business or Organization Name and Address *(Street Name and Number, City, State, Zip Code)*	Date *(month/day/year)*

Section 3. Updating and Reverification *(To be completed and signed by employer.)*

A. New Name *(if applicable)*	B. Date of Rehire *(month/day/year) (if applicable)*

C. If employee's previous grant of work authorization has expired, provide the information below for the document that establishes current employment authorization.

Document Title:	Document #:	Expiration Date *(if any)*:

I attest, under penalty of perjury, that to the best of my knowledge, this employee is authorized to work in the United States, and if the employee presented document(s), the document(s) I have examined appear to be genuine and to relate to the individual.

Signature of Employer or Authorized Representative	Date *(month/day/year)*

Form I-9 (Rev. 08/07/09) Y Page 4

If an operation offers retirement benefits, even if they are not available to the employee until after a specific period of time, that information also should be provided. Doing so is required by the federal government for some types of pension and healthcare programs.

Personnel Files

Both federal and state employment regulations require that most of the documents processed during hiring and orientation be kept on file. These records and other information should be kept securely in an employee's personnel file. This is a confidential file that contains documents related to hiring, training, evaluating, promoting, and if necessary, disciplining an individual. Information that should be kept in the file and that which should be kept separate is shown in *Exhibit 3.2*.

Exhibit 3.2

INFORMATION TO KEEP IN AND SEPARATE FROM A PERSONNEL FILE

Information That Should Be Kept in a Personnel File

Job application	Signed W-4 form and state and local tax forms
Cover letter and resume (if applicable)	Copy of driver's license (if applicable)
Competency or assessment test results	Proof of automobile insurance (if applicable)
Interview evaluation forms	Other internal documents related to employment decisions, such as test results from the screening process and new hire or orientation checklists
Signed employment letter or employment contract	
Job description	
Educational transcripts	
Copies of any certificates	
Letters of reference, or notes of reference checks done by telephone	

Items That Must Be Kept Separately

Benefits information, such as medical and retirement information	ADA accommodations
I-9 form	FMLA certifications
Work injury records	Drug test results (if applicable)

When an employee resigns or is terminated, information about the departure, such as a resignation letter and an exit interview form, should be added to the file. It is also helpful to obtain a permanent address so future tax information can be sent to the employee.

Personnel files should be stored in a safe, secure, and private space protected from fire, theft, and damage. The files should be kept in a locked cabinet or room so unauthorized persons cannot access them.

HIRING AND ORIENTATION ACTIVITIES

Some managers make a distinction between document processing and other orientation activities. In this case, tasks relating to employment and benefits documents are considered **hiring**. Those related to introducing the new employee to the establishment and the job are considered **orientation**. In practice, both types of related activities are done at the times and in the sequence established by the operation.

Timing of Hiring and Orientation Activities

As is true for the recruitment, screening, and selection activities discussed in chapter 2, organizations manage hiring and orientation procedures differently. For example, some operations send tax forms and other documents to a newly hired employee as soon as the job is accepted. Others wait until the employee begins orientation on the first day of work. The order in which many of these steps occur does not matter, as long as they are done within a short time after the employee starts. *Exhibit 3.3* shows when activities might occur.

Regardless of when hiring and orientation activities are done, the end results will include the processing of documentation. Also, the new employee will become oriented to the operation.

Hiring and Orientation Checklists

As suggested by *Exhibit 3.3*, there are many steps in the hiring and orientation process. Each must be managed, and it may also be necessary to confirm that some or all were completed. An effective tracking and filing system can help to address these concerns.

Manager's Memo

In large operations, human resources professionals will be involved in many hiring and orientation steps. However, regardless of the operation's size, managers will have some involvement. In addition, they will also be responsible for some of the many planning activities that support an employee's hiring and orientation:

- Developing support tools and materials such as checklists and orientation materials

- Planning the orientation program and job training

- Preparing the employees who will conduct parts of the orientation or job training

- Evaluating the orientation program and job training

Exhibit 3.3

HIRING AND ORIENTATION ACTIVITIES

Activity	Hiring	Orientation
Make job offer	X	
Send employment letter or contract	X	
Distribute job description	X	X
Distribute employee handbook	X	X
Distribute orientation handbook	X	X
Explain job expectations and probationary period	X	X
Notify unsuccessful candidates	X	
Check background	X	
Check physical abilities	X	
Conduct drug test	X	
Complete tax forms	X	X
Request proof of eligibility to work	X	X
Request certificates and licenses	X	X
Process job eligibility documents	X	X
Request proof of age	X	X
Request permission for minor/work permit	X	X
Explain benefits and distribute summary plan descriptions	X	X
Complete benefit enrollment forms	X	X
Create and use personnel file	X	X
Create and use new hire checklist	X	X
Explain organizational policies and procedures	X	X
Explain company vision, mission, and history	X	X
Distribute company contact numbers	X	X
Distribute work and payroll schedule	X	X
Introduce employee to staff	X	X
Create and use orientation checklist	X	X
Conduct orientation meeting		X
Provide tour of work area and facilities	X	X
Conduct training		X
Collect feedback		X
Evaluate program effectiveness		X

Checklists provide an easy way to track and manage hiring and orientation. Effective checklists, when used carefully, will help ensure that all legal, payroll, and policy requirements are met. They also minimize challenges for new employees (*Exhibit 3.4*).

Exhibit 3.4

Two types of checklists are commonly used: new hire checklists and orientation checklists. Given the overlap between the steps, some operations use only one checklist. When an operation uses both, the new hire checklist generally focuses on getting the employee and the operation ready for the employee's first day. The orientation checklist is then used to manage what happens on the first day and during follow-up.

To ensure that all steps are covered and each new employee is treated equally, checklists should include a way to identify who was responsible for each step and when it was done. When a step is completed, the person who performed it or ensured it was completed should sign or initial the form and enter the date. In this way, especially if employees sign or initial, the checklists can be used to show that an employee received certain information such as information about a health insurance policy. Keep completed checklists in employees' personnel files.

NEW HIRE CHECKLIST

Exhibit 3.5 shows a sample **new hire checklist**. It is especially useful for ensuring that all hiring documents are produced or completed.

Exhibit 3.5

SAMPLE NEW HIRE CHECKLIST

New Hire Checklist

Name: _Jamie Park_   **SSN:** _999-00-1234_

Activity or Task	Name	Date
Personnel file created	M. Martinez	9/2/13
Job offer extended in writing	M. Martinez	9/2/13
Job description distributed	M. Martinez	9/2/13
Job offer accepted in writing	M. Martinez	9/6/13
Signed copy of job description received	M. Martinez	9/6/13
Completed job application form on file	M. Martinez	9/2/13
Letter of welcome distributed	C. Kantas	9/1/13
Employee handbook distributed (and signed for)	C. Kantas	9/1/13
Uniform and dress code policy distributed	C. Kantas	9/1/13
Nondiscrimination policy distributed	C. Kantas	9/1/13
Employee referral policy distributed	C. Kantas	9/1/13
Tax forms distributed	C. Kantas	9/1/13
Proof of identity provided	C. Kantas	9/1/13
Proof of eligibility to work in the U.S. shown	C. Kantas	9/1/13
Job eligibility documents shown	C. Kantas	9/1/13
Proof of age shown (or N/A)	—	
Sanitation certification shown	C. Kantas	9/1/13
Other document shown (please list): _RAS cert._	C. Kantas	9/1/13
Other document shown (please list): N/A	—	
Health benefits plan and form distributed	C. Kantas	9/1/13
Health benefits explained	C. Kantas	9/1/13
Retirement plan and form distributed	C. Kantas	9/1/13
Retirement benefits explained	C. Kantas	9/1/13
New employee gift distributed	C. Kantas	9/1/13
Uniform issued	C. Kantas	9/1/13
Orientation schedule developed		
Orientation schedule distributed		

KEEPING IT SAFE

A well-planned and organized orientation program helps ensure that every new employee receives the same information. This consistency is important for many reasons, and one relates to safety and legal obligations. Everyone should receive the same information, learn the same safety practices, have the same opportunities to learn about the operation, and meet the same key people. This consistency helps ensure that every employee starts with an equal chance of success, an integral concern of equal employment opportunity laws.

Orientation sessions should address the types of emergencies a new employee is likely to encounter on the job. For example, fires may be possible in all establishments, but earthquakes are likely only in operations in some areas. These emergency situations must be identified and carefully considered as procedures are developed and delivered in training programs. While training should be ongoing, critical safety training should be conducted during orientation.

Exhibit 3.6

SAMPLE ORIENTATION CHECKLIST

Orientation Checklist
Hourly Employees

Name: _Terry Blazek_   Start date: _03/01/13_

Activity or Task	Name	Date
Initial orientation meeting	E. Silverstein	03/01/13
Received health benefits orientation	E. Silverstein	03/01/13
Signed health enrollment form	E. Silverstein	03/01/13
Signed tax form	E. Silverstein	03/01/13
Received retirement orientation	E. Silverstein	03/01/13
Interview with personnel assistant		
Interview with general manager		
Tour of facility		
Received Employee Handbook		
Received policy orientation		
Received procedures orientation		
Received policy of nondiscrimination		
Signed equal treatment agreement		
Received work schedule		
Received job description		
Orientation to responsibilities of new job		
Initial meeting with trainer		
Week 2 meeting with trainer		
Week 3 meeting with trainer		
Week 4 meeting with trainer		

ORIENTATION CHECKLIST

Managers develop **orientation checklists** to ensure that each new employee has the same orientation experience and a chance to learn about the same topics. A checklist is a way of guaranteeing equal opportunity. It also helps monitor each person's progress through the program, such as visiting certain departments or meeting with key supervisors or managers.

While it is similar to a new hire checklist, an orientation checklist focuses on a broader range of activities. This checklist should note the activities to be addressed during orientation. A sample list is shown in *Exhibit 3.6* to the left. In some establishments, the new employee must maintain the list. In other organizations, the individual works with another staff member or someone from human resources to ensure that all tasks are completed.

ORIENTATION PROGRAMS

An effective orientation program meets the needs of the new employee and the operation. It has two main purposes: to provide information a new employee needs to function effectively, and to make the employee feel welcome. To do this, orientation programs help set the employee's expectations and address questions.

A good orientation program demonstrates the customer focus that managers want all employees to practice. Managers want employees to feel comfortable, be happy in their work, and maintain a focus of meeting the customers' needs. That means the orientation program should establish a hospitality emphasis from the very beginning of employees' experiences with the establishment (*Exhibit 3.7*). Said simply, managers should treat employees in the same thoughtful manner as they expect the employees to treat customers.

Managers in operations with high turnover rates may find it difficult to justify a comprehensive orientation program. However, the lack of effective orientation often contributes to unacceptable turnover because new employees are not comfortable in their position. If new employees do not believe they are respected and appreciated, they will not like their work. In turn they will either leave, or remain and be unproductive and uncaring toward customers or peers. A well-planned orientation program is an important first step in developing the kind of employees all managers desire.

THINK ABOUT IT . . .

Do you think a new employee's orientation experiences affect his or her ideas about what it will be like to work for the establishment? Explain your answer.

Exhibit 3.7

Planning Orientation Programs

The best orientation programs are much more than a meeting to discuss benefits, fill out forms, and receive an employee handbook. These tasks are important, but they are only part of a comprehensive program that includes numerous activities. When planning an orientation program, it is important to consider the time frame, the program's content and structure, necessary materials and resources, and those who will conduct it.

TIME FRAME

Depending on the new employee's position and the operation's size, an orientation may be as short as several hours or as long as several weeks or longer. Orientation and onboarding programs for professional employees and managers can sometimes last several months. Entry-level employees typically have shorter orientations since they have fewer and more specific responsibilities. In small organizations, the orientation period may be very short, and the employees themselves provide much of the information. Managers rely more on documents and one-on-one meetings than on group orientation events.

It is necessary to consider content and delivery methods when determining the time required for orientation programs. Remember that the primary objective is not to make the program as short as possible. It is to determine what information a new employee requires to help the establishment meet customers' needs.

CONTENT AND STRUCTURE

Orientation programs are generally composed of two main areas: information everyone should know about the operation and what a specific employee should know about a position. In some operations, a separate induction program is used to provide specific information that an employee must know about his or her department and position. In a program that includes a number of new employees, everyone can participate equally in the part that relates to the entire organization. This is typically the first portion of the program and should include several activities:

- Review of the operation's vision, mission, culture, goals, and history
- Identification of key managers and organizational structure
- Explanation of benefits and benefit schedules, when applicable
- Completion of any outstanding hiring paperwork
- Explanation of company policies and procedures
- Distribution and review of the employee handbook, if not already done

The first activity listed is among the most important in the entire orientation process. Done correctly, it will not be a lecture session or a one-time review of the establishment's vision, mission, culture, goals, and history. Instead, the

Manager's Memo

Some operations make a more formal distinction between what all employees must know about their organization and what each employee must know about a specific position. These companies develop orientation programs for all staff members and induction programs that provide department and position information.

This is another example of how companies plan their new employees' first on-the-job experiences. Regardless of how the initial experiences are carried out, the information new employees obtain should be the same. Using the orientation and induction approach makes it easier to assign specific tasks to individuals. Human resources staff or a manager can address orientation, while those in specific departments can present more in-depth information about departmental and position concerns.

Neither approach—combined or separate—is perfect for every situation. Their common concern is the need to identify what new employees must know and provide a formal and organized method of supplying this information.

culture of the operation will be obvious when those facilitating the orientation show genuine enthusiasm, respect, and concern for the new employees. They will exhibit pride in what the organization has accomplished. Also, they will pledge an ongoing interest in helping the new employees feel comfortable and providing the knowledge and skills required for success. In other words, they are role models for attitudes and expectations. When a supervisor or manager is a role model, he or she performs in a way that meets the standards expected for employees' behavior.

The organization's culture will also be evident when new employees meet other managers and coworkers. They are not greeted with an offhanded "Hi, how are you?" Instead, they are genuinely welcomed to the team. They learn that their coworkers are there to answer questions, help in any way they can, and be supportive as the new employee transitions into the team.

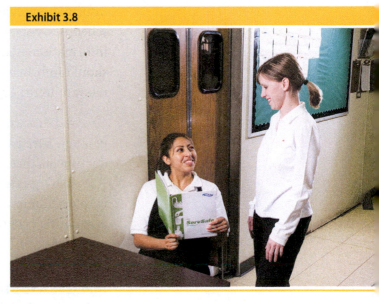

Exhibit 3.8

After the general orientation, new employees need to learn about the specific demands of their job. This may include an overview of how their department fits into the operation. Starting with a job description, the person learns what responsibilities are part of the position, when tasks must be done, and what materials are provided. Often, the new employee's manager provides at least part of this information (*Exhibit 3.8*). He or she should also address specific questions.

At a minimum, this phase of the orientation process should include several activities:

- Review and distribution of the job description
- Information about training and performance expectations
- Review of the employee's work schedule for the first week
- Distribution of contact numbers
- Introduction to coworkers and other staff
- Tour of facility, including the new hire's work area
- Distribution of uniforms, name tags, personal equipment, tools, or materials supplied by the establishment

The last two points cover basic logistics. The tour should include office, break room, time clock, restrooms, employee parking facility, employee entrance, and storage locations. The new employee also should receive his or her uniform, name tag, locker information, keys, and any other equipment or tools supplied.

Longer orientations often include time for periodic meetings with a supervisor to review how the employee is doing and what he or she is learning on the job. Some organizations may use a probationary period. A **probationary period** is the time used by the manager to assess whether a new employee can successfully perform the job's tasks.

MATERIALS AND RESOURCES

After orientation information and activities are known, it is possible to determine the tools, documentation, and staff that are needed for the orientation. In addition to the job description and other hiring documents, information reviewed typically includes organizational charts, work schedules, copies of menus and promotional materials, and contact information. A schedule for orientation activities should be provided, as should information about any probationary period and other legal documents relevant to the organization.

To avoid overwhelming new employees, some operations organize documents in a **new hire packet** given before or during orientation. It contains a copy of documents that are needed and will be discussed during orientation sessions. A trainer's guide is an essential tool that helps contributors get ready to assist with orientation activities. This guide should include a detailed outline of the orientation program and all the materials needed to complete the orientation checklist.

TRAINERS AND OTHER CONTRIBUTORS

Orientation builds a strong first impression and provides a foundation for employee attitudes. The people who present orientation sessions provide new employees with some of their first points of contact with the operation. Therefore, the impressions made will likely have long-lasting effects on employees' attitudes, behaviors, and morale.

Many trainers and orientation contributors are chosen for their expertise or their position in the operation. For example, a human resources professional may present information on company policies and benefits, while the general manager may discuss the organization's vision, mission, culture, and values. Decisions about who will present depend on many factors. These include the operation's size, the number of people being oriented, and the availability of the potential contributors. In addition to trainers, others who may have roles include meeting facilitators, administrators, coaches, and **orientation buddies**: those who serve as advisers during orientation.

In small operations, role distinctions will be less important since the general manager or another manager often conducts the entire orientation. Regardless of their role, orientation trainers and contributors must want to help new employees learn the operation's culture, policies, and procedures.

THINK ABOUT IT . . .

To successfully lead orientation meetings, a person should be able to present information clearly and handle questions with diplomacy. What other types of skills are necessary?

Employee Handbooks

A current copy of the **employee handbook** should be given to new employees. This helps ensure that new employees understand job requirements and the establishment's policies. Many operations have new employees sign a form indicating that they have received the employee handbook. If the employee handbook has not been updated for some time, any updates should also be provided. Note that restaurant and foodservice operations are increasingly posting employee handbooks on the establishment's intranet, and online manuals allow easy and ongoing updating. *Exhibit 3.9* shows the table of contents for a sample employee handbook. Note that it provides a broad overview of the types of information with which new employees should become familiar.

Exhibit 3.9

SAMPLE TABLE OF CONTENTS FOR EMPLOYEE HANDBOOK

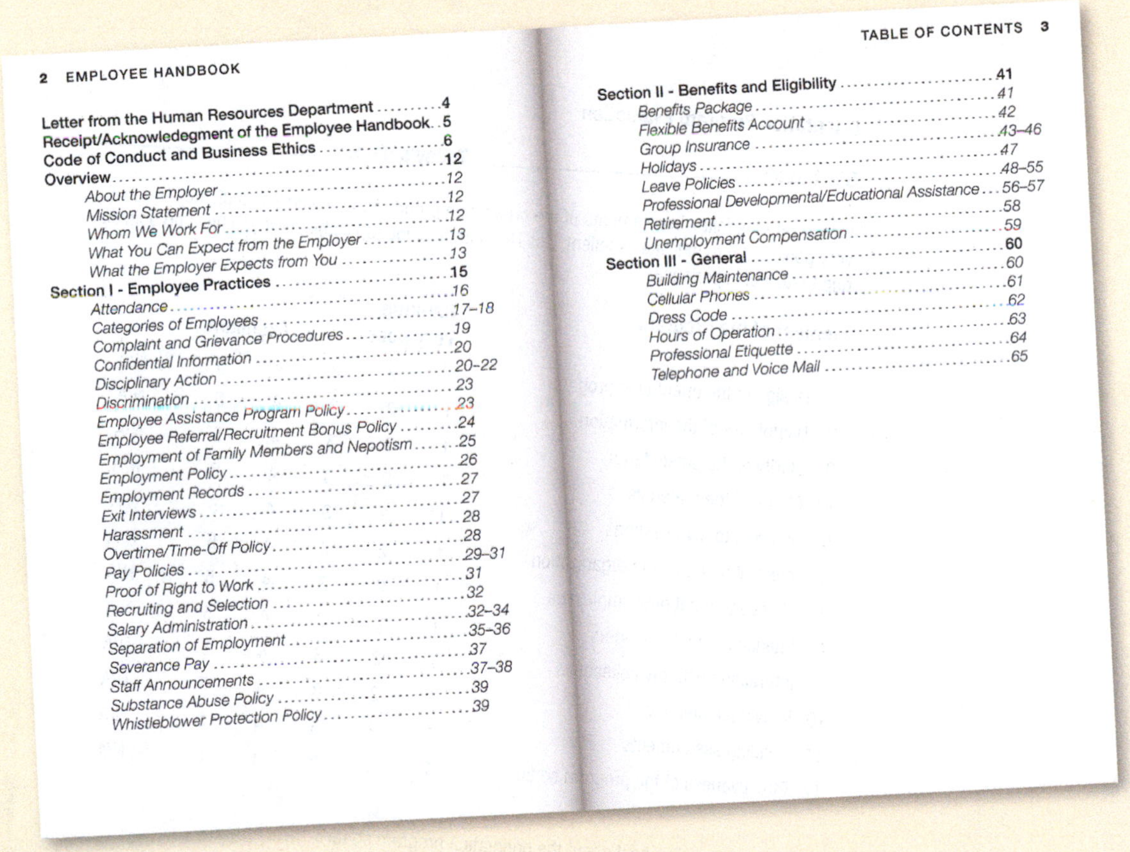
2 EMPLOYEE HANDBOOK

TABLE OF CONTENTS 3

Evaluating Orientation Programs

Managers evaluate orientation programs for several reasons. First, they want to know whether the participants liked the program and felt that it was useful. Second, they want to know whether the participants learned what was intended; that is, whether it helped them become more knowledgeable about the operation and their role. Managers also want to know if the program accomplished its objectives cost-effectively. The ultimate purpose of evaluation is to improve the orientation program.

One way to evaluate an orientation program occurs as managers talk with new employees to see if the process is effective. The managers can then share this feedback with the person responsible for orientation. These conversations also support the orientation because the manager can answer questions that were not addressed.

In addition, those responsible for orientation can use evaluation forms during or at the end of orientation. *Exhibit 3.10* shows examples of questions that can be used to rate various aspects of the orientation program and obtain general

Exhibit 3.10

SAMPLE ORIENTATION EVALUATION FORM

Orientation Program Evaluation

Start date: _____   Today's date: _____

Please rate the following elements of the orientation program by circling 1 to indicate very poor, and 5 to indicate excellent. Use N/A if item is not applicable, or if you have no opinion due to lack of experience.

Element of the Program	Ranking Very poor			Excellent		
1 Design of the orientation program	1	2	3	4	5	N/A
2 Usefulness of the information	1	2	3	4	5	N/A
3 Clarity of the presenter(s)	1	2	3	4	5	N/A
4 Clarity of the materials	1	2	3	4	5	N/A
5 Answers to my questions	1	2	3	4	5	N/A
6 Information about the organization	1	2	3	4	5	N/A
7 Chance to meet new employees	1	2	3	4	5	N/A
8 Chance to meet managers	1	2	3	4	5	N/A
9 Interaction with my colleagues	1	2	3	4	5	N/A
10 Individual interviews	1	2	3	4	5	N/A
11 Reading assignments	1	2	3	4	5	N/A
12 Effectiveness of the program so far	1	2	3	4	5	N/A

13 What do you like best about the orientation program so far?

_____

_____

14 What do you like least about the orientation program so far?

_____

_____

information. Evaluations also can be used to obtain feedback about trainers' performance and to gauge how well employees feel they are performing after orientation.

Beyond participant reactions, managers normally ask trainers or other persons responsible for orientation how they think the program is proceeding and what changes might be made. Combining their insights and the results of evaluation instruments can provide a clear picture of how orientation may be made more effective.

In some large operations, human resources professionals or managers may evaluate the overall effectiveness of orientation annually. For example, all employees hired within the past year may be polled to collect viewpoints about the orientation process. By comparing this information and data from other evaluations against the estimated or actual costs of the program, managers can begin to assess the program's cost-effectiveness.

Given the considerable time required for and the importance of orientation, this evaluation time is well spent. In small organizations, the evaluation is typically done more casually and with fewer cost calculations, since there is little staff time or other resources available for a detailed analysis.

EMPLOYEE TRAINING PROGRAMS

Training is an investment, not an expense, because its benefits are paid back over a period of time. Implementing training is similar to buying an oven; it will pay back dividends over its lifetime of use. Therefore, although effective training costs money, it will pay back dividends that are greater than its costs.

To use training effectively and receive a good return on the investment, managers must know how and when to train. Basic principles can guide managers as they make training decisions.

Benefits of Training

Training helps improve the skills and knowledge employees need to do their jobs. When training is focused and done well, it improves the quality of employee work, promotes employee growth, keeps employees challenged and satisfied, and creates talent to help the organization grow.

Although it is sometimes unappreciated and is often the first area affected by budget cuts, effective training is essential to the success of an operation. There are several reasons it is important.

THINK ABOUT IT . . .

Does training time "walk out the door" when an employee leaves? If so, are effective supervision practices a reliable method of reducing turnover? Why or why not?

JOB SKILLS IMPROVEMENT

Employees must be trained when they begin work, when job requirements change, and in several other situations:

- **Training provides basic skills:** Many restaurant and foodservice employees are first-time, entry-level, or unskilled workers. Often they have no previous experience in the industry. These employees must be trained to attain the required skills.

- **Training prepares employees for new assignments:** When employees move from one assignment to another, training is generally the quickest way to provide the skills and knowledge required for the new tasks. The alternative, allowing employees to learn by trial and error, is likely to yield low productivity and unhappy customers.

- **Training is needed for new equipment:** Computers and software programs are increasingly complex and more frequently used in equipment and throughout operations. New and long-term employees must be trained to function effectively in this environment.

- **Training is needed for new procedures:** New recipes and new procedures for food preparation are constantly being introduced in many establishments, and training can expedite the transition. Training teaches all employees to do things the right way from the start and reduces errors, waste, and rework. It can make a real difference in success or failure of launching a new procedure.

- **Training increases job proficiency:** Skilled employees are required to provide positive dining experiences for customers. Training helps ensure that effective customer service is provided.

- **Training increases sales and profitability:** Well-trained employees sell more and work more efficiently than others who are not as well trained.

OTHER BENEFITS

The primary purpose of training is to teach employees how to do their jobs well. Additionally, training offers other benefits. For example, training can help employees with poor English skills. Many organizations have found that some employees have difficulty reading and writing English, so they have developed in-house programs to ensure a minimum level of literacy. Other organizations use literacy training experts or send employees to literacy training classes.

Training also transfers values. It can help employees understand and buy into the vision, mission, and values of an operation. Training materials and activities should reinforce these concepts.

Training also creates consistency in products and service. Following the same standards creates consistency of look, feel, and taste across a company or between locations. Brand consistency is also important for single operations so customers enjoy the same experience every time they visit.

Training increases employee morale and confidence. Employees can be confident that they are working the right way and that they will be appreciated by managers. This confidence boosts morale, motivation, and commitment to an operation.

Training also reduces turnover. When an employee leaves, his or her replacement usually starts at a lower skill and knowledge level than a fully productive employee. Training improves the ability to attain standards, and it increases productivity. It also shows employees that they are supported, and it often increases job satisfaction and commitment.

Legal liabilities are reduced when employees are trained. Providing the same chances for employment and promotion is the cornerstone of equal opportunity laws. Since training is both an opportunity and a vehicle for other opportunities, having all employees in the same role participate in the same training ensures equal treatment. This helps ensure that all of them have an equal chance at success and promotion.

Training employees to properly handle food and potentially hazardous equipment, materials, and situations reduces safety risks to employees and customers (*Exhibit 3.11*). For example, employees must be trained to avoid slips, trips, and falls, and the costs of accidents far outweigh the costs of training on safety procedures. Good training makes the workplace safer, and it reduces the risk of liability if an accident or other unsafe situation should occur.

Training increases customer satisfaction and profitability. Customers are not usually lost through high prices, but through poor service. Customer retention and repeat business are the mainstays of most successful establishments. Well-trained kitchen and service staff can provide the level of service that customers want to receive.

Principles of Training

The best training programs focus on what an employee must know or be able to do to meet job standards. They address only those tasks that employees are currently not able to perform, and they provide as much hands-on work as is practical to reinforce the learning.

In addition, effective training is organized to maximize learning. It incorporates several important elements.

THINK ABOUT IT . . .

Which costs more money and takes more time: regaining customers lost because of inconsistent product and service standards or training employees to meet standards so guests remain loyal? Why?

Exhibit 3.11

CONTENT BASED ON JOB GUIDELINES

Training is meant to teach a qualified employee how to perform all tasks in a position. Therefore, the guidelines, standards, procedures, and practices of that job must be the foundation for the training. If the training is about part of a job such as setting a table or preparing an entrée, then only the essential functions for that task are needed.

CLEARLY STATED LEARNING OBJECTIVES

The skills and knowledge that trainees should learn as a result of the training are called **training objectives**. They are used to guide the development of the training activities and as the basis for evaluation of the training. The objectives should be stated in terms of what the trainee will be able to do after the training is completed, not what the instructor will do. To help trainees prepare for learning, they should be informed of the objectives when sessions begin.

The best training objectives contain four parts:

- Performance—What the trainee will be able to do
- Conditions—The situations in which the trainee will be able to perform
- Standards—How well the trainee will be able to perform
- Repetition—How often or how long the trainee will be able to perform

Here is an example of a learning objective. Notice how each part just listed is included:

> Prepare and bake six loaves of French bread in the bake shop using the standardized recipe and meet all doneness, firmness, texture, and taste standards as judged by the baker in the time allowed for this recipe.

QUALIFIED AND THOROUGHLY PREPARED TRAINERS

Those who train must be very knowledgeable and skilled in the tasks being presented, and they should also be good at training others. They must understand how to interact with a trainee and go through all the steps necessary to make him or her proficient. There are several important skills that trainers must use:

- Motivating the learner
- Providing an overview of training content and importance
- Organizing the information or skill into manageable pieces
- Allowing the trainee to learn at his or her own pace
- Giving constructive feedback

Manager's Memo

Employees must have the knowledge and skills required to do the job before they can train others. However, some managers think that the best trainers are those who are excellent performers or who have been with the organization the longest. In fact, neither of these factors can guarantee that a person will be a good trainer.

In addition to knowledge, skills, and experience, effective trainers must want to train and know how to train. They should be relieved of some duties to provide time required for the training. They know how to train because they have participated in a train-the-trainer program which allowed them to learn basic principles useful in teaching employees how to do their jobs. Such a program helps them learn training skills in the same way a program for entry-level employees addresses performance skills.

- Observing the extent of understanding and learning
- Adjusting the topics or procedures based on the extent of learning
- Helping the trainee transfer the learning back to the job

SUFFICIENT PRACTICE

Trainees learn best by doing. The more they do, the more likely they will learn and retain what they have learned (*Exhibit 3.12*). Watching and listening involve very little mental exercise, but actually doing something involves a tremendous amount of mental and physical activity. Since most training for entry-level employees involves on-the-job training, this principle can be easily implemented.

EFFECTIVE TRAINING EVALUATION

An important training principle addresses the need to evaluate the training effort. The trainee will want to know if he or she meets standards after training. Also, the manager and trainer will want to know if the training has been successful or if it must be repeated or modified. Typically, training evaluation covers every training objective.

Exhibit 3.12

To use the bread-baking example from the earlier discussion, the trainee could be taught how to use all equipment and tools required when the standardized recipe is followed. Then the trainer can review all recipe steps and coach the trainee as he or she works through the recipe. The recipe will serve as a checklist for both the trainer and the trainee. After the bread is prepared, the trainer can discuss how the finished product compares to the establishment's standards.

Validation of training is important to ensure that the training teaches what is actually needed. Validation means comparing training content and evaluation methods to the actual job of an employee who can do the work. This helps confirm consistency between actual procedures and those taught in training sessions. Validation may be best ensured when the input of those who do the work is obtained as training is developed. Managers can also compare training materials with the observation of actual work procedures.

The training and evaluation can also be used to recognize trainers as certified to teach specific subjects. Remember that a qualified trainer has a thorough knowledge of and the skills necessary to do the tasks addressed. Another way for a manager to certify a trainer occurs when an employee receives a performance appraisal. Certified trainers should normally receive a very high performance rating.

Determine Training Needs

It is obvious that a great amount of training effort must focus on helping new employees meet performance standards. However, all employees in the operation require ongoing training. Examples include learning new work procedures or operating new equipment. Additionally, training may be required when there are challenges with existing operating procedures and as some employees participate in professional development programs.

Several strategies can be used to identify training needs for experienced employees:

- **Observing work performance:** Managers may notice work procedures that differ from the standard operating procedures (SOPs) that specify how the work should be done. These might be corrected with training activities.

- **Receiving input from employees and customers:** Employees can be asked about challenges that can be addressed with training, and performance appraisal sessions are one time when this can be done. The use of comment cards or other systems for obtaining customer input are examples of how suggestions from guests can be obtained.

- **Making inspections:** Formal inspections such as those related to safety may identify problems that training can help. Informal inspections made by managers before, during, and after work shifts can also identify training needs.

- **Analyzing information:** Differences between budgeted financial results and actual performance may suggest areas where training can be helpful. For example, food costs may be too high because of ineffective inventory control practices that can be addressed by training.

- **Conducting exit interviews:** Formal or informal discussions with employees who are leaving may identify issues for training. If training is effective, it may reduce turnover rates and improve operating procedures.

Develop Training Plans and Training Lessons

Managers develop **training plans** to organize the content of training programs. These plans show how individual training lessons should be sequenced so trainees can learn the required information. **Training lessons** contain the information and methods used to present one session in a training plan.

A well-organized training plan helps managers in several ways. First, it provides an introduction telling why the training is important, and it includes an overview of training content. It also organizes training lessons to progress from simple to complex. This progression helps make trainees feel comfortable with the training. An organized training plan uses a logical order. In other words, it indicates what must be taught first as a basis for other knowledge or skills.

Managers who use training plans can do several things:

- They can schedule dates and times for all lessons.
- They can think about the sequence for each topic.
- They can determine who will present each lesson.
- They can identify the specific trainees for whom specific lessons are needed.

A training lesson tells the why, what, and how of a specific training session:

- Why = the training objectives
- What = the content
- How = the methods to be used for training

A training lesson about proper operation of the dishwasher is being planned. Here are some steps that might be used:

- **Step 1: Develop the lesson's objective:** "Dish washers will be able to operate the dish machine according to the procedures specified in the manufacturer's operating manual by the completion of the training session."
- **Step 2: Determine how to provide knowledge and skills to meet objectives:** The trainer will demonstrate proper procedures for using the dish machine, which are explained in the operating manual.
- **Step 3: Consider topic sequence:** The lesson will begin with an introduction, explain why proper procedures are important, and continue with a step-by-step demonstration. Then the trainee will use the proper operating procedures, and a discussion will review specific learning points.
- **Step 4: Select the training method:** The trainer will use a demonstration method followed by the trainee using the proper operating procedures.
- **Step 5: Consider time requirements for each topic:** The trainer's demonstration should last about ten minutes. The trainee's activities should take another ten minutes, and the follow-up discussion should last about five minutes.

Manager's Memo

It is always easier to implement a training program when trainees help develop the training. They can suggest new ways of doing things and areas in which they need to know more.

Trainees are best motivated when they are told what to expect, why the training is needed, and ample time is provided. The best managers explain that training will directly relate to the trainee's work and then review how the trainee will be evaluated. These managers also plan the training. When time is effectively scheduled, the minimum time will be required. This will reduce the pressure for trainees to participate while needing to complete all of the work tasks normally required.

- **Step 6: Identify training resources:** No resources other than the operator's manual supplied with the equipment will be needed to teach employees how to operate the unit.

- **Step 7: Evaluate and revise the training lesson:** The manager's experience with previous training sessions confirms that the planned approach should be effective.

- **Step 8: Consider the evaluation method:** The trainer will compare the procedures used by the trainee to the procedures outlined in the operator's manual.

Four-Step Training Method

The best way to organize training is to develop a plan that breaks down all required training into lessons addressing specific aspects of the job. For example, if a trainer is teaching someone how to bake bread following a standardized recipe, the recipe could be broken down into separate training elements. These might include separate sections for measuring and mixing, kneading, rising and rekneading, and panning and baking. Then, each section could be taught in sequence during one or several training sessions.

Many operations use the **four-step training method**, which consists of the following steps: preparation, presentation, practice, and performance. This process works well because an experienced employee will know how to do the training. It is also good for the trainee because it can be done one-on-one. Then the trainer can focus on the specific needs of the person being trained.

The four-step training method is an excellent way to train under certain important conditions:

- The trainer has the knowledge and skill to perform the task correctly.

- The trainer knows how to train and is given the time to do it.

- The trainer wants to help the trainee learn and is committed to following all four steps.

PREPARATION

There are two concerns in preparing for training. The first is that the topic, activities, and materials must be known and available. Managers, supervisors, and human resources staff develop training plans and training lessons to help those who will actually do the training. Then, for example, if an experienced entry-level employee will train others, he or she can review these resources.

THINK ABOUT IT . . .

Some managers think effective training consists of telling an employee, "Follow that employee, do what he or she does, and you will know how to do the task."

Do you think that approach is an effective one? Why or why not?

A second aspect of training preparation relates to getting the trainee ready to learn. The goal is to motivate the trainee to pay attention and learn what is being taught. This is easiest when the trainer relates the content to the person's success on the job. Trainers should also communicate their expectations by clearly indicating the learning objectives and previewing what the trainee will learn during the session.

To use the bread-baking example, the trainer might introduce the topic of measuring and mixing by indicating who is responsible for bread baking, why proper measuring and mixing are important, and which tasks in the recipe involve measuring and mixing.

PRESENTATION

Presentation is the part of the training process in which the trainer conveys new information and demonstrates skills. The trainer typically does the task, explains what he or she is doing, and provides tips about the most critical aspects.

Exhibit 3.13

Whenever possible, provide pictures, diagrams, and handouts that reinforce information demonstrated. This gives the employee a better chance of remembering what was taught. It is also appropriate to ask the employee about what he or she knows about the task. Demonstration of a skills-based task could also help the trainer to personalize the training even more. The task breakdowns discussed as part of position analysis in chapter 2 are an excellent example of the tools that help trainers prepare and help trainees learn the task.

Most people learn best by watching and doing as opposed to just reading or listening. Therefore, demonstration and hands-on activities are central to success in one-on-one training. (See *Exhibit 3.13.*) Additionally, trainers might encourage the trainee to take notes during the presentation. Allow plenty of time for questions and answers; this is another way that a trainee can be an active learner.

In the bread-baking example, the trainer's presentation for measuring and mixing might involve demonstrating and discussing the proper tools to use and way to measure ingredients and then the proper tools or equipment to use and way to mix them.

PRACTICE

After the trainer has shown the employee what to do and explained the key points, the trainee should be allowed to practice the task while the trainer observes. This approach allows the trainer to provide the trainee with feedback and correct any errors or misunderstandings immediately and repeat the demonstration if necessary. This process can help the trainee realize that what looked simple might actually be more difficult than it appeared. The trainer can then answer any additional questions and correct behavior if necessary. In doing so, the trainer helps shape the employee's work habits.

Returning to the bread-baking example, an activity could occur as the trainee measures and mixes the ingredients with observation, feedback, and corrections, if necessary, by the trainer.

PERFORMANCE

Performance relates to the trainee's on-the-job use of the new skill. After a trainer has explained the task, demonstrated it, and watched the employee practice it once, some managers and trainers think training is over. However, observing and following up as the trainee routinely performs the task is critical. Ongoing observation and feedback help the employee learn how to do the task correctly. The period just after training is a critical time when the trainee can develop bad habits and sloppy work without realizing it.

Returning to the bread-baking example, the performance for measuring and mixing might involve the trainee measuring the ingredients. Then the trainee can mix them without correction by the trainer being necessary.

INTEGRATIVE PRACTICE

Performance is the last step in the four-step training method. However, it is a good idea to also use **integrative practice**: a training strategy in which a trainee combines and demonstrates several steps in a job task that has already been learned. In the bread-baking example, the trainer could use an integrative practice activity at the end in which the trainee takes a different bread recipe and prepares it from start to finish. This concept is illustrated in *Exhibit 3.14*.

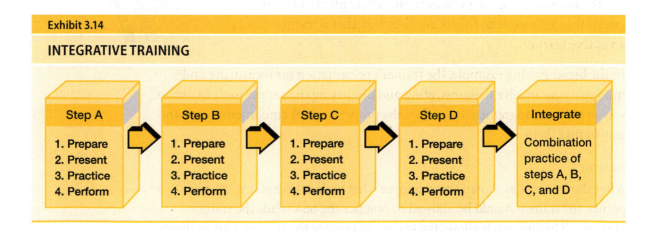

Exhibit 3.14

INTEGRATIVE TRAINING

Step A	Step B	Step C	Step D	Integrate
1. Prepare 2. Present 3. Practice 4. Perform	1. Prepare 2. Present 3. Practice 4. Perform	1. Prepare 2. Present 3. Practice 4. Perform	1. Prepare 2. Present 3. Practice 4. Perform	Combination practice of steps A, B, C, and D

The steps in *Exhibit 3.14* do not refer to the four steps of training. There can be any number of steps in a job task. For example, training on how to use a dishwasher might include three steps: loading the machine, operating the machine, and unloading the machine. The number of steps into which training is broken relates to task complexity: the more complex the task, the more steps before integrative practice. However, the best practice is to limit the number of steps to no more than seven.

Group Training

Group training is a method used to teach the same job-related information to more than one trainee at the same time. This method can save time when more than one staff member must receive the same information, such as for new product rollouts, new operating procedures, or information updates.

Exhibit 3.15

The same basic planning steps used for one-on-one training can be used for group training (see *Exhibit 3.15*). Objectives must be considered, and they will drive decisions about content, timing, use of resources, and training activities.

There are two popular group training methods for small numbers of trainees. Trainers can use the lecture method with visual aids or handouts. Question and answer components may be incorporated. Trainers can also use the demonstration method to show trainees how operating procedures should be performed. Group training also occurs when trainees practice a task that they have learned about in a group training session. The best group training methods often include some oral presentations supplemented with demonstrations, question and answer sessions, case studies, and other training activities.

When beginning a group training session, the trainer should give an introduction such as "I've got some news to share with you." An overview of the session can then be used to explain the session's objectives, tell why the information is important, and indicate how it will affect the trainees. Many trainers will take a moment at the beginning of a session to ask the learners what they hope to gain from the class.

Planning will help the manager or trainer stay organized. He or she will know the specific training points and how they should be presented. The speaker should use the same strategies that would be used if talking to a community organization or a group of customers. Some trainers prefer to discuss a

THINK ABOUT IT . . .

Group training allows multiple employees to learn the same information at the same time. What are some other advantages of groups?

What are some potential disadvantages as compared to one-on-one training using a four-step method?

RESTAURANT TECHNOLOGY

There are numerous Web-based programs that allow persons to enroll in everything from courses leading to a college degree to specific training programs on topics such as service quality, team building, and managerial accounting. One potential advantage to these programs is that trainees can learn according to their personal schedule and at their own pace. Other advantages relate to how the course is organized. Some, for example, involve project collaboration with persons located around the world. Others include chat rooms in which trainees can participate.

Traditional activities, such as assigned readings, use of case studies, and project-based instruction, can all be easily integrated into a Web-based course. Increasingly, managers take these types of courses and many are reimbursed by their employer after successful completion of a course with subject matter applicable to the establishment.

training point and then ask for questions and facilitate a discussion before moving on to the next point. Other trainers direct questions at trainees on a frequent basis throughout the entire session.

Basic principles can help trainers guide discussions:

- Ask for questions, consider discussion points, and use them to determine if the trainees understand the material.
- Treat trainees as professionals, not subordinates. Successful organizations promote teamwork, and this is just as important during training as at any other time.
- Ask clear and direct questions. A generic "Any questions?" is much less helpful than an open-ended question such as, "Why is it important to place the order for the lamb chops as soon as possible?"
- Allow only one person to talk at a time. This rule is important to control the training environment. Trainers might use a comment such as, "I would like to know what you think. Who wants to be first?"
- Listen carefully and show respect for all ideas. Listen closely to trainees' remarks to fully understand what is being said before formulating a response.
- Keep the discussion focused. An effective trainer knows when to direct the discussion back to the topic: "That's a great point, but we need to focus on suggestive selling."

Industry-Recognized Training

Before spending the time and money to develop their own training programs, many managers consider materials that are already available. There are numerous **off-the-shelf** training programs that can be used. This term refers to ready-made training materials that have been developed by associations and other external organizations. Some resources are purchased and used by the establishment, and some involve training in which employees participate electronically.

To best use off-the-shelf training materials, managers must have a clear sense of the objectives that need to be met and the skill levels and preparation of trainees. It is critical to analyze the operation's training needs and consider the program's design to find training that best meets the needs of the operation and its employees. With careful analysis based on an understanding of what makes good training, managers can find numerous useful resources. There are many sources of external training:

- Internet searches can be useful in finding good sources for Web-based training programs.

- Workshops offered by a variety of training companies can be helpful for general topics such as interpersonal skills, team building, customer service, or understanding financial statements. These programs provide training at relatively low cost with minimal travel expenses.

- Training opportunities are also provided by professional organizations such as the National Restaurant Association and the American Culinary Federation, among others. These organizations provide workshops as part of their annual conferences, and some offer classes at locations around the country.

- Local colleges may offer useful workshops in their continuing education or business development programs. These resources may expand what can be offered to employees.

- For employees experiencing difficulty with reading or writing, the Literacy Volunteers of America and other social service organizations provide one-on-one tutoring and assistance in learning English. Other local organizations may offer education in areas such as harassment, diversity training, teamwork, customer service, and payroll systems. The chamber of commerce and community colleges are also good local resources.

SUMMARY

1. **Review basic procedures that should be used for employment and payroll documentation.**

   Major hiring documents are those for employment and payroll and for benefit enrollment. Employee documents include the W-4 form, state and local tax forms, and the I-9 form. Other documents may be required depending on age and position. Job eligibility documents and permission documents to check references and background may also be needed.

   Benefit enrollment documents enable employees to enroll in life insurance or other benefit plans. Information about retirement benefits, if any, should also be provided.

   Most hiring and orientation documents should be kept in a personnel file. These confidential files should be stored in a safe, secure, and private place.

2. **Explain basic procedures that should be included in hiring and orientation activities.**

Managers must ensure that all required paperwork is completed and that the mission and culture of the establishment have been emphasized. Company policies, procedures, and the employee handbook should be reviewed and the new employee should receive a uniform, name tag, tools, and so on as appropriate. A facility tour should be provided, the new employee should be introduced to coworkers, and information about job responsibilities, expectations, and the first week's work schedule should be addressed.

Organizations manage hiring and orientation differently, but both tasks are necessary within a short time after employees begin work. Regardless of procedures used, the documentation of new employees will be processed, and they will be oriented to the organization. Some establishments use checklists to manage the flow of documents and activities. These help ensure that all legal, payroll, and policy requirements are met.

3. **Describe how to plan and evaluate orientation programs.**

The two main purposes of orientation programs are to provide the information a new employee needs, and to make the employee feel comfortable. Consistency is important to meet safety and legal obligations. Every new employee should receive the same information, learn the same safety practices, have the same opportunities to learn about the operation, and meet the same key people.

Managers and others planning orientation should consider the time necessary, program content and structure, materials and resources needed, and the trainers who will conduct the program.

Employee handbooks address basic information including policies. Employee handbooks should be kept updated.

Orientation programs are evaluated to determine whether participants completed all documents and gained the knowledge needed to start their new jobs. Managers can talk with new employees to obtain feedback, and employees can also complete evaluation forms.

4. **Explain procedures for planning and delivering training programs.**

Training is required for new employees and is useful for experienced staff. Effective training helps employees buy into the operation's values. It creates product and service consistency, increases employee morale, and helps reduce turnover and legal liabilities. Employees can learn how to properly handle food and potential hazards. Customer satisfaction and profitability increase.

Each task should be explained to the new employee, and he or she should be shown how to complete the task. The employee should then be observed performing the task and feedback should be provided.

Clearly stated learning objectives based on a job's essential functions drive training programs. Sessions should be conducted by qualified and prepared trainers. Managers can determine training needs by observing work performance, receiving input from employees and customers, making inspections, analyzing information, and conducting exit interviews. Training plans organize program content and individual lessons that provide a "road map" for the training. Training must be evaluated and validated to ensure effectiveness.

A four-step training method involves preparation, presentation, practice, and performance. In addition, integrated practice allows trainees to combine and demonstrate several steps that are part of a job task.

Group training can be used when more than one employee must receive the same information. The basic planning steps used for one-on-one training can be used. Popular group methods include lecture, demonstration, and practice, if applicable. A good trainer uses all of these tactics.

Many managers use off-the-shelf training materials. Sources of external training include the Internet, workshops by training companies, and training opportunities by professional associations. Other sources include local colleges and social service organizations that provide assistance in learning English.

APPLICATION EXERCISE

Break into groups of three to practice the four-step training method. One person should be the trainer, the second the trainee, and the third an observer.

The trainer should select a simple task for training. Examples include folding a napkin or setting one place setting on a table. Bring necessary items to class or cut pieces of paper into the approximate shapes and label them.

The trainer should plan how he or she will conduct the training. Then the trainer can teach the trainee how to do the task. The trainee should practice the task. When training is completed, the observer should begin a discussion by commenting on each of the four steps, including what the trainer did correctly and incorrectly and how the training might be improved.

If time permits, change roles and repeat the activity.

REVIEW YOUR LEARNING

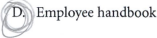

Select the best answer for each question.

1. Which form does an employee complete to signify eligibility to work in the United States?
   A. I-9 form
   B. W-4 form
   C. State tax form
   D. Local tax form

2. Which item(s) should be kept separate from an employee's personnel file?
   A. Job application
   B. Signed tax forms
   C. Medical information
   D. Signed employment contract

3. One of the purposes of an orientation program is to
   A. explain company policies.
   B. implement an emphasis on diversity.
   C. replace a four-step training program.
   D. determine training needs of new employees.

4. Basic information for all employees in a position is presented in what type of program?
   A. Orientation
   B. Four-step training
   C. Group training
   D. Induction

5. Which document ensures that new employees are aware of an establishment's policies?
   A. Hiring checklist
   B. Employment letter
   C. Orientation checklist
   D. Employee handbook

6. The skills and knowledge that a trainee should learn from training are called
   A. conditions.
   B. objectives.
   C. standards.
   D. lessons.

7. What process ensures that training teaches what is actually needed?
   A. Induction
   B. Validation
   C. Emulation
   D. Orientation

8. Which tool organizes the content of a training program?
   A. Task list
   B. Training plan
   C. Training lesson
   D. Task breakdown

9. Trainers convey new information and demonstrate skills in what phase of training?
   A. Practice
   B. Preparation
   C. Presentation
   D. Performance

10. The training strategy in which a trainee combines several steps that are part of a job task is called
    A. validation.
    B. repetition.
    C. integrative practice.
    D. secondary demonstration.

FIELD PROJECT

A. This chapter provides information about employee orientation and training. You and your project team can continue your study of these topics as you identify applicable interview questions for the restaurant and foodservice operations you will visit later in the course.

For example, orientation questions might include:

- Who conducts entry-level employee orientations in your operation and how long (hours or days) does the orientation process typically take?
- What basic topics are discussed in your orientation program?

Sample questions for employee training programs could include:

- How do you determine the content for training programs provided for new entry-level employees?
- How are your training programs evaluated?
- What are the qualifications of those who train new employees?

Note: *Save the questions you have developed. Later in this course, your team will conduct interviews with the managers of restaurant or foodservice operations selected by the team. These interviews will include the questions you have developed in this chapter, as well as questions from other chapters. You may want to use the interview form (template) in the Field Project Information Handbook at the end of this book, or develop an interview form of your own to list your interview questions. This form can then be used to record the managers' responses when you conduct your interview.*

B. Continue learning about employee orientation and training by conducting an Internet search. Make a list of several suggestions for orientation and training from each of at least four Internet resources. Examples of terms that can be entered in your favorite search engine include:

- Employee orientation checklist
- Employee onboarding
- Role of supervisor in orientation
- Training objectives
- Training lessons
- Four-step training method

These suggestions can be recorded in Part II (Internet Resources) for chapter 3 in the Field Project Information Handbook at the end of this book.

4

Foundations of Effective Employee Performance

CHAPTER LEARNING OBJECTIVES

After completing this chapter, you should be able to:

- Describe special concerns when an entry-level employee is promoted to a supervisory position.

- Explain basic employee motivation strategies.

- Describe procedures for building and maintaining effective teams.

- Discuss the development and management of employee recognition and incentive programs.

KEY TERMS

benefits, p. 104

career ladder, p. 105

compensation, p. 104

continuous quality improvement (CQI), p. 110

cross-functional team, p. 112

diversity, p. 105

employee incentive program, p. 116

employee recognition program, p. 116

entry-level employee, p. 100

esteem needs, p. 104

fast-track employee, p. 106

harassment, p. 105

income statement, p. 117

Maslow's hierarchy of needs, p. 103

open-ended question, p. 115

physiological needs, p. 103

pre-shift meeting, p. 108

role model, p. 100

safety needs, p. 103

self-actualization, p. 104

social needs, p. 103

stakeholder, p. 114

work team, p. 111

zero tolerance, p. 105

CASE STUDY

"I used to think Aldan was such a nice guy," said Sabrya, "but I was sure wrong!"

Sabrya was a server at Green Wall Café, and she was talking to Quincy, another server.

"Yes," said Quincy, "Aldan was a great guy when he was part of our team. He always helped out, he took shifts no one wanted, and he worked quickly."

"Well that's all changed since Aldan has become the dining-room supervisor," replied Sabrya. "It's almost like he doesn't know us. He seems kind of friendly in a standoffish way, but he doesn't join us for after-work activities, and he spends a lot more time with other supervisors. I guess now he is a big shot!"

1. What is the main problem being expressed?
2. What should Aldan do or say to the members of the server team that he now supervises?

THE ROLE OF SUPERVISOR

Operations cannot be successful without excellent managers, supervisors, and entry-level employees. Managers direct the work of supervisors, and supervisors direct **entry-level employees**: those who work in positions that require little experience and have no supervisory duties.

Exhibit 4.1

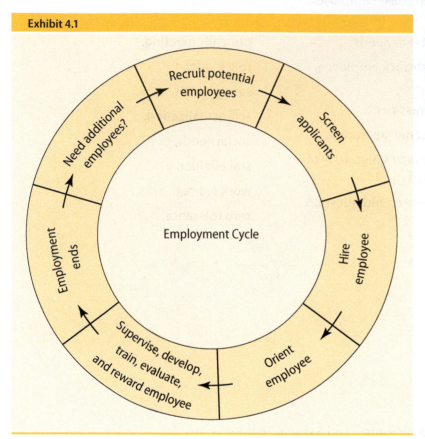

Employment Cycle

- Recruit potential employees
- Screen applicants
- Hire employee
- Orient employee
- Supervise, develop, train, evaluate, and reward employee
- Employment ends
- Need additional employees?

As seen in *Exhibit 4.1*, supervision impacts several areas of the employment cycle. These include providing ongoing supervision, developing and training employees, and evaluating and rewarding them. While supervisors are accountable to their own managers, helping their own employees succeed should be their ultimate goal. Supervisors can only be as successful as those they lead.

Supervisors have numerous responsibilities. One is to encourage productivity and quality by creating an environment that allows employees to use their knowledge and skills. Supervisors plan for success, communicate with individuals and groups, and encourage teamwork.

For good or bad, supervisors also set the tone of an operation by the way they treat employees, and through the behaviors and attitudes they exhibit as a role model.

A **role model** is a person displaying the behavior and attitudes that are appropriate for his or her employees.

Providing the right environment is only part of helping employees be successful. Another priority concern is motivating them to do their best work. What motivates people depends on the person, so the best supervisors learn about their employees. Then they can use effective motivational techniques as they interact with their staff.

Many of a supervisor's responsibilities focus primarily on the "people" aspects of management. Then, with further promotions come higher-level monitoring and planning activities. However, ongoing interactions with employees are part of everyone's job in the labor-intensive restaurant and foodservice industry.

THINK ABOUT IT . . .

What are some characteristics of good supervisors? Of poor supervisors? How do supervisors influence the behavior and attitudes of their employees?

THE TRANSITION TO SUPERVISOR

Good employees typically are promoted to supervisory positions on the basis of their performance in a specific job. Their ability to perform technical tasks with ease and expertise, and the potential they have to lead others, are primary reasons they are promoted. Relatively few operations have detailed assessment programs and well-organized orientation and training programs for new supervisors. Many persons are promoted and provided with support, but they are usually expected to learn the position on the job. In other words, they learn how to supervise by supervising.

Changing the Focus

One challenge that confronts many new supervisors occurs when they experience confusion between working and leading. Entry-level employees can usually see the results of their work immediately: the pots are washed and put away, the customers are happy, or the food has been prepped for service. Many people rightfully feel a high level of satisfaction from getting specific things done on time and in a visible way. Supervisors, however, can sometimes lose that sense of accomplishment and concrete results.

Discovering that technical tasks such pre-prepping food and setting tables are no longer the focus of work can be intimidating. Many of the tasks new supervisors must do are not "work" as they have known it, and they may be unclear about what they are supposed to do.

New supervisors need to remember that their job now is to set and monitor standards of quality, productivity, and efficiency and to begin to think about the larger picture of the entire operation. What they are doing is planning the work of their staff, focusing on the people who will get the work done, motivating their team, and monitoring its performance.

Sometimes when supervisors coordinate work, they may notice that things are not going as well as they should be. At these times, they must be ready, willing, and able to assist (*Exhibit 4.2*). If plates are backed up in the kitchen, a supervisor who carries them to tables shows employees that he or she is part of a team with one goal. If a cook is behind, a production supervisor who helps is also a role model while preventing a potential problem. The assistance provided shows the supervisor is not above doing technical work alongside employees.

As supervisory experience becomes more extensive, it is easy to feel further removed from the actual work. The supervisor should still know how to do the work. Supervisors must know the work standards, which describe how well and how often the work should be done, and must consistently follow all applicable policies. As this is done, supervisors will be respected by those whose work they facilitate. This shift in focus can be difficult for some new

THINK ABOUT IT . . .

Do you think of work as a physical thing like washing dishes or waiting on tables? Do activities like scheduling employees or conducting performance appraisal sessions seem like work to you? Why or why not?

Exhibit 4.2

supervisors. However, as they build professional relationships with their employees and focus on meeting their responsibilities, they will start to think like a supervisor and perform accordingly.

Managing Employee Relationships

Supervisors must develop a relationship of trust and respect with the members of their team. If they were promoted from the ranks of those they now supervise, they must adjust to being the team leader. Some employees may, through their actions, challenge the new supervisor to see how strict he or she will be. All supervisors must make the right decisions for the right reasons. Then they must stand by their decisions and not be influenced by their previous relationships with employees. Some new supervisors may try to rely on past friendships to motivate their employees to do the work. Unfortunately, this strategy will not work. A supervisor must make decisions and maintain good relationships with every employee, not just those with whom they were friendly before the promotion. Treating each staff member fairly is essential to successfully managing the team.

Building good working relationships involves being clear and honest. Supervisors typically have access to information that employees may not have. Therefore, they may sometimes see things differently. Explaining the situation from the view of the establishment rather than just the department can help in some cases. The employees will then know the decisions were made for the right reasons, and team members will likely adjust and work productively. Integrity is a most important quality; employees support supervisors they trust. Supervisors who walk around the operation, talk with employees, listen to their concerns, and share their perspectives are building good relationships. Supervisors should avoid taking sides in disputes if it is not necessary to intervene. Especially in a small operation, everyone must work together in a cooperative spirit.

Gaining Experience

Supervisors improve by remembering what they have done and how it impacted the employees and the operation. When mistakes occur, they learn from them to avoid making the same mistakes in the future. When something goes well, it is also important to understand why it went well so successful strategies can be repeated. While this reflection helps all supervisors, those who have been recently promoted should especially examine their work and its effects.

Good supervisors also learn to consider the potential effects of their actions *before* they act. They think before they speak, and they consider their options in every situation. Thinking before acting makes it easier to respond to employee requests, customer demands, and establishment pressures in thoughtful ways. This behavior also helps supervisors model the appropriate actions to employees.

EMPLOYEE MOTIVATION BASICS

The issue of motivation can be very complex. In reality, supervisors cannot motivate their employees; motivation must come from within each person. Supervisors can direct employees, but if employees are not motivated to work, the desired response is unlikely. The employees may do the work but not as well, as quickly, or as enthusiastically as they could. When employees are unmotivated, customer service, morale, work quality, teamwork, and ultimately profits can all suffer.

While supervisors cannot force employees to become motivated, they can create conditions that employees usually find motivating. People are motivated by different needs including money, social interaction, and job satisfaction. These needs may change over time. Everyone is different, which is why it is important for supervisors to know their employees as individuals. However, there are some factors that commonly motivate employees.

Maslow's hierarchy of needs states that people have five basic needs that typically arise in a certain order. When one need is fulfilled to the extent desired by the person, he or she is motivated to fulfill the next need. The five needs are shown in *Exhibit 4.3*.

Physiological needs are the most basic and relate to the need for food, water, air, and sleep. Employees' physiological needs are met through heating, air conditioning, lighting, meal and rest breaks, and limits on work hours. When these needs are met to an extent determined by each person, he or she is motivated to fulfill safety needs. These needs concern things that make people feel secure or keep them safe. These can be physical such as shelter or a dependable income, or they can be more personal such as freedom from stress. In the workplace, safety needs can be met by factors such as fair wages, healthcare and other benefits, the use of safety procedures, and safe operating equipment.

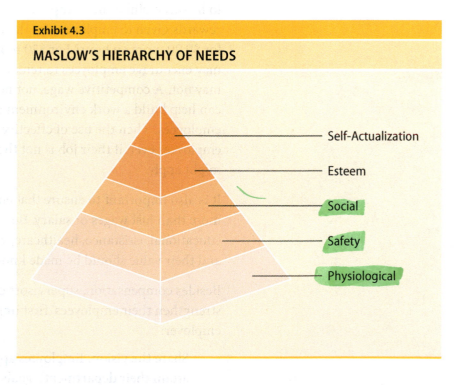

Exhibit 4.3

MASLOW'S HIERARCHY OF NEEDS

- Self-Actualization
- Esteem
- Social
- Safety
- Physiological

The next level in Maslow's model involves social needs. These relate to the need to interact with others. Social needs include love, belonging, and friendship. In the workplace, social needs can be met through friendship, teamwork, and a sense of belonging or acceptance, which are encouraged by a welcoming atmosphere. **Esteem needs** are at the fourth level and focus on how people feel about themselves and how they think others feel about them. Esteem needs in the workplace may be met by recognition, promotions, titles, appreciation, opportunities, and other factors.

At the highest level is the need for **self-actualization**: the drive to do the very best that one can do. This encourages people to push themselves, learn new things, and be creative. In the workplace, this need may motivate employees to become the most productive they can be, to produce the best quality work they can, or to develop themselves for other positions.

Each person considers "how much is enough" before he or she is motivated to address the next need. For example, one employee may want to be recognized with a promotion, while another may not care about job titles. Complicating this for managers is the issue that people's needs change; what motivates a person at one time may not motivate him or her later.

Make a Good First Impression

Almost all employees are concerned about their compensation, and this impacts their interest in their job and the extent to which they are motivated to be successful in it. **Compensation** is all of the financial and nonfinancial rewards given to employees for their work. Would employees change positions for $0.20 more an hour? For $20 more a week? Significant amounts of money may encourage employees to remain with their employer, but small amounts may not. A competitive wage, not necessarily the highest in the community, can help build a work environment in which supervisors can motivate employees. Then the use of effective management practices will help retain employees even if their job is not the very highest-paying one for which they might apply.

It is also important to ensure that employees know their total compensation is more than just wages or salary. **Benefits** that may include meals, uniforms, educational assistance, healthcare, vacation, and sick leave cost a great deal, and their value should be made known to employees.

Besides compensation, supervisors can use several other strategies to strengthen their employees' first impressions about their jobs and their employer:

- Share the vision. Employees appreciate knowing how their position helps attain their department's goals and what they and others must do to meet or exceed them.

- Help employees belong. New staff members are looking for things that will reinforce their decision to work at the establishment. They look to their supervisors to do and say things that increase their comfort level and sense of belonging to the team.

- Create a **career ladder**. A career ladder is a plan that explains how job advancement may occur. It shows employees how they can be promoted if they remain with the operation. The best supervisors consider each position they supervise and think about how a talented staff member in that job might advance. Then they develop a career ladder that shows the title, rank, and pay level for each new job. Sharing career ladders with staff members may encourage and motivate them. The best supervisors also provide a plan for additional training and education as employees move forward in their career.

- Explain the long-term benefits of staying. Examples include pay raises, extended vacation times, or other types of financial compensation and internal recognition. Supervisors should review these benefits during orientation programs and then frequently during their new employees' first months on the job.

Maintain a Professional Workforce

Employees want a safe place to work, and supervisors must guard against liability from harassment charges. **Harassment** relates to unwanted and annoying actions by one or more persons, including threats or demands. Supervisors ensure a quality workplace for all staff members by implementing zero tolerance for objectionable behavior (see *Exhibit 4.4*). **Zero tolerance** is a policy that allows no amount or type of harassing behavior. A harassment policy is included in the employee handbook and should be discussed at employee orientation sessions and other staff meetings.

Supervisors should also support a culturally diverse workplace that reflects the makeup of the community in which they work. **Diversity** is the concept that people are unique with individual differences and variations in race, ethnicity, gender, socioeconomic status, age, and physical abilities, among others. Diversity increases many employees' comfort level in the workplace. Another important benefit of diversity is that it often brings unique and useful ideas to the operation.

Supervise Effectively

The best supervisors direct the work of their employees in the same way they would like to be supervised. For example, policies are administered fairly and consistently. Employees do not like it when some workers are favored, and they watch carefully to see if this occurs. For example, it is not appropriate to allow some employees to arrive at work later than scheduled while others are punished. Policies should be reasonable, and everyone should be treated the same way.

Exhibit 4.4

Guarding against workplace harassment includes protecting employees from customers.

To support all employees, it is useful to give employees a personal copy of their work schedule. This can be done by circulating it through the operation's intranet, or texting or emailing the information to the staff members.

Supervisors should also know about available employee assistance programs. Some employees whose work is good still may need professional assistance because of problems, such as alcohol or substance abuse, and financial or other personal difficulties. These challenges can affect their attendance, their ability to meet required work standards, and their interactions with other members of the team. Supervisors can show their concern by directing them to places where professional assistance is available.

There are a number of strategies that supervisors can use to supervise effectively:

- Build a great team and praise it often. Members of winning teams want to be the best at what they do. To retain "star" players, ensure that all new employees know they have joined a successful team and will be treated like professionals.

- Reward employees who help out by working on nonscheduled days. Recognition, rewards, and extra benefits are among the ways to say thank-you for these efforts. Also, do not always ask the same employees to work extra shifts just because they are likely to say yes.

- Invite fast-track employees to attend some scheduled supervisors' meetings. **Fast-track employees** are those who meet work requirements in their present position and participate in professional development programs that allow them to advance quickly in the operation. Most employees like to know they provide value to their employer. When they know their supervisor has important plans for them, they are more likely to remain with the establishment and be motivated.

- Make the workplace fun. Ask staff members how to make the workplace more enjoyable. Consider ideas that will not reduce productivity but will positively impact employee attitudes. The workplace need not be boring; if it is, change the situation.

Plan for Success

Planning a positive, productive work environment involves a range of activities. It begins with creating a clear vision of the kind of workplace that is desired and then making plans to get there. Most supervisors' visions include a functional, profitable, and quality-based establishment that customers enjoy. Other things must be considered as well.

One aspect relates to the employees. Most supervisors want their staff to feel good about their work and their role in the operation. Smoothly functioning teams are also typically desired, and it is important for supervisors to envision

Manager's Memo

Supervisors do not work in a vacuum separate from other departments. The corporate culture of the operation will have a significant impact on how the supervisor thinks and what he or she does.

For example, it is very easy for a supervisor to interact with staff members in a fair and respectful way when doing so is inspired by the organization's vision, addressed in its mission statement, and expressed in measurable goals. When concern about employees is less of a focus, supervisors must put forth greater effort to develop a motivating work environment.

the context in which they lead their employees. These are among the considerations important as both day-to-day and longer-term plans are developed.

Help Employees Be Successful

Another aspect of planning for success involves developing ongoing training opportunities for employees. All staff members have the responsibility to develop the knowledge and skills that are required to be successful in their current position. When the employees can successfully do the work for which they were hired, their supervisors should assume the responsibility for providing additional opportunities for trainees that desire to learn more and to prepare for other positions, if practical. The best supervisors recognize the potential of their employees and help them attain it.

Reviewing an employee's work and goals should be an ongoing activity, and this should formally be done during performance appraisal sessions. Then supervisors can develop a personalized plan to move an employee toward a mutually determined goal. Helping employees become successful is rewarding, and the best supervisors know it is one of their most important responsibilities.

Be a Role Model

A supervisor's behavior and attitude set the tone for the department. If supervisors want employees to like and care about each other, for example, then getting to know them as individuals and showing respect for them sets that tone for the team. Supervisors should also follow the establishment's policies without exception.

Serving as a good role model requires a commitment to doing the right thing all the time. Supervisors must be constantly aware that what they do and say illustrates the range of acceptable behaviors for others. Although subtle, messages given through this type of modeling can be very powerful.

Being a role model inspires employees and communicates the importance of desired behaviors and attitudes. However, a supervisor's role also includes more direct methods of communicating with employees.

Communicate a Consistent Message

Clear and frequent communication about what employees should do and how it should be done makes it easier for employees to align their work with the supervisor's goals. Unfortunately, some supervisors do not take the time to discuss plans with employees or to tell them what is being done correctly or incorrectly. This lack of information often leaves employees guessing about priorities. For example, customer service is typically a clear priority, but food safety, good food, cost concerns, and personal safety are also very important.

> **THINK ABOUT IT . . .**
>
> What do these supervisory behaviors tell employees?
>
> - Picking up a piece of litter
> - Asking employees how they are
> - Throwing away food as soon as its holding time has expired

Exhibit 4.5

The clearer a supervisor can be about what needs to be done in what sequence for each shift, the easier it will be for employees to be successful.

Communicating with employees can be done several ways. One common method is the **pre-shift meeting**. This short employee meeting is held before the work shift begins to discuss plans and details and sometimes present short training information (*Exhibit 4.5*). Other communication methods include production meetings in which key employees meet with managers and supervisors to discuss production issues and plans for upcoming events. Sometimes a group meeting is held to provide a lot of information to everyone at the same time.

Another way to communicate information to all employees is by posting it on the employee bulletin board. Change the information regularly to encourage continued interest in looking at the board.

In large operations, supervisors and key employees may also participate in management group meetings to discuss common issues and events that will require significant coordination. These sessions involve a small but important group of employees and can be useful to present each department's viewpoint.

Acknowledge Employees

Routinely acknowledging employees by recognizing them as individuals is an often overlooked motivational strategy. Simple acts such as saying hello can make a big difference in setting a positive tone.

A good way to acknowledge staff members is to greet them at the beginning of every shift. Greet them by name, make eye contact, shake hands, and smile. These actions communicate to employees that their supervisor recognizes that they are important. Employees of supervisors who do not make these efforts often feel unappreciated. In fact, everyone in an operation is important, and an unintended message to the contrary is very harmful.

Offering a pleasant greeting also gives a supervisor the opportunity to *check in* with employees rather than *check on* them. This daily exchange allows the supervisor to ensure that everything is going smoothly and also verify that the employee is ready for work.

Also say goodbye at the end of the shift to acknowledge employees again. Mention something that went well, especially any contributions made by the employee. This gesture will be appreciated, even if employees are tired and do not show it.

Express Appreciation

Every employee appreciates a genuine thank-you for a job well done. There are also other methods that can be used in combination with this practice. The supervisor can extend personal thanks by sharing a copy of a personal note that will be placed in the employee's personnel file. The note will enable the supervisor to later recall significant situations, and this will be useful at the time of employee performance appraisal.

Supervisors can publicly express their own or a customer's appreciation to an employee. Some managers who conduct meetings to review policies, standards, and other operating information use these meetings to publicly thank individuals or the group. Smaller team or shift meetings provide the same opportunity. When a customer compliments an employee, share that compliment with the entire staff. Post a copy of the information received or read it aloud at a shift meeting.

The power of this recognition for the entire group cannot be overestimated. Although sometimes this activity can embarrass an employee, normally it makes him or her feel good. It also encourages everyone to work hard to get recognition.

Share Information

People like to know what is going on in their operation. This interest is natural because it satisfies a person's need to feel secure, valued, and involved. If new things are happening, employees should be informed. If there is a special group coming in or new tables, chairs, or linens are being purchased, tell the staff members. Some supervisors, especially those recently promoted, are excited to learn this information but do not share it. There is nothing to lose and much to gain by keeping employees informed.

Sharing information also creates a foundation for involving employees in the operation. Employees are more likely to cooperate with new policies and procedures if they understand why these changes are needed. Sharing information with employees also is the first step in asking for their help in solving a problem. For instance, one excellent way to encourage employees to carefully handle glassware and plates is to tell them about the cost of breakage. If they understand how the cost of breakage diverts money away from other things, such as new equipment or bonuses, they will be motivated to be more careful.

Express Interest

Supervisors who express interest in their employees show they care about them as individuals and as team members. Asking someone "How are you?" and listening to the answer demonstrates interest. Asking "What do you think about that?" demonstrates that a supervisor cares about employees' experiences at work and is open to hearing their perspectives and suggestions.

THINK ABOUT IT . . .

Has someone ever asked you a question and then not paid attention to your answer? How did you know they were not interested? How did that make you feel?

Exhibit 4.6

However, supervisors must be careful not to ask personal questions. There may be a fine line in an employee's mind between harmless interest and harassment or discrimination. Avoid discussing any topic that would be "off limits" in a job interview, such as marital status, race, ethnicity, religion, sexual preference, or disability. If unsure whether a question is appropriate, do not ask.

Involve Employees

Involving employees in the operation can motivate people for several reasons. When employees help with planning, problem solving, and decision making, they are being recognized as valuable individuals and team members (*Exhibit 4.6*). They are also being given opportunities for responsibility, contribution, creativity, and growth. In addition, soliciting employees' suggestions and feedback shows the supervisor's commitment to the team. Involving employees also typically produces better plans, resolutions, and decisions.

Employees can become involved in various ways, from informal discussions to formal committees, projects, and programs. Supervisors should obtain ideas from employees and consider their input. Listen to what is said and acknowledge ideas even if they cannot be used. Remember not to criticize employee suggestions.

When customers complain, share this information with employees and ask for suggestions to resolve the problems. Employees can help identify patterns in customer feedback. Honest employees who have the best interests of the operation at heart can make insightful comments. Those in customer contact positions may have especially useful ideas.

Establishments may have committees in which employees can participate, such as those for safety, menu planning, and **continuous quality improvement (CQI)**. CQI is a management philosophy that emphasizes that most work processes can be improved. Staff members can also participate in one-on-one conversations or short stand-up meetings while other things are going on.

Regardless of an operation's size, interested employees can participate in matters that affect them. Here are other examples of areas where employee feedback or involvement can be especially helpful:

- Saving money
- Setting team goals
- Practicing food safety
- Storing food
- Marketing
- Increasing revenue

THINK ABOUT IT . . .

You are a supervisor who has just received a suggestion from an employee. Unfortunately, it cannot be used.

What would you say to the employee?

TEAM BUILDING

Supervisors may facilitate the work of several types of work teams. **Work teams** are groups of employees who cooperate on the job to attain objectives and who hold themselves accountable for their success. Supervisors understand that the knowledge and creativity of an effective team often produces better results than can be achieved by individual persons.

While supervisors in a department may be committed to a team concept, the attitude about its importance must begin with top-level managers. The contributions of teams cannot be maximized unless high-level managers endorse them.

Types of Work Teams

One way to think about work teams is by what they do. Using this approach, teams can be classified as simple, relay, or problem-solving teams.

SIMPLE TEAMS

A simple team is a group of employees who do the same basic kind of work, as shown in *Exhibit 4.7*. Examples include dining-room servers and food-production staff. During slow times, a simple team of just a few employees may be needed to produce and serve meals. However, when business volume is greater, a supervisor must increase the size of the team to handle the increased workload.

Exhibit 4.7

All members of a simple team must be well trained. If one team member cannot do his or her job, the team's productivity will be affected. This means supervisors must ensure that their employees are consistently able to perform all required tasks correctly. Then teams can be flexible; members can help each other whenever assistance is required.

RELAY TEAMS

Operations use relay teams because of how work flows within the establishment. For example, the servers' team takes orders that must then be prepared by the food-production team. The prepared food is then delivered to the customers by either a delivery team or the servers' team. Most employees are part of at least one relay team. This means the work of employees takes on added importance because their work affects others in different departments.

Since most employees are members of relay teams, the work they do impacts customers as well as employees. Even if they do not directly serve customers, they serve other employees who are serving customers.

PROBLEM-SOLVING TEAMS

Members of a problem-solving team try to solve problems too big for one employee to address. One example may be when an establishment will begin to offer outside dining or takeout services. Persons from many, if not all, departments must help determine the procedures required to extend these services to customers.

Other, less complicated challenges may arise when there are problems with work tasks. Perhaps, for example, errors are being made when product inventories are counted. A first step is to determine the cause. Then the team might consider what can be contributing to the problem and use that information to resolve it.

Cross-functional teams are a special type of problem-solving team. They are composed of members representing different departments who work together to resolve problems. Consider, for example, a food cost problem. A team composed of only food-production employees might view the cause as spending too much to purchase products. The purchaser might think that costs are high because of wasteful food-preparation practices. When the purchaser and some cooks work together along with some servers who know how much leftovers customers are taking home, the problem can be identified and addressed.

Building Effective Teams

Successful teams do not happen by chance. Supervisors must develop and maintain an environment in which their employees can work together effectively. They must identify and make the best use of each member's strengths, and this requires coordination.

Supervisors who are effective team leaders share several traits:

- They have good interpersonal skills, or people skills.
- They allow team members to make decisions. When appropriate, they share responsibilities with team members who have the knowledge, skills, and experience for the task.
- They encourage active participation in problem solving and decision making, and they consider creative alternatives.
- They ask team members about work improvement strategies, productivity, and other issues that affect goals.
- They facilitate an environment that maximizes morale to minimize unnecessary turnover and best use limited resources.

> **THINK ABOUT IT . . .**
>
> One benefit of a cross-functional team is the varied skills of its members, each of whom brings different abilities and ideas to the decision-making process. How does this relate to the concept of diversity?

Successful supervisors are driven by their establishment's mission, and they share it with their team. Then they facilitate the development of a more specific departmental mission suggesting the department's role. This process allows their team members to know how they can contribute to the success of the operation.

Effective supervisors set expectations and monitor performance as work evolves. They ask team members for ideas about how to achieve predetermined goals. By involving the team, strategies to address challenges are better accepted, and team members have a significant interest in their success. Supervisors also ensure that their staff members are competent by providing access to training and professional development opportunities.

Good supervisors encourage team members to offer diverse opinions and ideas. They encourage communication, networking, and feedback, which become input for further discussion. They also reward their teams when new work methods are successfully implemented.

The best supervisors empower their team members by giving them authority to make decisions within their areas of responsibility. This helps give the team a sense of ownership for their jobs. Supervisors also manage and provide information to help their team plan and monitor progress toward goals.

Supervisors who build successful teams encourage team members to be service-minded. First, they serve as role models by exhibiting attitudes, words, and actions that emphasize customer service. Second, they provide service training to all staff members. Third, they reward team members who provide the levels of service envisioned in the establishment and department missions. This can include positive reinforcement on the job and favorable input during performance appraisals.

Developing Team Goals

Teams can be effective only when members understand their goals and the activities that have been planned to achieve them. An excellent way to gain team consensus occurs when team members work with supervisors as goals are defined and refined.

TYPES OF TEAM GOALS

Effective teams contribute to the achievement of four types of goals during a project. These goals relate to team building, obtaining information, planning and organizing, and determining and obtaining necessary resources.

Manager's Memo

A supervisor desiring to build a successful team should use several tactics. First, remember always to communicate effectively and clearly. Then conduct team-building exercises so team members understand the development process. The activities selected should be critical to team building and not "just-for-fun" events.

Work with the team to establish goals and facilitate a process that allows the team to determine how they should be attained. This strategy requires the effective communication just discussed. A process for reaching goals cannot be successful without ongoing communication between the supervisor and the team and among team members.

Finally, use effective management skills consistently to support the team. Success will be measured, in part, by the team's sense that the supervisor has facilitated and not obstructed the team's activities.

Exhibit 4.8

The first goal addresses team building:

- **Getting to know each team member:** Teams are most effective when they take time to discover each member's background, skills, and work style.
- **Learning to work together:** Teams need to identify the strengths of each member and set processes in place to work efficiently.
- **Setting ground rules:** Members need a common understanding of how the team will conduct itself and what is acceptable and unacceptable behavior.
- **Figuring out decision-making processes:** A characteristic of ineffective teams is that decisions just seem to happen. Teams need to discuss how decisions will be made to avoid conflicts (*Exhibit 4.8*).

A second type of goal focuses on information:

- Learning about the tools used to support the team's tasks
- Getting updates from team members on progress
- Communicating with **stakeholders**, which are those who can impact or be affected by the actions of the team

The third type of goal relates to what the project or activity is trying to accomplish. These goals relate to understanding the project and each member's assignment. Team members should be able to ask questions about their tasks and the stakeholders' expectations. Supervisors should be able to identify the business needs supported by the goals. If this cannot be done, team members will have greater difficulty working toward goals because they will not see the purpose of the assignment. For example, a team of servers is assigned to establish a routine for honoring customers who are celebrating birthdays. What is the purpose of this activity? How will it help the business?

In addition to understanding the "what" and "why" of the activity or project, team members also need to understand their specific responsibilities. The team leader should discuss plans with team members. Breaking the process into smaller steps and assigning duties will help build team collaboration. Teams should continue to review and revise these plans as they move toward their goals.

The final type of goal relates to learning what resources are needed. How much time does the birthday celebration team have to make suggestions? How much can be spent on each customer's birthday event? Knowledge of this information will minimize time wasted considering alternatives that cannot be funded.

Supervisors must provide ongoing leadership and communication to help ensure that the team understands its contribution. Acknowledging team members, for example, with personal thank-you notes supports the members' feelings of accomplishment. Such practices should be part of a continuous improvement process.

Team-Building Issues

A number of factors can contribute to a team's ineffectiveness:

- **Poor management style:** The consistent use of one management style with all team members all the time is not likely to encourage a high-performing team. For example, the discussion of Maslow's hierarchy of needs earlier in this chapter pointed out that each team member likely has different motivational needs and an individual's performance will improve if their personal concerns are addressed.

- **High turnover:** Low employee retention rates mean that members of a team regularly come and go. If team membership turns over too frequently, teams can lose the cohesiveness that has been developed.

- **Failure to maintain team priorities:** Supervisors should remember the need to focus on goals. For example, team-building activities may encourage some team members to be more concerned about building interpersonal relationships during team-building exercises than goal attainment.

In contrast to some teams that may take time to become effective and increase productivity, other work teams never realize their potential. There are several clues that indicate if a team is unlikely to achieve goals:

- Members do not understand the team's mission or goals.
- Supervisors make decisions without much input from team members.
- There are few accomplishments.
- The level of trust is low.
- Members blame each other when problems arise.
- There is little diversity on the team.

Solutions for improving performance depend on the type of team experiencing problems. For example, strategies useful for a simple team include offering more training and meeting individually with team members. Supervisors can also work with specific employees to observe potential issues, and they can ask open-ended questions to reveal problems. An **open-ended question** encourages a response that exhibits a person's knowledge or feelings. For example, a supervisor might ask, "Why do you think overtime hours are frequently required?"

Manager's Memo

Several factors can hinder the effectiveness of a team when setting goals. For example, a trusting environment is essential if teams are to be successful. Teams can fail if some members do not feel comfortable. Team-building activities can be helpful in eliminating this potential problem.

Poor communication can negatively affect goal setting. In extreme cases, lack of communication can result in team members not knowing about goals or not sharing them. Communication challenges can also result in a failure to connect goals with specific business activities or improvements. Supervisors must be sure that each team goal is a priority that links back to the mission of the operation.

When a relay team is experiencing problems, the supervisor should make sure employees know that what they do affects the rest of the team. Supervisors could invite employees from different departments to a meeting in which they explain how their work affects others. If team members participate in the activity and still do not understand how their jobs relate to others, more training is likely needed. Experienced supervisors know that employees must care about their performance. If they do not, they should be counseled to determine the reasons for their lack of concern.

If a problem-solving team is not effective, a first step is to ensure that the team knows how to solve problems. If it does not, training may be required. If team members do not get along, this can also impact results. Then it is necessary to discover and eliminate the reasons for the conflict.

EMPLOYEE RECOGNITION AND INCENTIVE PROGRAMS

Some operations use formal employee recognition programs or employee incentive programs as additional ways to motivate employees. **Employee recognition programs** provide a way for establishments to publicly express appreciation for employees, or to acknowledge and celebrate them as individuals. **Employee incentive programs** are designed to encourage employees to meet specified goals by offering some kind of reward. There is no clear line between recognition programs and incentive programs. Most incentive programs include some public recognition. For many employees, that recognition is an incentive to attain the required goals.

In multiunit operations, recognition and incentive programs are often designed by upper-level management and implemented in all units. However, supervisors at the local level and those in independent operations can develop these programs as well. These tools are motivators, and often the supervisors closest to the employees are in the best position to understand what motivates and challenges them. To develop effective programs, supervisors must plan for them and ensure that certain components are in place.

Planning Successful Programs

The range of possible recognition and incentive programs is very broad. However, there are several challenges that must be addressed as successful programs are planned. They include issues of realism and the ability to meet requirements, as well as the program requirements themselves. Length of the program, details of the reward, and measures of success are also factors.

GOALS AND PARAMETERS

Employees need to believe they have a realistic chance of meeting the goals successfully and that their efforts will make a difference. That means goals must be set high but be realistic, and supervisors must be very clear about those goals when the recognition and incentive program is rolled out. The goals should identify what the recognition or incentive program is designed to achieve. Examples include increasing bottled wine sales, increasing customer comment scores, or improving employee attendance.

Some recognition and incentive programs can have a dramatic impact on the establishment's income statement. An **income statement** is a summary of the operation's profitability that shows revenues generated, expenses incurred, and profits or losses realized during a specific accounting period. For example, positive results of recognition and incentive programs to increase the check average will improve revenue. Rewarding employees who suggest how to reduce food costs can decrease costs on the income statement.

If recognition and incentive program goals and requirements are not clear and well understood, employees will be confused. Then, contrary to the program's intent, employee morale and productivity may actually decrease. If, for example, the employees think goals are unattainable or the measurement of success is subjective, the program will lose its impact. Employees must understand what to do to succeed, and they must believe that success is possible.

Supervisors planning recognition and incentive programs must also consider other issues. These include eligible participants and tracking methods.

The resources available to reward employees should be determined early in the program planning process. An important first consideration is to determine what motivates employees. Surveys and one-on-one meetings may provide the answers. Experienced supervisors realize that a little money can go a long way. Consider, for example, the food cost for two meals and the purchase price of two movie tickets compared to revenue generated by $2 more per guest over a two-week period. Creative arrangements can reduce recognition and incentive program costs, such as bartering clothing store gift certificates in exchange for complimentary meals for store managers when they conduct meetings. Bartering is the process of exchanging products or services without using any money.

It is also important to determine the behaviors or accomplishments for which employees should be recognized or rewarded. Examples include length of employment, attendance, increased check average, and reduced dish breakage. The specific rewards to be given depend on the resources available and the importance that managers and supervisors attach to accomplishing the goals of the recognition and incentive program. The rewards can also relate to the improved performance that was achieved. For example, a recognition and incentive program might include tiered rewards. Perhaps a basic reward is given to servers who attain a specified check average and the reward is increased in stages as each employee's check average increases.

Details about the recognition and incentive program must be carefully developed. These include the time frame, specific rules including who will participate, specific and measureable goal statements, and program results.

Manager's Memo

Supervisors should be aware that efforts to build teamwork may be set back if programs are developed in which only one employee is rewarded. It is far better to establish success factors that enable multiple rewards. For example, instead of rewarding the server with the highest check average for a specified time period, all servers who generate an average above a specified amount are rewarded. A second example concerns reducing accidents by working more safely. If the goal is to reduce accidents by a specified amount, everyone can be rewarded if the safety goal is met.

Supervisors must determine how to track participants' progress. For example, if a recognition and incentive program is developed to increase wine sales or check averages, progress can be measured with the establishment's point-of-sale (POS) system. If a program to encourage attendance is in place, payroll records can be accessed.

An employee recognition or incentive program can also lose its impact if the intended behavior is not rewarded quickly enough. A program can lose focus and employees may tire of it. That is why many programs run for short time periods and then are repeated. In this way, employees see the benefit of their efforts quickly.

However, not all recognition and incentive programs need to be short to be effective. In a long and more complex program such as one relating to reduced accidents or dish breakage, it is important to periodically report on efforts during the competition. Doing so will help keep employees motivated. Regular communication with participants should inform them about their progress. Otherwise, the employees may think the program has been terminated and abandon it themselves.

IMPLEMENTING THE PROGRAM

After an employee recognition or incentive program has been developed, it must be implemented. There are several ways to inform employees, but the most common method is to announce it during a meeting. Depending on the complexity and length of the program, a supervisor might also post information on the employee bulletin board, distribute a written explanation, or use electronic media.

Regardless of the method used, it is important to clearly explain all details of the recognition and incentive program. Verify that employees understand what the goal is, who can participate, what must be done to attain the goal, how long the program will run, and what the rewards will be.

Exhibit 4.9

REWARDS AND CELEBRATION

The rewards set for any recognition and incentive program must reflect the effort employees have to expend. For example, improving customer comments over the period of a week or two may result in a cash reward or gift certificate. In contrast, improving safety records over three months may require monthly reports and a large cash reward at the end of the program.

Celebrating the end of a recognition and incentive program and recognizing the employees who accomplished its goals is another reward. Such a celebration provides a way to publicly recognize the efforts and accomplishments of all employees who participated (*Exhibit 4.9*).

Supervisors should consider how they can most effectively recognize the employees who attain recognition and incentive program goals. Examples include group meetings; postings on the company's intranet, newsletter, or bulletin board; and email and social media postings.

Evaluating the Program

Tracking employee progress is important not only for motivating employees, but also for helping evaluate the success of recognition and incentive programs. While employee progress in large part determines whether a program worked or not, there are other issues to consider:

- Did the recognition and incentive program motivate most or all of the intended employees?

- Did employees like the program?

- Did the program achieve its goals?

- Were the benefits of the program worth the effort and expense?

- Was there anything about the recognition and incentive program's plans or implementation that could have been improved on?

Considering the answers to these and related questions can help with planning and implementing future recognition and incentive programs. As in many situations, supervisors who can identify the strengths and weaknesses of the program can learn from their mistakes and build on their successes.

Examples of Incentive Programs

Supervisors can create numerous types of recognition and incentive programs. Examples include those that target service, sales and productivity, customer satisfaction, safety, and longevity.

SERVICE AWARDS

Employee-of-the-month (or quarter, or year) recognition and incentive programs are relatively common and provide public recognition of employees who provide exceptional service. Sometimes these programs involve peer nominations, and sometimes winners are nominated by supervisors and managers. Typically there is a significant reward such as money, a gift certificate, or a special perk including a reserved parking space or a public transportation pass if the establishment is in an urban area. To enhance the value of such recognition and incentive programs, operations often have a short ceremony in which the employee is applauded and recognized. This is followed by posting the employee's name in a public location, often for customers to see.

In establishments that do not have a large number of employees, there may be an expectation that all employees will receive the recognition sooner or later.

THINK ABOUT IT . . .

In some establishments, certain employees meet incentive and recognition goals almost all the time, and many other employees seldom do so.

What would you do to encourage every employee to meet program goals?

Supervisors in these operations may grant quarterly awards or design a recognition and incentive program in which an award is given only when there have been examples of exceptional service.

SALES AND PRODUCTIVITY AWARDS

Recognition and incentive programs designed to increase sales or productivity might focus on increasing check averages, decreasing food costs, or improving safety records. For example, supervisors who want to increase the check average may communicate that broad goal, or establish more specific goals such as increased sales of appetizers or upscale wines and liquors. The average guest check is the average amount of money spent per visit by one guest.

CUSTOMER SATISFACTION AWARDS

Those who want to assess customer satisfaction may employ mystery shoppers, or persons who visit the establishment posing as customers and rate employee performance. The best mystery shoppers do not just focus on what is going wrong but also on what is going right. Other systems to measure actual customer satisfaction can be challenging because they depend on voluntary feedback. Comment cards and customer letters, for example, normally get only the fringe responses: those who are very happy and those who are very unhappy.

SAFETY AWARDS

Safety awards are often given to employees who have made improvements in their individual safety record or suggestions that lead to overall safety improvements. These improvements can be tracked using an accident log, which documents each time an employee is injured, and a record of safety in various departments. Safety programs can be organized in several ways:

- Severity of accidents measured by time lost
- Number of accidents in a specific time period
- Length of time between accidents
- Type of accidents and frequency

LONGEVITY AWARDS

Other strategies that motivate employees might include service awards that recognize how long an employee has worked at the establishment. Some operations provide birthday bonuses and other gifts. For example, an establishment may pay $20 to employees on their birthday and $50 on their service anniversary. Many operations thank all employees by hosting company picnics and annual parties and by giving special gifts or food items during holiday seasons. These special celebrations and gifts are ways to recognize all employees, thank them in a public manner, and build the morale of the entire team.

SUMMARY

1. **Describe special concerns when an entry-level employee is promoted to a supervisory position.**

   New supervisors often face challenges, such as confusion between working and leading, knowing when to assist with tasks, and interacting in the new relationship.

   Supervisors must develop trust and respect with team members. This involves being an effective communicator and being consistently honest and fair. Experience helps supervisors better meet their responsibilities.

2. **Explain basic employee motivation strategies.**

   Motivation is an inner drive, but supervisors can create conditions that employees typically find motivating, including making a good first impression and maintaining a professional workforce. They also support a culturally diverse workplace.

   Supervisors should direct the work of their employees as they would like to be supervised. They prepare for success by providing a clear vision and making plans. They help employees succeed as they develop ongoing training opportunities and review employees' work. They know that appreciation is a powerful motivator.

   Supervisors serve as role models. Their own behavior and attitude set the tone for the department. They communicate a consistent message about what employees should do and how.

   Strategies to encourage a motivational environment include acknowledging employees and expressing appreciation. Sharing information and involving employees in problem solving are also important. Supervisors demonstrate an interest in employees as individuals. Employees who are involved in planning and decision making know they are valuable.

3. **Describe procedures for building and maintaining effective teams.**

   Members of simple teams have similar work. Relay teams interact with each other, as when servers take orders and cooks produce them. Problem-solving teams work together to resolve problems.

   The best way to build teams is to maintain an environment in which employees can work together effectively. Good team leaders use several tactics including the use of interpersonal skills, allowing team members to make decisions, and creating an environment to reduce turnover and use available resources.

   Effective teams know their establishment's mission and their role. They develop carefully planned goals focused on team functioning, information flow, specific assignments, and necessary resources.

   Teams cannot be effective if supervisors use a poor management style, high turnover exists, or teams fail to focus on goals. If simple teams are not performing, more training may be required. When a relay team has problems, employees should be reminded that their work affects the entire team. If problem-solving teams are ineffective, corrective procedures are used and conflicts resolved.

4. **Discuss the development and management of employee recognition and incentive programs.**

Employee recognition programs provide a way to publicly express appreciation. Incentive programs encourage employees to meet specific goals by offering a reward. Planners should determine what motivates their employees and what resources are available to reward the employees. They must also determine what behaviors or accomplishments should be recognized, determine the specific rewards for specific behavior and results, and communicate the recognition and incentive program information to the employees.

Those planning recognition and incentive programs must also determine time frames and program rules and results. They must also decide how those who achieve program goals should be determined, and how the effectiveness of the program will be evaluated. It is also important to continuously implement other recognition and incentive programs based on the evaluation results. Examples of incentive programs include awards for service, sales and productivity, customer satisfaction, safety, and longevity.

APPLICATION EXERCISE

You are a dining-room supervisor in an independently owned establishment known for its friendly service, relaxed ambience, beautiful décor, and great food. Victor, the owner, has asked you to develop an incentive program to help introduce a new appetizer. The operation is open for dinner seven days a week. During the week the operation typically serves 120 customers each night, and Friday through Sunday about 160 are served nightly. On average, approximately 20 percent of the customers order appetizers.

Victor wants to sell at least 150 orders of this new appetizer within the next month. To encourage this, he is offering it at a special introductory price and has created table tents announcing the item. The budget for the incentive program is $200.

For the next month, Victor wants every server to take three specific actions:

- Use suggestive selling to sell the new appetizer to all customers.

- Ask customers who try the new item how they like it.

- Report any customer feedback during pre-shift meetings.

1. What parameters should be set for the program?

    - Time frame:

    - Rules:

    - Goals:

    - Eligible employees:

    - Measures of success:

    - Tracking methods:

2. How will you introduce the program?

3. Describe the training, if any, that you will provide.

4. You want all servers to be able to earn rewards; what must each server do to achieve his or her goal? Be specific.

5. How and when will you communicate participants' progress?

6. What rewards and celebrations will you have when the program ends?

REVIEW YOUR LEARNING

Select the best answer for each question.

1. Supervisors can best motivate employees by
   A. offering an average local entry-level wage.
   B. providing a positive working environment.
   C. reviewing available disciplinary alternatives.
   D. making an example of unsuccessful employees.

2. Which problem are new supervisors most likely to face?
   A. They do not know how to perform specific tasks.
   B. Their work does not produce concrete results.
   C. They are unable to assist with technical work.
   D. They are unfamiliar with quality standards.

3. What should new supervisors do when they interact with employees who previously were their peers?
   A. Treat all employees respectfully and fairly.
   B. Let the employees know they will be strict.
   C. Ask past employee peers to make their own decisions.
   D. Tell the employees special conditions will apply to them.

4. What is an example of a payroll benefit?
   A. Tips
   B. Wage
   C. Salary
   D. Insurance

5. What is the first step in planning a positive, productive work environment?
   A. Selecting a team leader
   B. Creating financial goals
   C. Developing a clear vision
   D. Establishing training programs

6. What aspect of job success is most difficult to improve with training?
   A. Knowledge
   B. Attitudes
   C. Abilities
   D. Skills

7. What type of team involves members from different departments who meet to address problems?
   A. Relay
   B. Simple
   C. Participative
   D. Cross-functional

8. What can cause a team to be ineffective?
   A. Low turnover
   B. High turnover
   C. Diverse opinions
   D. Individual assignments

9. What problem can arise when only one employee is rewarded in a recognition and incentive program?
   A. It causes the program to last longer.
   B. It increases the cost of the reward.
   C. It does not achieve program goals.
   D. It can discourage teamwork.

10. How should a supervisor determine which employees should receive rewards in a recognition or incentive program?
    A. They should reflect the employees' efforts.
    B. They should be determined by employees' peers.
    C. They should be given to all employees eventually.
    D. They should be given to only full-time employees.

5

Facilitating Employees' Work Performance

INSIDE THIS CHAPTER

- Communication
- Coaching
- Managing Conflict
- Managing Change
- Employee Performance Appraisals
- Progressive Discipline Procedures
- Employee Termination

CHAPTER LEARNING OBJECTIVES

After completing this chapter, you should be able to:

- Explain basic communication skills and challenges for restaurant and foodservice managers.

- State procedures for coaching employees.

- Describe procedures for resolving employee conflicts.

- Explain procedures for managing change.

- State basic procedures for conducting performance appraisals.

- Explain steps in a progressive discipline program.

- Describe procedures for employee termination.

KEY TERMS

CASE STUDY

"I know what Carmichael's meeting was about yesterday!" said Jasmine, the bar manager at Rusty Nail Bistro.

"How could you know?" asked Mariano, a long-time bartender.

"Carmichael came in today and began talking about the need for mystery shoppers to randomly and routinely visit to learn what we're doing right and wrong."

"I know," replied Mariano. "Whenever the boss goes to a meeting, he comes back with new ideas. We put them into practice immediately, and they are a big deal until either they don't work or he goes to another meeting and learns another idea that works someplace else."

"You're absolutely right, Mariano. Get ready for a team meeting that rolls out a mystery shopping program."

1. Why do you think Jasmine and Mariano are speaking negatively about the mystery shoppers program?

2. What procedures would you use to implement the program if you were Carmichael?

COMMUNICATION

Basic Communication Skills

Managers of restaurant and foodservice operations must be effective communicators. This means that they must consistently use basic speaking, listening, and writing skills.

SPEAK LIKE A PRO

Restaurant and foodservice managers speak to many people every day. In today's business environment, most managers use informal communication more often than formal communication.

Successful speakers use basic principles to deliver their messages. They do so to help ensure listeners will be receptive and will understand them. Some of these principles are shown in *Exhibit 5.1*.

Exhibit 5.1

PRINCIPLES OF EFFECTIVE SPEAKING

Speak Clearly

- Deliver concise messages.
- Tell *who, what, where, when, why,* and *how*.
- Pronounce words correctly.

Use Suitable Language

- Minimize use of jargon.
- Define technical terms.
- Do not make negative comments.
- Do not use slang.

Interact with Listeners

- Verify understanding.
- Repeat to ensure understanding.
- Create a relaxing environment.
- Maintain eye contact.

Remember Nonverbal Communication

- Ensure body language does not interfere.
- Use appropriate gestures.
- Use reasonable facial expressions.
- Act like a professional.

Personalize Message for Listeners

- Consider cultural differences.
- Overcome language barriers.
- Think about listeners' age and education.

Vary Speech Patterns

- Change voice tone and pitch.
- Pause after important points.
- Speak at a steady pace.

Successful speakers know they must focus on and understand the listener. They also know that effective communication requires interaction. What they think was clearly communicated may not be what the listener heard or understood. Speakers can do several things to help ensure listeners understand their messages:

- Ask questions about the topic and use responses to determine whether listeners understand.

- Repeat important points using different words.

- Encourage listeners to provide feedback.

Sometimes managers make formal presentations, such as when they speak to many employees or represent their establishment at a community business meeting. In these situations, they must think about how they will include all needed information in a clear and concise way.

One way they can do this is to plan the presentation to answer the 5 *Ws* and *How* questions:

- Who will be listening to the presentation?
- What do the listeners need to know?
- Where should the content begin and end?
- When in the context of other information will this information be presented?
- Why is the information important?
- How do we best present the information?

When managers plan presentations to answer these questions, they will have developed the content. Then it is important to practice the presentation, think about how their voice sounds, and consider whether they use any actions that may distract listeners. Also, managers should think about how listeners can interact with them to better understand the message being presented.

USE THE TELEPHONE LIKE A PRO

Managers should use the proper procedures when they use the telephone. They should also teach these procedures to all employees who must use them on the job (*Exhibit 5.2*):

- Say the establishment's name and your name and then offer assistance; for example, "Good afternoon, this is Rusty Nail Bistro, Shola speaking. How may I help you?"
- Listen carefully and wait until the caller has finished speaking before responding.
- Maintain a positive and courteous attitude.
- If the caller has a long message, take notes. Be sure to ask the 5 *Ws* and *How* questions to take a complete message: who, what, where, when, why, and how.
- Repeat the caller's basic message to ensure everything was heard correctly. Ask questions to clarify information, if necessary.
- If you cannot provide the necessary information, transfer the call to a person who can help the caller. Before transferring, obtain the caller's name and phone number in case the call is lost. Do not say "Wait a minute" or "Hold on." Instead, say something like, "I think Mr. Brahnson will be able to assist you; may I place you on hold and transfer the call?"
- Close the conversation by asking the caller if there is anything else you can do: "I am glad to help, Mrs. Addison; may I assist you with anything else?" A polite "Thank you for calling" is a good way to end the call.

THINK ABOUT IT . . .

Most people speak all day without thinking about it. Do you think that managers should take the time to learn how to speak professionally in ways that might be different from normal? Why or why not?

Exhibit 5.2

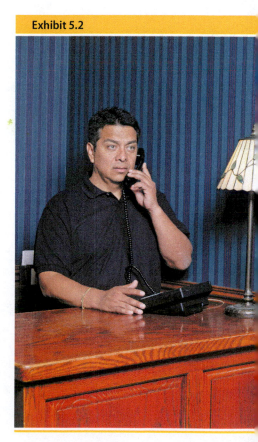

THINK ABOUT IT . . .

When some managers deal with an angry customer, they think, "This person is having a bad day. I will try to make it better."

Do you think this is possible when a customer is angry?

Sometimes callers become angry or rude. Managers must remember that they represent the operation, and they must remain polite and in control. Using effective listening skills and trying to understand the caller's position can often help manage these kinds of calls.

LISTEN LIKE A PRO

Some people think it is the sender's responsibility to ensure that a message is understandable. However, communication is a two-way process. While the speaker must communicate clearly, the listener must listen effectively. Listening is the ability to focus on what a person is saying to understand the message being spoken.

Almost everyone has had the experience of trying to listen but finding their thoughts wandering. The result is a message that has not been understood. Listeners must focus actively on listening. If they do not, the information may be lost, and the listener may leave the impression of not caring about the speaker or the message. An effective listener is involved in the communication process in several ways:

- Maintain eye contact with the speaker.
- Try to avoid interrupting.
- Ask questions for clarification.
- Restate the message to ensure understanding.
- Use effective body language such as nodding the head in agreement.
- Lean toward the speaker to indicate interest in the message.
- Take notes if necessary.
- Give the message to others, if necessary, without losing its meaning.

WRITE LIKE A PRO

Written communication, like spoken communication, must be understandable to be helpful. Writing is often more formal than speaking. Managers must be comfortable with all forms of written communication, including business letters, memos, and email. They must also know how to write policies, procedures, job descriptions, and numerous other types of business documents. Therefore, an important first step is to know the basic parts of a written message:

- **Introduction:** This is used to capture the reader's attention, state the message's purpose and introduce its topic, and tell the writer's point of view.
- **Body of message:** This is an organized discussion of the content.
- **Conclusion:** This reviews important points and may call for action.

Good writers plan what they want to say before they begin writing. They also use an organized process to develop their ideas into a clear, concise, and readable document. *Exhibit 5.3* reviews steps in an organized writing process.

Exhibit 5.3

ORGANIZED WRITING PROCESS

1. Think about the reader.

2. Think about what you want to accomplish. Write down what you want to happen as a result of the written message.

3. Identify the message benefits. How will it help the company, the reader, your customers and employees, and you?

4. Think about the situation. Ask yourself the five *W*s and *How* questions and write the answers.
   - Who?
   - What?
   - Where?
   - When?
   - Why?
   - How?

5. Identify the topics and group the details underneath them.

6. Order the topics in a logical flow.

7. Write the body of the message first, then the introduction, and then the conclusion.

8. Read the draft of your message. Edit and revise the content and flow to ensure it is easy to read. Check for spelling and correct sentences.

9. If the document is important, ask someone to read it and make suggestions as necessary to improve it.

10. Write the final draft and distribute the message.

Use these ideas to be a more effective writer:

- Be clear and complete. Sometimes writers leave something out of the message. Review your writing to be sure all ideas are complete and understandable.

- Be concise. The more you write, the more the reader must read and the more likely that problems can result. Long explanations make messages more difficult to understand. The best written messages make their points and then move on without using unneeded words.

- Keep it simple. Complex sentences are hard to read. Use short sentences and simple words where possible. If you must use words that are not commonly used in day-to-day conversation, define them.

- Check your work. If possible, use the grammar and spell-check functions in your computer's word processing program.

- Express a positive attitude. Even if your message must deliver troubling news, try to mention some long-term benefits.

- Write often. As is true with most skills, writing skills improve the more they are used.

Manager's Memo

The writing principles being discussed suggest the need for planning, organization, careful writing, and review of a written message before it is distributed. Managers can typically perform these tasks very quickly, perhaps only in seconds, if the message is simple to write and understand. An example may be a handwritten memo posted on the employee bulletin board to remind employees that the establishment will be open one hour later for a holiday.

In contrast, much time may be needed to properly write messages on topics that have significant implications for the operation. An example may be a letter to an attorney or customer about an alleged food safety problem.

One of a manager's most important challenges is to determine the importance and priority of each task, including writing. Then time and appropriate principles should be used to address the challenge.

Emails, faxes, tweets, and text messaging are just some ways that technology enables communication. These methods are fairly casual, but managers should use the same basic writing principles that they use with other types of messages.

Barriers to Effective Communication

The ability of a manager to communicate effectively is made difficult by many barriers that can get in the way of spoken and written messages. These barriers make it harder for messages to be correctly received and understood:

- **Word meaning:** Message receivers may not know the meanings of some words or phrases or may interpret them differently than the sender.

- **Jargon:** Jargon refers to technical language, and it can create communication challenges.

- **Gestures:** Body movements can cause distractions to listening, and gestures can convey different messages to different people.

- **Cultural differences:** The usual distance between two people when speaking differs among cultures. Praising someone in public is not considered appropriate in some cultures. Managers, through their experience and training, should acquire and use knowledge about the cultural backgrounds of their employees as they communicate with their staff.

- **Assumptions:** Some managers assume their team members know how to solve a problem when they really do not. In these cases, difficulties may occur because the manager did not provide enough information.

- **Fixed ideas:** Managers may think some employees never listen. Then they repeat themselves and cause the employees to lose interest in what they are saying.

- **Opinions:** Some managers hold opinions based on experience that may not reflect the current situation. These attitudes influence how they send messages.

- **Distracting workplace:** Environmental noise is any sound, such as loud talking or blaring radios, that interferes with communication.

Additionally, even the best business writers can make mistakes. Try to avoid the following common writing pitfalls:

- **Failure to plan:** Even if there is little time available, think through the message's purpose and main points before you begin writing.

- **Uncertain purpose:** Readers' interest quickly decreases when they do not understand the reason for the written message. State the purpose of the written communication in its introduction.

- **Forgetting the audience:** Always remember who will be reading the message. Then use the correct approach and write a message readers will understand. Understanding who the readers will be and why the message is being written are important keys to successful writing.

- **Using an incorrect style:** Write in everyday language and make points that the reader will understand.

Writing challenges confront many managers. However, use of the principles just discussed can help capture readers' attention and ensure that they understand the intended message.

Managing the Grapevine

Each operation has an informal channel of communication that relies on word of mouth to transmit information. This system, commonly referred to as the **grapevine**, can be a good way to transmit information if it is used in a positive manner. Then it can foster an environment that encourages information sharing and respect.

However, informal communication systems can also cause numerous problems. Negative comments and gossip are two of the most harmful issues. If allowed to spread, negative communication can create a stressful work environment and destroy relationships between coworkers.

Sometimes there is little that an employee can do about other employees' negative communication. However, all employees have control over their own communication. Gossip and negative comments will quickly die if they are not repeated. Managers must determine the type of work environment desired. Then they must set the standard, monitor, and be prepared to follow up if employee behaviors fail to meet the standard.

Rumors involve information without a source. Supervisors can use several techniques to manage rumors:

- First, question whether the rumor may be untrue. Ask questions such as "Why am I being told?" and "Would the person telling me gain something by saying something untrue?"

- Consider the source of the rumor. Ask, "Does the person have access to information? Can the information be confirmed?"

- If the rumor appears to be gossip, ask the person why you are being told, and indicate that communication about the topic should cease. In some instances is may be appropriate to inform the subject of the rumor. Finally, do not repeat the information.

Managers should plug into the grapevine and obtain as much information as they can from it.

Manager's Memo

New employees notice negative communications. They are just as likely as others to hear rumors, and what if the rumors are about them? These experiences run counter to the welcoming environment the manager is trying to establish. At the least, new employees are likely to judge these actions to be unprofessional. At the worst, new employees may begin to wonder if their decision to join the establishment's team was a good one.

New employees present another communication challenge. Managers and other trainers must communicate work requirements effectively while creating an atmosphere that encourages questions. Confusion can be created when new employees learn that some communication is good while some is not. The challenge of distinguishing between acceptable and unacceptable communication can create more difficulties for those who are already trying to learn as much as they can as quickly as they can.

Information that can be confirmed as truthful can be useful input for problems being resolved and decisions being made. Information that is incorrect may be countered by use of the strategies just noted.

Nonverbal Communication

Nonverbal communication refers to a speaker's expressions and movements that tell additional information about the message. It occurs during one-on-one conversations, but it is often most noticeable when someone is giving a speech.

Examples of uncontrolled nonverbal communication occur when a speaker paces back and forth or gestures in a certain way. Nonverbal communication also occurs when, for example, a manager is interacting with an employee about something that is important only to the employee. If the manager yawns, stops to make or take telephone calls, or looks at a wristwatch, these actions convey feelings that the conversation is not important.

These examples show that people can communicate even when they do not use words. Nonverbal communication can turn any message into a miscommunication.

Exhibit 5.4 shows some examples of nonverbal communication. Managers need to be aware of these things when they are talking.

One way for managers to minimize the use of distracting nonverbal communication is to practice speaking in front of a mirror. They could also ask someone to give them honest feedback on their delivery. Effective speakers want to know what nonverbal messages they may be using and try to eliminate the negative ones.

In addition, nonverbal cues are also seen in written emails, texts, or other written communications. The use of all capitals, bold fonts, or loud colors is associated with yelling or anger in the written word. Lack of capitalization or fully spelled words indicates hurried responses that may mean the writers question or query is not worth the time to respond properly. Managers need to use good writing cues to convey their messages.

Nonverbal signals have different meanings for different cultures. Sometimes, a nonverbal behavior can mean something positive in one culture and something negative in another culture. In some cultures and with some persons the following nonverbal behaviors send a negative message:

- Biting lips signals nervousness
- Slouching in chair shows disinterest
- Raising eyebrows indicates disbelief or amazement
- Gesturing with hands can be distracting
- Pointing with finger comes across as scolding or lecturing

Exhibit 5.4

EXAMPLES OF NONVERBAL COMMUNICATION

Facial expressions

Crossed arms

Gestures

Back-and-forth pacing

Posture

Touching

Invasion of personal space

Clothing and appearance

Eye contact

THINK ABOUT IT . . .

Nonverbal communication is a subtle way that a person communicates.

How do you feel if a speaker stands just a few inches in front of you? If a person on a platform looks down at you?

In some cultures and with some persons the following nonverbal behaviors can signal something positive:

- Sitting on edge of chair and leaning forward expresses interest.
- Smiling shows confidence and enthusiasm.
- Giving a "thumbs up" suggests agreement (*Exhibit 5.5*).
- Winking an eye indicates recognition.

Cultural differences mean that the same behavior can convey multiple different meanings. For example, sharing gifts, arriving at meetings on time, and even crossing the legs when seated can mean very different things in different cultures. Managers must be aware of these factors as they interact with persons of different cultural backgrounds.

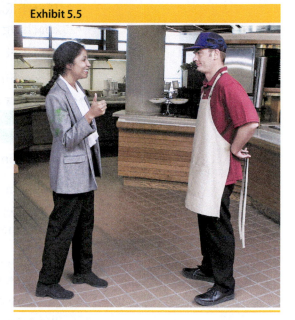

Exhibit 5.5

COACHING

Experienced managers know that coaching is one of the best ways to improve employees' work. Coaching involves informal efforts to improve job performance. The process takes considerable listening skills, patience, and focus, but it can produce improvements that are worth the effort.

Overview of the Coaching Process

Steps in the basic coaching process are shown in *Exhibit 5.6*.

Much coaching is done as managers "manage by walking around." As they do so, they can compare an employee's performance to expected performance as described in a job standard such as standard operating procedures (step 1).

When employees are observed doing something right, managers should reinforce their performance (step 2). This can be a simple comment such as "Great job!" or "That's a tough task, and you always do it correctly; thanks!"

Sometimes, managers will note employees doing something incorrectly. In this case, coaching involves correcting negative performance. A manager might, for example, tell why the action is incorrect, show the employee the correct way to do it, or inform the employee's manager, who can help the employee improve.

Correcting errors should normally be done in private or at least quietly at the workstation. The purpose is to correct the performance, not to embarrass or punish the employee.

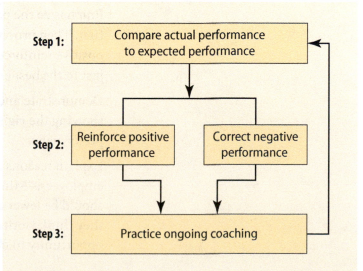

Exhibit 5.6

STEPS IN THE COACHING PROCESS

Step 1: Compare actual performance to expected performance

Step 2: Reinforce positive performance / Correct negative performance

Step 3: Practice ongoing coaching

If an informal coaching discussion does not correct the problem, a second coaching session may be needed. The manager may need to revise his or her coaching technique to make it more effective.

If coaching reveals that the employee does not want to do the task, the manager may decide to move from coaching to progressive discipline efforts. **Progressive discipline** involves a series of corrective actions that become more serious as unacceptable performance continues. It assists an employee in improving performance by bringing it up to established standards.

Step 3 in *Exhibit 5.6* suggests that the manager should perform ongoing coaching. This means that the process of comparing actual to expected performance should continue, as well as reinforcement or correction.

The manager acting as a coach provides input and makes suggestions for changes. He or she also provides feedback about the employee's ideas and responses and helps the employee improve performance. These actions are not simply giving orders and criticizing mistakes.

Coaching is not a one-time activity. It involves a commitment to help an employee grow and an interest in helping the employee determine how to accomplish this. The function of the coach is to think about how to help employees solve their own problems.

Coaching Principles

Coaching helps employees learn how the manager views their work on a timely and ongoing basis. Employees like this input, there is no expense, and it takes little time. Several principles can help ensure that a coaching activity is effective:

- Be tactful when providing correction. Focus on the behavior, not on employees themselves.

- Emphasize the positive. Try to find something good, and mention it first. Then proceed with any necessary corrective discussion. Direct positive reinforcement to all employees who perform a task correctly, not just to the best employees.

- Demonstrate and review appropriate procedures. Spend much more time showing the right way to do something than discussing the incorrect performance.

- Explain reasons for changes, if possible, from the viewpoint of employees: "Mina, we have changed how this should be done. Now there should be fewer errors and less stress for you." Also, ask employees how they think work can be improved. A coaching discussion can be another opportunity to obtain useful ideas from employees.

- Maintain open communications with staff members. Ongoing coaching discussions reduce concerns such as "Now what does the boss want to talk to me about?"

- Conduct discussions of negative behavior in private. Praise employees for proper performance in public and have performance improvement conversations in private.

- Evaluate work by comparing performance against standards. The review of performance should consider how an employee's performance compares to what is expected, not how it compares to others' performance.

THINK ABOUT IT . . .

Which of the following statements would you prefer your boss to say to you? Why?

"I just trained you yesterday! Why don't you know how to do this?"

"Let's go over this procedure again."

MANAGING CONFLICT

Managers must sometimes deal with conflicts that arise among employees. Therefore, they must know and practice skills of conflict resolution in the work environment. **Conflict resolution** refers to processes that encourage finding solutions to problems before more formal grievance procedures are needed (*Exhibit 5.7*).

Exhibit 5.7

Conflict Resolution Strategies

Typically, conflicts occur because of disagreement about a work situation or personality clashes between employees. An effective conflict resolution process can develop understanding and cooperation that leads to an agreement that works for those involved. The process should allow employees to avoid embarrassment or other situations that might interfere with solving the problem.

Managers can use several forms of conflict resolution, including **negotiation**, **mediation**, and **arbitration**:

- **Negotiation:** discussion between involved persons with the goal of reaching an acceptable agreement

- **Mediation:** a process in which a neutral third party facilitates a discussion of difficult issues and makes suggestions about an agreement

- **Arbitration:** a process in which a neutral third party listens and reviews facts and makes a decision to settle the conflict

Conflict Resolution Steps

All three forms of conflict resolution follow similar basic steps, which are reviewed in *Exhibit 5.8*. Ultimately, the best process to use is one that results in a solution that the concerned persons can accept and feel good about. Additionally, allowing employees to resolve conflict with one of these methods gives them greater control over their own work situation.

Exhibit 5.8

RESOLVING EMPLOYEE CONFLICTS

1. Identify concerns as well as all persons involved and their feelings about the situation or individuals.

2. Determine the facts.
   a. Define the conflict and impact of the problem.
   b. Verify the sources and facts of the conflict.
   c. Review and enforce operation policies.
   d. Identify other persons who should be involved, such as higher-level managers.
   e. Interview all involved persons separately.

3. Develop a resolution that best meets the needs of all parties.
   a. Work together to identify critical factors.
   b. Ensure that the resolution complies with existing policies and is fair, legal, and will resolve the issue.
   c. Confirm that all parties are comfortable with the resolution.

4. Communicate the resolution.
   a. Be sure all involved parties are aware of the resolution.
   b. Be sure all parties understand the resolution.

5. Document the agreement reached.
   a. Accurately record all important information and resolution details.
   b. File the information in employee files or another place where it can be reviewed if necessary.

6. Follow up on the agreement.
   a. Discuss any other details to ensure the issue is resolved.
   b. Monitor the agreement, if necessary.

The steps in *Exhibit 5.8* can be used to review how an employee conflict might be resolved. Think about an example in which there is uncertainty about whether removing bags of garbage at the end of the shift is the responsibility of the closing cook or the dish washer.

Step 1. Identify concerns

Both employees indicate they are very busy with cleanup duties and do not have time to remove the garbage.

Step 2. Determine the facts

Both employees are very busy at the end of most shifts. However, there are serious food safety and cleanliness issues. Since there are no existing policies, the matter must be resolved.

Step 3. Develop a resolution

The manager meets with the chef, who is the manager of both employees. The manager and the chef agree that teamwork is the best way to resolve the problem.

Step 4. Communicate the resolution

Currently, the dish washer moves garbage bags about two hours before the end of the shift. Garbage that accumulates from that point until the end of the shift often remains in the cans overnight and is removed about mid-morning. The chef meets with the closing cook and the dish washer, and they agree to a compromise. The dish washer will remove garbage from all kitchen areas, and the closing cook will be responsible for mopping the floor in food-production and serving line areas. The dish washer will clean all other back-of-the-house floors.

Step 5. Document the agreement reached

A new policy will be developed, and the kitchen's closing checklist will be modified to include these assignments. The procedures will be included in training material for new employees in both of these positions.

Step 6. Follow up on the agreement

The chef and the manager will monitor the closing checklist information and review the cleanliness of kitchen work areas when they arrive for the early morning shift. If cleanliness standards are not met, the chef will suggest corrective actions that will involve the closing cook and/or dish washer and confirm that they are effective.

MANAGING CHANGE

Many managers agree that the only thing constant in the restaurant and foodservice industry is change. Changing customer preferences and an ever-increasing emphasis on value along with changing perceptions of the employee workforce are examples of the human side of change. Technology innovations as well as economic, legal, and competitive pressures have an ever-changing influence on the operating procedures of all operations.

The best managers and their employees recognize that change for the sake of change is not always good. They also recognize that purposeful change is necessary for survival. An attitude of accepting change rather than resisting it is perhaps the most important ingredient in a change management recipe.

The Challenge of Change

Change may affect just a few employees, such as receptionists who must learn how to operate a new automated reservation system. Alternatively, it may affect almost all employees if a new menu is implemented. Operations are composed of departmental teams, so many staff members can be affected when even a "simple" change is made. For example, when a salad bar is added, production and serving staff will both be affected. Fortunately, some basic procedures can be used to manage all types of change. Managers will frequently need to use them.

An operation is complex and typically has numerous pressures that impact it all the time. For example, each establishment has an organizational culture that affects the way employees are treated, the level of concern for customers, and perhaps its role in the community. It has policies and procedures to guide decision making, and it has organizational charts that show relationships between departments and employees and job descriptions that indicate what employees are supposed to do.

At the same time, change pressures affect the operation. Some are internal, such as the need to better serve customers, pressures to meet budgeted costs, and the impact of technology. Technology provides information and influences its flow and its use in decision making. Over time, the contributions of managers and employees yield changes that improve the operation.

In addition to internal pressures, operations face external pressures for change. Consider the evolving wants and needs of customers and the impact of new products and equipment, as well as regulatory issues that require operating changes.

One of the most important responsibilities of managers and their teams is to keep alert to the need to develop goals in light of changes. These goals bring the establishment closer to attaining its mission. The ways to do this can change, and managers must assess whether and when changes are needed. Then they must use available resources wisely to attain the goals.

Change Strategies

A frequently discussed model for change suggests that managers can use three strategies to manage it. *Exhibit 5.9* shows the steps that can be used to implement change.

Step 1: Unfreeze the Situation.

Managers must be aware of the existing situation, the pressures that defend it, and those that prompt change. This will help them determine how a change might be managed.

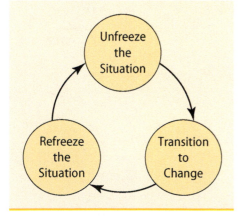

Exhibit 5.9

THREE-STEP CHANGE PROCESS

For example, consider an establishment in which each department head orders products needed for the department. The manager thinks that time and cost savings could result if purchasing activities were centralized. The manager also understands that department heads will not like the change because they currently purchase what they want, when they want to. Also, they have established relationships with vendors and enjoy the authority to make purchasing decisions.

The manager invites the department heads to a meeting to discuss their concerns and explain how the change in the purchasing process could benefit them. For example, they will have more time for other duties and will still be a primary influence in selecting products. In addition, this change will allow the establishment to remain competitive and generate additional revenues, some of which will be allocated to compensation increases.

Step 2: Transition to Change.

The second step involves interacting with affected team members. This group can help with revising policies and procedures, training staff, and addressing numerous questions and concerns, especially with significant change.

The transition to the desired change is easier when managers have long, professional relationships with affected employees. In a work environment of trust and respect, employees know the manager wants to make changes that benefit the operation. They do not suspect other motives.

In the purchasing example, the manager and department heads will develop an overview of how a centralized purchasing process might work. It will address issues such as who will be responsible for purchasing, how purchase requests will be routed, and what should be done if several departments use the same products. Other issues could involve how vendors will be selected, how the ordering process will work, and how the revised system will be evaluated.

Step 3: Refreeze the Situation.

All concerns about the change should have been addressed, and necessary policies, procedures, training, equipment, and tools should be in place. Even so, situations may arise that require the manager's attention. Effective planning will minimize these issues, and the new situation will not be affected by lingering problems.

In the purchasing system example, the department heads will feel comfortable if the decision was a good one. There may be some awkward situations, such as concerns about how paperwork from deliveries will flow to the accounting office. However, these issues should be limited when proper planning has been undertaken.

THINK ABOUT IT . . .

Suggesting creative ideas may make some employees feel important or feel that they contribute.

Do you think managers can motivate employees and obtain creative ideas at the same time? Why or why not?

Overcoming Resistance to Change

Employees' resistance is often an obstacle to be overcome as change is managed. Employees who are used to doing something one way may resist changes. A standard concern is expressed in the statement, "We have always done it this way!"

Employees may be uncertain how they will be affected by the change. They may not want to take time to learn new ways of doing things. Also, they may think there will be closer and more frequent coaching and supervision as the change is implemented and evaluated. Managers who understand and address the human nature to resist change will be more likely succeed with it.

A manager can use multiple approaches to address resistance. All will be more effective if the manager has a history of involving employees and explaining why change is necessary. Managers who have predicted successful changes in the past will likely meet with less resistance because employees know that those changes led to improvements.

Several strategies can be useful in reducing resistance to change:

- Involve employees in the decision-making process. A **participative management** style improves the quality of decision making and makes change implementation easier because the decision was a consensus. Participative management is a leadership method that increases the quality of decision making by involving employees. Managers using this approach typically discover another advantage: it improves the employees' job satisfaction.
- Inform employees in advance about changes that will impact them.
- Select an appropriate time to implement the change. Trying something new during an extremely busy shift is never a good idea.
- Share past successes. Review related changes that have benefited employees and the organization.
- Reward employees for sharing ideas in the decision-making process that benefit the establishment and the employees.

THINK ABOUT IT . . .

Have you ever had a job that was always the same? Do you think it would be more enjoyable to work in an environment in which the usual ways are challenged? Why or why not?

Managers as Change Agents

A **change agent** is a person who leads change in an organization. At first it might seem that all managers are change agents because they must manage changes that are made. However, some managers resist change as well. They may think it is good for other establishments but not theirs, or they may believe they will make changes some other time. In contrast, a change agent is always alert for changes that will benefit the operation, even if only in a small way. They see the analysis of opportunities and activities required to implement change as an important part of their job. Change agents encourage all employees to think about better ways of doing things. They encourage open communication, whether formally in meetings or performance appraisal sessions or in informal coaching or other situations.

Many change agents like to benchmark. **Benchmarking** is any activity that helps identify and analyze best practices to discover ways to improve performance. Managers and their employees benchmark as they think about how operating procedures are done at other establishments. They consider their own operation as they read trade magazines, talk with peers in association meetings, and dine out in other operations. The objective of benchmarking is to learn best practices and to ensure that the procedures used at an operation are at least as good as the best practices identified.

Change agents know how to use the three-step model for change. They encourage and reward their employees for input, and they do not punish them if reasonable suggestions do not work. Change agents must also share information with their employees to receive maximum benefit from their ideas. It is also helpful to suggest how employees will benefit from changes. Examples may include less work, greater safety, less stress, and the knowledge that staff are using the best work practices.

Steps for Implementing Change

Broad strategies for managing change were reviewed in the three-step change process in *Exhibit 5.9*. Managers can use specific procedures to implement change. *Exhibit 5.10* provides an overview of these procedures.

In reviewing each step in the process, think about whether the strategies noted are useful. Consider how an employee affected by the change might react.

Step 1: Discuss Need for Change.

Employees like to feel that they are "in on things," and managers should alert them about pending changes as soon as possible. Managers should provide as much information as they can and help employees understand the "why" and "how" of the change. When possible, they should also review how the change will help employees and explain how it is in line with the establishment's mission.

Managers should provide as much detail as possible. For example, provide timelines, mention potential challenges, and explain what the situation will be like if the change achieves its goal. This becomes an objective of the change, which can be used later to determine if the change is successful.

Manager's Memo

Managers who believe in the benefits of reasonable change often lead employees in continuous quality improvement (CQI) activities. These involve ongoing efforts to better meet or exceed customer expectations and to define ways to perform work with better, less costly, and faster methods.

These managers know that regardless of how small a change may be, the establishment improves when any change helps better meet the organization's mission and goals. Employees in a CQI environment will be conditioned for change, and they will look forward to it because they know the benefits that can be realized. CQI typically works "from the bottom up" because employees closest to the situation are likely to have ideas to help improve it. In CQI efforts the manager is typically a facilitator who helps define problems and then uses a team approach to make decisions and implement necessary changes.

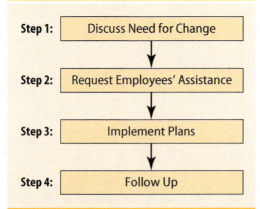

Exhibit 5.10

PROCEDURES FOR IMPLEMENTING CHANGE

Step 1: Discuss Need for Change

Step 2: Request Employees' Assistance

Step 3: Implement Plans

Step 4: Follow Up

Exhibit 5.11

Step 2: Request Employees' Assistance.

Managers should ask employees about their viewpoints. These will be freely given if the establishment's culture supports a relationship of cooperation (*Exhibit 5.11*). Ideally, meetings and conversations with individual employees will enable employees to understand details about the change. Many affected employees may agree with it; however, this may not be the case. Employees' comments and actions may suggest concerns, and managers who know about them are in the best position to address them. When managers take the opportunity to obtain employee ideas, there is likely to be less resistance to change.

Managers should ask employees to support the change. Personal conversations with some employees to address their specific concerns may be helpful. Also, employees who appear influential can be asked for their support and assistance in promoting the change.

Step 3: Implement Plans.

Small changes like revisions to recipes and use of new serviceware may not create significant challenges. However, the implementation of on-site production of items previously purchased ready-made may seriously impact kitchen employees. The roll-out of a new point-of-sale system may create significant anxiety for servers.

Managers can minimize these problems by developing plans that are reviewed by affected employees. For example, the preparation of new menu items according to standardized recipes and extensive training on new point-of-sale (POS) systems will be necessary before changes in existing procedures can be implemented. Perhaps limited quantities of new menu items can be produced while production staff are being trained. A company representative or the dining-room manager may be able to help servers with initial use of the new POS system. Implementation of new items and systems in times of slow business volume can also be helpful, as can scheduling additional labor hours to address potential lowered productivity.

Step 4: Follow Up.

Recognition of employees' success is an important follow-up activity. This is not the time to say "See, I told you it would work!" Instead, it is a time for the manager to genuinely compliment and thank employees for their cooperation, creative ideas, and other help with the transition.

Evaluation of the change implementation process will also be useful. This is best done by considering the objectives discussed in step 1. For example, the objective of on-site food item preparation is to reduce labor hours without affecting quality. Were labor hours reduced? What do customer comment cards say about the new menu item? If the objective of the new POS system is the generation of more useful reports, is this occurring?

In both examples, managers should determine whether there were any unexpected spin-off problems. If so, they should be addressed. Also, managers and their teams can review the strategies used to manage the change in efforts to learn what should and should not be done as further changes are implemented.

EMPLOYEE PERFORMANCE APPRAISALS

Employee performance appraisals are a critical aspect of an environment that enables employees to stay motivated. They are very important for several reasons. Employee appraisals allow managers to interact with employees for specific purposes:

- Discuss and document past performance
- Ask employees how they think work can be improved. A coaching discussion can be another opportunity to obtain useful ideas from employees.
- Review any other job-related issues
- Talk about employee development opportunities and establish goals

Performance appraisals typically focus on performance, important issues and facts, and agreement about opportunities and goals. An operation's policy usually indicates how often formal performance appraisals should be conducted. In many establishments, discussions about changes in the employee's compensation occur before, during, or after the session. This topic is very important to employees, and performance appraisal polices in some companies require a separate meeting to discuss compensation changes such as the amount of wage or salary increases, if any. Compensation is discussed in chapter 9.

Performance Appraisal Procedures

As seen in *Exhibit 5.12*, the performance appraisal process is cyclical. A review of past performance is followed by its evaluation, which is followed by goal setting for future performance.

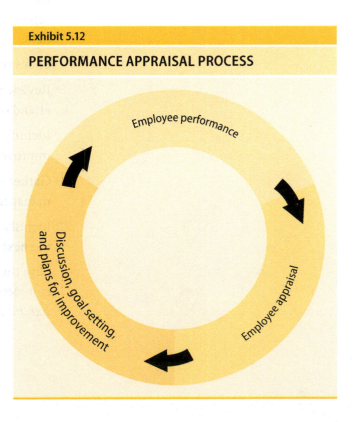

Exhibit 5.12

PERFORMANCE APPRAISAL PROCESS

Employee performance

Employee appraisal

Discussion, goal setting, and plans for improvement

Too many managers approach the appraisal process in a hurried manner and focus on the most recent examples of an employee's performance. Add in a lack of ongoing feedback and little emphasis on goal setting, and it is easy to see why many employees have negative feelings about appraisal meetings.

Effective managers understand the importance of performance appraisal to the development of their staff and operation, so they know evaluations must be done carefully and correctly. Several steps should be followed to ensure the appraisal process is productive and helps everyone gain the most benefits from the meeting.

Step 1: Preparing for the Meeting.

Set a time and place for the appraisal meeting and notify the employee in advance. The employee will want to prepare, just as the manager must.

Select and complete a performance review form in a format consistent with the company philosophy. Gather the facts needed to evaluate the employee's performance. Review the employee's file and ask team leaders who work with the employee for their input. At the same time, the employee should complete a self-evaluation appraisal form to discuss during the meeting. It should focus on the employee's strengths, opportunities, accomplishments, and future development goals.

Use these suggestions to prepare for the performance appraisal session:

- Review job descriptions, current development plan goals, project reports, employee file information, and any other performance data.

- Focus on performance measures and not personality traits.

- Review the employee's background including skills, training, and attendance records.

- Identify the employee's performance strengths and areas needing improvement.

- Gather information about performance from all of his or her managers.

- Identify areas in which you think the employee can improve during the next appraisal period.

- Give the employee a self-evaluation form and request that he or she complete it and bring it to the meeting. A sample form is shown in *Exhibit 5.13.*

SAMPLE EMPLOYEE APPRAISAL FORM

SAMPLE EMPLOYEE APPRAISAL FORM

Employee name: Nadlee Cooper   Position title: Cook's Helper

Appraisal period: From 1/1/2012 to 6/30/2012   Today's date: 7/5/2012

PART I: PERFORMANCE OF JOB TASKS

Job Description Task	Performace (*circle one:* 1 = unsatisfactory; 5 = exceptional)				
1. Obtains necessary products needed for food preparation	1	2	3	4	5
2. Cleans fresh produce	1	2	3	4	5
3. Cleans fresh vegetables	1	2	3	4	5
9. Properly stores food preparations	1	2	3	4	5
10. Follows postshift cleanup procedures	1	2	3	4	5

PART II: JOB-RELATED BEHAVIORS (*circle one:* 1 = unsatisfactory; 5 = exceptional)

1. Cooperation	1	2	3	4	5
2. Attitude	1	2	3	4	5
3. Dependability	1	2	3	4	5
4. Judgment	1	2	3	4	5
5. Job knowledge and skills	1	2	3	4	5
6. Interpersonal relationship	1	2	3	4	5
7. Other: _____	1	2	3	4	5

PART III: IMPROVEMENT and PROFESSIONAL DEVELOPMENT

A. Last Period's Goal	Achieved	Not Achieved	Comments
1.	❏	❏	
2.	❏	❏	
3.	❏	❏	

B. Next Period's Goal	How Success Will Be Measured
1.	
2.	
3.	

PART IV: COMMENTS

Supervisor:

Employee:

Signatures:

Supervisor   (Date)   Employee   (Date)

Step 2: Conducting the Meeting.

The performance appraisal session allows the manager and the employee to have an open discussion about how the employee has performed since the last appraisal meeting. Start by asking for the employee's view of his or her performance. Also, ask about challenges to performance or reaching goals and ask if he or she has any questions. After the employee has provided his or her views, managers should share feedback about the employee's strengths and opportunities for improvement.

After both employee and manager have discussed the employee's performance, gain agreement about past performance and how the employee will improve. The manager must be sure to ask how he or she can help.

An employee development plan should be discussed. Goals should be considered, and the employee can refine them further to include timelines and resources needed. There are strong reasons to involve the employee in the goal-setting process during performance discussions:

- Involvement creates ownership for the employee's development.
- The goal-setting process can be a motivation tool to help develop the employee's leadership skills.
- The employee gains a better understanding of how he or she is helping the operation reach its goals.
- The process allows the employee to find pride in his or her work.
- The manager gains information about the employee's views.

Use these principles when conducting a performance appraisal meeting:

- Create an open and friendly atmosphere.
- Explain that employee input is desired.
- Try to put the employee at ease.
- Discuss job requirements, strengths, and opportunities and compare the employee's actual performance against goals set for this appraisal period (see *Exhibit 5.14*).
- Be prepared with questions to engage the employee.
- Take notes during the meeting.
- Encourage the employee to suggest ideas for an employee development program, and offer suggestions.
- Reach agreement on goals, a schedule, and any needed resources.

Exhibit 5.14

Step 3: Closing the Meeting and Following Up.

The manager closes the meeting by providing a summary, and asks the employee about any comments or suggestions. The manager tells the employee he or she will support the employee's development plan and offer ongoing assistance. The supervisor should monitor the employee's progress toward attaining goals. For example, informal performance appraisal sessions can be conducted before the date of the next formal appraisal meeting to discuss performance progress or issues.

End on a positive and friendly note, and let the employee know if any follow-up meetings are needed. The time frame for the next performance appraisal meeting should be established. Document the meeting, including a summary of past performance, information about the employee development plans, and any commitments. Be sure to give the employee a copy of the summary report.

A final activity in the performance appraisal process is for the manager to think about how he or she managed the meeting and consider whether there are things he or she could have done better. This analysis can help the manager plan and conduct future performance appraisals.

Discussing Performance Problems

Discussions about performance problems can occur during informal coaching sessions, in special conversations, or as part of a performance appraisal meeting. The time spent meeting about the issue and the type of meeting depend on how serious the problem is.

A standard operating procedure (SOP) is a set of written instructions that document a routine activity done by employees of the restaurant or foodservice organization. If an employee fails to follow standard operating procedures, a six-step process can be used to address this problem:

Step 1: Compare observed performance with SOPs.

These job standards are the basis for training employees to do specific tasks and are the benchmarks that actual performance is compared to.

Step 2: Identify gaps between observed behavior and the SOPs.

A gap can be relatively minor, such as an error in folding a napkin, or very serious, such as putting a soiled knife in the pot-and-pan sink.

Step 3: Determine the reason for the gap.

Perhaps the employee did not know the SOP (a training problem), forgot (a performance issue), or does not care (a discipline issue).

147

Step 4: Correct the negative behavior.

A simple coaching conversation or retraining may be the first step in a progressive discipline program. The decision about the method to correct the problem will be based on how serious the gap is and on the manager's view of why it occurred.

Step 5: Monitor employee behavior to ensure the problem is corrected.

Managers can do this by observing work as they move throughout the operation, with coaching conversations, or during performance appraisal meetings.

Step 6: If the performance problem is not corrected, follow-up disciplinary action may be needed.

This will be determined by operation policies and by the factors creating the problem.

The basic message in a discussion to correct performance problems should be that the manager and employee will be partners in improvement plans. The manager should ensure that the approach used to correct the problem is one that eliminates misunderstandings and makes clear what is expected of the employee.

PROGRESSIVE DISCIPLINE PROCEDURES

Sometimes managers encounter challenges with some employees that may be caused by things the manager does or fails to do, or by the actions of the employees themselves. A well-planned and implemented progressive discipline strategy is often important in correcting these problems.

What Is Progressive Discipline?

Progressive discipline is a series of corrective actions that assist an employee in improving performance by bringing it up to established standards. Throughout the process, managers must consider retraining, coaching, and determining the potential need for new equipment or tools. Broader issues to be considered include whether the employee has the ability and interest to perform the job or whether a transfer to another position would be helpful. Progressive discipline has several objectives:

- Prevent or minimize misunderstandings between the employee and the manager
- Ensure that the employee is given specific evidence of unacceptable performance, guidelines for improvement, assistance as required, and sufficient time and opportunity to improve

- Reduce the number of situations that result in terminations
- Ensure that documentation is available to support the organization's position if a terminated employee later brings a complaint

Some employers use a formal progressive discipline process for improper behavior. Their process consists of a series of steps that may include coaching, oral warnings or discussions, written warnings or reminders, probation, and final warnings before termination. Other establishments may include other steps such as suspension, often without compensation, and demotion to a position with lesser responsibilities and pay.

Sometimes an employee's behavior or a policy violation makes it necessary to terminate an employee immediately. Defining the actions that may result in immediate termination, and developing the procedures for it, are important. These should be addressed in the establishment's progressive discipline program.

Common Steps in Progressive Discipline

Three steps are commonly included in progressive discipline programs: oral warning, written warning, and probation. Each step has the same basic goals: to improve the employee's performance and to retain him or her. Managers should always recall that the purpose of discipline is to correct improper behavior. It is not to "show who's the boss." Therefore, managers should always remain professional, be sincere, and ensure that the employee knows the goal is to correct behavior, not to criticize the employee as a person.

A final step in the progressive discipline process, termination, is also a major concern. Ideally, it can be avoided as earlier steps are implemented. There are many procedural and legal concerns applicable to termination, which are addressed later in this chapter.

ORAL WARNING

The first step in the progressive discipline process is to discuss the problem informally but directly with the employee. These discussions should not be one-way directions given by the manager. Two-way conversations and agreement between the manager and the employee are important. The outcome should be a program designed to bring the employee's performance up to standard.

For example, a discussion could clarify a misunderstanding between the employee and manager, or it could result in the manager assisting the employee in improving the quality or quantity of work. Examples include an employee with an untidy uniform or a server who does not complete pre-opening tasks within the time allowed.

THINK ABOUT IT . . .

All new and experienced employees must know about the establishment's progressive discipline process. If you were a manager, how would you educate employees about the discipline procedures used at your establishment?

The progressive discipline discussion should cover several concerns:

- Identification of and agreement about the problem and its apparent causes
- The employee's role in solving the problem
- Specific actions to be taken by the employee and the manager
- A timetable for assessing progress
- Notice of the specific disciplinary action that will occur if performance does not improve

The manager should keep a record of all formal or informal discussions with the employee. A useful tool is a form such as that shown in *Exhibit 5.15*.

Exhibit 5.15

PROGRESSIVE DISCIPLINE REPORT

Progressive Discipline Report

Employee _____ Position _____
Store/Location _____
Supervisor _____ Date _____

Copies to: General Manager, Personnel File

The following serves as written documentation to the above employee for the incident(s) described below.

CURRENT INCIDENTS
Describe the situation (behavior, performance, policy violation, etc.) that occurred. Include date(s), time(s), location(s), people involved, witness, effects of the incident on the staff member's work or other staff members, and all other relevant circumstances or contributing factors. Please provide specific examples, whenever possible.

PREVIOUS INCIDENT(S) CORRECTIVE ACTIONS
List type of action (verbal warning, written warning, etc.), offense, and date for any previous incident.

GOALS AND TIMEFRAME FOR IMPROVEMENT
What specific actions—within what timeframe—are to be accomplished to improve behavior or performance? Within five (5) working days, supervisor and staff must jointly submit a personal development plan to address each of the crucial areas. This plan may be submitted under separate cover.

CONSEQUENCES
What will happen if the staff member fails to meet the goals set within the designated timeframe?

PLANNED FOLLOW-UP REVIEW DATE(S)
After each follow-up meeting, the supervisor provides a written summary to the employee and HR.

Progressive Discipline Report

FOLLOW-UP COMMENTS
The supervisor summarizes the employee's progress and determines if he or she is in good standing, or if further disciplinary action is required.

Date _____
Comments _____

STAFF MEMBER'S COMMENTS (Attach additional pages if needed.)
The employee may submit a response within five (5) business days.

_____
_____
_____
_____
_____
_____
_____
_____

Supervisor's signature _____ Date _____
Division/Department head signature _____ Date _____
*Staff member's signature _____ Date _____
Human Resources signature _____ Date _____

*Staff member's signature, with date, indicates the employee met with the supervisor indicated to discuss the incidents cited; it does not necessarily signify that the employee agrees with the Counsel and FeedBack report. In addition, this form does not alter the "at will" employment relationship in any way.

Note that the progressive discipline report in *Exhibit 5.15* records important information:

- Date the conversation took place and the individual(s) involved
- Description of the problem in specific detail (critical incidents)
- Previous incident(s) and corrective actions
- Goals, time frame, and development plan to address the problem agreed to by the employee and manager
- Consequences
- Date for follow-up and progress report completion

When the manager initiates these steps, further action usually is not necessary. However, in some cases additional steps must be taken.

WRITTEN WARNING

If a performance issue continues, the manager must take more formal action. These actions should include the second step in progressive discipline: a written warning provided to the employee in a formal meeting. This meeting should be held privately in the manager's office. The written report serves as documentation and should be the focus of the meeting. At a minimum, the documentation should include several items of key information:

- The date and time of the meeting
- A clear statement of the problem
- A comparison of the employee's behavior against the standard or expected behavior
- A plan of action to improve the performance or solve the problem
- The expected outcome that can be evaluated in a measurable way
- A deadline for achieving these results

The report should be reviewed with the employee, who should be allowed to express his or her thoughts in writing. The report should then be signed and dated by the employee and the manager, and placed in the employee's file. A copy should also be given to the employee, who has a right to see information in the file related to performance or any grievance. Examples of behavior that could result in a written warning are continued use of inappropriate language and excessive instances of reporting to work late.

PROBATION

If the first two steps, oral and written warnings, are not effective, the manager must move to the third step. **Probation** is a specific time period during which an employee must consistently meet job standards or other reasonable conditions imposed by the manager as a condition for continued employment.

Manager's Memo

An oral warning that is part of a progressive discipline program is not the same as ongoing coaching conversations. Coaching is an informal process by which desired performance is reinforced. Managers coach when they acknowledge proper performance and when they make suggestions to improve performance.

It is likely that several or more coaching conversations will have taken place before a formal oral warning is given. Oral warnings are serious because they are the first step in the process by which an employee could be terminated. They are also serious because they suggest that a manager's previous attempts at corrective action have not been successful.

There's a saying, "There are two sides to every story." By the time a manager gives an oral warning, the manager should be fully aware of the employee's perspective, and the employee of the manager's perspective.

Manager's Memo

The development of progressive discipline programs is a very serious process. Taken to its conclusion, the employee may lose his or her job. Also, the operation will incur significant time and expense to recruit, select, and bring a new employee up to required job standards. It is also an important undertaking because lawsuits with time and cost implications are an ever-present concern even after the employee is terminated.

For these reasons, it is important that managers seek the advice of a competent attorney as the progressive discipline policy and procedure is developed. This is also important as the process is implemented with specific employees and perhaps immediately before terminating an employee.

The employee should be informed about disciplinary probation with a written notice. The notice should provide the reason for the probation and the length of the probationary period. It should also include a corrective action plan that must be successfully completed during that time.

The manager should meet with the employee to discuss the details of the probation. At this time, the employee should be asked to sign the probation notice to confirm that he or she has been informed. A copy should be placed in the employee's file, and a copy can be given to the employee. If the employee refuses to sign, the manager should note that the employee was given the opportunity and refused.

During and at the end of the probationary period, the manager should meet with the employee to review performance improvements. If at the end of the probationary period the employee has not met the requirements detailed in the probation notice, he or she will be terminated.

Improvement Timelines

The first three steps in progressive discipline focus on encouraging employees to improve their performance. Thought must also be given to the amount of time that will be allowed for the employee to meet improvement goals. Time frames must be reasonable. They should provide enough time for the employee to improve, but they must also recognize that the operation is affected until the performance goals have been met. Managers must be careful as they consider how long they are going to allow a part of the operation to be substandard.

For example, the problem might involve a server who makes frequent errors when taking orders. This issue would probably need to be corrected more quickly than a problem with slow service. The first server affects both the customers who receive the wrong orders and the establishment, which incurs food and labor costs for an order that cannot be sold. While both problems must be corrected as soon as possible, one problem is more serious.

Consistent Management Actions

All workplace rules and standards must be clearly written and comply with legal standards. For example, there cannot be one set of rules for an older worker and a different set for younger workers. Likewise, unless there is a reason, there cannot be one set of rules for those in front-of-the-house positions and another set for employees in the kitchen. One example of a reasonable difference in rules is the requirement that kitchen employees wear a hair restraint or other approved covering.

In addition, managers must apply the rules consistently. One manager cannot loosely interpret them while another manager enforces them very strictly. Achievable and measurable goals, rules, and standards are easier to consistently enforce than those that are not measurable.

Helping Employees Be Successful

Managers have the responsibility to help their employees improve. They must discover why employees do not meet standards and then assist in finding a solution. They should also be available as the employee tries to implement the solution.

For example, a bartender can barely keep up with customer demand. The manager notices the employee has trouble ringing up sales and making change. The manager discovers that the employee cannot work faster because he or she does not know how to use the POS system.

At the end of the shift, the employee agrees to remain for a while "on the clock" so the manager can provide instruction about using the POS system. This strategy is successful, and the manager notices the bartender's speed increasing over the next several shifts.

EMPLOYEE TERMINATION

Employee terminations affect customers, employees, and the establishment's profitability. A manager's actions, including those discussed in this chapter, can help keep termination rates low.

Operating Impacts of Termination

Employee vacancies caused by termination must be filled. Ideally, employees who leave voluntarily will provide one or more weeks' notice so procedures to fill the position can begin. If so, strategies for routine recruitment and selection will be helpful. However, there will likely be times that a new employee will not be found and almost certainly that a new staff member cannot be trained in a short time period. Even in the best case, operating challenges will occur.

The manager can schedule extra hours for existing employees if a termination occurs on short notice. Perhaps, for example, a part-time employee will work a few extra hours until a permanent replacement for the terminated employee can be found. Some managers are lucky enough to have "on-call" persons who will fill in when additional assistance is needed. Regardless of the strategies used, managers will frequently have to be creative in scheduling required hours until a new staff member is able to work to job standards.

Managers have some ability to determine when they will terminate an employee as part of a progressive discipline process. While there is never a good time, a manager may determine in some cases that it is better to delay termination for a short time rather than to have it occur, for example, immediately before a busy period. Many factors can influence the manager's decision, such as the availability of other employees, the type of work done by the departing employee, and the type of performance problems that were experienced.

Voluntary Termination

Voluntary termination occurs when an employee decides to leave the organization for personal reasons. These may include desiring to change careers, finding a better position in another organization, retiring, starting a family, leaving the area, or returning to school.

Voluntary termination is often both a happy and a sad occasion (*Exhibit 5.16*). Managers may be happy for the person leaving as he or she pursues new opportunities. At the same time, the manager may be losing a valuable member of the team.

Fellow employees are also affected when someone leaves. They may have developed professional and personal friendships with the departing employee, and they may be uncertain how they will get along with his or her replacement. Employees may also have concerns about needing to do more work for a while.

This type of turnover is expected and cannot be avoided. Voluntary termination is generally easier to manage than termination resulting from progressive discipline procedures, although both types have challenges. All operations should have written policies and procedures regarding both types of terminations. These guidelines should support a legal defense in the event a former employee either files for unemployment or sues.

Managers should conduct an **exit interview** with employees who leave voluntarily and also complete a separation checklist. An exit interview is a meeting between an employee who is leaving and a manager or someone from the operation's human resources department. Both of these activities are discussed later in this chapter.

Involuntary Termination

Involuntary termination is a situation in which managers terminate an employee for one or more of these four reasons: lack of work for the employee, lack of funding, unsatisfactory performance, or violation of a company policy. In other words, unlike voluntary termination, which generally occurs to benefit the employee, involuntary termination is done for the well-being of the organization.

The decision to terminate an employee should be made only after thorough consideration of the facts and circumstances leading to the decision. Prior to an employee being terminated, focused efforts should be made via progressive discipline to make that person a productive member of the team, or to find another position for him or her.

Managers know their investment in the employee will be lost on termination. Also, there could be significant costs associated with recruiting, hiring, and training a new employee. Additionally, significant time and legal costs can be incurred in possible cases of wrongful discharge. A **wrongful discharge** claim is a legal action taken by a former employee against a previous employer. It alleges that the discharge was in violation of state or federal antidiscrimination laws, public policy, or an implied contract, agreement, or written promise.

COMMON CAUSES

Involuntary termination can occur as the final step in a progressive discipline program or as the result of a **terminable act**. A terminable act is an action by an employee that typically causes immediate termination. The following behaviors are among those that usually justify discharge without an extensive discipline process:

- Disruptive or destructive behavior
- **Insubordination**, which is the failure to follow reasonable instructions
- Theft of the operation's or customer's property or funds
- Harassment of employees or customers
- Alcohol or illegal drug abuse
- Inappropriate conduct toward coworkers or customers
- Conduct harmful to the company's image either on or off the job

Some organizations have identified other terminable acts. Owners or managers may wish to seek legal advice when identifying terminable acts. All such violations should be explained in writing in the employee handbook. Employees should be required to sign a document showing their agreement. As with any worker dispute, violations of company policy should be documented in writing and kept on file in case of later legal proceedings.

Lack of work or funding are other reasons for involuntary termination. If an employee is facing a layoff because of lack of work or lack of funding to keep that person employed, the manager should attempt to find suitable employment for the person within the organization. This strategy is probably most useful in a chain organization that may have better-performing units relatively close to the property with financial problems. If the organization is large enough, the human resources department may be able to assist the employee in finding an opportunity that matches his or her skills.

Finally, managers of financially successful operations may involuntary terminate underperforming employees and those who violate company policies. The manager, department head, supervisor, or others including a human resources representative should have first implemented activities to identify and address performance deficiencies.

If a skills mismatch has been identified, the employee may be offered a transfer to a new position. If an employee's performance continues to be unsatisfactory after repeated warnings and even probation, termination procedures should be initiated.

Termination Process

The same basic steps should be used to terminate employees for voluntary or involuntary reasons:

Step 1: Identify the cause for terminating the employee.

There should be a legal, policy-based cause for which the employee is being terminated. When the reason is voluntary, the cause relates to personal reasons of importance to the employee. When the reason is involuntary and relates to lack of work and funding, there will be adequate operating and accounting data to support the termination decision. When the reason involves inadequate performance or behavior, the employee's file should include documentation about the activities undertaken as part of the progressive discipline process. Additionally, there should be company handbook or policy information to support the termination. Managers should confirm that the termination cause is legal and in line with company policy, and that all proper procedures including warning, write-up, and probation have been taken.

Step 2: Ensure that proper documentation has been completed as part of the disciplinary process.

Laws and company policies will dictate the type of documentation needed. This information will be found in the company handbook or policy, and other required information such as performance appraisal and disciplinary documentation should be in the employee's file. It is important to confirm that the correct procedures and documentation are being followed. Managers should also confirm that the actions taken are consistent with similar situations in the past.

Step 3: Obtain necessary approvals from management and human resources and seek legal advice, if necessary, for termination.

Company policies should address this point. Managers often seek legal advice to confirm that the cause, applicable disciplinary process, and documentation are sufficient to justify termination.

Step 4: Assemble termination package documents and information.

Payroll and benefit concerns, necessary forms, and other activities should be considered.

Step 5: Conduct the termination meeting.

The meeting should be conducted in private with a third-party observer acting as a witness. The manager should review all necessary information and documentation to be fully prepared for the meeting. Remember that its purpose is neither to place blame nor to allow the employee to request a second chance. Instead, the manager should restate the specific reason for the termination and go over necessary documentation with the employee.

Step 6: Ensure that the employee surrenders company property and receives his or her personal property, if any.

Step 7: Make adjustments to security as needed.

The terminated employee should be escorted outside the establishment. Door locks and computer passwords that were previously accessible to the terminated employee should be changed as necessary. Many operations have policies that provide specific information about this requirement.

Exit Interviews

Exit interviews are used to help managers learn about any employee concerns, reasons for leaving, and suggestions about how the company can improve. Exit interviews should be conducted for several reasons:

- To determine the real reason an employee is leaving and to retain a desirable employee whenever possible
- To discover any grievances the employee may have regarding work conditions so that corrective action can be taken
- To retain the goodwill of the employee and his or her family and friends toward the organization
- To learn about any difficulties the employee may have had with his or her manager

Information from effective exit interviews can be helpful in many ways:

- Reducing turnover
- Developing procedures to improve employees' work experiences
- Identifying any broad employee-related issues that should be addressed
- Assisting the departing employee's manager with developmental needs, if necessary
- Improving the effectiveness of general management practices
- Identifying and addressing any problems within a department or the organization

Exhibit 5.17

Exhibit 5.17

THINK ABOUT IT . . .

Exit interviews may help managers discover correctable problems. However, some persons become defensive if departmental procedures are criticized.

What are some things you as a manager could do to help supervisors look objectively at procedures?

An exit interview can point out unknown problems and opportunities to the management team (*Exhibit 5.17*). Often, current employees may not be comfortable discussing complaints, observations, or concerns with their current manager. If employees are concerned that their input is not wanted, this may contribute to the turnover rate.

In contrast, someone who is leaving the company has little to lose and is more likely to speak frankly with a manager. The employee's comments could offer insight into concerns such as unpopular company procedures, insufficient pay scales, inadequate working conditions, dissatisfaction with other employees, and favoritism.

Keep in mind during the interview that if the departing employee does not like a situation or policy, many other employees may not like it either. While some employee comments may be incorrect or overstated, it is still important to listen carefully to learn about situations that may exist.

Exit interviews can use a free-flowing **unstructured interview** approach, in which the manager conducts a conversation with the employee without prepared questions. Alternatively, they can use a **structured interview** approach, in which the manager asks a set of specific questions.

Three basic types of questions can be used in an exit interview:

- Open-ended questions ask for more than a one-word response and permit a free expression of ideas.

- Close-ended questions are those for which there are only short-answer responses or yes-or-no answers.

- **Multiple-choice questions** ask the departing employee to select the response that best represents his or her thoughts.

Exit interview questions can be oral or written. Many managers use elements of both structured and unstructured interviews in their meeting with employees.

A properly conducted exit interview can be a powerful tool that provides insight into the operation's organizational culture. On the other hand, the departing employee could have been happy at the organization and have few, if any, complaints. This observation will support the continuation of current policies and procedures.

Exhibit 5.18 shows sample exit interview questions. Not all of these questions might be asked of each employee. Instead, the questions used would be based on company policy or the factors causing the employee to leave. The employee might complete the exit interview as a written interview, or the person conducting the interview might ask the questions and record the employee's responses on the interview form.

Exhibit 5.18

SAMPLE EXIT INTERVIEW QUESTIONS

Listed below are samples of the types of exit interview questions that employers commonly ask departing employees.

Open-Ended Questions
- What would you improve to make this company's workplace better?
- What could your immediate supervisor do to improve his or her management style?
- Based on your experience with us, what do you think it takes to succeed at this company?
- How do you generally feel about this company?
- What does your new company offer that this one does not?

Close-Ended Questions
- Did you receive sufficient feedback about your performance between merit reviews?
- Were you satisfied with this company's merit review process?
- Can this company do anything to encourage you to stay?
- Before deciding to leave, did you investigate a transfer within the company?
- Did anyone in this company discriminate against you, harass you, or cause hostile working conditions?

Multiple-Choice Questions
U = Unsatisfactory   F = Fair   S = Satisfactory   G = Good   E = Excellent
- Pay levels at this company were generally _____
- The amount of training I received when I first came here was _____
- The extent to which I had the opportunity to use or develop my potential was_____
- The level of cooperation among the employees in my department was _____
- Generally speaking, I would rate this company as _____ to work for
- The level of concern for employees here was _____
- As compared to other companies, our benefit package was_____

Written Questions
- What did you like most about working here?
- What did you like least about working here?
- What are your suggestions for improving this company as a place to work?
- Any other additional comments?

The manager conducting the exit interview must be a good listener and encourage the employee to share opinions. If the employee feels uncomfortable, he or she will not be completely honest.

The employee might be given some options about who will conduct the interview. For example, the interviewer could be the employee's immediate manager, the department head, or even the general manager. Some employees may provide more information when interviewed by a top-level manager because the employees may believe that their comments will be taken seriously.

The interview should be held in a location in which the employee is most likely to feel comfortable and provide honest responses. It should occur shortly after the employee's resignation notice so that the employee may be more willing to provide valuable responses. The employee should be informed that all information obtained from the exit interview will remain private and secure with the interviewer and other managers. At the completion of the interview, the employee can be asked to provide any additional input that may not have been covered in the questions.

A sample exit interview form is shown in *Exhibit 5.19* on next page. The departing employee could complete it, or the manager conducting the interview could ask the questions and record responses on the interview form. The exit interview form, along with any notes by the manager conducting the interview, may provide information useful in identifying problems contributing to employee turnover.

SEPARATION CHECKLISTS

Completion of a **separation checklist** is an important component of any termination process. A separation checklist is a list of activities to be completed for employees who are leaving the organization. *Exhibit 5.20* on page 162 shows a sample employee separation checklist.

When reviewing *Exhibit 5.20*, it will be helpful to know some additional information for activities 1, 2, 4, 5, 7, and 8:

- **Activity 1. Accrued vacation or sick leave calculated and paid according to policy:** The amount of vacation and sick leave, if any, and any other financial benefits due to the departing employee must be calculated and paid according to the operation's policy.

- **Activity 2. Employee reference release signed:** The employee should be required to complete an employee reference release form if he or she will be using the operation as an employment reference and wants the manager to provide information to a potential employer.

- **Activity 4. COBRA information provided: COBRA** refers to the Consolidated Omnibus Budget Reconciliation Act. It gives workers who lose health insurance benefits the right to continue group health benefits for limited periods under certain situations. These situations include voluntary or involuntary job loss, reduction in hours, transition between jobs, and other life events. Former employees who are qualified may be required to pay the entire health insurance premium up to 102 percent of the cost of the plan.

Exhibit 5.19

SAMPLE EMPLOYEE EXIT INTERVIEW FORM

Employee name: _____   Date: _____

Interviewed by: _____   Employee ID no.: _____

1. What factors influenced you to accept your position with us? (Check all that apply)

   ☐ Compensation   ☐ Fringe benefits   ☐ Location   ☐ Reputation of the organization

   ☐ Career change   ☐ Job responsibilities ☐ Schedule   ☐ Other:_____

2. Why are you leaving? (Check all that apply)

   ☐ Compensation   ☐ Fringe benefits   ☐ Location   ☐ Reputation of the organization

   ☐ Career change   ☐ Job responsibilities ☐ Schedule   ☐ Other:_____

3. What is your level of satisfaction about your
   experience with the organization?

   <u>Very Unsatisfied</u>   <u>Very Satisfied</u>

   ① ② ③ ④ ⑤

4. What did you find least satisfying about your experience with the organization?

   _____

   _____

   _____

   _____

   _____

5. Do you think you were treated fairly on your performance reviews?   ☐ Yes   ☐ No

6. Were you told about opportunities for advancement?   ☐ Yes   ☐ No

7. Would you recommend us as an employer to your friends and family?   ☐ Yes   ☐ No

8. Please give us any other feedback you would like to provide to help us improve as an employer.

   _____

   _____

Thank you for answering these questions.

Exhibit 5.20

SAMPLE EMPLOYEE SEPARATION CHECKLIST

Employee name: _____   Employee ID no.: _____

Last date of employment: _____

Separation Activities	Completed	Manager's Initials	Comments
1. Accrued vacation or sick leave calculated and paid according to policy.	☐ Yes ☐ No		
2. Employee reference release signed.	☐ Yes ☐ No		
3. Exit interview completed.	☐ Yes ☐ No		
4. COBRA information provided.	☐ Yes ☐ No		
5. Company property returned (if applicable). ☐ Keys ☐ Uniforms ☐ Tools ☐ Company identification ☐ Other: _____ ☐ _____ ☐ _____	☐ Yes ☐ No		
6. Repayment of any advances collected.	☐ Yes ☐ No		
7. Verification of emergency contact information or address: _____ _____ _____ _____	☐ Yes ☐ No		
8. Final paycheck received.	☐ Yes ☐ No		

This is to certify that all of the above separation activities have been completed.

_____   _____
Employee's Signature   Date

_____   _____
Manager's Signature   Date

Important: This completed employee separation checklist should be placed in the employee's human resources file.

- **Activity 5. Company property returned:** Departing employees must return company property. This includes such things as keys, tools, uniforms, and corporate identification. The manager should have a procedure in place to document property in employees' possession, and this information should be included in employees' human resources files. On termination, all company property should be returned.

- **Activity 7. Verification of emergency contact information or address:** Employers will be required to send former employees copies of their **W-2 income tax forms**. A W-2 form is an information form completed by employers and sent to the federal taxing authorities. It is used to report wages and salaries paid to employees and taxes withheld. The employer must send copies of the federal W-2 form and applicable state and local tax forms to employees. Emergency contact information provided by a departing employee may provide a more permanent address that can be used to contact former employees.

- **Activity 8. Final paycheck received:** Some companies have a policy of not issuing the employee's final paycheck until all company materials have been returned. It is important to confirm that this action is within the guidelines of applicable state laws before implementing such a policy.

Note that the employee separation checklist should be signed by the departing employee and his or her manager after verifying that all necessary separation activities have been completed. The completed checklist should be placed in the employee's file for future reference.

SUMMARY

1. **Explain basic communication skills and challenges for restaurant and foodservice managers.**

   Managers represent the operation, themselves, and their employees. They must use effective speaking and listening skills during personal interactions, with groups, and on the telephone, and they should recognize that what they say may not be what is understood.

   Managers should write by using an introduction, organized discussion, and conclusion and avoiding writing pitfalls. Many barriers can interfere with communication including misunderstandings about the meaning of words, jargon, gestures, cultural differences, and assumptions. Other communication problems include attitude issues, a distracting workplace, timing, clarity of the message, and tone of voice.

   Each establishment has an informal "grapevine." The manager should know how to counter rumors. Examples include questioning whether the rumor is true and whether the person spreading the rumor has access to the information on which the rumor is based. Another tactic is to not repeat the information.

Nonverbal communication refers to expressions and movements, which provide additional information. Examples include pacing, slouching, and pointing. Managers should try to eliminate nonverbal communication practices that are negative.

2. **State procedures for coaching employees.**

Coaching involves informal efforts to improve performance and should be ongoing to reinforce proper behavior and correct negative performance. Effective practices include being tactful, focusing on behavior, emphasizing the positive, demonstrating procedures, and explaining reasons for changes. Managers should maintain communication with employees, conduct negative coaching in private, evaluate work against standards, reinforce all correct performance, and ask employees how work can be improved.

3. **Describe procedures for resolving employee conflicts.**

Conflict resolution encourages finding solutions before more serious procedures are needed. Conflict typically occurs because of disagreement about work or personality clashes, and resolution strategies include negotiation, mediation, and arbitration. Steps to resolve conflict include identifying concerns, determining facts, developing and communicating the resolution, documenting the agreement, and following up.

4. **Explain procedures for managing change.**

Change may affect few employees or all. A common model for change incorporates three strategies: unfreezing the situation, transitioning to change, and refreezing the situation. Many employees resist change because they do not want to learn new ways of doing things or are fearful of closer supervision during changes. Strategies to reduce resistance include using a participative management style, informing employees about changes that affect them, setting an appropriate time for the change, and sharing past successes. Employees may be rewarded for sharing beneficial ideas.

Managers must be change agents and recognize that each change improves the operation. The best managers believe in the continuous quality improvement (CQI) process. Implementing change begins with discussing the need and requesting employees' assistance. Final steps are implementing plans and following up with recognition and evaluation.

5. **State basic procedures for conducting performance appraisals.**

Managers use performance appraisals to discuss performance, establish goals, review issues, talk about development, and document performance. Basic procedures involve preparing by gathering information and allowing the employee to complete a self-evaluation form. During the meeting, the employee should be asked to review performance and then discuss possible areas of improvement and development plans. At the close, the manager should provide a summary, ask for comments, and determine whether any follow-up meetings are needed.

In discussing problems, observed performance should be compared with standard operating procedures and the gap identified. Reasons should be determined, conversations or retraining should be used, and behavior should be monitored to ensure the problem is resolved. If not, follow-up disciplinary action may be needed.

6. **Explain steps in a progressive discipline program.**

Progressive discipline assists in bringing performance up to standards. Its objectives are to minimize misunderstandings, ensure the employee is given evidence and opportunity to improve, reduce terminations, and ensure documentation. Common steps include oral warning, written warning, probation, and termination.

Timelines should be reasonable but recognize that the operation is affected until performance goals are met. Workplace rules and standards must be clearly written and comply with legal standards, and all goals should be achievable and measurable. Managers have the responsibility to help employees improve, and this can be done through training followed by coaching.

7. **Describe procedures for employee termination.**

Establishments benefit when employees who leave voluntarily provide reasonable notice. Managers can determine when employees who will be involuntarily terminated are removed. Employees are involuntarily terminated for one or more of four reasons: lack of work, lack of funding, unsatisfactory performance, or violation of company policy. First, managers must use progressive discipline to help employees become productive or find another position, taking steps to prevent wrongful discharge. Involuntary termination can occur as the final step in progressive discipline. It can also occur as a result of a terminable act that causes immediate termination. The cause of termination must be identified and the manager must ensure proper documentation. Necessary approvals and legal advice should be obtained, termination package documents must be assembled, and a meeting with the employee should be held. The employee must surrender all company property, and security changes should be made as needed.

Exit interviews help managers learn about concerns, reasons for leaving, and suggestions. These interviews can use an unstructured approach or a structured approach in which the manager asks specific questions. Separation checklists provide a list of activities that must be completed for departing employees. The completed checklist should be placed in the employee's file.

APPLICATION EXERCISE

Divide into teams of three. One person will be a manager, the second will be an employee, and the third will be an observer. The manager should conduct a coaching session with the employee about several of the following situations, depending on time limits and instructor assignments. The observer should comment on the coaching sessions when they are completed. If time permits, rotate assignments to enable each person to be manager, employee, and observer.

Situation 1: The manager observes the employee performing a very complicated task correctly after a training session yesterday.

Situation 2: The manager notices the employee cleaning a meat slicer without unplugging the unit in violation of establishment policy.

Situation 3: The manager notices the employee, a server, wearing sandals in violation of establishment policy.

Situation 4: The manager notices the employee arriving at work about 10 minutes late for the third time this week.

Situation 5: The manager notices the employee helping a teammate with a task that is not the employee's responsibility.

Situation 6: The employee, a bartender, is spending a lot of time on a relatively slow night with a bar customer who appears to be a very good friend.

Situation 7: The employee has incorrectly completed an issue requisition form for the third time in two weeks.

Situation 8: The manager just heard a rumor that appears to have come from the employee suggesting that another employee is dishonest.

REVIEW YOUR LEARNING

Select the best answer for each question.

1. **What can an effective listener do to be involved in the communication process?**
   A. Begin thinking about the response before the speaker finishes
   B. Interrupt to tell the speaker the message is understood
   C. Shuffle through notes to help develop a response
   D. Maintain eye contact with the speaker

2. **A sound that interferes with communication is called**
   A. listening hurdle.
   B. conversation noise.
   C. environmental noise.
   D. conversation barrier.

3. **Which item relates to a company's informal channel of communication?**
   A. Intranet
   B. Grapevine
   C. Policy
   D. Procedure

4. **What nonverbal communication may be a sign of nervousness?**
   A. Sitting on edge of chair
   B. Raising eyebrows
   C. Slouching in chair
   D. Biting one's lips

5. **Managers do coaching when they**
   A. manage by walking around.
   B. conduct negotiation sessions.
   C. give employees an oral warning.
   D. conduct performance appraisals.

6. **What is the process in which a neutral third party facilitates a discussion and makes suggestions about an agreement?**
   A. Negotiation
   B. Arbitration
   C. Mediation
   D. Probation

7. **The first part of the change process is**
   A. revising procedures.
   B. transitioning to change.
   C. refreezing the situation.
   D. unfreezing the situation.

8. **When should an employee complete a self-evaluation performance appraisal form?**
   A. Before the session
   B. During the session
   C. In a follow-up meeting
   D. At the end of the session

9. The first step in any termination process is to
   A. conduct an exit interview.
   B. complete a separation checklist.
   C. identify the cause for termination.
   D. ensure documentation is complete.

10. What is a legal action against a previous employer alleging that termination violated antidiscrimination laws?
    A. Insubordination
    B. Wrongful discharge
    C. Exit interview response
    D. Unemployment compensation claim

FIELD PROJECT

A. Managers facilitate their employees' work performance by managing change and conducting performance reviews. Continue obtaining information for your team's field project by identifying several questions for your restaurant or foodservice manager's interviews. Examples of questions can include the following:

- How do you overcome employee resistance to change?
- What role do entry-level employees play in the change process?
- What is the biggest challenge in managing change?

Identify questions that you will ask managers about their performance review procedures. Examples of questions include these:

- How often are formal performance reviews given to entry-level employees?
- What are common errors that some restaurant or foodservice managers make when they evaluate the performance of their employees?
- What role, if any, do job descriptions play in your performance reviews?

Note: *Save the questions you have developed. Later in this course, your team will conduct interviews with the managers of* *restaurant or foodservice operations selected by the team. These interviews will include the questions you have developed in this chapter, as well as questions from other chapters. You may want to use the interview form (template) in the Field Project Information Handbook at the end of this book, or develop an interview form of your own to list your interview questions. This form can then be used to record the managers' responses when you conduct your interview.*

B. Learn additional information about managing change and conducting performance reviews by conducting an Internet search using your favorite search engine. These are examples of search terms for managing change:

- Managing change in organizations
- Overcoming employee resistance to change

Make a list of suggestions for managing performance reviews by entering search terms such as these:

- Entry-level employee performance reviews
- Preparing for performance reviews
- Performance review procedures

These suggestions can be recorded in Part II (Internet Resources) for Chapter 5 in the Field Project Information Handbook at the end of this book.

6

Meeting Workshift Standards

CHAPTER LEARNING OBJECTIVES

After completing this chapter, you should be able to:

- Explain why operating standards are important and how managers can enforce them.

- Identify, implement, and review sales and service goals for the front of the house.

- Identify, implement, and review production and quality goals for the back of the house.

- Describe a nine-step process for scheduling employees.

- Explain how checklists can be used to monitor quality.

- Explain how communication logs help monitor quality.

KEY TERMS

communication log, p. 201

crew schedule, p. 174

Family and Medical Leave Act (FMLA), p. 188

floater, p. 185

fringe benefit, p. 176

labor cost, p. 174

pro forma budget, p. 177

salary, p. 176

scheduling, p. 174

standard, p. 170

standard operating procedure (SOP), p. 170

wage, p. 174

CASE STUDY

"I guess it's just common sense that we need more employees when we're going to be busy and fewer employees when business will be slow. The trick is to figure out what business will be like," said Casey, co-owner of Blue Star Vegetarian Delite Restaurant.

"Yes, that is the challenge," replied Destiny, the other co-owner.

"We started our business as a good fit with the many people in our community who like vegetarian meals," Destiny continued, "and it seems to be working out. We have lots of customers sometimes, and now we have a few months of operating information to help us determine when we need more employees. We also know when we should schedule fewer employees so we don't lose money on labor costs."

1. How do customer estimates help managers plan labor schedules?

2. How might these co-owners evaluate the effectiveness of their scheduling plans?

IMPORTANCE OF OPERATING STANDARDS

Restaurant and foodservice operations require guidelines to best ensure that customers are consistently pleased and that financial and other goals are attained. Employees can do their jobs properly only if they know what to do. They must also be trained and provided with the equipment, tools, and other resources needed to do the work correctly. The smooth operation of each shift depends on the coordination of many people doing many specific jobs and meeting quality expectations.

To guarantee this coordination, managers must develop standards. They must also develop the routine procedures required to attain the standards consistently.

What Are Standards?

Standards indicate the level of quality, speed, food safety, or hospitality that employees should demonstrate. When standards are followed, customers receive a consistently good experience. Standards also indicate how staff members should do work tasks including how well, how often, and how quickly. For example, standards specify equipment settings, measurements, frequencies, and other factors that define the desired quality of products and services. When these are in place, the establishment will have a standard way of setting a table, standard procedures for preparing foods and beverages, and a standard way to mix sanitizing solutions for cleaning. Standards should be in place for all areas of an operation. They may be written, which is usually preferred, or discussed during training sessions.

An example of a standard that indicates a goal for how tables should be set up for lunch is shown in *Exhibit 6.1*. When a table is set up correctly, it will have all of the serviceware in the positions specified in the diagram, which can be given to trainees. The dining-room manager can determine whether tables are set correctly by comparing them to this diagram.

After standards are established, an operation can develop standard operating procedures (SOPs). These tools explain how tasks should be done so the standards will be met.

Standard Operating Procedures Implement Quality Requirements

SOPs explain what employees must know and do when they perform the work specified in their job descriptions. Although SOPs can be used to handle unusual situations such as emergencies, they are most often thought of as the routine procedures that employees do every day. For example, cooks often have certain ways to clean walk-in coolers, and servers must do specified

Exhibit 6.1

EXAMPLE OF TABLE SETUP STANDARD FOR LUNCH

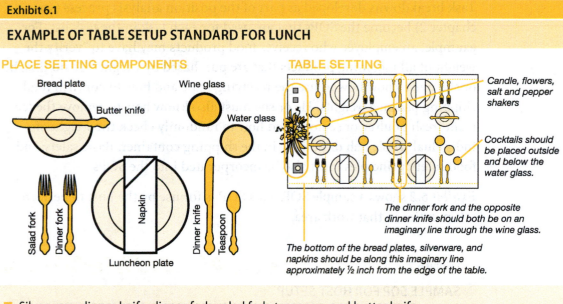

PLACE SETTING COMPONENTS

Bread plate
Butter knife
Wine glass
Water glass
Salad fork
Dinner fork
Napkin
Luncheon plate
Dinner knife
Teaspoon

TABLE SETTING

Candle, flowers, salt and pepper shakers

Cocktails should be placed outside and below the water glass.

The dinner fork and the opposite dinner knife should both be on an imaginary line through the wine glass.

The bottom of the bread plates, silverware, and napkins should be along this imaginary line approximately ½ inch from the edge of the table.

- Silverware: dinner knife, dinner fork, salad fork, teaspoon, and butter knife.
- The coffee cup should be placed in the same position as the wine glass, if coffee is ordered with the meal. Remove the wine glass.
- Candle, flowers, and salt and pepper shakers should always be on the other side of the table from the entrance of the room.
- Align the tables according to the dining-room table placement diagram, and align the wine and water glasses on the tables according to the required place setting diagram.

Adapted with permission from David R. Wightman, ECE

things to get ready for service. When employees know what they and their coworkers are supposed to do, there are fewer surprises, and work can be done more effectively.

SOPs must be reviewed and updated as necessary. Customer complaints, unexpected costs, quality problems, and employee feedback can all help identify concerns. Priorities should be established, and a process to revise procedures should be implemented. Drafts of procedures should be reviewed, and ideas from employees who do the tasks should be received and evaluated before final approval by the general manager. The revised SOPs are then put into use and become important tools to ensure quality in daily operations.

Sometimes SOPs are developed to improve a specific step in a task. For example, an operation used to have a bartender open a bottle of wine before a server took it to a customer at a table. In an effort to project a more upscale image, that step is changed so that the server opens the bottle tableside.

A second approach is to determine how an entire task should be done and then develop the SOPs that make up the task. For example, an SOP could be developed to indicate how a table-mounted can opener will be cleaned and sanitized.

Task breakdowns developed as part of the position analysis process (see chapter 2) become the SOPs that are used for each task in the task list. For example, an employee who receives food products may have to "verify the weight of all incoming products that are purchased by weight." To do this, he or she must know how to use the receiving scale and how to confirm total shipping package weights. He or she must also know how to remove the ice from fresh poultry or seafood and how to randomly check the weight of individual whole fish or poultry in the shipping container. Basic safety and food safety principles must also be incorporated into the SOPs.

Exhibit 6.2 shows a sample SOP. This SOP is for use by the host to perform setup duties in that work area.

Exhibit 6.2

SAMPLE SOP FOR HOST SETUP

Setup Duties

- Check the waitstaff schedule to see who is working.
- Check supplies: pencils (sharpened), pens, grease pencils, and message pads.
- Retrieve the reservation book from the bartender and transfer the phone to the host station.
- Turn on music and set to correct level; appropriate music is classical or jazz with no vocals.
- Ensure the lights are at the correct level and dimmed at 5:30 p.m.
- Ensure the light in the buser's station is dimmed.
- Check for cleanliness of host station, foyer, and establishment; pay special attention to the floor.
- Ensure all empty coat hangers are to one side.
- Check glass in entrance door and doors to kitchen; clean as needed.
- Ensure the reception stand looks neat and orderly.
- Inform the servers about any special table setups.
- Check the reservation book five days ahead to see whether there are any special situations that need to be communicated to the kitchen or a manager.

Standards are also of critical importance in the back of the house and at the bar. Food and beverage production standards are expressed in standardized recipes. In effect then, the recipes are standard operating procedures. When they are consistently used, and this should be a requirement in all operations, the necessary product quality levels will be consistently attained.

Food and beverage production employees learn about the importance of and procedures to follow standardized recipes beginning with their initial training experiences. Compliance with the recipes is also emphasized during ongoing coaching and performance appraisal activities. Pre-shift line-up meetings can be used to address any recipe challenges and to help ensure that no "shortcuts" will be taken as the standard operating procedures (recipes) are implemented.

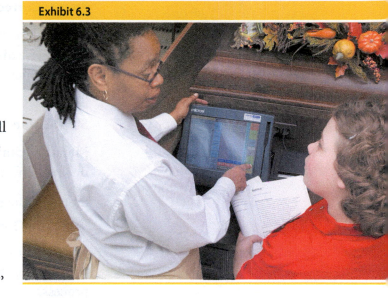

Exhibit 6.3

Enforcing Standard Operating Procedures

Since SOPs are so critical to helping the establishment attain standards consistently, in most cases they must be followed without exception. Typically, this is not a problem, especially when the SOPs describe a reasonable procedure. Likewise, compliance is generally easier when employees have provided input into the development of the SOP. However, when a manager notices that SOPs are not being followed, some type of corrective action is needed.

Discussions about performance problems can occur during informal coaching sessions, in special conversations, or as part of a performance appraisal meeting. Standard operating procedures are useful training tools because they tell how a task should be done (see *Exhibit 6.3*). The time spent meeting and the type of communication depend on how serious the problem is.

If an employee consistently fails to follow SOPs, a six-step process can be used. These steps can be integrated into the progressive discipline process discussed in chapter 5:

> **Step 1: Compare observed performance with the applicable SOP that was the basis for training.**
>
> The SOP is the benchmark against which actual performance is compared.
>
> **Step 2: Identify gaps between observed behavior and the SOP.**
>
> A gap can be relatively minor, such as an error in folding a napkin, or very serious, such as improperly cleaning an electric slicer.
>
> **Step 3: Determine the reason for the gap.**
>
> Perhaps the employee did not know (a training problem), forgot, or does not care (a discipline issue).

Step 4: Correct the negative behavior.

A simple coaching conversation or retraining may be the first step in progressive discipline. The method for correcting the problem will be based on how serious the gap is and on the manager's view of why it occurred.

Step 5: Monitor employee behavior to ensure the problem is corrected.

Managers can do this by observing work, in coaching conversations, or during performance appraisal meetings.

Step 6: If the performance problem is not corrected, follow-up disciplinary action may be needed.

This will be determined by the operation's policies, the factors creating the problem, and procedures identified in the progressive discipline process.

The basic message in correcting performance should be that the manager and employee will be partners in improvement plans. The manager should ensure that the approach used to correct the problem eliminates misunderstandings and makes clear what is expected. That expectation is the consistent use of SOPs for all tasks that have them.

SCHEDULING EMPLOYEES

Managers must schedule the correct number of employees in the right positions at the right times to produce products and services meeting expected quality and quantity standards. They must do this while staying within labor cost goals. **Labor cost** refers to the money and benefit expenses paid to employees for their work.

Managers must use an effective **scheduling** process that determines which employees will be needed to serve the expected number of customers during specific times. The **crew schedule** that results is a chart that informs employees who receive wages about the days and hours they are expected to work during a specific time period, usually a week. **Wages** are the money earned by employees who are paid based on the number of hours they work.

The crew schedule is not just a list of employees' names and times. Instead, it is a well-thought-out plan that considers the expected volume of business, the employees required, and the labor costs incurred. The crew schedule also recognizes that employees have personal lives. It tries to balance the needs of the operation and its customers with the needs of employees. Unfortunately, the best-planned crew schedules may need to be changed because of unexpected business volume or employee-related problems. Backup plans consider these types of events to minimize problems that impact customers.

Several steps should be followed to plan, manage, and evaluate employee work schedules:

Step 1: Determine budgeted labor cost.

Step 2: Create a master schedule.

Step 3: Develop sales, service, production, and quality goals.

Step 4: Assign individual responsibilities.

Step 5: Develop a crew schedule.

Step 6: Distribute and adjust the crew schedule.

Step 7: Monitor employees during shifts.

Step 8: Analyze after-shift labor information.

Step 9: Monitor weekly labor costs and adjust as necessary.

Numerous concerns become important as managers implement these scheduling and control steps. The following sections discuss each step in detail.

Determine Budgeted Labor Cost

The first step in developing an effective employee schedule is to determine how much money can be spent for labor during each work shift. This amount is found in the approved budget. Managers should not spend more for labor than budgeted, and strategies to meet this goal begin when the employee schedule is planned.

Consider Ophelia, the owner and manager of Factory Road Café. Her establishment is located on the edge of the largest industrial park in her community. It is open from 6:00 a.m. to 2:00 p.m. during the work week, which is Monday through Friday. The operation serves about 175 customers per day, and it also does a carryout business of approximately 75 customers each day.

Ophelia has developed an operating budget for the current year. It was developed by estimating revenue and expenses for each month separately and then combining the monthly budgets to obtain the yearly budget.

Ophelia develops her budget in late fall for the next year. While this makes it fairly current for the early months, the budget for the later part of the year can be outdated when the actual month arrives. For example, if the budget for November was planned last November, the information will be about 12 months old. Therefore, Ophelia updates each monthly budget as necessary using past, current, and even future estimates of the number of customers to be served based on factors discussed later in this chapter.

Ophelia's approved budget allows her to spend $13,250 for waged employees in March 2012. This budgeted labor cost will be adjusted, if necessary, based on more current financial information and then will be used to drive the development of the employee schedule.

Ophelia's budget estimates fringe benefits separately from wages. **Fringe benefits** are monies paid indirectly in support of employees for purposes such as vacation, holiday pay, sick leave, and health insurance. This means that Ophelia's schedule does not need to consider the cost of benefits.

The employee schedule will also not include the money or benefits paid to managers who receive a salary. A **salary** is a fixed amount of money for a certain time period that does not vary based on the number of hours worked. Salaried employees are not included because adjusting labor hours does not affect the money that they are paid.

Ophelia plans her waged employee schedule on a weekly basis for the number of workdays in that week. This number is usually five unless there is a holiday when most businesses in the industrial park close. The amount that she can spend on employee wages on an average day in March 2012 is easy to calculate:

$$\begin{array}{ccccc} \$13,250 & \div & 22 & = & \$602 \\ \textbf{March labor} & & \textbf{Workdays} & & \textbf{Average} \\ \textbf{(wage) budget} & & \textbf{in March} & & \textbf{daily wage} \end{array}$$

If the *average* hourly wage rate, not including benefits, is approximately $13, Ophelia can schedule about 46 hours for waged employees on an average workday in March:

$$\begin{array}{ccccc} \$602 & \div & \$13 & = & \textbf{46 hours (rounded)} \\ \textbf{Average} & & \textbf{Average hourly} & & \textbf{Average hours} \\ \textbf{daily wage} & & \textbf{wage rate} & & \textbf{per day} \end{array}$$

Her labor budget also allows Ophelia to use no more than 230 waged hours in an average week:

$$\begin{array}{ccccc} 46 & \times & 5 & = & 230 \\ \textbf{Average hours} & & \textbf{Days open} & & \textbf{Average hours} \\ \textbf{per day} & & \textbf{per week} & & \textbf{per week} \end{array}$$

These calculations will help Ophelia develop her schedule for waged employees because she knows she can spend an average of $602 for waged employees each day. She also knows the average number of hours she can schedule each day (46) and each week (230).

Ophelia knows that "average" means more labor hours can be scheduled when more customers are expected and fewer labor hours when customer counts should be lower. It also means that some employees such as cooks can be paid more than $13 per hour, and others such as servers will be paid less. Also,

THINK ABOUT IT . . .

Ophelia, like many restaurant and foodservice owners, receives a salary for her work.

What are some reasons a business owner might receive a salary instead of just profits from the business?

recall that Ophelia is developing a schedule for employees who receive wages. Employees who receive a salary (including her) are carried in a separate labor expense account, as are all employee benefits expenses.

Create a Master Schedule

When an operation is initially planned, it is difficult to identify staffing needs unless the property is part of a multiunit organization that can use operating information from other properties with the same menu. Small business owners like Ophelia have to think about the operation's concept. For example, Factory Road Café serves traditional breakfasts and lunches at reasonable prices with table service (*Exhibit 6.4*), and carryout service to employees working nearby.

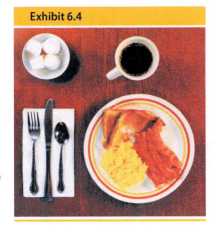

Exhibit 6.4

With previous experience, Ophelia might have some ideas about the number of meals that can be produced and served within a selected time frame such as one hour, or in one six-hour shift. If she does not, she will need to rely on "rules of thumb" she might find in Internet searches or written information about restaurant and foodservice start-ups. She might also obtain some general information from friends in the business or she might hire a consultant to provide start-up information including labor estimates. She will need estimates of labor hours because they relate to labor cost, which will be a significant part of the pro forma budget. A **pro forma budget** is an estimate of revenues, expenses, and profit developed before a business opens. It is used to help justify beginning the business and to obtain funding from a lending organization. This might be a bank or credit union, or even friends and family.

Since Ophelia has defined her business concept, she knows she will need cooks, service employees, and dish washers. She might need a counter attendant to serve as cashier, take carryout orders, and help customers when they arrive. As an on-site business owner, Ophelia intends to be available to assist with physical work tasks during busy times. She will do her management-related activities at other times.

As Ophelia further develops her financial plans, she will need to estimate the number of labor hours required to generate the forecasted revenue. These hours can then be translated into labor costs. Some planners are conservative, underestimating revenue and overestimating expenses including labor. This provides a margin of error, or cushion, as profitability is estimated.

After Ophelia's establishment is open for several months, she will likely have a much better idea about revenues, staffing needs, labor hours, and labor cost based on actual operating information. This will allow her to create a more accurate and meaningful master schedule that can be used for routine scheduling of labor.

Recall that Ophelia knows she can schedule an average of 46 hours of waged labor per day and 230 hours of waged labor each week. Based on her experience, she can develop a master schedule that provides guidelines about the expected number of customers. Then, she can allocate the number of hours allowed by the budget between the different positions in the operation. The master schedule shows the number of employees that will be needed in each position and the total number of hours that employees in these positions will be scheduled to work.

A master schedule has two purposes:

- It helps ensure the correct number of waged employees in each position will be available so customers will receive prompt, efficient service and properly prepared food.

- It helps in planning waged labor expenses to meet budget goals.

Exhibit 6.5 shows a master schedule that Ophelia developed for an average day at Factory Road Café. It provides a starting point, and she will make changes based on forecasted sales for each day.

Note that the master schedule shown in *Exhibit 6.5* is for an average shift. It is planned for the average number of customers (175 dine-in and 75 carryout), and it allows for 45 waged labor hours (one hour less than the average). The master schedule Ophelia will develop for each shift may differ from this master schedule because the number of customers served each day may differ. She will need more employees on busy days, and the total waged hours will increase. On slower days the total waged hours will decrease. When reviewing *Exhibit 6.5*, notice these points:

- The master schedule indicates the waged hours needed for persons in specific positions. It does not indicate the names of the employees.

- The master schedule indicates each hour that waged employees in the position must work. It also provides the average hourly rate and the total labor cost. For example, Server A will work 4.5 hours and is paid $8 per hour, for a total of $36 for the day.

- The master schedule indicates that 45 waged hours will be scheduled for this shift, and the estimated total wage cost will be $598.

The master schedule must be created carefully because the actual crew schedules are developed from it. When Ophelia correctly modifies the waged labor hours specified on the master schedule based on changes in business volume, she should have the right number of employees available at the right times to handle the estimated number of customers. She will also meet her goal of not exceeding the budgeted labor cost for waged employees.

Exhibit 6.5

MASTER SCHEDULE FOR FACTORY ROAD CAFÉ

Date: _____3/12/12_____   Total no. of expected customers: _____175 dine-in; 75 carryout_____

Time	5:00–6:00 a.m.	6:00–7:00 a.m.	7:00–8:00 a.m.	8:00–9:00 a.m.	9:00–10:00 a.m.	10:00–11:00 a.m.	11:00 a.m.–12:00 p.m.	12:00–1:00 p.m.	1:00–2:00 p.m.	2:00–3:00 p.m.	Total Wage Hours	Average Hourly Rate	Total Wage Costs
Position													
Server A	x*	x	x	x	x						4.5	$ 8	$ 36
Server B				x	x	x	x	x			5	8	40
Server C						x	x	x			3	8	24
Server D								x	x	x	3	8	24
Counter Attendant				x	x	x	x	x	x		6	15	90
Dish Washer				x	x	x	x	x	x	x**	6.5	12	78
Cook A	x	x	x	x	x	x					6	18	108
Cook B				x	x	x	x	x	x	x	7	18	126
Cook C							x	x	x	x	4	18	72
											45		**$598**

*5:30–6:00 a.m. **2:00–2:30 p.m.

Note: *The number of persons in each position, the number of hours to be worked, and the average hourly rates are examples only and should not be considered standards or guidelines.*

Much information is needed to develop a master schedule. For example, sales history information will be important. It tells the number of customers who have visited the establishment on different days in previous weeks. This information can be used to estimate customer counts for future dates, which will have to be considered when crew schedules are developed.

Develop Sales, Service, Production, and Quality Goals

Analyzing sales history information is important because what has occurred in the past is likely to occur in the future. Most operations have a pattern of business volume that, with some changes, repeats itself. Knowledge of historical patterns helps Ophelia develop sales forecasts to revise the master schedule for the expected level of sales. Modern point-of-sale (POS) systems make it easy to track customer counts.

POS systems collect information about revenue, number of customers served, menu items sold, and a wide range of other information. The system then generates numerous reports that help with management decision making. Accurate historical sales information is important. Inaccurate information can allow too many employees to be scheduled, which increases labor costs beyond budget goals and reduces profit. Inaccurate information can also result in too few employees being scheduled. Then production and service will be slow, and unhappy customers will not return and will tell others about their bad dining experience.

SALES FORECASTS

Accurate sales forecasts are critical to developing a good master schedule. Past sales records provide a baseline, which is then increased or decreased based on current trends. As the projected number of customers increases, the number of employee hours required will increase. As estimated customer counts decrease, required employee hours will decrease.

A master schedule is created with the idea that a certain number of customers will be served. As estimated customer counts change from that norm, either up or down, the master schedule should be adjusted.

For example, if a new office building will open across the street this year, sales would be projected to increase over the same time period last year. If a manufacturing plant in the industrial park is expected to close, Ophelia would probably lower her projections because she will lose those customers.

Experienced managers know that many factors impact the number of customers who will visit their property on a given day or for a specific meal period. The master schedule should reflect the expected customer count as closely as possible so the crew schedule can reflect the number of labor hours needed. Here are some factors that influence customer counts:

- **Holidays:** In many establishments, some holidays increase customer counts and others result in closing because there will likely be almost no business. Mother's Day is the highest-volume day of the year for many operations, while many properties close on Christmas Day. Since Factory Road Café serves business employees, it closes when the majority of businesses are not open, including all weekends.

- **Seasonal adjustments:** The weather often plays a critical role in customer counts. Extreme heat or cold will normally cause sales to drop. Hurricanes, tornadoes, and snowstorms all affect sales. In severe cases, the establishment may have to close. Other seasonal adjustments include the holiday shopping season, which typically increases sales, and income tax time, when sales in some operations slow. Lunch sales at Factory Road Café are affected by extremely cold weather, when more people tend to pack meals from home so they can stay indoors at midday.

- **Advertising and promotions:** These factors are known in advance, so their impact can be considered when the master schedule is planned. These events should cause sales to increase, and managers should plan for more employees. On the other hand, if competitors have a well-planned promotion, customer counts could be reduced, and this should be reflected in the master schedule. Ophelia offers daily specials, including Friday payday meals, and these strategies increase sales in the short term.

- **Community activities:** Fairs, festivals, and athletic events may get people out into the community. Depending on the location of the event, these activities can increase sales. The best managers know what is happening in their communities and how it will impact their business. Ophelia's business is typically not affected by these types of activities.

- **Economy:** Operations are affected differently by the economy. In tough economic times, business may slow in fine-dining operations and pick up in more casual service properties. When the economy is growing, many establishments enjoy increased business. The economy is an important concern when the master schedule is planned at Factory Road Café, because businesses in the industrial park hire and lay off employees depending on the economy.

TRENDS

Managers should study more than just past sales information when forecasting future revenue. They also need to consider current trends. Local trends are more important than national ones. However, the economy, unemployment rates, and other national and even international events may all affect customers' desire or ability to eat out. In the following example, Ophelia uses her knowledge of changes in her customer base to develop revenue projections for next year's budget. Information about budgeted revenues and labor costs will be used, in part, to develop the master schedule.

Ophelia considers the following factors as she develops her plans:

- A new business in the industrial park has just opened and employs about 75 persons. She is allowed to provide "Welcome to the Park" discount coupons, and she notices that six or eight customers present them each day for about two weeks. She begins to recognize some of these people and thinks her customer count will increase by about five carryout lunches per day.

- A fire at a small business in the park will close it for about one month. It provided about 10 customers for her operation daily.

- The city will begin some road construction in front of her establishment for two months. This construction will affect revenue levels because potential customers may have difficulty driving to her café. She believes this will reduce her business by about 20 customers daily, and she is optimistic that some of the construction workers will eat at her establishment so the customer count will not be reduced beyond this estimate.

Ophelia does simple estimates of the possible impacts of the business changes and road construction. *Exhibit 6.6* shows her projections for the next three months based on this information.

In addition to the customer count changes reviewed in *Exhibit 6.6*, Ophelia knows that her customer count has increased by about 5 percent each year. When she develops her budget, she will also factor this information into her projections. Ophelia knows that the information is as accurate as it can be. However, she also knows that remodeling after fires and road completion projects are not always completed on time. She will, therefore, update her customer count information as necessary.

Exhibit 6.6

SALES PROJECTIONS FOR THE NEXT THREE MONTHS FOR FACTORY ROAD CAFÉ

Month 1

• Add customers from new business	5
• Deduct customers from business with fire	−10
• Deduct customers because of road construction	−20
Customer Count Change	**−25**

Average daily customer count (month 1)
$250^* − 25 = 225$

Month 2

• Add customers from new business	5
• Deduct customers because of road construction	−20
Customer Count Change	**−15**

Average daily customer count (month 2)
$250^* − 15 = 235$

Month 3

• Add customers from new business	5

Average daily customer count (month 3)
$250^* + 5 = 255$

*175 drive-in + 75 carryout = 250 customers

CUSTOMER SERVICE NEEDS

Managers must estimate the number of customers they will serve on a monthly basis to develop the operating budget, and on a daily basis to create or revise the master schedule. Some establishments that serve two meals daily, such as breakfast and a midday meal, may require a separate master schedule for each meal period. This is because the schedule's purpose is to determine the number of employees in each position that must be scheduled for each meal period. In Ophelia's case, only one master schedule is needed. She has experience with her operation and customer counts, and the menus do not change significantly. Also, it is a relatively small-volume operation and employees can and do work both meal periods. Also, the cooks working one shift typically pre-prep food for the next meal period.

It would be easy if the number of customers arriving were approximately the same each hour. In fact, many establishments have a customer volume that varies greatly during a meal period. How then can a manager develop the master schedule and the resulting crew schedule? The answer goes back to the POS system, which can provide customer-count information by any time period requested. Also, managers typically know that, for example, they are likely fairly slow during the first part of a shift and perhaps the last hour, with the majority of customers arriving between those two time periods.

Using POS information and the manager's operating experience, the number of customers expected per hour can be determined. With this information, the number of employees required for each position in the master schedule can be determined. Returning to Factory Road Café, the master schedule in *Exhibit 6.5* indicates that Ophelia is estimating 250 customers per day. How were the numbers of employees in each position determined, and how did she know to schedule them for the hours shown? For example, since the establishment opens for breakfast at 6:00 a.m. and closes at 2:00 p.m., the last customers may be seated and final carryout orders taken at 2:00. Therefore, some customers will still be dining after the operation stops seating additional customers. Notice that Ophelia has scheduled one-half server hour before 6:00 a.m. to prepare for customer service, and one cook hour for kitchen prep. She has also scheduled one server hour from 2:00 p.m. to 3:00 p.m. to clean up and prepare for the next morning's shift.

On a typical breakfast shift, only a few customers are served during the first hour of operation (6:00–7:00 a.m.). Business increases until only a few are seated shortly between 10:00 a.m. and 11:00 a.m., when the lunch menu is offered.

Ophelia has scheduled one-half hour for the dish washer and one hour for the cook after closing to perform cleanup tasks. While there might be some production required for customers ordering meals shortly before 2:00 p.m., the majority of the scheduled time can be spent for closing duties.

Exhibit 6.7

AVERAGE NUMBER OF CUSTOMERS PER HOUR AT FACTORY ROAD CAFÉ

Time	% of Total Customers	No. of Customers (rounded)
6:00–7:00 a.m.	10%	25
7:00–8:00 a.m.	15	40
8:00–9:00 a.m.	10	25
9:00–10:00 a.m.	10	25
10:00–11:00 a.m.	5	10
11:00 a.m.–12:00 p.m.	15	40
12:00 p.m.–1:00 p.m.	25	65
1:00 p.m.–2:00 p.m.	10	25
	100%	**255**

Exhibit 6.7 shows the average number of drive-in and carryout customers served each hour of operation. The time frame covered is the last eight weeks, which is 40 days open for business.

Ophelia's review of recent POS system information and her long-term experience at Factory Road Café allow her to create estimated percentages of customers per hour, as shown in *Exhibit 6.7*. Ophelia is then able to translate those percentages into total customers for each hour. Ophelia used this information to develop the master schedule. Note in *Exhibit 6.5* that during the 6:00–7:00 a.m. time period, she has scheduled only one server, the same server who came in before opening.

The last hour of service, 1:00–2:00 p.m., is normally a slow time. Ophelia has kept one server during this period because as the customer count decreases, the server can begin end-of-shift cleanup tasks that can continue until he or she leaves at 3:00 p.m. The same type of factors used to plan server hours are also used to plan the number of hours required for the counter attendant, dish washer, and cook positions. Note again that Ophelia is determining the required number of hours for each position without indicating the specific employee.

PRODUCTION AND QUALITY GOALS

Schedules must include enough time for production personnel to adequately prepare the required number of portions according to standard recipes. Doing so ensures that quality standards will be met. Times must also allow the use of all food sanitation and safety practices without any shortcuts being taken because of time constraints. This includes time for necessary cleanup activities during and at the end of the shift. These types of concerns are built in to the number of waged production employees included in the master schedule.

THE MASTER SCHEDULE AND THE BUDGET

The draft of the master schedule should be compared with the average number of hours waged employees can work per day within budget. Recall that Ophelia can schedule, on average, approximately 46 hours each day. *Exhibit 6.5* indicates that Ophelia is planning to use 45 hours on an average day. Remember that the budget standard is an average: she should schedule more labor hours on shifts forecasted to be busy and fewer labor hours when fewer customers are expected. The hours worked by Ophelia, as the salaried owner and manager, are not included in the master schedule. She is able to help her employees with front- and back-of-the-house tasks as needed to ensure food-production and service standards are consistently attained.

Managers developing master schedules may be able to use one employee to fill more than one position during slow serving hours or meal periods. If they do so without affecting the quality of production or service, labor hours can be saved and reassigned to busier work shifts. For example, perhaps Ophelia's counter attendant can clear tables during slow periods. Also, a cook who has received food safety training may be able to assume a dish-washer position during very slow shifts (*Exhibit 6.8*). Also, dish washers might be trained to do some basic vegetable and other pre-preparation work to help during a slow shift. These examples show the benefits of cross-training employees to do tasks that are not normally part of their position. This is just one tool that experienced managers can use while always striving to meet customer- and profit-related goals.

Exhibit 6.8

Assign Individual Responsibilities

How should the specific employees required by the master schedule be selected when the crew schedule is developed? The first step is to identify which staff members can perform each position. Typically employees are hired to perform tasks in specified positions, such as cooks and dish washers, and those employees would fill these positions. Employees who are cross-trained for a cook's position might be able to do some of those tasks, but they would not normally be scheduled to do cooking tasks for an entire shift. Some establishments use **floaters**, employees who can perform all tasks in more than one position. These employees might be scheduled for different positions on different days.

The staffing needs for the shift being scheduled will be known from sales calculations and development of the master schedule. With this information, the schedule planner can determine the number of employees needed and when they must work.

Staff availability is an important concern if, for example, an employee is planning a vacation or will otherwise be away for the time period covered by the crew schedule. Procedures for addressing specific employee needs as crew schedules are developed will be discussed in the next section. Schedule planners will also know the days and hours that specific staff members have normally worked, and these additional factors are considered as scheduling decisions are made.

Develop a Crew Schedule

The master schedule is used to prepare the crew schedule. However, Ophelia must do more than insert a specific employee's name on each line. She must consider several factors to match necessary positions in her master schedule with specific employees in the crew schedule. First, there should be a balance between the needs of the establishment and its customers and the needs of employees. Ophelia will need employees at the times noted on the master schedule. However, the crew schedule should be developed with flexibility in mind.

What happens when an employee requests a day off for an important personal occasion or is scheduled for a several-day vacation? It can be stressful for a manager to learn that an employee cannot, or will not, work a shift when he or she is needed. Many of these situations can be avoided with clear policies and effective two-way communication.

COMMUNICATION AND CREW SCHEDULES

Communication plays an important role in scheduling employees. Most employees want to help the operation, and they know a team effort is needed to ensure success. Therefore, managers should keep employees informed. Employees should be told about plans such as a change in the menu or hours of operation or an upcoming promotion expected to increase business. Managers should, however, recognize that many employees accept employment with the understanding that they will work at certain times and for a specific number of hours each week.

Likewise, employees should learn about potential decreases in business caused by, for example, road repairs. Perhaps a line cook may decide to go on vacation that week, and this would benefit the employee and the establishment. One fewer line cook could be scheduled, and that person could have a well-deserved break. Open communication will not solve all scheduling problems, but it will help solve many of them. Most employees who know what is going on in an operation are more likely to schedule their personal time around events affecting their work.

TIME-OFF REQUESTS

Managers should establish and circulate a time-off request policy. The policy should explain the procedures and guidelines employees should follow when they want time off from work.

VACATION REQUESTS

Managers must follow their property's policies for granting vacation time. Employees should be aware of these policies from orientation and training sessions, the current employee handbook, and from coaching sessions if they ask about vacation concerns.

One way to determine when vacation time is available is to determine which weeks during the year could have heavy revenue volumes. These weeks could be "blocked off" the vacation calendar and request form. Some managers also allow no more than a specified number of persons from a department or other work area to take time off at the same time. Vacation requests are normally fulfilled according to seniority: employees working for the operation the longest have first choice. Vacation request forms should be submitted in writing and in advance according to the process defined by the operation. Then managers will have time to prepare for the employee's absence. Managers who have cross-trained their employees will have fewer problems dealing with these absences.

DAY-OFF REQUESTS

Guidelines are also needed for employee day-off requests. Since these requests are usually for only one or a few days, receipt of the requests at least one week before the schedule is developed may be acceptable. Managers should also think about how many employees in a department or work area can be off at one time. If a conflict occurs, a guideline should be in place about whether requests will be honored by seniority or on a "first come, first served" basis.

Day-off requests are normally not an issue unless there is a major event that affects the same employees, such as a community-wide activity. These are times when a well-thought-out and consistently applied policy is needed. Special concerns are likely to arise for holidays. Some managers develop an annual schedule of holiday shifts, such as the sample seen in *Exhibit 6.9*. However, special exceptions should be made for employees requesting time off for religious holidays, when possible.

Exhibit 6.9

SAMPLE HOLIDAY SCHEDULE

HOLIDAY SHIFTS (x = time off requested)

Name	Position	New Year's Day	Valentine's Day	Easter	Memorial Day	Fourth of July	Ramadan	Labor Day	Rosh Hashanah	Yom Kippur	Thanksgiving	Christmas Eve	Christmas Day	New Year's Eve
Sarah	Server			x		x				x	x		x	
Lon	Server	x	x		x		x							x
Armando	Server	x	x	x	x			x						
Mila	Server				x	x				x	x	x		
Venn	Host/Cashier	x		x		x				x	x			
Kai	Host/Cashier			x	x			x				x	x	
Roane	Bus person/ Dish washer			x	x	x		x			x		x	
Hamza	Bus person					x	x	x						x
Jami	Line cook	x	x	x						x				
Jeremy	Line cook					x		x			x	x	x	
Jake	Pantry	x				x	x	x						x
Adie	Pantry		x		x					x			x	

Ophelia does not have a significant problem with holiday schedules at her property because it closes for the most commonly celebrated holidays. As at many other businesses, some employees schedule days off immediately before and after some holidays. Since these are usually low business volume days, these requests can be handled easily.

FAMILY AND MEDICAL LEAVE ACT

The **Family and Medical Leave Act (FMLA)** is a federal law that allows eligible employees to take off an extended amount of time for medical and other personal reasons. FMLA applies to businesses employing 50 or more persons. Requirements of FMLA do not affect Ophelia's business because she has fewer employees. However, it will impact scheduling decisions in larger operations. FMLA will be discussed further in chapter 8.

EMPLOYEE ABSENCE POLICY

Managers should have policies and procedures in place to manage time-off requests made formally before the crew schedule is developed. Sometimes, however, employees need time off without warning because of sickness or a family or other emergency. Employee absence policies are guidelines and procedures that explain how employees should inform managers if they are unable to work. These policies often require employees to contact their manager as soon as they know they cannot work and also to indicate how long they think it will be before they will return to work. Many operations have a policy that if employees are ill for more than a specified number of days, they must obtain a doctor's release prior to returning to work. This is important in the restaurant and foodservice industry since diseases and infections may spread.

SCHEDULING MINORS

The Fair Labor Standards Act (FLSA) is a federal law that, among other things, establishes scheduling standards for young persons. This topic is discussed further in chapter 8.

OTHER SCHEDULING CONCERNS

Most operations have some great employees, some good employees, and some employees whose skill levels need to be improved. Each employee's abilities should be considered when employees are scheduled for specific shifts. For example, those whose skill levels need improvement might be placed with other employees who can mentor and help them. More experienced and productive employees are often scheduled during times of high business volume.

Every employee will not be available every day for every shift. Sometimes arrangements are made when an employee is hired. For example, a server might request Tuesday and Thursday evenings off to attend a college class. Some operating factors may need to be considered when the crew schedule is written because they were not considered in the master schedule. For example, perhaps large food deliveries are received on Fridays because the weekend shifts are the busiest (*Exhibit 6.10*). Who is going to receive them, and how much time will be needed? Can someone do this work and still complete their other responsibilities? What if equipment is out for service; will that lower productivity?

Employee training may be another concern. Perhaps a recently hired employee who must be trained will be scheduled, or another staff member must relearn a specific task. An experienced employee who is mentoring this person may be taken away from regular tasks, and perhaps an additional person will need to be scheduled to maintain efficiency. Employee meetings are another activity that sometimes is not considered on the master schedule. If managers want to conduct a meeting, that time should be set aside on the crew schedule.

Those planning crew schedules should not take advantage of their best employees. For example, if the operation is busiest on the weekends, the excellent nontipped employees should not be scheduled to work every weekend unless they prefer this schedule. In other words, they should not be "punished" for being good at their job. Those planning crew schedules should also recognize that employees who work at the beginning and end of shifts likely have some setup and cleanup duties. Employees in the same position should normally be scheduled in a way that all employees will share in these duties.

MORE ABOUT CREW SCHEDULES

After the manager has developed the master schedule and considered the factors just discussed for specific employees, the crew schedule can be developed. Ophelia uses the basic master schedule for each day in the week beginning March 12. Her worksheet is shown in *Exhibit 6.11* on the next page.

When reviewing *Exhibit 6.11*, note that the schedule for Monday shows the employees who are scheduled for the time blocks required by the master schedule in *Exhibit 6.5* on page 179. The weekly schedule also considers the one request made by a server who wanted two days off. Fred is taking off March 15 and March 16, and Shawna, an on-call server who has helped out for several years, will be working Fred's two shifts. Since Ophelia was able to use the shift times specified in the master schedule for each shift, the number of waged labor hours scheduled for the week will not exceed budget. Recall that an average of 230 waged labor hours can be used each week, and only 225 waged labor hours are scheduled.

Exhibit 6.10

Manager's Memo

Overtime refers to the number of hours of work, usually 40, after which an employee must receive a premium pay rate. This rate is usually 1.5 times the basic hourly rate. Some employees may have to be paid overtime if customers arrive near closing time and prevent those scheduled to leave from doing so. Others may work overtime because another employee did not report to work and did not inform the manager, thus making him or her a "no-show." This term applies to employees who, when they are scheduled to work, neither tell managers they will not work nor report for their assigned shift.

Overtime should never be planned into a crew schedule because it is a waste of payroll dollars. The best managers also try very hard to minimize overtime during actual work shifts.

Exhibit 6.11

CREW SCHEDULE WORKSHEET FOR FACTORY ROAD CAFÉ (3/12–3/16)

	1 3/12 Monday	2 3/13 Tuesday	3 3/14 Wednesday	4 3/15 Thursday	5 3/16 Friday	6 Scheduled Hours
Server						
Lani	5:30–10	5:30–10	5:30–10	5:30–10	5:30–10	22.5
Jacelyn	7–12	7–12	7–12	7–12	7–12	25
Candy	10–1	10–1	10–1	10–1	10–1	15
Fred	12–3	12–3	12–3			9
Shawna				12–3	12–3	6
						77.5
Counter Attendant						
Frieda	8–2	8–2	8–2	8–2	8–2	30
						30
Dish Washer						
Edgar	8–2:30	8–2:30	8–2:30	8–2:30	8–2:30	32.5
						32.5
Cook						
Cory	5–11	5–11	5–11	5–11	5–11	30
Carlo	7–2	7–2	7–2	7–2	7–2	35
Jack	11–3	11–3	11–3	11–3	11–3	20
						85
				Total waged labor hours		**225**

Distribute and Adjust the Crew Schedule

Crew schedules should clearly indicate what all employees must know about their planned work schedules:

- Dates and days of the week covered by the schedule
- Employees' names
- Scheduled days to work and to be off from work
- Scheduled start and stop times, indicating a.m. and p.m.
- Date of schedule preparation and name of the manager preparing it

Crew schedules should be distributed approximately one week before the first day of the schedule period. *Exhibit 6.12* shows a crew schedule developed from the worksheet in *Exhibit 6.11*. Notice that it includes all of the information that should be on a crew schedule.

Exhibit 6.12

CREW SCHEDULE FOR FACTORY ROAD CAFÉ (3/12–3/16)

	1 3/12 Monday	2 3/13 Tuesday	3 3/14 Wednesday	4 3/15 Thursday	5 3/16 Friday
Server					
Lani	5:30 a.m.–10:00 a.m.	5:30 a.m.–10:00 a.m.	5:30 a.m.–10:00 a.m.	5:30 a.m.–10:00 a.m.	5:30 a.m.–10:00 a.m.
Jacelyn	7:00 a.m.–12:00 p.m.	7:00 a.m.–12:00 p.m.	7:00 a.m.–12:00 p.m.	7:00 a.m.–12:00 p.m.	7:00 a.m.–12:00 p.m.
Candy	10:00 a.m.–1:00 p.m.	10:00 a.m.–1:00 p.m.	10:00 a.m.–1:00 p.m.	10:00 a.m.–1:00 p.m.	10:00 a.m.–1:00 p.m.
Fred	12:00 p.m.–3:00 p.m.	12:00 p.m.–3:00 p.m.	12:00 p.m.–3:00 p.m.		
Shawna				12:00 p.m.–3:00 p.m.	12:00 p.m.–3:00 p.m.
Counter Attendant					
Frieda	8:00 a.m.–2:00 p.m.	8:00 a.m.–2:00 p.m.	8:00 a.m.–2:00 p.m.	8:00 a.m.–2:00 p.m.	8:00 a.m.–2:00 p.m.
Dish Washer					
Edgar	8:00 a.m.–2:30 p.m.	8:00 a.m.–2:30 p.m.	8:00 a.m.–2:30 p.m.	8:00 a.m.–2:30 p.m.	8:00 a.m.–2:30 p.m.
Cook					
Cory	5:00 a.m.–11:00 a.m.	5:00 a.m.–11:00 a.m.	5:00 a.m.–11:00 a.m.	5:00 a.m.–11:00 a.m.	5:00 a.m.–11:00 a.m.
Carlo	7:00 a.m.–2:00 p.m.	7:00 a.m.–2:00 p.m.	7:00 a.m.–2:00 p.m.	7:00 a.m.–2:00 p.m.	7:00 a.m.–2:00 p.m.
Jack	11:00 a.m.–3:00 p.m.	11:00 a.m.–3:00 p.m.	11:00 a.m.–3:00 p.m.	11:00 a.m.–3:00 p.m.	11:00 a.m.–3:00 p.m.

Date Prepared: March 1   **Prepared By:** Ophelia

Exhibit 6.13

DISTRIBUTION OF CREW SCHEDULE

Crew schedules can be distributed to employees in several different ways. In some properties they are posted on employee bulletin boards and in other central locations (see *Exhibit 6.13*). They also can be included with paychecks. Increasingly, managers email schedules or make them available on the operation's intranet system. An intranet is a network of computers for a single organization that can be at the same or different locations.

REVISE CREW SCHEDULE AS NEEDED

Crew schedules are never really final because employees may become ill, be no-shows, show up late, or even resign after the schedule is developed. Unexpected changes in customer estimates can occur, which would change the number of labor hours needed. Managers must be skilled negotiators and problem solvers as they interact with employees to keep the schedule in line with the number of customers served.

In Ophelia's case, recall that she is able to supplement the schedule where necessary because she has blocked out customer service times to be free for assistance where required. Recall also that some employees may be floaters who can perform more than one job regularly and fill in for employees taking time off. They provide a great deal of flexibility when the manager needs an employee with a range of abilities.

Monitor Employees during Shifts

Managers try to schedule in a way that best ensures that all required quantity and quality standards will be met during the shift. However, careful planning is not useful unless there is follow-through while employees are working.

Managers can use several methods to emphasize the importance of meeting standards during work shifts. For example, dining-room managers can review sales and service goals during pre-shift line-up meetings. A line-up meeting is a brief training session held before the work shift begins. Line-up meetings are often used to update employees about expected business, daily specials, and other operating concerns.

Emphasizing goals that connect the mission statement to daily operations can set the pace for performance during the shift. Managers will also observe employees as they work. Then they can identify problems and coach employees to address them. When they see employees doing things correctly, they can use positive feedback for reinforcement. Experienced managers allow their experience to guide them as they monitor quality during work shifts. Some managers of full-service establishments say they can evaluate how well service is going by the amount of water in customers' glasses. If water glasses are full, service is as it should be. If water glasses are not full, servers do not have time to fill them, and this suggests that problems may be occurring.

Food-production managers use their experience to monitor quality as well. They use temperature and taste checks, compare production plans with quantities of food produced, and are always alert to food safety procedures.

Some managers schedule meetings only when there are problems. While such meetings are necessary, meetings to plan and evaluate goals and to thank employees for meeting or exceeding standards are also important.

Analyze After-Shift Labor Information

Professional managers know that the control of labor costs involves more than just planning an employee schedule that meets standards. They must also analyze actual labor costs after work shifts are completed to learn how well their plans worked out. Labor costs for employees who receive wages are managed by using the labor cost standard in the approved operating budget. If the budget goal is not met, the difference between the budgeted expense and the actual expense is called a variance. *Exhibit 6.14* on the next page shows Ophelia's analysis of waged labor hours for the week of March 12. It is the same as her worksheet in *Exhibit 6.11* on page 190 except that she completed columns 7 and 8 after the week ended.

When reviewing *Exhibit 6.14*, note the last three columns:

- Column 6 shows the number of hours scheduled for each employee.

- Column 7 shows the number of hours actually worked by each employee. This information is taken from employee time records.

- Column 8 shows the variance, or difference in the number of scheduled and actual hours for employees in each position. The bottoms of columns 6 and 7 show that while 225 labor hours were scheduled for all employees, 230.5 hours were actually worked. This created a variance of 5.5 hours:

$$\underset{\textbf{Actual hours}}{230.5} \quad - \quad \underset{\textbf{Scheduled hours}}{225} \quad = \quad \underset{\textbf{Hours}}{5.5}$$

How much higher will labor costs be than expected? This question can be answered by considering where the costs were incurred. First, note that two variances did not increase labor costs:

- Jacelyn, a server, was scheduled to work 25 hours but worked only 23 hours because it was somewhat slower than expected in the dining room on Thursday. However, it was still a good sales day because of a larger-than-expected number of carryout lunches.

- Renee, an on-call employee, filled in for Frieda, the scheduled counter attendant, on Thursday and Friday because Frieda was ill.

Exhibit 6.14

REVIEW OF SCHEDULED AND ACTUAL LABOR HOURS AT FACTORY ROAD CAFÉ (3/12–3/16)

	1 3/12 Monday	2 3/13 Tuesday	3 3/14 Wednesday	4 3/15 Thursday	5 3/16 Friday	6 Scheduled Hours	7 Actual Hours	8 Variance
Server								
Lani	5:30 a.m.–10:00 a.m.	5:30 a.m.–10:00 a.m.	5:30 a.m.–10:00 a.m.	5:30 a.m.–10:00 a.m.	5:30 a.m.–10:00 a.m.	22.5	22.5	
Jacelyn	7:00 a.m.–12:00 p.m.	7:00 a.m.–12:00 p.m.	7:00 a.m.–10:00 p.m.	7:00 a.m.–12:00 p.m.	7:00 a.m.–12:00 p.m.	25	23	(2)
Candy	10:00 a.m.–1:00 p.m.	10:00 a.m.–1:00 p.m.	10:00 a.m.–1:00 p.m.	10:00 a.m.–1:00 p.m.	10:00 a.m.–1:00 p.m.	15	15	
Fred	12:00 p.m.–3:00 p.m.	12:00 p.m.–3:00 p.m.	12:00 p.m.–3:00 p.m.			9	9	
Shawna				12:00 p.m.–3:00 p.m.	12:00 p.m.–3:00 p.m.	6	6	
						77.5	75.5	(2)
Counter Attendant								
Frieda	8:00 a.m.–2:00 p.m.	8:00 a.m.–2:00 p.m.	8:00 a.m.–2:00 p.m.			30	18	
Renee				8:00 a.m.–2:00 p.m.	8:00 a.m.–2:00 p.m.	0	12	
						30	30	0
Dish Washer								
Edgar	8:00 a.m.–2:30 p.m.	8:00 a.m.–2:30 p.m.	8:00 a.m.–5:00 p.m.	8:00 a.m.–4:00 p.m.	8:00 a.m.–4:00 p.m.	32.5	38	5.5
Cook								
Cory	5:00–11:00 a.m.	5:00–11:00 a.m.	5:00–11:00 a.m.	5:00–11:00 a.m.	5:00–11:00 a.m.	30	30	
Carlo	7:00 a.m.–2:00 p.m.	7:00 a.m.–2:00 p.m.	7:00 a.m.–2:00 p.m.	7:00 a.m.–2:00 p.m.	7:00 a.m.–2:00 p.m.	35	35	
Jack	11:00 a.m.–3:00 p.m.	11:00 a.m.–3:00 p.m.	11:00 a.m.–3:00 p.m.	11:00 a.m.–5:00 p.m.	11:00 a.m.–3:00 p.m.	20	22	2
						85	87	2
					Total hours	225	230.5	5.5

There were two causes of excess labor costs:

- Edgar, the dish washer, worked 5.5 hours more than expected during the week (38 actual hours − 32.5 scheduled hours). The reason is explainable: There were problems with the dishwashing machine, and dishes were washed by hand in the three-compartment sink Wednesday through Friday. This variance problem should be entered in the manager's communication log for future reference.
- Jack, a cook, worked two more hours than expected on Thursday. The reason involved some deep cleaning in the kitchen that Ophelia forgot to include when the schedule was developed.

The impact of these extra hours can be calculated using the average hourly rate for the positions (see *Exhibit 6.5*):

$$\text{Edgar:} \quad 5.5 \text{ hours} \times \$12 \text{ per hour} = \$\ 66$$
$$\text{Jack:} \quad \ \ 2 \text{ hours} \times \$18 \text{ per hour} = \underline{\quad 36}$$
$$\$102$$

If the issues continued for one year, the excess labor costs would be significant:

$$\$102 \qquad \times \qquad 49 \qquad = \qquad \$4{,}998$$

Weekly excess labor costs	weeks*	Total annual variance

Fortunately, there were no overtime hours used during the week. If that had happened, the cost of the excess labor hours would have been much greater. Edgar's overtime rate is 1.5 x $12 per hour, which is $18 per hour. If the five extra hours of labor for Edgar were beyond 40 hours per week, this would be the calculation:

$$\text{Edgar:} \quad 5.5 \text{ hours} \times \$18 \text{ per hour (overtime rate)} = \$\ 99$$
$$\text{Jack:} \quad \ \ 2 \text{ hours} \times \$18 \text{ per hour (regular pay)} = \underline{\quad 36}$$
$$\$135$$

Edgar's overtime would have increased the excess labor costs by $33:

$$\$135 \qquad - \qquad \$102 \qquad = \qquad \$33$$

Excess cost of labor including overtime	Excess cost of labor without overtime	Difference

If this labor cost continued for one year, the total increased labor cost would be $6,615:

$$\$135 \qquad \times \qquad 49 \qquad = \qquad \$6{,}615$$

Excess labor costs per week with two overtime hours	Number of work weeks assuming 15 holidays per year	Total annual labor cost increase

*Assume Factory Road Café is closed a total of three work weeks, or 15 workdays, during the year for holidays.

As calculated previously, the two overtime hours would increase the excess labor costs by $1,617 per year:

$6,615	−	$4,998	=	$1,617
Excess labor costs with overtime		Excess labor costs without overtime		Additional excess labor costs because of overtime hours

Ophelia might have avoided the excess labor hours if an effective preventive maintenance program was in place for the dishwashing machine, and she should now determine whether this corrective action is needed. She should also be sure to consider additional tasks, such as deep cleaning, when she develops schedules. In this case, the variance in labor hours can be explained. However, there may sometimes be unclear reasons for excess labor hours. Then a careful analysis is needed to quickly identify the problems causing variances and correct them to bring labor costs back under control.

Monitor Weekly Labor Costs and Adjust as Necessary

Ophelia controls her labor costs for waged employees by managing labor hours. Recall that she first determines the number of waged labor hours allowed by her budget, and then she schedules accordingly with more waged labor hours for busy times and fewer during low-volume periods.

Ophelia knows that excess waged labor costs reduce her profits, and she uses another labor control strategy to monitor waged labor costs during the entire month. Her employees must check in and check out of work shifts through her POS system. This allows her to generate additional information to help her with waged labor control. For example, she completes a weekly labor cost recap for waged employees as shown in *Exhibit 6.15*.

Exhibit 6.15

WEEKLY LABOR COST RECAP: WAGED EMPLOYEES

				March				
	No. of Work	**Expected Waged Labor Costs**		Actual Weekly		**Monthly Waged Labor Cost Tally**		
Week	Days	Daily	Weekly	Waged Labor Costs	Variance	Expected	Actual	Variance
(1)	(2)	(3)	(4)	(5)	(6)	(7)	(8)	(9)
3/1–3/2	2	$602	$ 1,204	$ 1,300	$ 96	$ 1,204	$ 1,300	$ 96
3/5–3/9	5	602	3,010	3,150	140	4,214	4,450	236
3/12–3/16	5	602	3,010	3,095	85	7,224	7,545	321
3/19–3/23	5	602	3,010	2,915	(95)	10,234	10,460	226
3/26–3/30	5	602	3,010	2,900	(110)	13,244	13,360	116
			$13,244	$13,360	$116			

When reviewing *Exhibit 6.15*, notice that there were only two workdays (3/1–3/2) in the work week beginning on March 1 (column 2). Ophelia knew from her earlier analysis that she could spend, on average, $602 daily for waged labor (column 3). Since there were two workdays during the first week, she expected to spend no more than $1,204 ($602 × 2 days) for waged labor costs. In fact, payroll records indicate that she spent $1,300 for those two days (column 5). This resulted in a variance of $96 (column 6):

$$\underset{\substack{\text{Actual weekly} \\ \text{waged labor cost}}}{\$1,300} \quad - \quad \underset{\substack{\text{Expected weekly} \\ \text{waged labor cost}}}{\$1,204} \quad = \quad \$96$$

During the second week (3/5–3/9), there were five days, so her expected cost was $3,010 (column 4). However, her actual cost was $3,150 (column 5), which was $140 more than expected (column 6).

Ophelia runs a monthly waged labor cost tally as seen in columns 7, 8, and 9. For example, she had expected to spend $4,214 (column 7) for waged labor from 3/1 to 3/9. This is the sum of $1,204 for 3/1 to 3/2, plus $3,010 for 3/5 to 3/9 (column 4).

Unfortunately, her actual waged labor cost for 3/1–3/9 was $4450. This is the sum of $1300 for 3/1–3/2, plus $3150 for 3/5–3/9 (column 5). Therefore, Ophelia spent $236 more than she expected in waged labor cost for those seven workdays:

$$\underset{\substack{\text{Actual waged} \\ \text{labor cost} \\ \text{(column 8)}}}{\$4,450} \quad - \quad \underset{\substack{\text{Expected waged} \\ \text{labor cost} \\ \text{(column 7)}}}{\$4,214} \quad = \quad \underset{\substack{\text{Variance} \\ \text{to date} \\ \text{(column 9)}}}{\$236}$$

Continuing through the month, notice that excess waged labor cost reached a peak by 3/16 (a variance of $321 in column 9). Ophelia was able to work that number down to $116 by the last workday in March.

Exhibit 6.16

Ophelia constantly remembers two major factors when she monitors her waged labor cost during the month:

• She can never reduce waged labor hours in efforts to reduce cost when this will create quality problems that impact customers.

• She can manage her waged labor costs by spending more than average on days when more customers are served, balancing that out with lower labor hours on slower business days (*Exhibit 6.16*).

The approach that Ophelia uses eliminates "surprises" at the end of the month. First, she knows the number of waged labor hours scheduled and actually worked each week. She also knows her actual waged labor cost each week, and she takes corrective action as necessary to remain close to budget expectations.

USING CHECKLISTS TO MONITOR QUALITY

Supervisors and managers use checklists to help them ensure that standards are met and routine operating procedures are performed consistently during work shifts. There are several types of checklists, and each has a specific purpose. Some remind staff to perform all necessary tasks in a timely and comprehensive way, and others ensure quality operations and consistent record keeping.

Checklists are designed for use at specific times and in designated areas. For example, an opening checklist for the back of the house could address turning on ovens, checking cooler temperatures, and ensuring that work stations are ready to use. A manager's opening checklist might include verifying that all employees have arrived in proper uniform and checking the heating or air conditioning. Regardless of the shift, area, or role, checklists should include items relating to finance, front-of-the-house service readiness, back-of-the-house sanitation, and the facility.

Employees develop good work habits when they follow checklists. Checking all parts of the operation becomes a regular part of daily work and ensures a consistent approach to taking care of customers, the facility, and equipment.

There are many types of checklists that can help managers and their teams. *Exhibit 6.17* shows a sample pre-shift checklist for a manager. With all of the things a busy manager must do before a shift begins, it is easy to see how this checklist can help ensure that no responsibilities are forgotten.

Opening and pre-shift checklists help ensure that everything is ready to help customers as soon as the doors open or the shift begins. Employees and managers may use different checklists. Managers should conduct a walk-through of their areas to make sure all items have been satisfactorily completed:

- **Facility opening and pre-shift checklists:** Monitoring the interior and exterior of the establishment is necessary to be sure it is clean, safe, and presentable. The facility's appearance is an important factor for potential customers, and their initial impression can influence their experience.

- **Front-of-the-house opening and pre-shift checklists:** These checklists address concerns such as ensuring all tables are ready, linens are clean, side stations are ready to use, music is on, and lighting is adjusted.

Exhibit 6.17

SAMPLE PRE-SHIFT CHECKLIST

ALUMNI HOUSE

Exterior of Building
- ❏ Parking lot is clean and free of debris
- ❏ Front walk is clean and free of debris
- ❏ Loading dock is clean and free of boxes, garbage, etc.
- ❏ Dumpster and recycling receptacles are clean and picked up
- ❏ Exterior lights are working
- ❏ Patio is ready for service

Kitchen
- ❏ All staff members are present according to schedule
- ❏ All product has been received, with temperatures recorded and dated, put away, and rotated
- ❏ All refrigeration equipment is holding temperature
- ❏ Line is clean and free of debris
- ❏ All kitchen equipment is working properly
- ❏ Equipment is cleaned
- ❏ Cooks are checking the temperatures of food for cooking, heating, and cooling
- ❏ Reach-ins are neat and organized, with foor stored properly
- ❏ Floors are clean of spills, water, and other slip/trip hazards
- ❏ Lights are working

Kitchen
- ❏ Dish machine is at correct temperature
- ❏ Titration of soap and sanitizer is correct
- ❏ Tray of machine is free of clutter
- ❏ Walls, floors, and machine are free of buildup and clean
- ❏ Machine is delimed

Front of the House
- ❏ Coffee station is clean and organized
- ❏ Messages have been checked
- ❏ Reservations have been plotted
- ❏ Server's reach-in is clean and organized
- ❏ Opening checklist is being followed
- ❏ Side work is completed
- ❏ Cash-handling procedures are being followed

Service
- ❏ Kitchen is ready
- ❏ Specials are posted
- ❏ Pre-shift staff meeting is held, specials are discussed, uniforms are checked
- ❏ Bar is ready
- ❏ Lights are set
- ❏ Music is set
- ❏ Dining room has been inspected and tables, chairs, lights, floor, and menus are clean and ready for service
- ❏ Inventories have been taken as scheduled
- ❏ Orders are placed as needed
- ❏ Schedules are posted

Adapted with permission from David R. Wightman, CEC

- **Back-of-the-house opening and pre-shift checklists:** The chef or kitchen manager must confirm that the kitchen is ready to prepare and serve foods.

- **Financial opening and pre-shift checklists:** Financial activities involve managing cash, checks, gift certificates, and payment card receipts so nothing is lost or stolen. Effective financial practices include checks and balances so each person who handles funds has someone to double-check calculations or counts.

With so many things to track, managers often use a midshift checklist to remind them about critical activities. However, these checklists are only reminders. Following a checklist periodically during a shift is no substitute for continuous monitoring:

- **Front-of-the-house midshift checklists:** The dining-room manager should monitor server courtesy, service speed, attentiveness of servers to their tables, table resetting, and customer satisfaction. Checklist items during the shift should remind managers and others to look for situations that might be forgotten or neglected.

- **Back-of-the-house midshift checklists:** The chef or manager must monitor food preparation, safety, staffing, and food inventory. He or she should continuously monitor the speed of food production, confirm employees are working efficiently, and ensure proper operation of equipment.

- **Financial midshift checklists:** Managers should monitor how employees write orders, process payment cards, and handle funds, including cash, personal checks, payment card receipts, coupons, and gift certificates. Periodically during the shift, the manager should conduct cash drops: counting and removing cash and depositing it in the safe.

Numerous activities must be done to ensure that the operation is ready for the next shift and the appropriate records have been completed. Many of the same concerns assessed before the shift or opening should be rechecked at shift-end or closing:

- **Front-of-the-house shift-end and closing checklists:** These checklists can include tasks such as confirming that all side work is completed, side stands are clean and restocked, and self-serve sections are clean and stocked.

- **Back-of-the-house shift-end and closing checklists:** These checklists might confirm that production sheets are completed and are compared to the actual quantity sold, and that discrepancies are noted.

- **Financial shift-end and closing checklists:** Financial tasks encompass both front- and back-of-the-house activities. For example, are revenue accountability forms completed, and are payment card slips reconciled? Is the amount of currency and change required for the next shift available?

- **Facility shift-end and closing checklists:** These checklists typically involve checking the inside of the facility. Are restrooms cleaned and restocked, and have decorative objects been dusted? Checklist items for the outside of the facility might include some of the same checks that are done before opening.

Checklists must be developed to fit the needs of the specific operation. However, their purpose is always the same: to ensure that all of the many details required to begin, manage during, and complete a work shift have been attended to.

USING COMMUNICATION LOGS TO MONITOR QUALITY

Communication logs are documents used by managers to record information about what has happened during a shift and share it with the managers of future shifts. Sometimes paperwork systems can get very complicated and detract from a manager's ability to respond to customers. However, all communication logs provide several benefits:

- They help managers communicate across shifts so the operation runs smoothly.
- They capture information that can help show patterns and identify problems.
- They capture information to help protect the operation from liabilities.

Using daily communication logs can be a challenge since there is so much paperwork involved in any manager's workday. However, general managers can inform other managers and key employees how the log can help them. Also, each manager should understand that the shift is not done until the log is completed.

The chef's communication log allows him or her to record information about covers, recipe ideas, customer reactions to specials, allergic reactions, unusual equipment performance, and reminders for the next shift. This log may also be used to record notes about the efficiency of back-of-the-house staff.

Three other types of communication logs are in common use:

- **Dining manager's communication log:** This log records information such as the weather, customer service patterns, and the balance between reservations and walk-ins. It may also be used to record special issues during a shift such as accommodating late reservations, responding to an unexpected crowd, and managing difficulties.
- **Banquet and catering log:** This log is kept by banquet or catering staff when the operation provides such services. It is used to record special needs for a banquet or catered event and problems that have been resolved.
- **Manager's communication log:** This log contains information that affects the operation in general, although it also may contain some of the same information as other logs. Examples include significant changes in sales or cover counts and critical incident events that must be recorded in case of a claim or lawsuit, such as reports of possible foodborne illness.

REAL MANAGER

USING CHECKLISTS, ENSURING STANDARDS, DOCUMENTATION, PROVIDING SAFE FOOD

Documentation is often overlooked in daily restaurant and foodservice operations. Documentation can really mean any number of things—from using operational checklists during shifts to the documentation involved in employee performance. Too often, managers grow complacent about paperwork, believing that they "can do it in their sleep." I simply don't buy into that thinking. Consider providing safe food, for example. I believe that air travel provides a good analogy for restaurant and foodservice businesses in this regard. How many of us would continue to get on an airplane if the airline industry consistently had accidents? If planes crashed frequently, we would simply stop flying. But oftentimes, shifts "crash" in an establishment and what happens? It gets defined as a "bad shift." I think managers often set the bar too low regarding the guest experience. The manager's mission is to consistently and safely take the guests from point A to point Z in their individual experience and to do it flawlessly. This requires a plan of action and a set of tools to ensure that every part of the operation is ready to go every shift without fail. If you have very tight processes and systems, if everyone understands their unique role and what they must do to ensure success, and if there is a committed "pilot" in charge, then guest service problems should be preventable. I believe in shift checklists, quality audits, communication logs, employee one-on-ones, and so on. All of these are the tools of our business.

Communication logs must be accessible to various people, so remember that the information is relatively public. Therefore, it is important to eliminate personal judgments or comments and other entries that are not supported by facts and might be misinterpreted.

SUMMARY

1. **Explain why operating standards are important and how managers can enforce them.**

   Standards indicate the level of quality, speed, food safety, or hospitality that employees should demonstrate so customers will receive a consistently good dining experience. Standards also specify how, how often, and how quickly employees should do work tasks, and they should be in place for all areas of an operation.

   Standard operating procedures (SOPs) explain what employees must know and do when they perform work, and they are used to implement standards. SOPs must be reviewed and updated as necessary. Sometimes this involves addressing a specific step and sometimes an entire task. Corrective actions to enforce SOPs include informal coaching sessions, special conversations, or discussions during performance appraisal meetings.

2. **Identify, implement, and review sales and service goals for the front of the house.**

   Sales goals are established as part of the process to schedule employees. When the estimated number of customers to be served is known, the number of waged labor hours can be scheduled to best ensure service goals will be met. Standard operating procedures indicate how things should be done to attain service goals, For example, when a customer's table is set up correctly, it will have all of the serviceware in the positions specified by the SOP for this task. The correct table setup can be diagrammed and used to train new servers. Additionally, the dining-room manager can determine whether tables are set correctly by comparing them to the diagram.

3. **Identify, implement, and review production and quality goals for the back of the house.**

   Production goals center around the preparation of food products that meet required standards. These standards are met when standard recipes help ensure that quality standards are consistently attained. Production personnel are also concerned about following food sanitation and safety concerns. Production goals also relate to control of waged labor costs, and these are controlled as an effective waged labor scheduling process is implemented.

4. **Describe a nine-step process for scheduling employees.**

   A nine-step process is used to plan, manage, and evaluate work schedules for waged employees. The first step is to determine budgeted labor costs. The second step involves creating a master schedule that provides guidelines based on the expected number of customers. In the third step, the manager develops sales and service goals and production and quality goals. In the fourth step, managers assign responsibilities to employees. In step 5, a crew schedule is developed by matching employees needed with those available. In step 6, the crew schedule is distributed and adjusted if needed. Step 7 involves monitoring employees during shifts to confirm that standards are met. In step 8, the manager analyzes after-shift labor information to determine variances between scheduled and actual labor hours. In the last step, the manager monitors weekly labor costs and adjusts future schedules.

5. **Explain how checklists can be used to monitor quality.**

   Checklists help ensure standards are met and routine operating procedures are performed consistently. Opening and pre-shift checklists can be developed to check the facility's interior and exterior, to ensure that the front of the house is ready for customer service, and to confirm that back-of-the-house staff are ready for food production. Financial concerns can also be addressed in a pre-shift checklist.

   Midshift checklists help managers review the operation of all stations and positions during each shift. Front-of-the-house checklists help managers monitor service speed and attentiveness, table resetting, and customer satisfaction. Back-of-the-house checklists monitor food safety and sanitation and ensure that required ingredients are available and production is not slowed. Financial checks include ensuring that all payments are processed and accounted for and cash drops are managed.

   Closing checklists help ensure the operation is ready for the next shift and appropriate records are completed. Front-of-the-house checklists can include activities such as cleaning and restocking, and a back-of-the-house list helps confirm that all kitchen and storage-related activities are completed. Financial checklists help confirm that all revenue is accounted for according to production, and prepare funds for deposit. Facility checklists involve concerns on the building's interior and exterior and include some of the same checks done before opening.

6. **Explain how communication logs help monitor quality.**

   Communication logs are used to record what happens during a shift so the information can be shared with managers of future shifts. Chefs' logs record information about the number of customers, recipe ideas, reaction to specials, and other information. Dining-room managers' logs record information about customer patterns, reservations, and walk-ins. Banquet and catering logs record information about special needs and problems resolved. A manager's communication log contains general information, such as changes in sales or customer counts and critical incidents.

APPLICATION EXERCISE

Divide into groups of two or three and brainstorm strategies that managers and supervisors should use when they observe SOPs not being followed in the following situations. Select one person to record the strategies suggested. If time permits, he or she can make a report to the class.

- **Situation 1:** A server still in training is observed setting a table incorrectly.

- **Situation 2:** A dish washer is observed following procedures accurately during slow times but taking shortcuts when business volume increases.

- **Situation 3:** A long-time server who has never created any problems has been written up in several recent customer comment cards for inattentive service.

- **Situation 4:** A long-time receptionist arrives at work with several facial piercings in violation of company policy.

- **Situation 5:** A server who began work several months ago and completed all required training consistently has difficulty operating the POS system.

REVIEW YOUR LEARNING

Select the best answer for each question.

1. **Which management tool implements standards?**
   A. Job descriptions
   B. Job specifications
   C. Performance appraisal forms
   D. Standard operating procedures

2. **What are developed as part of the position analysis process that will become SOPs?**
   A. Task lists
   B. Job descriptions
   C. Task breakdowns
   D. Performance standards

3. **What is the first step in planning, managing, and evaluating employee work schedules?**
   A. Create a master schedule.
   B. Develop a crew schedule.
   C. Determine budgeted labor cost.
   D. Develop production and quality goals.

4. **A manager has budgeted $39,540 for waged labor in April. The operation is open seven days a week. The average employee is paid $12 per hour. What is the average number of labor hours that can be scheduled per day?**
   A. 110
   B. 125
   C. 140
   D. 155

5. **What information is provided in a master schedule?**
   A. Actual labor cost to be incurred during the shift
   B. Names of employees to be scheduled for each position
   C. Number of hours of salaried labor required for the shift
   D. Number of hours needed for employees in specific positions

6. **When should employee day-off requests normally be submitted?**
   - A. One week before the schedule is developed
   - B. Within one day of the schedule's distribution
   - C. Within three days of when the day off is needed
   - D. One day in advance of need unless business volume is heavy

7. **A labor variance is a difference between**
   - A. staffing needs and budgeted labor cost.
   - B. historical information and current forecasts.
   - C. scheduled hours and actual hours worked.
   - D. positions needed and staff members available.

8. **A cook is paid $12 per hour and works two hours of overtime during a specific week. How much is the cook paid for the two hours of overtime?**
   - A. $24
   - B. $32
   - C. $36
   - D. $42

9. **What is a benefit of using a checklist to monitor quality?**
   - A. Employees do not need to be trained.
   - B. Managers help ensure standards are met.
   - C. The need for on-site supervision is eliminated.
   - D. The operation will automatically meet quality requirements.

10. **Critical incidents should be noted in which log?**
    - A. Chef's communication log
    - B. Manager's communication log
    - C. Dining manager's communication log
    - D. Banquet and catering communication log

7

Professional Development Programs

CHAPTER LEARNING OBJECTIVES

After completing this chapter, you should be able to:

- Explain the importance of professional development.

- Describe basic professional development strategies.

- Identify procedures for professional development planning meetings.

- Provide information about professional development programs for managers.

- Explain three commonly used professional development methods.

- Identify other professional development methods.

- Describe basic procedures for developing succession plans.

KEY TERMS

certification, p. 219

cross-training, p. 211

delegation, p. 222

developmental goal,
p. 216

knowledge or skill gap,
p. 208

mentoring, p. 224

on-the-job training (OJT),
p. 211

professional
development, p. 208

succession planning,
p. 228

CASE STUDY

"I really like this work and the people at Glass Top Restaurant," said Joe, a server. "But I think I could do more if I had the chance!"

"Well," replied Bino, a cook, "we are a small restaurant, but employees do come and go. There's always a chance to take on another position."

"I've been here awhile," Bino continued, "and I would like to continue cooking. I can see, however, that others might like to learn different tasks and earn more money. Why don't you talk to Estella? Our boss may have some ideas for you."

1. Do you think Estella has a responsibility to explain training opportunities at Glass Top Restaurant to employees? Support your answer.

2. The restaurant is a small operation without a large training budget or access to corporate resources. What are some practical things Estella might do to help employees improve their knowledge and skills and perhaps reduce turnover?

IMPORTANCE OF PROFESSIONAL DEVELOPMENT

Professional development refers to experience, training, and education provided to help employees do their current jobs better and prepare them for other positions. In other words, it involves the things people do to further their careers. The term refers both to actions taken for a single employee and actions the operation takes to improve employees in general. A professional development program can involve formal activities such as group training or informal activities such as coaching. The term typically refers to planned activities after an employee has participated in orientation and the basic training for a specific position.

Managers and supervisors use the same basic procedures to plan and manage activities for employees and, often interacting with their manager, to develop programs to improve their own knowledge and skills. This chapter covers planning and facilitating professional development programs for both employees and managers.

Overview of Professional Development

The corporate culture of many operations emphasizes the importance of employees to the establishment's success. Continuous learning is a key to professional development, and it is important for everyone who wants a fulfilling career path in the restaurant and foodservice industry.

There are several reasons why managers and their employees often want to improve their skills and knowledge:

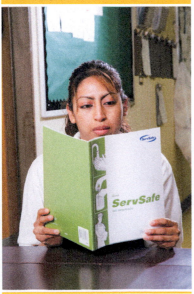

Exhibit 7.1

- They have the basic skills but can improve productivity with more advanced skills.
- They have been assigned a new job that requires additional skills.
- There are changes such as new tasks, procedures, or equipment.
- They want to qualify for a different job requiring different or additional skills.
- New requirements have been mandated by upper management or the government.

Each of these reasons relates to a **knowledge or skill gap**: a difference between the knowledge or skills a manager or employee already has and those that are needed. Studying resource materials from professional associations is just one way to narrow a knowledge gap (*Exhibit 7.1*).

There are several ways that knowledge or skill gaps can be identified by managers:

- Personal observation
- The employee's own beliefs

- Reports by a manager

- Reports or complaints by other workers, customers, or vendors

- Routine performance evaluations

- Additional knowledge and skills identified for higher-level positions

Generally, the information from all of these sources is assembled into a description of the various knowledge and skill gaps for each employee. Then the manager can facilitate a discussion with the employee to suggest goals. It is important to agree on the knowledge and skills that are an improvement priority and on the goals. This information can then be used to plan professional development activities.

Professional development goals guide the planning of training and education programs. Developmental activities should support the establishment's mission, and the operation should not be expected to provide knowledge or skill development in areas unrelated to the employee's work. However, most operations require persons with a broad range of competencies, so that requirement is not generally a limiting factor. Interested managers and employees might be able to learn about a variety of technical topics such as cooking, quality service or management, and intellectual skills, such as a foreign language or financial analysis.

Responsibilities for Professional Development

The operation, the immediate manager, and the employee all share some responsibility for professional development. They all have different responsibilities, and they will all benefit differently from the attainment of goals.

- The operation is responsible for providing professional development methods and opportunities, including paying for the costs. In return, an employee will be better able to help the establishment succeed.

- The immediate manager is responsible for assessing development needs, recommending and assisting in the development of goals and methods, and assessing progress. In return, he or she will benefit from an employee who is easier to supervise and who can handle more assignments.

- The employee for whom the program is being planned is responsible for achieving the agreed-on goals. In return, he or she will receive increased knowledge and skills, which will lead to greater recognition and possible career advancement.

The participant carries the most responsibility for his or her development. This responsibility will be evidenced in the commitment to successfully complete the assignments.

PROFESSIONAL DEVELOPMENT STRATEGIES

Every employee has more potential that can be developed. Managers can work with employees to plan and implement an organized series of actions designed to expand skills and knowledge. *Exhibit 7.2* shows the steps in the professional development process.

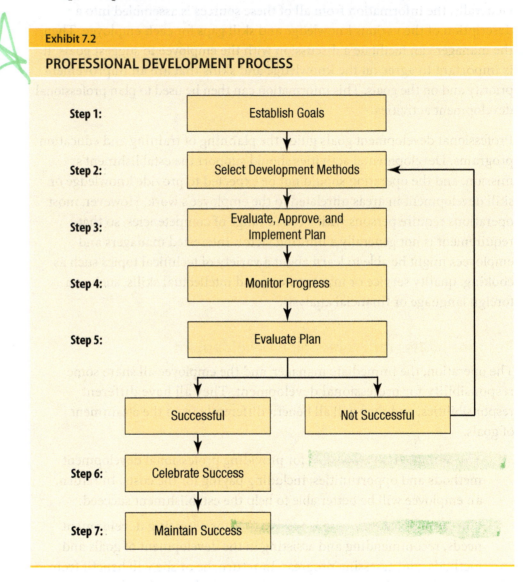

Exhibit 7.2

PROFESSIONAL DEVELOPMENT PROCESS

Step 1: Establish Goals

Step 2: Select Development Methods

Step 3: Evaluate, Approve, and Implement Plan

Step 4: Monitor Progress

Step 5: Evaluate Plan

Successful

Not Successful

Step 6: Celebrate Success

Step 7: Maintain Success

Establish Goals While Considering the Budget

The first step in the professional development process is to establish goals. These should focus on the operation's needs first and then the employee's goals. Frequently, these will be the same, since a motivated employee helps himself or herself while benefiting the company.

An operation's training and professional development budget is often a concern when knowledge and skill improvement plans are considered. The budget may not be affected at all when, for example, a learning activity involves participating in a managers' meeting or completing a project at the operation. The budget will likely be impacted if the activity involves signing up for an online course or attending a restaurant association workshop in another city. Managers should be aware of the amount budgeted for professional development and then consider priorities when developing plans for specific employees.

Effective managers inform their eligible employees about professional development opportunities that are available based on the plans discussed. Employees should also know that funds are limited and priorities based on the operation's needs will guide decision making.

When goals are established, the purposes of the professional development plan will be known. Specific, measurable goals are needed. For example, an establishment is beginning to offer banquets, and the kitchen manager has limited experience with them. To improve knowledge and skills for his present position, he must learn about banquet menus. One goal may be "to develop prearranged banquet menus with a food cost of 34 percent or less." Another operation wants to promote a server to a department head position, and one of her goals will be "To complete all required management reports from the point-of-sale system."

In a formal program, goals would be written as part of the plan, which would be signed by the manager and employee after agreement. In an informal program, an oral statement and agreement would be used.

Select Development Methods

After goals are agreed on and budgets are approved, methods to acquire the necessary knowledge and skills must be identified. Generally, the manager should be aware of opportunities within the operation. Examples include special projects designed to help with the employee's development, cross-training in which an employee learns how to do work normally done by someone in a different position, and programs available from human resources departments in large businesses. Since cross-training often occurs at an employee's work station, it is usually considered on-the-job training (OJT): a one-on-one approach to training conducted at the worksite.

Educational opportunities that relate to the goals of the program might also exist outside the establishment:

- Local trade school, community college, or four-year educational programs
- Trade or professional association resources
- Books, videos, and computer-based training programs
- Classes and materials available on the Internet

Alternative professional development methods will be discussed later in this chapter. While specific opportunities vary, there are likely to be alternatives available regardless of the establishment's location.

Several questions should be addressed as the professional development plan is designed:

- How will different activities in the plan be prioritized?
- How much time will the employee spend on each activity? This question introduces the idea that the employee must be committed to the plan. It also suggests that some personal time away from work might be needed to complete some learning activities.
- What does the operation expect as a result of successful completion of the activity? A specific, measurable goal should be established for each activity. Then it will be easier to evaluate success.
- How will the plan be evaluated?

The actual plan can be a relatively short statement that addresses these topics:

- Plan goals
- Determination of whether budgeted funds will be needed and, if so, assurance that funds are available
- The plan's time frame
- Development activities
- How success will be measured
- When progress checks will be done

Exhibit 7.3 shows a worksheet that a manager can use to assist an employee in attaining knowledge and skills for another position. A series of these development plans can be used over time to address transfers or advancements.

Evaluate, Approve, and Implement Plan

After the development program is planned, it should be evaluated and approved by the manager. The extent of program evaluation required will depend, in large measure, on the amount of input the manager had when the plan was developed. The plan should include the employee's suggestions about how it can be achieved. However, the best ideas of both the employee and the manager will likely yield the most workable plan. Success will then depend on the manager providing the agreed-on resources, including time and budgeted funds, and the employee following through with all commitments.

Exhibit 7.3

PROFESSIONAL DEVELOPMENT PLAN

Employee: _____ Manager: _____

Present position: _____

Desired position: _____

Goal (include time frame to complete plan): _____

Development Plan

A. For additional knowledge:

	Knowledge Needed	How to Attain (Development Activities)	Target Completion Date
1			
2			
3			

B. For additional skills:

	Skill Needed	How to Attain (Development Activities)	Target Completion Date
1			
2			
3			

C. Additional development activities:

D. Dates for progress review:

Plan Revisions and Schedule:	Planned	Actual

_____   _____
Employee   Date   Manager   Date

Exhibit 7.4

Monitor Progress and Evaluate Plan

Throughout the program, the manager and employee should meet to discuss progress and ways to overcome any obstacles. The manager should do several things during these sessions:

- Observe the employee's new and existing behaviors (*Exhibit 7.4*).
- Provide feedback about what is observed and whether it is satisfactory.
- Discuss the progress being made to achieve goals and whether it is acceptable.

Formal monitoring of activities can occur at the time of performance review sessions. In some operations, educational goals are included with performance goals and the appraisal addresses both types of activities.

Evaluation of progress is easier if the developmental activities are measurable. For example, the development plan for a cook might include learning how to precost recipes. A specified number of recipes can be costed, and the cook and manager can then determine if the calculations were done correctly and how they impact selling prices and food cost percentages. Similarly, a server's ability to complete management reports according to the operation's procedures can be easily evaluated.

Celebrate and Maintain Success

After activities have been evaluated, the manager and employee can determine whether each activity was successfully completed. If so, they may discuss additional activities or even begin revising the employee's development plan to include additional tasks and responsibilities.

If the planned knowledge or skill goals are not met, it may be necessary to select additional development methods. The manager must determine whether it is more important to provide additional money for this employee's second attempt or to invest in other employees. This decision will be easier as the manager considers the employee's history of attaining career development plans and whether the employee is actually motivated.

The employee may be asked to provide an oral or written summary of the learning experience, which can be useful in determining if it might be beneficial for other employees. If applicable, documentation of attendance at events, such as food vendor shows and hospitality association meetings, can also be requested. Ideally, information learned at these events will be brought back to and implemented at the operation.

Successful completion of agreed-on activities should be followed by recognition of success. This may range from a simple "Congratulations!" to a job promotion. A record of educational activities in which the employee has participated should be maintained. This information should be part of the employee's file.

The final step noted in *Exhibit 7.2* is to maintain success. Ideally, this means that the employee has enjoyed the professional development process. He or she will want to continue to learn more and advance up a career ladder to increasingly more responsible positions in the organization and the industry.

PROFESSIONAL DEVELOPMENT PLANNING MEETINGS

A professional development planning meeting is usually held in conjunction with, but separate from, an employee's performance appraisal. It is generally best that the two subjects not be discussed at the same time. Since performance appraisals affect compensation and employment status, some employees may perceive professional development conversations to be criticisms of their present levels of knowledge and skills. This creates the opposite of the atmosphere desired. Professional development meetings should be a cooperative effort in which the manager helps the employee grow.

Here are some suggestions for a constructive professional development planning meeting:

- Select the meeting's location carefully and allow ample time.
- Establish a relaxed and cooperative atmosphere.
- Provide feedback about the employee's current level of knowledge and skills.
- Listen to the employee's needs, concerns, and interests.
- Discuss career options.
- Discuss knowledge and skill goals.
- Discuss available methods to develop new or improved knowledge and skills.
- Select a program of action and establish review dates.

Meeting Preparation

The best meeting location for a discussion of professional development plans is a quiet, uninterrupted space. An office is ideal, but a corner of the dining room can be used between shifts as long as it is quiet and without interruptions.

To prepare for the meeting, establish a clear agenda and length of meeting and inform the employee ahead of time. Gather all data related to the employee's developmental needs. Write a brief outline of the points to be covered.

THINK ABOUT IT . . .

What are some reasons an employee who can do his or her current job might not want to participate in professional development activities?

What should the manager of such an employee do?

Start the Meeting

The manager should encourage an informal, relaxed mood by indicating his or her interest in helping the employee improve and be happier in the job. An informal conversation about career goals will help enable the employee to relax. This, in turn, will help ensure an honest and productive discussion about development.

Listen to the employee's needs, concerns, and interests to help determine if he or she has thought about possible career plans and the knowledge and skills required. The manager may learn about additional topics for further discussion and then offer other suggestions.

Set Developmental Goals

Developmental goals describe the knowledge and skills that need to be gained or improved on to eliminate or reduce the employee's knowledge and skills gap. One purpose of the meeting is to uncover the goals that will drive professional development activities.

There are two kinds of developmental goals. One type relates to learning specified knowledge or a certain skill, and the second addresses improvement. For example, a baker might have a learning goal of learning how to bake several new products. Later, the baker might have an improvement goal of increasing productivity as the products are prepared. The two types of goals allow for four categories of professional development goals as shown in *Exhibit 7.5*.

Exhibit 7.5		
FOUR CATEGORIES OF PROFESSIONAL DEVELOPMENT GOALS		
Kind of Goal	**Knowledge**	**Skill**
Learning	Learning new knowledge	Learning a new skill
Improvement	Improving knowledge	Improving a skill

Each employee's professional development goals will often be unique because each employee typically has a unique set of knowledge, skills, and experiences as well as knowledge and skill gaps. In each case, the manager should work with the employee to establish professional development goals. In a formal program, the goals will likely be written in a planning document such as that shown earlier in *Exhibit 7.3*. The document would be signed by both the manager and the employee. In an informal program, an oral statement and agreement would be sufficient.

Manager's Memo

An employee's professional development goals differ from an establishment's performance goals. Professional development goals often focus on issues beyond current job performance, such as gaining knowledge for another position. In contrast, performance goals focus on tasks an employee must perform as part of the current job.

Managers must set and help employees attain performance goals, but they can also help employees clarify professional development goals and align them with performance goals. For example, an employee wants to gain new skills and be promoted. The manager can help the employee identify the positions he or she might prepare for and the knowledge and skills needed. Then the employee can address knowledge and skill gaps that are common to the current and desired positions.

Managers should use their knowledge of the operation, existing development opportunities, and other positions that the employee might want to prepare for. It is important to help the employee understand what knowledge and skills are needed for advancement. In a discussion about career development options, managers can share information about the career ladder in their operation. If there is no formal career ladder, they can share stories about how people got promoted and which position would normally lead to another. These conversations may encourage employees to think about expanding their knowledge and skills and moving up in the organization.

THE MANAGER'S PROFESSIONAL DEVELOPMENT PROGRAM

Managers must be concerned about their own professional development for the same reasons they are concerned about assisting employees. Managers' daily tasks become more complex as they acquire more responsibility, and they will need new knowledge and additional skills to keep pace with these changes. Continuous learning and improvement of knowledge and skills to attain specific career goals is a critical part of every manager's growth.

As noted earlier, the basic steps that managers use to facilitate professional development programs for employees should be used as they plan their own activities:

- Determine professional development goals.
- Identify education and training activities that align with the goals.
- Determine what the budget will allow for professional development.
- Choose activities that align with the goals, budget, and learning activities available.
- Participate in the selected activities.
- Maintain records of the activities.

As when managers interact with their employees to plan and manage development activities, the assistance of a manager's own manager will be very helpful. These interactions will significantly impact the success of the professional development program.

Managers considering career advancement goals may need to think about events and activities several years or more in the future. Then they can develop plans and take actions in the near term that will move them toward their longer-term goals. Planning professional development goals is an important first step in thinking about a career path (*Exhibit 7.6*).

Exhibit 7.6

When establishing professional goals, managers should identify goals that will further develop their knowledge and skills and contribute to career growth. To help with goal setting, they should consider what they learned from past performance appraisals, think about standard or common industry career paths, and ask other professionals at different organizational levels for advice. Managers should consider what they like and do not like to do, and should remember that not all promotions are beneficial.

Professional goals sometimes change for personal and professional reasons. Managers should remain flexible and recognize that a review of their career goals and associated learning activities will be useful on a routine basis. The most appropriate learning activities should be identified as managers consider their goals, the budget, and the time they have available. Then they can establish priorities for activities based on how well each will meet their professional development goals.

Managers should keep a record of their successful completion of each professional development activity. This information will be helpful when seeking promotions and when updating their resume.

Professional goals are not likely to be attained unless an individual is committed to them. The priority that a manager attaches to a plan may be the most important factor in attaining it.

Details of a professional development plan can be written down to help participants remain organized. *Exhibit 7.7* shows a plan developed by a head cook with the assistance of the manager. Note that a knowledge and skills goal, learn how to plan menus, has been decided on mutually. The purpose of obtaining this knowledge and these skills recognizes that menu planning is an important duty for a head cook. The menu drives many of a head cook's responsibilities and work activities. The manager and cook have also determined a completion date.

Exhibit 7.7

PROFESSIONAL DEVELOPMENT PLAN

Name: _____   Present position: _____

Employer: _____   Desired position: _____

Knowledge or Skills Goals	Purpose	Goal Completion Date
1. Learn how to plan menus.	Menus drive many of the head cook's responsibilities and tasks.	May 1

How will the head cook learn about menu planning? That question is addressed in *Exhibit 7.8*.

Exhibit 7.8

PROFESSIONAL DEVELOPMENT LEARNING METHOD

Knowledge or Skills Goal	Apprenticeship	Coaching	Informal Learning	Job Rotation	OJT	External Training	Self-Study	Special Project	Team Assign	Other
#1 Menu Planning								✓		

Notice that the desired knowledge and skills goal, menu planning, is listed along with several alternative professional development methods. The menu planning activity will be accomplished by use of a special project. That project will involve sitting in on menu discussions and, ideally, contributing to revisions of the menu during the next several weeks.

Sometimes the employee participating in a professional development program interacts with his or her manager to develop a series of learning activities and a sequence for their completion. At other times a goal such as advancement to a different position is first determined. Then, when the tasks required for that position are known, knowledge or skills goals can be developed over time with consideration given to the availability of learning methods as they occur.

Continuous Improvement

Continuous improvement through professional development is essential for success in restaurant and foodservice management. Becoming certified is one way to do this. **Certification** requires an individual to demonstrate a high level of skill and to meet specific performance requirements by participating in a rigorous process.

The National Restaurant Association has several certification programs for people working in the industry:

- Foodservice Management Professional® (FMP®)
- ServSafe® food protection manager certificate
- ServSafe Alcohol® certificate
- ManageFirst Professional® (MFP™) credential

Additional certifications are available from several other sources. Certifications are usually administered through professional organizations. Some certification programs require membership in the sponsoring association. Many certifications also require work experience as a demonstration of competence in the field.

Membership in professional organizations is another way to remain current with the restaurant and foodservice industry. Weekly or monthly newsletters, workshops, and conferences are just some of the benefits of belonging to a professional organization. The following organizations may be beneficial to join:

- National Restaurant Association
- The state and local restaurant association
- International Food Service Executives Association (IFSEA)
- Women's Foodservice Forum (WFF)
- American Culinary Federation (ACF)

Other resources to consider for professional development opportunities include industry publications such as *Nation's Restaurant News*, *Food Management*, *QSR Magazine*, and *Restaurant Business*.

The Internet also provides a wealth of information for restaurant and foodservice management professionals. It is beneficial to keep up with the ever-increasing variety of electronic resources for furthering continuing education.

Networking

Managers, supervisors, and employees must stay connected to their industry. They can do so, in part, by networking with other industry professionals. Networking is a process in which persons build relationships to help with their career advancement, keep updated about the industry, and seek advice about common operating challenges. One method of networking is to attend trade shows and interact with others. Here are other methods for networking:

- Attending designated networking sessions during conventions, seminars, and conferences
- Participating in community events and sharing information about the operation
- Attending state and local association meetings and social events
- Participating in community career days, forums, charity events, and service projects
- Attending local chamber of commerce meetings
- Volunteering as a community mentor and getting to know key community leaders
- Becoming an active member of a professional organization

Networking is also valuable because it helps keep all employees current with industry trends. They can develop contacts through memberships in various professional organizations, and they can establish a contact list of peers, vendors, and government employees.

Employees who network can share information, contacts, or opportunities with others in the network. The reverse is true as well; they can also share best practices with other professionals in their network.

Another networking opportunity occurs when managers seek help in dealing with complex problems. Colleagues can offer insights about challenging situations they may be encountering. This helps them develop a stronger relationship that can be beneficial to everyone in the network. Networking also promotes important ongoing conversations within the entire industry.

THINK ABOUT IT . . .

The Internet provides information about professional sites for networking that connect professionals to trusted contacts and allows them to exchange knowledge, ideas, and opportunities.

What are some advantages of using these networking tools?

PROFESSIONAL DEVELOPMENT METHODS

Managers have many alternatives to help their employees and themselves grow professionally. Three of the most common are cross-training, delegation, and mentoring.

Exhibit 7.9

Cross-Training

Cross-training allows managers or their employees to learn a job related to their own, often by working closely with an employee who is currently doing that job (see *Exhibit 7.9*). Many operations would benefit from developing cross-training activities as part of professional development programs.

Cross-training benefits the establishment because employee absences and sudden increases in business volume can often be met with available staff. The process allows employees to discover different interests as they consider their career goals. In addition, cross-training can help with scheduling challenges, may reduce overtime, and often boosts teamwork and morale.

An important step in developing cross-training programs is to identify the employees who will be cross-trained. Some establishments use cross-training only as a method to help an employee achieve professional development goals. In this case the participant, working with his or her manager, will have determined that cross-training is the best way to achieve a professional development goal. In other cases, cross-training in selected tasks can provide a general development opportunity to improve teamwork or morale. If so, cross-training activities can be offered to all employees. Providing equal access in this situation is important for building morale, and it is also required to comply with equal opportunity laws. The same equal opportunity guidelines that apply to screening during the recruitment process also apply to promoting from within or moving an employee into a different position. When considering candidates for general cross-training, managers should think about missing knowledge or skills identified in performance appraisal sessions. They should also think about which employees are self-starters with organizational skills.

When implementing cross-training opportunities, review work schedules for the affected employee and also consider slow business volume times. Recognize that productivity may be low when a person is being cross-trained. Encourage and thank the employee selected to do the training and explain the need for him or her to be patient while the trainee learns.

The cross-training plan should include time frames, knowledge and skills to be learned, and ways to measure success. If the trainee does not master the skills or if new developmental needs arise, additional cross-training activities may be planned.

Delegation

Delegation is a process of working with and through others to complete a task or project. It shares authority and entrusts employees to accomplish the tasks assigned to them.

Delegation is often thought of as a time management alternative. For example, a manager can make time for priority responsibilities by delegating tasks of lower priority. However, it can also be used as a professional development method to help employees attain goals involving work tasks and responsibilities that are not a normal part of their position.

Several types of tasks are most appropriate for delegation and may be useful in the professional development programs for some employees:

- **Fact-finding tasks:** One important element in problem solving involves analyzing the problem, and to do that, facts must be gathered. This task can be assigned to an employee wanting to gain experience in problem solving.
- **Detail work:** This type of work can be important for employees wanting to learn complicated tasks such as analyzing point-of-sale (POS) data.
- **Repetitive tasks:** Employees wanting to learn about the completion of weekly production reports, sales monitoring, and inventory counting could learn these things by completing delegated tasks.
- **"Standing in" tasks:** Those participating in professional development programs may achieve some of their learning goals by representing their manager at some management meetings. This provides more time for the manager while providing new job perspectives to the participant.

THINK ABOUT IT...

Some managers may not delegate because they think their job is safer if they don't. Others recognize they cannot be promoted unless another person is capable of doing the work.

What do you think about these two viewpoints?

Several steps should be used if the delegation process is to be effective. These steps are preparation, planning, execution, assessment, and appreciation.

In the preparation step, the manager and the participant work together to select the task to be delegated, and then the manager clearly defines it. Initially, tasks should be fairly simple and straightforward. As an employee develops confidence and skills, tasks can become more complex. It is often helpful to create a checklist for each task so it can be monitored easily. Additionally, discuss the results anticipated, resources needed, relevant information to be considered, and time frame for completion.

The next step in delegation involves planning. The manager should meet with the employee to describe the assignment in detail and discuss all the facts and required results. Information about other people involved, equipment, budget, and materials, if any, should be shared. Any constraints should be identified and suggestions to overcome them should be discussed.

It is important to consider the level of involvement the employee must have to attain the professional development goal. As seen in *Exhibit 7.10*, delegation levels can be increased until an employee has a high degree of freedom and decision-making authority. Share and discuss the level of delegated authority the employee will have while completing the assignment. Additionally, notify all employees who may be affected.

In the execution step of delegation, the manager turns over the project or task to the employee. As the task progresses, he or she must monitor the situation and discuss any requested adjustments to the original plan. Discussions should include problems or issues and plans for resolving them. During this step, feedback and encouragement is vital. The coaching activities should be balanced between telling the employee exactly what to do and offering no support at all.

The final steps of delegation, assessment and appreciation, occur after the task is successfully completed. A meeting to discuss the results, process, and lessons learned is very important. Acknowledge the employee to recognize his or her efforts, acknowledge the contribution, and provide motivation for future assignments.

Exhibit 7.10

LEVELS OF DELEGATION

Takes action without direct supervision
Highest level of confidence

Takes action and follows up with manager
Confidence in abilities, follows up to ensure that any potential risks are resolved quickly

Decides and proceeds, yielding to manager's advice
Controls more actions but requires checks and measures to flag any potential risks

Decides course of action, waits for approval
Trusted to judge options correctly but needs approval before taking action

Gives recommendation with options
Manager checks thinking before a decision is made

Finds information, manager decides
Investigates, analyzes, but makes no recommendations

Waits to be told
No delegated responsibility

Exhibit 7.11

Mentoring

Mentoring is a process in which an experienced employee provides advice to less experienced employees about concerns relating to the job, establishment, and profession (*Exhibit 7.11*). Mentoring is used for several reasons in many operations. These include helping new employees experience the establishment's organizational culture and addressing performance problems that are identified. However, long-term mentoring relationships can also provide input and continuity for an employee's professional development program.

While the benefits of mentoring to employees are clear, mentors themselves can also benefit from the relationship. For example, it provides a feeling of giving back to the establishment. Mentors would not be chosen unless they were good "corporate citizens," and this feeling of self-esteem can be very rewarding. Mentors who are managers of specific employees are, in effect, helping to train their successors. Then both parties, the mentor and the employee being mentored, will be able to expand their network of contacts for assistance in the future.

A wide range of knowledge and skills can be addressed in an effective mentoring program, and many times the relationship is not established to address one specific goal. Instead, a mentoring relationship can become one in which the employee discusses many issues over a long time period.

In effect, mentors serve in many roles as they interact with the employees assigned to them. First, they are a coach providing specific task and job-related information. Second, they can be a counselor providing ideas about the entire industry and the employee's career. They can also serve as a role model because their behavior probably is judged favorably by the establishment. Finally, they can support the employee when higher-level discussions about job opportunities and possible promotions occur.

Effective mentors have significant experience in the operation. They are in a higher-level position than the employee being mentored, and they enjoy a favorable reputation in the organization. They also are accessible. They have the time and interest in helping the person being mentored.

Mentors are good communicators with effective interpersonal and listening skills. They are also good motivators, and this becomes possible as they learn more about the employee and understand his or her goals. They know when information should be kept confidential and they provide honest information, not just what the employee wants to hear.

Employees have several responsibilities when they agree to interact with a mentor. First, they must do it because they want to, not just because their manager suggests or requires it. They must be honest when providing information on which the mentor will base suggestions. They must also meet reasonable deadlines imposed by the mentor. Also, they must take the initiative to seek the mentor's advice when necessary, and they must be able to objectively evaluate the information provided against their own interests and feelings.

Those participating in a long-term mentoring relationship for professional development purposes often go through several stages. These are addressed in *Exhibit 7.12*.

THINK ABOUT IT . . .

Some persons believe that mentoring is a one-way conversation—telling the employee what to do. Others say the mentor is responsible for the employee's success.

Do you think either idea is correct? Why or why not?

Exhibit 7.12

STAGES IN LONG-TERM MENTORING RELATIONSHIP

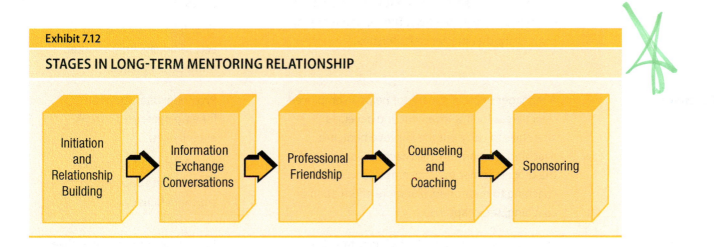

Initiation and Relationship Building → Information Exchange Conversations → Professional Friendship → Counseling and Coaching → Sponsoring

The first stage, initiation and relationship building, allows both parties to get to know each other and to feel comfortable in question-and-answer conversations. In the second stage, information exchange, the employee begins to ask questions and the mentor begins to give responses in much the same way that friends provide advice to each other.

In the third stage, professional friendship, the mentor begins to provide more generalized advice that is less role and task related. In the next stage, counseling and coaching, the employee begins to more easily accept and even initiate acting in ways encouraged by the mentor. During this stage the relationship becomes more long term, and this stage can last for many years. Finally, in the sponsoring stage, the mentor recognizes the worth and contributions that can be made by the employee and serves as a sponsor, or reference, to help the employee move forward in his or her career.

THINK ABOUT IT . . .

As an employee matures professionally, he or she may actually become a mentor for the next employees.

Do you think mentored employees have a responsibility to "give back" during their career? Why or why not?

Other Professional Development Methods

Besides cross-training, delegating, and mentoring, there are many other ways that professional development goals can be attained. *Exhibit 7.13* summarizes the more popular methods.

Exhibit 7.13		

ADDITIONAL PROFESSIONAL DEVELOPMENT METHODS

Method	Description	Pros and Cons
Apprenticeship	A form of training in which a master craftsperson assumes responsibility for the total development of a person new to the field. The result after many years is another master craftsperson.	*Pro:* Thorough training under a master. *Con:* Takes years and can accommodate only a limited number of students.
Coaching	A manager or other supervisor helps an employee select areas for improvement and develops strategies to carry out the improvement. In a coaching relationship, the coach takes charge of the process rather than the employee. Compare coaching to mentoring. (For more information on coaching, see chapter 5.)	*Pro:* Individual attention for employee; uses coach's experiences. *Con:* Takes a lot of coach's time; success depends on the coaching skills.
Informal learning	Employees learn how to do their jobs from their colleagues and through trial and error. This is unstructured development that may or may not result in the proper skills being learned.	*Pro:* Cheap and easy to initiate. *Con:* No guarantee that right things will be learned; great risk that wrong methods will be learned.
Job rotation	An employee is assigned to another job in the organization and one or more methods are used to learn the new job. This results in broadening the employee's understanding of the original job, the organization as a whole, and how all the parts of the organization work together. Job rotation can be a formal system in which the sequence of jobs is planned for all employees, or it can be more impromptu. Job rotation differs from temporary assignment because it involves the intentional changing of jobs on a regular basis until all or most jobs have been learned.	*Pro:* Develops well-rounded employees who know the "big picture." *Con:* Relies on existing employees to train person being rotated; can build resentment in those who train others, but are not selected for rotation.

Exhibit 7.13

(CONTINUED)

Method	Description	Pros and Cons
On-the-job training (OJT)	Traditionally the most prevalent form of employee development, OJT involves learning something new by doing it under the supervision and guidance of an expert. OJT differs from informal learning by being more formal and organized. In OJT, the trainee is assigned to the expert, and the expert is directed to teach the trainee specific things.	*Pro:* Teaches employee how to do the job; quick and easy to set up. *Con:* No guarantee that right methods will be learned; great risk that wrong methods will be learned.
Outside training and education	The employee is sent to college courses, commercial classes, or the company school for formal training and education. Classes can be attended instead of regular work (e.g., a weeklong cooking workshop), or on the employee's own time (e.g., evening classes at a local college).	*Pro:* Usually thorough and effective; covers topics the operation is not equipped to handle. *Con:* Takes time away from the job or personal life; can be expensive.
Self-study	The employee studies one or more forms of individualized materials on the topics to be learned. Materials can take many forms, from print workbooks to e-learning.	*Pro:* Usually thorough and effective; covers topics an organization is not equipped to handle; relatively cheap. *Con:* The student must be well disciplined.
Special project	The employee is given a special work project that is somewhat outside of his or her skill set, but within reach. For example, a cook might be assigned to develop a new menu from concept through printing. Additional self-study and research are usually necessary to successfully complete the project. Other employees are also available to help or advise the employee.	*Pro:* Broadens skills well; produces usable results. *Con:* Relies on individual research and other employees.
Temporary assignment	The employee is temporarily assigned to another job with the purpose of learning that job. For example, a pastry chef might be assigned to work in the salad department. Temporary assignment differs from job rotation in that it is typically a one-time situation, not an overall plan to rotate through a series of jobs.	*Pro:* Develops new skill set; easy to set up. *Con:* Relies on other employees to train the temporary employee.

RESTAURANT TECHNOLOGY

Electronic technology has dramatically increased opportunities to participate in a wide variety of professional development activities. Programs offered by educational organizations, professional associations, and businesses may be excellent alternatives for many managers and other staff. Online programs can be pursued at whatever time is convenient and in any place that has Internet access. Some operations have one or more dedicated computers at the work site.

These programs are often very affordable. Some establishments may reimburse total or partial costs to employees who successfully complete each program. In some programs, especially company-sponsored programs, feedback from tests, projects, or other activities is provided to trainees and managers.

Most of these programs offer general topics such as leadership, financial management, safety, and marketing. Relatively few are useful for specific skills such as taking inventory.

Vendors of POS systems, food-production equipment, and dishwashing chemicals also have materials useful for group or individual study.

Managers familiar with the methods in this chapter should have many ideas for activities to help attain their employees' and their own professional development goals. Some developmental methods, such as cross-training, delegation, and mentoring, are readily available if the management team approves their use. Only the manager's creativity and the establishment's policies and procedures limit the extent of their use. Other developmental methods, such as external education and training alternatives, have larger budget implications. After determining the availability of these programs, financial concerns will need to be addressed.

One or more developmental methods should be assembled into a program for the employee. The sequence of methods may have to be considered. Methods in which the work depends on prior knowledge or skills must be used after the knowledge or skills have been mastered. For example, a special project in menu planning would depend on the employee knowing about food costing, equipment concerns, and food preparation.

DEVELOPING SUCCESSION PLANS

Succession planning is a process used by many organizations to ensure that employees will be recruited for and prepared to fill key positions when they become vacant. Many managers are not involved in developing succession plans. However, they may become involved in the process if they are among those recruited for "fast-track" positions to learn the knowledge and skills required for higher-level positions. Several important steps should be used to develop succession plans:

Step 1: Review job descriptions to determine which positions to include in the plan.

Upper-level staff, including unit managers and department heads, are among those for whom succession planning is important. Other positions requiring specialized skills, including those in accounting, financial management, and purchasing, are often hard to fill.

Do general managers in single-unit locations develop succession plans for their position? If the operation is family-owned and -operated, long-term plans are often in place. By contrast, when an owner hires a general manager, the owner may be very concerned about finding a replacement for that position on short notice. While networking may be helpful, the time required to acquire all knowledge and skills likely increases with greater responsibilities and specialized expertise. Finding someone for the top position in a single-unit organization is often a challenge, and owners using a promote-from-within strategy must ensure that someone will be available if the position becomes vacant.

Step 2: Write the succession plan.

Several tools will be helpful in developing the plan. These include the organizational chart, job descriptions, and job specifications, which indicate the personal qualities including experience, certification, and knowledge and skills required for the positions in the plan.

For small-volume operations, a succession plan may involve only one person to be prepared for vacancies in higher-level positions. In contrast, organizations planning expansions may need at least several persons for each position in the succession plan.

The time frame for the plan is another concern, and many factors affect it. For example, is there an assistant manager who already performs many of the general manager's responsibilities in the manager's absence? However, if both the manager and assistant manager have been employed for many years, they may retire within a short time of each other. In this situation, a midlevel manager may be considered for the unit manager position, although training and development times will be longer.

Step 3: Develop a training program and select or recruit employees for each position in the succession plan.

Training programs must consider the current knowledge and skill levels of persons who may be promoted in the future. A bookkeeper who might be promoted will already know the organization's accounting system and the policies and procedures required to work within it. In contrast, an employee with some accounting experience in another industry will have to learn how things are done at the organization.

In both cases, job requirements for the position identified in the succession plan must be known. The candidate identified must acquire the knowledge and skills he or she does not already have to become competent in the position quickly when it becomes vacant. All managers in higher-level positions must have a good command of job knowledge–based information and experience in problem solving, decision making, leadership and management, and financial control, among many other skills.

These types of experience, unlike specific activities such as decorating a cake or serving the correct order to each customer, may be obtained at another establishment, perhaps even in a different industry. The best succession plans are those that recognize what a person in the higher-level position must know and be able to do. Then a person who can do many of those tasks can be selected from within or can be hired. Specialized education and training activities can be planned to address areas where additional preparation is required.

Manager's Memo

The volume of business and the number of units in an organization are two primary concerns in succession plans. Managers generally require greater knowledge and skills as volume increases. Also, the number of positions at each level is greater as units increase. Very large organizations use sophisticated formulas to consider factors including expansion plans, positions of existing managers, and attrition rates. The attrition rate is the number of persons who leave. Planning should also consider the impact of positions becoming vacant as employees move up.

Young managers may leave and older managers stay, but the reverse can also occur. Some terminations are voluntary, others are unplanned, and still others can be made unexpectedly by owners or managers. Some managers think there is no way to plan for everything. However, this does not mean that programs cannot be in place to prepare staff for higher-level positions and to recognize when external candidates must be hired.

Step 4: Train the employees, evaluate trainees, and revise training activities as necessary.

Performance appraisals and on-the-job observations of participants should be closely reviewed by the owner and higher-level managers. Many of the professional development methods discussed earlier in this chapter may be useful as knowledge and skills improvement plans are developed. Special projects may be very useful, as may delegation of tasks normally the responsibility of persons at the highest organizational levels. Those who know they may be in line for promotion will likely be motivated to achieve professional development goals assigned with higher-level positions in mind.

Step 5: Evaluate the plan periodically to ensure it is still useful.

Staff changes, revisions in long-range and shorter-range business plans, technology, and changing customer preferences are among the many factors that require an operation to consider changes. As they are made, staffing needs may also change. With these changes comes the need for revisions to recruitment and professional development plans that are included in succession planning programs.

SUMMARY

1. **Explain the importance of professional development.**

   Professional development involves the experience, training, and education provided to employees to help them do their jobs and prepare them for other positions. The same basic activities can be used for employees and managers.

   Knowledge or skill gaps are apparent when staff need improved skills to be more productive, are assigned a new task, or want to qualify for different jobs. The operation should provide professional development. The immediate manager should help employees plan their program. The employee is most responsible for achieving goals.

2. **Describe basic professional development strategies.**

   The first step in professional development is to establish goals, which should focus on the operation's needs first. The budget is an important concern, and specific, measurable goals are required.

   The second step is to identify methods of acquiring the knowledge and skills. Some opportunities are likely available in the operation. External alternatives may include colleges, professional associations, and books, video, and computer-based training. Professional development plans consider goals, time frames, activities, evaluation, and progress checks.

   The final steps are to evaluate, approve, and implement the plan. Progress should be monitored to determine if goals are being achieved and whether corrective actions are necessary. Successful completion should be celebrated and recorded in the employee file. A summary should be made to help plan future activities.

3. **Identify procedures for professional development planning meetings.**

   Professional development planning should be held separate from an employee's performance appraisal. The manager should establish the agenda, meeting location, and time frame, and inform the employee. All information related to developmental needs should be gathered, and an outline will be helpful to organize the information collected.

   The manager can begin by asking about needs, concerns, and interests to determine starting points. Developmental goals, related to learning or improving specified knowledge or skills, should be established. Managers should work closely with the employee to develop a program that best meets the needs of the operation and the employee.

4. **Provide information about professional development programs for managers.**

   Advancement goals for managers may involve long-term planning with numerous activities. Details about advancement plans should be written down, and reasonable completion dates should be mutually agreed on.

   Alternatives include apprenticeship, coaching, informal learning, job rotation, and on-the-job training. Other possibilities include external training, self-study, special projects, and team assignments.

   Continuous improvement can be achieved through certification programs and organization memberships. Managers should network to build relationships that help with career advancement. Networking also keeps managers current with industry trends and can provide contacts for resolving problems.

5. **Explain three commonly used professional development methods.**

   Cross-training allows staff members to learn a related job, often by working closely with an employee in the job. Delegation is working through others to complete a project, and it shares authority and entrusts employees to accomplish assigned tasks. Mentoring is a process in which an experienced employee provides advice to less experienced employees about the job, establishment, and profession.

6. **Identify other professional development methods.**

   Other common development methods include apprenticeships, coaching, informal learning, job rotation, and on-the-job training. Other possibilities include outside training and education, self-study, special projects, and temporary assignments.

7. **Describe basic procedures for developing succession plans.**

   Succession planning can help organizations ensure that employees will be recruited for and prepared to fill key positions when they become vacant. First, job descriptions should be reviewed to determine which positions to include. Then the plan should be developed with help from tools including the organization chart, job descriptions, and job specifications. Training programs should be developed and employees selected. Current employees may be selected for some positions and external contacts may be used to recruit others. Trainees should be evaluated and training activities revised as necessary, and the succession plan should be evaluated periodically.

APPLICATION EXERCISE

Working with a classmate, conduct a developmental goal–setting session to learn about each other's professional development goals. One person should be the manager and the other the employee. The manager should make sure that all elements of goal setting are addressed as the employee provides information including work experience and career interests. The manager and employee can then interact to plan some developmental goals for the employee. Some examples include the following:

1. What does the employee want to learn?

2. What are the employee's career goals beginning with the next desired position?

3. What knowledge and skills are needed for the position, and what methods are available to acquire them?

4. What time frames seem practical?

Take about 10 minutes for the session, and then switch roles and conduct a session for the other person. Share your professional development goals with the class, if time permits.

REVIEW YOUR LEARNING

Select the best answer for each question.

1. **Professional development refers to**
   A. formal group activities such as employee orientation.
   B. training in the foundational tasks of a specific position.
   C. feedback from managers during coaching conversations.
   D. learning or improvement to address knowledge or skill gaps.

2. **Who is responsible for assessing professional development needs and progress?**
   A. The employee
   B. The employee's manager
   C. The establishment's owner
   D. Any establishment stakeholder

3. **Whose needs should be considered when professional development goals are established?**
   A. The immediate manager's
   B. The employee's
   C. The operation's
   D. The customers'

4. **Which item should be included in a professional development plan?**
   A. Performance appraisal results
   B. Employee background
   C. Years of experience
   D. Project time frame

5. **What is the best measurement of the success of a professional development program?**
   A. It maximizes use of one developmental method.
   B. It resolves current operational problems.
   C. It accomplishes the program's goals.
   D. It is the least expensive alternative.

6. **Where is cross-training usually conducted?**
   A. At the employee's work station
   B. At a local school or college
   C. In the manager's office
   D. On the Internet

7. **What is an important tactic when delegation is used for professional development purposes?**

   A. Focus on low-priority tasks.

   B. Move from simple to complex tasks.

   C. Be sure no one else wants to do the task.

   D. Ensure the employee is given total responsibility.

8. **In what stage of a mentoring relationship does the employee begin to ask questions?**

   A. Information exchange conversations

   B. Counseling and coaching

   C. Professional friendship

   D. Sponsoring

9. **Which planning tool is helpful in developing a succession plan?**

   A. Professional development plan

   B. Organizational chart

   C. Operating budget

   D. Mentor plan

10. **A succession plan would typically be developed for which position?**

    A. Manager

    B. General manager

    C. Part-time employee

    D. Entry-level employee

FIELD PROJECT

A. This chapter discusses professional development strategies, and your team's interviews with restaurant and foodservice managers and Internet searches will help you obtain more information about this topic.

Identify several questions your team will ask managers about professional development activities. Examples of questions include:

- What opportunities do entry-level employees have at your operation to advance in their careers?

- How do you determine if an employee is prepared to advance to another position?

- What type of information about professional development is normally discussed during performance reviews?

Note: *Save the questions you have developed. Later in this course, your team will conduct interviews with the managers of restaurant or foodservice operations selected by the team. These interviews will include the questions you have developed in* this chapter, *as well as questions from other chapters. You may want to use the interview form (template) in the Field Project Information Handbook at the end of this book, or develop an interview form of your own to list your interview questions. This form can then be used to record the managers' responses when you conduct your interview.*

B. Your team can also learn more about professional development programs through Internet searches. Use your favorite search engine to develop several suggestions about planning professional development programs using the following or other search terms:

- Cross-training

- Planning your career

- Planning professional development programs

These suggestions can be recorded in Part II (Internet Resources) for Chapter 7 in the Field Project Information Handbook at the end of this book.

8

Ensuring a Lawful Workplace

INSIDE THIS CHAPTER

- Laws Impact the Operation
- Federal Laws
- State and Local Employment Laws
- Providing Safe Food
- Serving Alcoholic Beverages Responsibly
- Protecting the Operation from Legal Actions
- Interacting with Unions

CHAPTER LEARNING OBJECTIVES

After completing this chapter, you should be able to:

- Explain the impact of laws that affect restaurant and foodservice operations.

- Explain the federal employment laws that affect establishments.

- Describe the state and local laws that regulate restaurant and foodservice operations.

- Describe the legal aspects of serving safe food.

- Review the legal aspects of serving alcoholic beverages.

- Identify the procedures that should be followed to protect the operation from legal actions.

- Explain how restaurant and foodservice operations should interact with unions.

KEY TERMS

affirmative action plan (AAP), p. 244

arbitrator, p. 261

bargain in good faith, p. 261

collective bargaining, p. 260

dram shop law, p. 256

Equal Employment Opportunity Commission (EEOC), p. 237

executive order (EO), p. 243

foodborne illness, p. 251

Food Code, p. 251

food safety management system, p. 253

grievance, p. 260

Hazard Analysis Critical Control Point (HACCP), p. 253

health code, p. 251

hostile work environment, p. 240

intoxicated, p. 255

labor contract, p. 260

labor union, p. 260

lawsuit, p. 236

mediator, p. 261

protected class, p. 237

reasonable care defense, p. 257

strike, p. 260

subcontractor, p. 243

third-party administrator (TPA), p. 247

unemployment insurance, p. 248

union dues, p. 260

union steward, p. 260

whistleblower, p. 258

workers' compensation, p. 246

zoning ordinance, p. 249

CASE STUDY

"I'm really glad I joined the local restaurant association and went to the meeting last night," said Authella, the manager of Greenhill Soup & Sandwich Shop.

"Was it interesting?" asked Colleen, the establishment's owner.

"Yes," said Authella. "The speaker was a local attorney who specializes in small businesses, and she presented an overview of federal, state, and local laws that affect all establishments. I didn't even know that some of the laws existed."

Authella continued, "Some large operations have a human resources department with the full-time job of keeping up with all these laws. How are busy managers in small operations supposed to keep up?"

"I don't know," answered Colleen. "But, it's one of the reasons I hired you. This operation is your responsibility."

1. How can Authella find out about laws that apply to her operation?

2. What could happen if a manager did not follow all regulations related to employing workers legally and serving customers properly?

LAWS IMPACT THE OPERATION

Managers of restaurant or foodservice operations must know the legal and regulatory environment in which they operate so they can ensure their establishment is always in compliance. Managers are not attorneys who understand the details of every law, but they must understand the intent of the laws and how they directly affect the operation. They must also recognize when to obtain additional information or defer issues to specialists such as a human resources staff or legal professionals.

Not knowing or following applicable laws can lead to complaints, fines, and lawsuits. A **lawsuit** is a claim or dispute brought in a court of law for adjudication. Operations, especially large corporate ones, must sometimes manage lawsuits that arise from not understanding or following policies or laws and regulations. Breaking these laws can result in criminal charges for owners, managers, executives, and sometimes even employees.

Since laws and regulations vary and can change regularly from state to state, managers must stay informed. Operations with human resources staff have some assistance, but managers in smaller operations will likely need to develop their own resources.

Laws and regulations impact all areas of an operation, and understanding them is an important aspect of a manager's job. For example, antidiscrimination laws can impact many aspects of daily operations including job descriptions, recruiting, screening, hiring, employee development, training, and promotions. Most company policies enforce these laws and contain zero tolerance statements. Such a statement means a policy has no exceptions.

There are many management concerns directly addressed by laws and regulations:

- Sanitation and alcoholic beverage service laws require, respectively, safe sanitation and foodhandling practices and the responsible service of alcohol.
- Scheduling and work assignments are affected by federal, state, and local laws that restrict work assignments and hours for minors. State and local laws define the meal and rest times required for various schedules.
- Federal and sometimes state laws mandate safety standards for restaurant and foodservice operations.
- Union relations are affected by federal laws that restrict how employers and unions can attempt to influence an employee's decision about joining a union.
- Wages and payroll are impacted by federal laws that establish minimum hourly wages for certain employees and when overtime wages must be paid. Also, antidiscrimination laws make it illegal to pay employees different amounts for essentially the same work based on certain characteristics.

- Federal and state laws require employee benefits in some situations and define how many types of benefit programs must be administered.

Basic information about federal, state, and local laws is provided in this chapter. Details about how the laws impact compensation and managing a safe and healthy workplace will be reviewed in chapters 9 and 10.

FEDERAL LAWS

Numerous federal laws and regulations govern what can and cannot happen in the workplace. The **Equal Employment Opportunity Commission (EEOC)** is the federal agency that enforces employment discrimination laws related to age, sex, race, national origin, disability, creed, and religion. There may be other federal or state laws that extend additional classes of protection. Discrimination is the unjust or prejudicial treatment of persons based on **protected classes**. A protected class is a group that lawmakers specifically protect from discrimination. It is also illegal to discriminate against a person because he or she complains about or files a charge of discrimination or participates in a discrimination investigation or lawsuit.

Laws Enforced by the EEOC

Several laws administered by the EEOC impact restaurant and foodservice operations:

- Title VII of the Civil Rights Act of 1964 makes it illegal to discriminate against someone on the basis of race, color, religion, national origin, or sex. The law also requires that employers reasonably accommodate applicants' and employees' sincerely held religious practices unless doing so would impose an undue hardship on the business.

- The Genetic Information Nondiscrimination Act (GINA) of 2008 protects Americans against discrimination based on their genetic information when it comes to health insurance and employment.

- The Pregnancy Discrimination Act amended Title VII to make it illegal to discriminate against a woman because of pregnancy, childbirth, or a medical condition related to pregnancy or childbirth (see *Exhibit 8.1*).

Exhibit 8.1

SOME REQUIREMENTS OF THE PREGNANCY DISCRIMINATION ACT

According to the Equal Employment Opportunity Commission (EEOC), this law in practice means that managers:

- Cannot "refuse to hire a woman because of a pregnancy-related condition as long as she is able to perform the major functions of her job."
- Cannot "single out pregnancy-related conditions for special procedures to determine an employee's ability to work."
- Cannot require an employee who is pregnant to go on leave or remain on leave until the baby's birth.
- Cannot prohibit an employee from returning to work for a predetermined length of time after childbirth.
- Must treat an employee who is temporarily unable to perform her job due to pregnancy the same as any other temporarily disabled employee. (At this point, the pregnant employee may also be eligible for time off under the Family and Medical Leave Act.)
- Must allow pregnant employees to work as long as they are able to do their jobs.

- The Equal Pay Act of 1963 makes it illegal to pay different wages to men and women if they perform equal work in the same workplace. The jobs need not be identical, but they must be substantially equal, and this is determined by job content. All forms of pay are covered by this law, including salary, overtime pay, bonuses, stock options, profit sharing and bonus plans, life insurance, and vacation and holiday pay.

- The Age Discrimination in Employment Act (ADEA) of 1967 protects people who are 40 years of age or older from discrimination because of age. Some states have laws that protect younger workers from age discrimination.

- Title I of the Americans with Disabilities Act (ADA) of 1990 makes it illegal to discriminate against a qualified person with a disability. The law requires that employers reasonably accommodate the known physical or mental limitations of an otherwise qualified individual with a disability who is an applicant or employee unless doing so would impose an undue hardship on the operation of the business.

While not administered by the EEOC, the Uniformed Services Employment and Reemployment Rights Act (USERRA) prohibits discrimination against people who serve or have served in the Armed Forces Reserve, National Guard, or other uniformed services. This act is administered by the Department of Labor and protects the right of veterans to return to their civilian jobs after being away for military service or training. Additionally, the Immigration Reform and Control Act (IRCA) of 1986 makes it illegal for an employer to discriminate with respect to hiring, firing, or recruitment or referral for a fee, based on an individual's citizenship or immigration status. The law prohibits employers from hiring only U.S. citizens or lawful permanent residents unless required to do so by law, regulation, or government contract. Numerous government agencies and offices enforce this law.

Managers should understand that discrimination is not allowed at any stage of the employment cycle:

- **Job advertisements:** Employers may not use an advertisement that discourages someone in a protected class from applying for a job.

- **Recruitment:** It is illegal for an employer to recruit new employees in a way that discriminates against some applicants. An employer may not refuse to give applications to people of a certain race.

- **Pre-employment inquiries:** As a general rule, information obtained and requested through the pre-employment process should be limited to that essential for determining whether a person is qualified for the job. Employers are explicitly prohibited from making pre-employment inquiries about disabilities. Inquiries about organizations, clubs, societies, and lodges of which an applicant may be a member should generally be avoided. Employers should not ask for a photograph of an applicant.

- **Application and hiring:** It is illegal for an employer to discriminate against an applicant in a protected class. Any required tests must be necessary and related to the job.

- **Terms and conditions of employment:** An employer may not discriminate when hiring, firing, promoting, or making compensation decisions. It is also illegal to discriminate when granting breaks, approving leaves, assigning work tasks, or setting any other term or condition of employment.

Similarly, discrimination against protected classes is not allowed after an applicant has been selected:

- **Job assignments and promotions:** Employers cannot make decisions about job assignments and promotions based on protected class. For example, an employer may not give preference to employees of a certain race when making shift assignments.

- **Pay and benefits:** An employer may not discriminate based on protected class in the payment of wages or employee benefits such as sick and vacation leave, insurance, overtime access and pay, and retirement programs.

- **Discipline and discharge:** If two employees commit a similar offense, an employer may not discipline them differently because of protected class.

- **Reasonable accommodation and disability:** The law requires an employer to provide reasonable accommodation to an employee or applicant with a disability unless doing so would cause significant difficulty or expense. A reasonable accommodation is any change in the workplace or in the ways things are usually done to help a person with a disability apply for a job, perform its duties, or enjoy the benefits and privileges of employment.

- **Training and apprenticeship programs:** An employer may not deny training opportunities to certain employees because of race.

- **Employment references:** An employer cannot give a negative or false employment reference or refuse to give a reference based on protected class.

Harassment and the EEOC

Harassment is unwelcome conduct that is based on race, color, religion, sex (including pregnancy), national origin, age (40 or older), disability, or genetic information. It violates the nondiscrimination laws that were mentioned earlier in this chapter.

THINK ABOUT IT . . .

Have you ever worked at an operation that provided reasonable accommodation for one or more employees? What were the reasonable accommodations?

Exhibit 8.2

The most common type of harassment is sexual harassment (*Exhibit 8.2*). Sexual harassment is defined as unwelcome conduct that is sexual in nature, or is a sexual advance, or request for sexual favors. The conduct can also be offensive remarks about a person's sex. To rise to the level of harassment, the conduct must:

- Be unwelcome
- Be frequent, severe, or pervasive
- Interfere with or create a hostile or offensive work environment or result in an adverse employment decision

Sexual harassment has been illegal since 1965. Millions of dollars in court settlements have since been awarded to male and female employees from companies whose managers were accused of sexual misconduct or mistreatment. Settlements have also covered work environments defined as hostile. For a workplace to be classified as a **hostile work environment**, the behaviors in question must be frequent, severe, and pervasive. Situations that have been ruled to constitute a hostile environment include the following:

- Posting sexually suggestive pictures in employee work areas
- Consistently telling sexual jokes or stories that all employees in the area can hear
- Tolerating employees who make sexually suggestive remarks within earshot of coworkers
- Allowing peer employees, customers, suppliers, or any other person to persist in unwanted attention, such as asking for dates
- Allowing the use of derogatory terms with a sexual connotation to describe coworkers
- Allowing frequent physical contact even when it is not sexual

The nonharassment rules apply to other protected categories also. For example, verbal comments or physical conduct related to a person's race, color, sexual orientation, or medical condition constitute harassment when they unreasonably interfere with the person's work performance or create an unhealthy work environment.

Other Federal Employment Laws

Several other federal laws impact establishments. They are administered by the United States Department of Labor.

FAIR LABOR STANDARDS ACT

The Fair Labor Standards Act (FLSA) establishes minimum wage, overtime pay, record-keeping, and child labor standards. Its regulations affect full-time and part-time workers in the private sector, including restaurant and foodservice operations.

For example, according to the FLSA, 14- and 15-year-olds may work the following schedules:

- Non–school hours
- Three hours on a school day
- Eighteen hours in a school week
- Eight hours on a non–school day
- Forty hours in a non–school week
- Between 7 a.m. and 7 p.m., except from June 1 through Labor Day, when nighttime work hours are extended to 9 p.m.

The FLSA has major implications for establishments that hire minors. Some state laws also regulate the work of minors, and managers must follow the law that has the highest minimum standard. More information about younger workers is found in chapter 10.

The Wage and Hour Division (WHD) of the U.S. Department of Labor (DOL) administers and enforces the FLSA. The FLSA sets basic minimum wage, as well as overtime pay standards for work in excess of 40 hours in a workweek. The FLSA regulates the employment of minors. It also sets compensation requirements for meal and rest periods when offered by employers. There are a number of employment practices that the FLSA does not regulate and leaves to the agreement of employer and employee:

- Vacation, holiday, severance, or sick pay
- Premium pay for weekend or holiday work
- Pay raises or employee benefits
- Discharge notice, reason for discharge, or immediate payment of final wages to terminated employees

However, where the federal regulations may be silent on these topics, many states have regulations that must be complied with. It is prudent to research your individual state requirements.

The FLSA does not provide wage payment or collection procedures for an employee's usual or promised wages or commissions in excess of those required by the FLSA. But some states do have laws under which such claims (sometimes including benefits) may be filed.

OCCUPATIONAL SAFETY AND HEALTH ACT

The Occupational Safety and Health Act of 1970 created the Occupational Safety and Health Administration (OSHA). Its mission is to help businesses protect their workers by reducing deaths, injuries, and illnesses in the workplace. This, in turn, reduces workers' compensation insurance costs and medical expenses, decreases costs of return-to-work programs, and lowers accommodation costs for injured workers.

OSHA uses several strategies to help reduce on-the-job injuries, illnesses, and deaths:

- It ensures OSHA regulations are followed.

- It provides safety-training resources and activities for employers and employees.

- It encourages partnerships and alliances through voluntary programs. For example, OSHA's Strategic Partnership Program (OSPP) provides the opportunity for OSHA to partner with employers, workers, professional or trade associations, labor organizations, or other interested stakeholders. Its Voluntary Protection Program (VPP) recognizes employers and workers in the private industry who have implemented effective safety and health management systems and maintain injury and illness rates below national Bureau of Labor Statistics averages for their respective industries.

OSHA promotes workplace safety and health in several ways that include implementing new or improved safety systems, undertaking workplace inspections, and establishing specific rights and responsibilities of employees and employers. It also establishes record-keeping and reporting requirements for employers and collaborates with states that operate their own occupational safety and health programs.

FAMILY AND MEDICAL LEAVE ACT

The Family and Medical Leave Act (FMLA) entitles eligible employees of covered employers to take unpaid, job-protected leave for specified family and medical reasons. During this time, group health insurance coverage is continued under the same terms and conditions as if the employee had not taken leave.

Eligible employees are entitled to 12 workweeks of leave in a 12-month period for the following reasons:

- Birth of a child and to care for the newborn child within one year of birth

- Placement with the employee of a child for adoption or foster care and to care for the newly placed child within one year of placement

- To care for the employee's spouse, child, or parent who has a serious health condition

- A serious health condition that makes the employee unable to perform the essential functions of his or her job

The leave can be taken as needed or on a reduced schedule when medically necessary. Employees must make reasonable efforts to schedule leaves so they do not disrupt operations. They must also provide 30 days' advance notice of leave when possible.

Manager's Memo

The FMLA applies to any employer who has 50 or more employees each working day during at least 20 calendar weeks in the current or last calendar year. To be eligible for FMLA leave, an employee must meet all of these standards:

- Be employed by a covered employer and work at a worksite within 75 miles of where that employer employs at least 50 people

- Have worked at least 12 months (they do not need to be consecutive) for the employer

- Have worked at least 1,250 hours during the 12 months immediately before the date leave begins

Covered employers must inform employees requesting leave whether they are eligible, and the notice must inform employees about their rights and responsibilities. If employees are not eligible, the employer must indicate the reason. In addition, many states also have similar state family leave laws that may offer additional leave rights to employees.

WORKER ADJUSTMENT AND RETRAINING NOTIFICATION ACT

The Worker Adjustment and Retraining Notification Act (WARN) offers protection to workers, their families, and communities by requiring employers to provide notice 60 days in advance of covered plant closings and covered mass layoffs. In general, private, for-profit employers are covered by WARN if they have 100 or more employees, not counting employees who have worked less than 6 months in the last 12 months or employees who work an average of less than 20 hours a week. Employees entitled to notice under WARN include hourly and salaried workers as well as managerial and supervisory employees.

EMPLOYEE POLYGRAPH PROTECTION ACT

The Employee Polygraph Protection Act (EPPA) of 1988 prevents employers from using lie detector tests, either for pre-employment screening or during the course of employment, with certain exemptions. Employers generally may not require or request any employee or applicant to take a lie detector test or discharge, discipline, or discriminate against an employee or applicant for refusing a test or exercising other rights under the act. In addition, employers are required to display the EPPA poster in the workplace.

Other Federal Requirements

Some operations may be governed by special EEO requirements:

- Organizations that contract with the federal government.
- Organizations that provide services or supplies as subcontractors to a business that contracts with the government. A **subcontractor** is a business or person who does work for a company (the contractor) as part of a larger project.
- Organizations that accept federal grants or funds, such as schools and hospitals.

For example, operations that supply government facilities such as airports, and establishments that operate within those facilities, may have to follow additional requirements. They are specified in federal statutes and by executive orders that apply to certain businesses.

Executive orders (EOs) are proclamations issued by the president of the United States, with implementing regulations issued by federal agencies such as the U.S. Department of Labor. EOs and other federal statutes may direct covered employers to take steps to eliminate existing discrimination, remedy the effects of past discrimination, and prevent future discrimination.

EEO-1 REPORT

Specific government reports must be completed for operations covered by special EEO requirements. In general, employers subject to Title VII of the Civil Rights Act of 1964, as amended, with 100 or more employees must complete an annual EEO-1 report that provides information about the race, sex, and job category of their employees. The report must also be filed by some companies with fewer employees and by nonexempt federal contractors with 50 or more employees who have contracts of $50,000 or more.

The EEOC prefers that employers complete the survey online using its secure Web-based form. There are different requirements for employers doing business at only one location and for those doing business at more than one location.

AFFIRMATIVE ACTION PLAN

An **affirmative action plan (AAP)** establishes guidelines for recruiting, hiring, and promoting women, qualified minorities, persons with disabilities, and covered veterans to eliminate the present effects of past employment discrimination. An employer must analyze current employment practices and the makeup of its workforce for any indications that women and minorities are excluded or disadvantaged. If problems are identified, new or different policies and practices must be developed to address them. Last, goals must be developed to measure progress in correcting the problems.

In general, employers that have 50 or more employees and that have contracts with the federal government or federal contracts of at least $50,000 must prepare and maintain an AAP. A plan must be developed within 120 days from the commencement of a contract. The program must be updated annually.

An AAP is designed to ensure equal employment opportunity and is intended to yield a workforce that reflects the gender, racial, and ethnic profile of the local labor market. It includes a written document that provides required information, management training, recruitment outreach, employee tracking, and other activities.

VETS-100 FORM

The Federal Contractor Program requires that any contractor receiving a contract from the federal government of $25,000 or more, or any subcontractor receiving a contract of $25,000 or more from a covered contractor, must file an annual VETS-100 Report. This report indicates the number of special disabled, Vietnam-era, and other protected veterans employed and the number hired during the reporting period. In addition, employers report the total number of employees and the total number of new hires.

COMPLETION OF REQUIRED GOVERNMENT FORMS

Covered employers must complete government-required forms for these programs and others and must maintain all applicable information to do so. For example, all solicited and unsolicited job applications must be kept for 12 months for an affirmative action plan (*Exhibit 8.3*). Local municipalities or states may have their own document retention policies. Knowledge of the records to be obtained is very important. Some owners and managers study requirements to determine this information. Others hire a specialized company to set up their programs or maintain them. A document destruction policy is also helpful. For example, the policy might be to destroy unneeded applications after 12 months.

Exhibit 8.3

Access to census data is required for affirmative action plans, and material related to internal employment referral plans may also be needed. Most federally required forms are related to workforce planning. For example, documentation of reasonable accommodations under the ADA may be needed.

A second step in completing forms involves determining which forms must be completed and deadlines for their completion. For example, an organization with 100 or more employees must complete forms including an EEO-1 report including a consolidated plan and one for each location, an affirmative action plan, and a VETS-100 form. Workers' compensation and unemployment insurance forms must be completed as needed.

The third step in the document management process is to complete the required forms. If outside assistance has been contracted, that organization will do this. If the establishment has an automated human resources information system, this process may be done automatically. If not, the manager or human resources professional must complete the form manually.

After completion of required forms, a review and audit should be undertaken prior to submitting them. Most organizations submit these forms electronically.

STATE AND LOCAL EMPLOYMENT LAWS

Employment within states and local communities may be regulated by federal, state, and local laws. Managers must be familiar with the laws that apply to their locations.

Some issues, such as mandatory union membership and minimum wages, are regulated by different federal and state laws. If so, the law most favorable to employees must be followed. Other issues, which may include overtime, are addressed only by federal law or state law but not both.

Most state and some local EEO laws prohibit discrimination in the workplace. These laws are often broader and more extensive than federal laws. For example, some state and local laws prohibit workplace discrimination based on sexual preference, marital status, parental status, and appearance. In addition, these laws often provide greater penalties and offer different administrative procedures for settling or resolving claims.

In a sense, equal opportunity laws define the floor of unacceptable discriminatory behavior in employment practices. Managers, however, want to promote positive behaviors and nurture an environment that recognizes differences and treats everyone appropriately at all times.

Workers' Compensation

Workers' compensation is a system that states use to compensate employees when they are injured at work. Each state has its own laws. Fault and negligence, or failure to use reasonable care, by the employer are not considered for an employee to receive benefits. Instead, regardless of who caused the injury, the workers' compensation system generally compensates the employee for medical costs, lost wages, and other losses. The injury or illness must have occurred in the course of employment for the system to provide benefits.

Punitive damages, which is compensation designed to punish a defendant and deter bad conduct, are not available to an employee for injuries covered by workers' compensation. Also, the legal defenses normally available to a defendant in a civil action are not available to the employer in workers' compensation. This means, among other things, that the employer cannot claim the operation should not have to pay because the employee caused his or her own injury.

Workers' compensation coverage is typically required by states for every employee. However, state law may allow specific exemptions for some businesses with very few employees and for some types of employees. Few restaurant and foodservice operations are exempt from these laws.

Managers should investigate the causes of workers' compensation claims. They can do so by developing an accident investigation process. In the event of an accident that injures an employee, the process should begin with providing appropriate medical attention, and then completing an injury and illness incident report. An example has been developed by OSHA called OSHA's Form 301 (see *Exhibit 8.4*).

It is important to determine in advance who will provide medical care and at what site. Also, details about the accident investigation process should have been developed through an applicable policy and set of procedures. For example, a "slip and fall" investigation will be different from an "equipment" investigation. Procedures for these and other situations should be considered before accident investigation procedures are developed.

KEEPING IT SAFE

Managers have the responsibility to maintain a safe working environment by providing employee training about potential safety hazards. They also conduct formal and informal ongoing inspections of the facility and equipment.

Workers' compensation laws and those issued by OSHA provide additional reasons for a manager's consistent emphasis on safety. An establishment's payments into the state-administered workers' compensation fund increase as employees make claims. Also, significant management time and attorney expenses can be required to prepare for and attend hearings. Managers know that there are no good reasons to neglect safety and many good reasons why this concern should be emphasized consistently.

Exhibit 8.4

INJURY AND ILLNESS INCIDENT REPORT

OSHA's Form 301
Injury and Illness Incident Report

Attention: This form contains information relating to employee health and must be used in a manner that protects the confidentiality of employees to the extent possible while the information is being used for occupational safety and health purposes.

U.S. Department of Labor
Occupational Safety and Health Administration

Form approved OMB no. 1218-0176

This *Injury and Illness Incident Report* is one of the first forms you must fill out when a recordable work-related injury or illness has occurred. Together with the *Log of Work-Related Injuries and Illnesses* and the accompanying *Summary*, these forms help the employer and OSHA develop a picture of the extent and severity of work-related incidents.

Within 7 calendar days after you receive information that a recordable work-related injury or illness has occurred, you must fill out this form or an equivalent. Some state workers' compensation, insurance, or other reports may be acceptable substitutes. To be considered an equivalent form, any substitute must contain all the information asked for on this form.

According to Public Law 91-596 and 29 CFR 1904, OSHA's recordkeeping rule, you must keep this form on file for 5 years following the year to which it pertains.

If you need additional copies of this form, you may photocopy and use as many as you need.

Completed by _____

Title _____

Phone (___) ___ - ___ Date ___ / ___ / ___

Information about the employee

1) Full name _____

2) Street _____
   City _____ State ____ ZIP _____

3) Date of birth ___ / ___ / ___
4) Date hired ___ / ___ / ___
5) ☐ Male
   ☐ Female

Information about the physician or other health care professional

6) Name of physician or other health care professional _____

7) If treatment was given away from the worksite, where was it given?
   Facility _____
   Street _____
   City _____ State ____ ZIP _____

8) Was employee treated in an emergency room?
   ☐ Yes
   ☐ No

9) Was employee hospitalized overnight as an in-patient?
   ☐ Yes
   ☐ No

Information about the case

10) Case number from the Log _____ *(Transfer the case number from the Log after you record the case.)*

11) Date of injury or illness ___ / ___ / ___

12) Time employee began work _____ AM / PM

13) Time of event _____ AM / PM ☐ Check if time cannot be determined

14) **What was the employee doing just before the incident occurred?** Describe the activity, as well as the tools, equipment, or material the employee was using. Be specific. *Examples:* "climbing a ladder while carrying roofing materials"; "spraying chlorine from hand sprayer"; "daily computer key-entry."

15) **What happened?** Tell us how the injury occurred. *Examples:* "When ladder slipped on wet floor, worker fell 20 feet"; "Worker was sprayed with chlorine when gasket broke during replacement"; "Worker developed soreness in wrist over time."

16) **What was the injury or illness?** Tell us the part of the body that was affected and how it was affected; be more specific than "hurt," "pain," or sore." *Examples:* "strained back"; "chemical burn, hand"; "carpal tunnel syndrome."

17) **What object or substance directly harmed the employee?** *Examples:* "concrete floor"; "chlorine"; "radial arm saw." *If this question does not apply to the incident, leave it blank.*

18) **If the employee died, when did death occur?** Date of death ___ / ___ / ___

Public reporting burden for this collection of information is estimated to average 22 minutes per response, including time for reviewing instructions, searching existing data sources, gathering and maintaining the data needed, and completing and reviewing the collection of information. Persons are not required to respond to the collection of information unless it displays a current valid OMB control number. If you have any comments about this estimate or any other aspects of this data collection, including suggestions for reducing this burden, contact: US Department of Labor, OSHA Office of Statistical Analysis, Room N-3644, 200 Constitution Avenue, NW, Washington, DC 20210. Do not send the completed forms to this office.

The first report of injury form should be completed in cooperation with the **third-party administrator (TPA)**. The TPA is the insurance claims adjuster or an organization that manages insurance claims for a self-insured organization. Ongoing communication must be maintained with the TPA throughout the process. This is especially important if there are any changes of status, such as physical condition or resignation of the employee. If applicable, post-accident drug testing may be done if policy and state law permit.

The cause of the accident should be determined. Was there an unsafe condition? An unsafe action? A combination of both? (See *Exhibit 8.5*.) Managers should photograph the accident location and document all details. For example, was there a sharp object, or was the floor wet? The manager should take notes and review historical information about the employee or accident site to determine whether a pattern can be established.

The manager should create a file that contains all information, notes, and documentation relating to the accident and the claim, including medical data and employee work release. A separate workers' compensation file should be established for each claim and maintained in a secure location.

Exhibit 8.5

Many accidents that involve workers' compensation occur because of an unsafe condition and an unsafe action.

The manager should collect names of all witnesses to the accident and interview them. The manager, working with others in the department in which the accident occurred, should develop a corrective action plan to prevent a reoccurrence. Current standard operating procedures (SOPs) and all documentation collected during the accident investigation will be helpful in determining the corrective action. It will also be helpful to review historical information such as OSHA-300 logs.

For example, more-than-occasional slips and falls after cleaning require revised procedures to limit access to these areas after they are cleaned. Likewise, cuts from knives or equipment may signal the need for additional safety training.

It is also important to review the accuracy of the workers' compensation claim. Documentation collected during the investigation will be helpful. Every detail should be checked for accuracy and any inconsistencies, and the information in the claim should be consistent with medical reports.

If the claim is accepted, determine whether it is a lost time situation or a modified duty situation. Lost time occurs when the employee is not able to work after the accident. Modified duty means the employee may still work but cannot perform some required tasks. Managers should follow directions of the TPA and keep in contact with the employee.

In a lost time situation, knowledge of the employee's pay history is necessary to determine temporary total disability because compensation paid is usually a percentage of weekly wages until the worker returns to the job. For a modified duty situation, knowledge of work restrictions is necessary, and a return to work authorization from a physician will be required. The goal should be to work toward a full duty release based on medical advice. The TPA should be made aware of the employee's revised duties. The employee's current responsibilities will be known by a review of the job description. Knowledge of the employee's current capabilities to perform duties will be based on medical and other applicable advice. In each case, the return to work program should be tailored to meet the needs of the individual employee. In all workers' compensation cases, the employee's contact information will be needed.

If notice is received that the employee is litigating, or taking the claim to court, this information should be reported to the TPA. The next step will be for the manager to participate in a hearing. This topic is addressed later in this chapter.

Unemployment Insurance

The federal–state **unemployment insurance** program provides benefits to workers who are unemployed through no fault of their own as determined by state law. Eligibility requirements and other requirements vary from state to state.

The amount of compensation received depends on the amount an employee earned while working during an established period of time referred to as a base period. In addition, there are eligibility requirements to qualify, including the need to work a certain number of weeks. If an employee is determined to be ineligible for benefits, there is an appeals process available.

Unemployment insurance payments are intended to provide temporary financial assistance to unemployed workers who meet requirements. Each state administers a separate program within guidelines established by federal law. In almost all states, benefit funding is based on a tax imposed on employers.

Those receiving unemployment insurance benefits must file weekly or biweekly claims and respond to questions about continued eligibility. They must also report any earnings from work during the week(s) and any job offers or refusals of work.

State employment service offices have current labor market information and provide a number of reemployment services free of charge. Employment service staff attempt to refer those receiving payments to job openings and/or training programs.

Benefits can be paid for a maximum of 26 weeks in most states. Additional weeks of benefits may be available during times of high unemployment, and some states provide additional benefits for specific purposes. Benefits are subject to federal income taxes and must be reported on the employee's federal income tax return.

Local Licenses and Permits

Managers must ensure that they apply for all required local licenses and permits on a timely basis. An important first step is to determine if there are any factors that may prevent the operator from receiving them. Examples of factors that may prevent successful application for liquor licenses and live entertainment licenses include felony convictions and misdemeanor narcotic convictions. Prior revocation of licenses may prevent some companies from receiving licenses and permits.

The concept of the operation will be an important concern as applications are made. For example, is the operation a bar that also serves food, or is it a restaurant? Will there be live entertainment? After the concept is determined, owners and managers must learn whether local community zoning ordinances and liquor licenses will allow their type of business in that location. A **zoning ordinance** is a legal declaration of land use policies for a city, district, or county that indicates for what purposes specific land areas can be used.

THINK ABOUT IT . . .

Have you ever received unemployment insurance benefits? What steps did you have to take to receive the benefits?

The next step is to determine the required licenses. Building or renovation permits; food safety certifications; certificates of occupancy; alcoholic beverage permits; cabaret or live performance licenses; and business, insurance, and other licenses may be needed. A review of license requirements ensures that the establishment's physical facility, business plan, and intended use meet all conditions. If they do not, adjustments in plans will be necessary.

It is also important to ensure that the timeline takes into account lead times. Some permits, such as liquor licenses and sometimes building permits, may have minimum required waiting times.

The licenses and permits may be issued by a number of separate state and local entities. The owner or manager must ensure that all required licenses are obtained. It may be appropriate to hire a lawyer or other third party familiar with local laws to help determine the licenses and other documents required. Other sources of information include the local chamber of commerce, specific issuing agencies, or state or municipal licensing centers.

Managers should file or submit applications for all required licenses and permits. Some certifications, such as food safety, may require training or testing. In some areas, it may be possible to purchase an existing license and transfer it to a new operation. However, an application may still be required. Some licenses and permits will require an inspection of the facility or business plan. Filing an application may result in additional inspection or review by other government entities, such as the local fire department.

If an application is denied, the owner or manager may be able to file an appeal. Additional steps may include making adjustments to the business plan, making corrections to the physical facility, or addressing community concerns, such as hours of operation, noise, and traffic patterns.

After receiving all necessary permits and applications, managers will need to take any actions required by "conditional approval." This means that a license will be granted if certain conditions are addressed. Actions can include, for example, making changes to the facility to comply with code requirements, adjusting business hours because of noise, or changing parking lot lighting.

Existing certifications can expire, and permits and licenses may require periodic renewal. Managers should develop a calendar that documents all necessary licenses, permits, and insurance policies along with the required renewal or resubmission dates. It is also important to consider how much lead time will be required for processing documents so that the license or permit will not have expired before filing is complete. Managers should periodically review and update the calendar to ensure that it is always current.

PROVIDING SAFE FOOD

A manager has no more important responsibilities than to serve customers safe food and to train employees in safe foodhandling practices. Safe foodhandling helps an operation avoid **foodborne illnesses**, diseases that are carried or transmitted to people by food. Serving safe food also helps comply with **health codes**, which are local laws designed to ensure food safety. As *Exhibit 8.6* shows, there are many reasons to do this. To stay in business, an operation must comply with applicable health or sanitation codes.

Exhibit 8.6

COSTS OF A FOODBORNE ILLNESS VERSUS BENEFITS OF SAFE FOODHANDLING

Costs of a Foodborne Illness	Benefits of Safe Foodhandling
• Loss of customers and sales	• Higher profits
• Negative public relations	• Repeat business
• Loss of prestige and reputation	• Better food quality
• Embarrassment	• Reduced health code violations
• Possibility of lawsuits and related fees	• Reduced chance of lawsuits
• Increased insurance premiums	• Reduced or minimized insurance costs
• Need for employee retraining	• Reduced food waste
• Lowered employee morale	• Increased job satisfaction
• Employee absenteeism	

Food Sanitation Laws

Government control of food is exercised at federal, state, and local levels. At the federal level, agencies directly involved in inspection are the U.S. Department of Agriculture (USDA) and the Food and Drug Administration (FDA). Among other responsibilities, these two agencies regulate organizations that operate in two or more states.

The FDA also writes the **Food Code**, which is the federal government's recommendations for foodservice regulations to prevent foodborne illnesses. Currently, these recommendations are updated every two years to reflect developments in the restaurant and foodservice industry and the field of food safety. Operations that are inspected by the FDA or USDA must follow the Food Code. Other operations must follow their state or local health department regulations.

Many state and local regulations are based on the Food Code, but these governments adopt and interpret the Food Code recommendations differently. Consequently, Food Codes may vary widely between states and, in some cases, from one locality to another.

State and local governments may also differ in the recommended frequencies of inspection. Local health departments should be contacted to determine regulations that apply to specific operations.

Keeping Food Wholesome

Managers must keep food safe and wholesome throughout the operation at all times. The FDA recommends that local and state health departments hold the person in charge of the operation responsible for knowing and demonstrating specific information:

- Rights, responsibilities, and authority the local code assigns to employees, managers, and the local health department.

- Diseases carried or transmitted by food and their symptoms.

- Points in the path food takes through the operation (see *Exhibit 8.7*) where hazards can be prevented, eliminated, or reduced, and how these procedures meet local code requirements.

- Relationship between personal hygiene and the spread of disease, especially relating to cross-contamination, hand contact with ready-to-eat food, and hand washing.

- How to keep injured or ill employees from contaminating food or food-contact surfaces.

- The need to control the length of time that particular food products remain at temperatures in which disease-causing microorganisms can grow. These food products are called Time and Temperature Control for Safety (TCS) food.

- Hazards involved in the consumption of raw or undercooked meat, poultry, eggs, and fish.

The FDA also charges managers with additional responsibilities:

- Using safe cooking temperatures and times for food items such as meat, poultry, eggs, and fish

- Maintaining safe temperatures and times for storing, holding, cooling, and reheating TCS food items

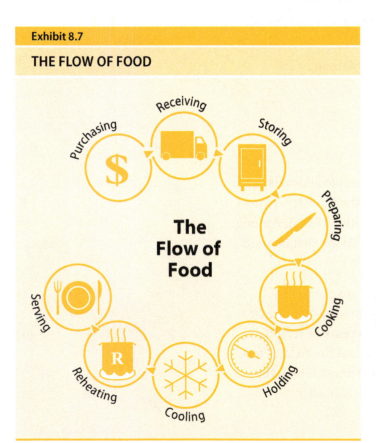

Exhibit 8.7

THE FLOW OF FOOD

The Flow of Food

Purchasing · Receiving · Storing · Preparing · Cooking · Holding · Cooling · Reheating · Serving

- Using the correct procedures for cleaning and sanitizing utensils and food-contact surfaces of equipment

- Controlling the types of toxic materials used in the operation and knowing how to safely store, dispense, use, and dispose of them

- Confirming that equipment is sufficient in number and capacity to handle food safely and is properly designed, constructed, located, installed, operated, maintained, and cleaned

- Using water that is safe to drink or for use as an ingredient in food and knowing the importance of keeping water clean and safe

Managers must know this information, and they need to ensure all their employees can safely handle food. They should also keep a copy of the local or state sanitation regulations and be familiar with them. It is important to compare the code to procedures regularly and adjust the food safety management system as needed. A **food safety management system** is a group of programs and procedures designed to control hazards throughout the flow of food. A strong food safety management system incorporates the principles of active managerial control. This process addresses common risk factors as managers continuously monitor employees to ensure policies and procedures are being followed. It is important for managers to remember, however, that code requirements are only minimum standards for keeping food safe.

Ensuring Food Safety

Serving safe food is vital to an operation's success. The best way to protect the operation and its employees and customers is to develop and maintain a sound food safety management system and ensure all employees follow it.

A **Hazard Analysis Critical Control Point (HACCP)** system focuses on identifying specific points within the flow of food that are essential for preventing, eliminating, or reducing a biological, chemical, or physical hazard to safe levels. To be effective, a HACCP system must be based on a written plan that is specific to an establishment's menu, customers, equipment, processes, and operations. Managers must ensure all policies and procedures are followed (see *Exhibit 8.8*).

Managers should keep a copy of their local or state sanitation regulations and be familiar with them. They should compare the code to procedures regularly and adjust the food safety management system as needed. As noted earlier, remember that code requirements are only minimum standards for keeping food safe.

Exhibit 8.8

Providing Adequate Training

A food safety management system provides a foundation for safe foodhandling, but managers must ensure that everyone follows this system. To do so, managers must ensure that all employees are properly trained in food safety. A food safety training program should consist of components for new and experienced employees and include assessment tools to identify the need for ongoing food safety training. The best programs also have a selection of resources to support training including books, videos, posters, and technology-based materials. Records to document completion of training should be maintained.

Performing Self-Inspections

Managers and their staff should continuously perform self-inspections to ensure that the food safety management system is working and food is safe. Managers in operations with high sanitation and food safety standards consider local health department inspections as a supplement to their own self-inspection program. A good self-inspection program provides many benefits:

- Safer food
- Improved food quality
- A clean environment
- Higher health department inspection scores
- Increased public interest in the establishment

SERVING ALCOHOLIC BEVERAGES RESPONSIBLY

Just as establishments that serve food have legal responsibilities to ensure food safety, so do operations that serve alcohol. Managers must understand the responsibilities that they, their operation, and their employees have in consistently complying with alcoholic beverage laws. They must ensure employees understand the risks that breaking these laws pose to them, the establishment, and the community.

If someone in an operation breaks laws related to the responsible service of alcohol, the manager, the employee, and the operation could face serious consequences ranging from lawsuits to criminal charges, including fines or even imprisonment. In addition, the establishment could lose its liquor license. This, in turn, could lead to a significant loss in revenues that could force the operation to close. When it comes to serving alcohol, all employees must understand and comply with applicable laws.

THINK ABOUT IT . . .

Do you think many people realize the responsibilities of food and beverage employees to protect those in the community? Serving safe food affects the customers, but safely serving beverages can impact others who could become involved in alcohol-related accidents.

Each state's liquor board or liquor authority develops and enforces its own regulations for alcoholic beverage service. In addition, these agencies are responsible for issuing and monitoring liquor licenses, issuing citations for violations, and holding hearings for those who violate the liquor code.

Since the laws pertaining to the sale and service of alcohol vary widely, managers must become familiar with those that apply to the establishment. Here are some common concerns addressed by state and local alcoholic beverage laws:

- **Legal age to drink:** In all 50 states, a person must be 21 years old to purchase alcohol. In some states, it is legal for a parent or legal guardian to purchase alcohol and serve it to a minor child.

- **Legal age to serve:** In general, a person must be 21 years old to serve alcohol. However, this law can vary. For example, some states allow those under 21 to bring alcohol to the table but not to pour it. Others allow underage servers to take the order and payment for the drink but not to serve it. Some states require an underage server to apply to the liquor authority for permission to serve alcoholic beverages. In all cases, persons who are younger than 21 and serve alcohol must be supervised by someone older.

- **Legal age to enter the establishment:** In some areas, the law does not allow minors, or those under the legal age to drink alcohol, to enter a tavern or a restaurant's bar area (see *Exhibit 8.9*).

- **Serving intoxicated guests:** It is illegal to serve a guest who is intoxicated or shows signs of intoxication. A person is **intoxicated** when his or her blood alcohol concentration (BAC) is above the limit specified by the state in which the alcoholic beverage is sold or served.

Exhibit 8.9

- **Serving a pregnant guest:** It is illegal to deny alcohol service to a woman because she is pregnant because doing so would be considered sex discrimination. Many states, however, require establishments to post signs warning of the effects of alcohol on a fetus.

- **Hours and type of service:** Local liquor authorities control the hours for the legal sale and service of alcohol and the type of alcohol that may be sold or served, such as hard liquor or carryouts.

- **Happy hours and other promotions:** Some states, counties, and municipalities regulate or forbid "happy hours" and other drink promotions. These laws may prohibit serving a guest any of the following:

  - Two or more drinks at a time
  - An unlimited number of drinks for a fixed price
  - Reduced-price drinks for a specified period of time
  - Drinks containing additional alcohol without an increase in price
  - Drinks as a prize for a game or contest conducted at the establishment

- **Certification to serve:** Some states, counties, and municipalities require that people who serve alcohol be certified in safe alcohol service practices. These certifications may be earned through local educational institutions and other organizations, such as the ServSafe Alcohol® Certification offered by the National Restaurant Association Educational Foundation.

Another factor that affects alcohol service is **dram shop laws**. These regulations vary from state to state, but they hold the server and the establishment responsible for the actions of those they have served. They are also called third-party liability laws. For example, the drinker (first party) hurts someone (third party) and the seller of alcohol (second party) is held liable for the injuries. The penalties and liabilities for violating these laws differ by state. These laws and the insurance premiums required for serving liquor have led many managers to establish detailed training programs for employees who make cocktails, tend bars, and serve liquor.

Even employees who are not directly involved in the production or service of alcoholic beverage will likely require training. Consider employees at the entrances to some establishments who check customers' identifications. How should this be done to ensure that no underage customers enter the establishment? What about valet auto parkers or receptionists, who are often the last employees to see customers as they leave the establishment? What should they do if they notice a customer who appears to be intoxicated?

Managers must monitor compliance with liquor laws. They should determine the most common operational issues associated with alcoholic beverage service. This information may be obtained from liquor control authorities and the operation's own records. Common violations may include unsanitary bottles, taps, and beer lines; sale of alcohol to minors; and failure to post business tax certificates or health warnings. Other violations may involve record keeping, such as failure to maintain invoices and records to prove that alcohol was not purchased at retail. Advertising practices and promotions including happy hour laws, drink specials and discounts, quantity specials,

Manager's Memo

Restaurant and foodservice managers in the United States must follow dram shop laws, which relate to third-party liability. Assume a customer has several drinks at an operation and then drives away and injures someone crossing the street. Dram shop laws allow the third party (the injured person) to sue the first party (the intoxicated customer) and the second party (the operation that sold or provided the alcoholic beverage).

and advertising discounts are additional common problems noted by liquor authorities. Overcrowding and capacity restrictions in the establishment are also commonplace.

Managers should ensure that they always cooperate with public officials including police and fire departments and liquor inspectors. They should also be "good neighbors" with parking, noise during late hours, and alcoholic beverage service near churches and schools.

The operation's attorney, marketing manager, and representatives of local or state Alcoholic Beverage Control (ABC) Commissions will likely be able to provide information and make suggestions about policies and procedures to help address problems that are identified.

Alcoholic beverage laws may change, sometimes frequently, and it is important that managers remain knowledgeable. Many control agencies send out newsletters highlighting legal updates. Restaurant and other associations may also provide this information to their members. As soon as changes are known, the property's policies, procedures, and training programs should be changed and implemented to reflect current laws. Special training programs can then be planned and implemented. These training sessions provide a great opportunity to ensure that applicable employees have current service certificates as required by local or other laws or regulations.

PROTECTING THE OPERATION FROM LEGAL ACTIONS

Despite the best intentions of operations, some customers file lawsuits to obtain compensation for injuries they believe they have suffered as a result of food they were served. Operations using a food safety management system as discussed earlier can use a **reasonable care defense** against a food-related lawsuit. A reasonable care defense is one that involves proof that an establishment did everything that could be reasonably expected to ensure the food served was safe. The keys to this defense are documented standards, training practices and procedures such as a HACCP plan, and positive inspection results. Since decisions in these suits follow state law, managers should typically hire a qualified attorney.

General Guidelines

Although federal, state, and local laws often differ, many have several elements in common. These can be used to develop general guidelines to protect an operation from liability and ensure the rights of employees:

- Follow policies and practices. Those of most operations are based on applicable laws.

- Keep current on workplace laws. Laws and regulations vary by location, and they change. Always interact with human resources staff or develop personal resources to stay up-to-date.

257

FEDERAL AGENCIES AND ACTS THAT REQUIRE POSTERS

- Equal Employment Opportunity Commission (EEOC)
- Occupational Safety and Health Administration (OSHA)
- Employee Polygraph Protection Act (EPPA)
- Fair Labor Standards Act (FLSA)
- Family and Medical Leave Act (FMLA)
- Uniformed Services Employment and Reemployment Rights Act (USERRA)

- Monitor employees for compliance. Managers are responsible for what their employees do on the job, and they should monitor and coach to ensure that all policies, procedures, and applicable laws are followed consistently.

- Provide an "open door" for employees. Make sure employees know they can discuss issues, and when they do, respond in a timely and professional manner.

- Allow employees to exercise their rights. Many laws contain provisions to ensure that employees are protected when they:

  - Request or exercise their rights under a law.

  - Report a violation or possible violation. These employees are commonly called **whistleblowers**: persons who expose wrongdoing within an organization in the hope of stopping it.

- Post required notices. Several federal and many state laws require that notices be posted in the workplace (see *Exhibit 8.10*). If some employees speak another language, it may be necessary to display posters in that language.

- Keep accurate records. Keep records required by law and documents that may reduce risks of liability. For example, keep new hire paperwork, disciplinary action records, performance reviews, and time cards.

Additional Strategies

The best managers do two additional things to help protect their operation from lawsuits: prepare themselves when it is necessary to participate in legal hearings, and maintain all certifications required by local regulations.

PARTICIPATE IN HEARINGS

Managers may need to participate in hearings on topics involving wages or medical bills for employees. Conflict with medical practitioners, such as when doctors do not agree on the nature or severity of an employee's injury, is another common reason for hearings.

Attorneys generally suggest that the hearing be attended if it is voluntary. Managers should prepare for a hearing by reviewing all applicable documents including adjusters' notes, photographs, and statements of information that will likely be suggested by the attorney. The purpose of this review is to update and refresh the manager's knowledge about the case files and history. When reviewing information, managers should ensure that there are no gaps.

Managers should discuss procedures with counsel when preparing for and reviewing information before the hearing. If preparation has been effective, the manager will have the tools needed to present a clear and compelling argument. When being questioned, it is important to answer every question but additional information should not be volunteered. A manager's task is to provide answers to the questions that are posed, and he or she should always follow the advice of the attorney.

Managers may need to collect additional documentation or records as requested by the attorney. Examples include witness statements, history of vacation and other leave, and payroll documents. These data are intended to give the attorney and manager the information required to explain and defend the company's position.

When attending the hearing, the manager should act professionally. This includes answering all questions clearing and concisely and always following counsel's advice.

MAINTAIN CERTIFICATIONS

Applying for licenses and permits was discussed earlier. Managers must also maintain the certifications required by local regulations. A license and a certificate are not the same thing. A license is the right to do an activity, and a certificate is the evidence of that right.

Managers should ensure they are aware of and maintain all certifications required by local regulations. It is often advisable to retain an individual with specific knowledge of local regulations because they change between jurisdictions. For example, a local attorney can help determine which certificates are required and can identify the appropriate issuing authorities. Examples of certificates include those for health and sanitation, alcohol safety and service, and occupancy and compliance with building codes. Other requirements include warning signage and licenses including for amusement and live music or cabaret. There are many issuing agencies, and a study of county and community Web sites can be used to help determine which are applicable.

Managers should also confirm that all licenses are current. Many have expiration dates and must therefore be renewed. Managers should be aware when certificates should be updated and obtain any that are missing or expired. Some licenses, such as for food service, may require employees to receive training or pass an exam. Managers should confirm that these requirements are met.

Exhibit 8.11

It is important that all certificates be posted according to applicable laws and that records are maintained to meet necessary requirements (*Exhibit 8.11*). Backup documentation should be filed separately from originals.

Managers should document the expiration and review dates for all licenses, and a schedule can be developed for obtaining or renewing them with ample time before expiration. Additional time may be required for ongoing training as well.

INTERACTING WITH UNIONS

Employee labor unions have historically influenced workplace regulations about fair labor practices. Originally created to win basic rights and protections from powerful employers, **labor unions** are organizations designated by employees to negotiate their employment terms such as wages, benefits, discipline, and job security. In 2011, 4.0 percent of employees in food preparation and serving occupations were union members. This membership rate is smaller than the national average of 11.8 percent of employees who belonged to a union.[1]

THINK ABOUT IT...

Employees in states with right-to-work laws cannot be forced to join a union or pay dues. Unions argue that all workers at union shops benefit from contracts negotiated by the union. What do you think?

Role of Unions

In operations with unions, employees may be required to join, depending on the agreement between the union and the employer. Workplaces where employees must join the union are known as union shops. Employees who join unions must pay **union dues**, which are fees to help pay for the administration of the union. Members are entitled to elect their union representatives.

The terms of employment that a union negotiates for its members are written into an employment agreement or **labor contract** with the employer. Labor contracts are written for a specific time period, typically two or more years. When a labor contract is set to expire, union and company representatives often renegotiate the terms of the contract in a process called **collective bargaining**. Once a new contract is written, the union members must vote to approve or reject it. In some establishments, the employment terms negotiated for union members automatically apply to some nonunion members in the same establishment. For example, the wages, benefits, and other terms of a labor contract negotiated for union dish washers and bus staff will also apply to nonunion dish washers and bus staff.

If a contract is rejected, the union may call a **strike**. A strike is an order to all union members at one or more locations to stop working. Strikes also may be called at other times to protest conditions that often begin as grievances.

Grievances are complaints filed against an employer for breaking the terms of the labor contract. They may be filed by an individual and escalated as needed by the union or filed by the union on behalf of all its members. When an individual files a grievance, the complaint is handled through a process defined by the labor contract. Often the first step is for the employee, the employee's manager, and a union representative called a **union steward** to meet and try to resolve the grievance. A union steward is an employee who is elected by his or her coworkers to represent them to their employer. If the

[1] *Bureau of Labor Statistics News Release*, January 27, 2010, *www.bls.gov/news.release/union2.nr0.htm*.

grievance cannot be resolved at this level, the issue is escalated to higher levels of management and union representation.

Unresolved grievances are eventually escalated to a third party called an arbitrator or mediator. An **arbitrator** is an impartial person who hears each party's side of the case, weighs the evidence, applies the law, and makes a decision that is usually binding. A **mediator** is an independent third party who helps those involved in a dispute talk to each other and allows them to resolve the dispute.

Understanding Responsibilities and Limits

Given the problems that can result from grievances, managers in union operations need to fully understand their employees' labor contracts and the laws that control union–employer relations. The terms of a labor contract are usually broad. In day-to-day interactions with union employees, the contract may determine, for example, work schedules, how employees are trained, and how promotions are made. Other impacts may include how job postings are communicated, how managers discipline or terminate employees, and other aspects of the relationship between the manager and employees.

Regardless of procedures to comply with the labor contract, managers will want to build good relationships with their employees, whether they are supervisors, union leaders, or regular employees. Make sure these relationships include open communication because this is especially important with union leaders. The better the relationships managers create with all employees, the more effective they will be.

One of the oldest and most important acts that legislates union and employer interactions is the National Labor Relations Act (NLRA) of 1935. This act, also known the Wagner Act, established the National Labor Relations Board to enforce its provisions:

- The right of employees to join or not join a union
- The right of employees to have their union negotiate a labor contract on their behalf
- The requirement that employers and unions **bargain in good faith**, which is a duty to approach negotiations with a sincere resolve to reach a collective bargaining agreement

To comply with the NLRA, employers cannot prevent employees from joining or forming unions or engaging in a group activity to change working conditions. Employers cannot use threats, coercion, or discriminatory work practices to try to dissuade employees from union activities. They also cannot attempt to influence union operations, such as by bribing union leaders. Finally, as with many employment laws, employers cannot punish or discriminate against employees who exercise their rights or file charges under the law.

The U.S. Congress amended the NLRA with the Labor-Management Relations Act of 1947, also known as the Taft-Hartley Act. This act provides certain rights to employers and employees when dealing with unions and puts limits on union actions. Among its many provisions, the act prohibits unions from requiring job applicants to join the union as a condition of employment, unless the union has this arrangement in their labor contract, and prohibits unions from coercing employees to join the union. The act allows managers to talk to employees about the advantages and disadvantages of union membership, but does not allow managers to threaten or bribe employees to influence their decision to join a union.

SUMMARY

1. **Explain the impact of laws that affect restaurant and foodservice operations.**

   Failure to follow applicable laws can lead to complaints, fines, and lawsuits. Regulations are sometimes amended, so managers must keep current. Laws and regulations impact a wide range of concerns including sanitation and alcoholic beverage service, scheduling and assignments, safety, union relations, wages and payroll, and benefits.

2. **Explain the federal employment laws that affect establishments.**

   The EEOC enforces federal discrimination laws. Title VII of the Civil Rights Act of 1964 makes it illegal to discriminate against someone on the basis of race, color, religion, creed, national origin, or sex. Other laws relate to pregnancy and age discrimination, equal pay, employees with disabilities, and citizenship or immigration status. Harassment is unwelcome conduct based on a protected class factor.

   The U.S. Department of Labor administers some federal employment laws. The FLSA establishes minimum wage, overtime pay, record-keeping, and child labor standards. The OSHA helps businesses reduce workplace deaths, injuries, and illnesses. The FMLA provides leave for specified family and medical reasons. The WARN requires notice 60 days in advance of certain plant closings and mass layoffs. Other laws protect persons who have served in military services and prevent employers from using lie detector tests, with certain exemptions.

   Operations that contract with the federal government or serve as subcontractors must complete an EEO-1 report relating to discrimination; an affirmative action plan that establishes guidelines for recruiting, hiring, and promoting women and minorities; and a VETS-100 form applicable to special disabled, Vietnam-era, and other protected veterans employed.

3. **Describe the state and local laws that regulate restaurant and foodservice operations.**

   State and local laws may address some of the same topics as federal laws. The law applies that provides the most benefit to employees. States administer workers' compensation laws and unemployment insurance programs. Managers should use an accident investigation process to determine causes of workers' compensation claims. A third-party administrator such as an insurance claims adjuster may assist in completing a report of injury form. The cause of the accident should be determined, and the manager should keep a file of all information relating to the accident.

   Operations must typically maintain a wide variety of local licenses and permits for building, renovation, food safety, occupancy, alcoholic beverage service, cabaret or live performance, and numerous others. Managers must apply for all required local licenses and permits on a timely basis. The operation's concept is an important concern as applications are made. The required licenses must be determined and processing lead times must be considered. If an application is denied, the manager may be able to file an appeal. Any actions related to conditional approval must be addressed.

4. **Describe the legal aspects of serving safe food.**

   Safe foodhandling helps an operation avoid foodborne illnesses. Local health codes are driven by the FDA's Food Code.

   Managers must implement policies and procedures to keep food wholesome and to ensure food safety. Some use a Hazard Analysis and Critical Control Point (HACCP) system and food safety training. They also perform self-inspections that supplement those made by local health departments.

5. **Review the legal aspects of serving alcoholic beverages.**

   Serious consequences including fines or imprisonment result if alcoholic beverage laws are not followed. State or local laws address the legal age to drink and to serve alcoholic beverages and the legal age to enter an establishment that serves alcohol. Other concerns relate to serving intoxicated or pregnant guests, hours and type of service, and drink promotions. Dram shop laws hold the server and the establishment responsible for the actions of those they have served.

6. **Identify the procedures that should be followed to protect the operation from legal actions.**

   Managers must consistently follow policies and practices, keep current on workplace laws, and monitor employees' compliance. They must post required notices, keep accurate records, and allow employees to discuss issues and exercise their rights. They must also effectively participate in hearings and maintain numerous certifications to provide evidence of licenses.

7. **Explain how restaurant and foodservice operations should interact with unions.**

   Some operations are unionized; the union negotiates for its members. A collective bargaining process renegotiates contract terms. Union members may file grievances against an employer for breaking the terms and, if not resolved, may escalate to higher levels.

   Managers must fully understand labor contracts and the laws that control union–employer relations. The NLRA addresses the rights of employees to join a union, a union's negotiation of labor contracts, and good-faith bargaining. The Labor-Management Relations Act prohibits unions from requiring job applicants to join as a condition of employment unless stated in the contract. It also prohibits unions from coercing employees and allows managers to talk about advantages and disadvantages of unionization.

APPLICATION EXERCISE

You are a manager preparing for a meeting with supervisors in which you will provide basic information about federal employment laws. Use a search engine to research the following agencies and laws. (Make sure to select the Web site maintained by the applicable federal government agency. These will include *.gov* in the Web address.) Note five important elements on each Web site for your meeting:

- Equal Employment Opportunity Commission
- Pregnancy Discrimination Act

- Equal Pay Act of 1963
- Age Discrimination in Employment Act
- Americans with Disabilities Act
- Fair Labor Standards Act
- Occupational Safety and Health Act
- Family and Medical Leave Act

REVIEW YOUR LEARNING

Select the best answer for each question.

1. **Which practice is allowed by EEOC regulations?**
   A. Testing applicants on job content
   B. Requesting a photo with applications
   C. Focusing recruiting on certain applicants
   D. Asking if applicants require accommodation

2. **Which item does the Fair Labor Standards Act regulate?**
   A. Holidays
   B. Meal breaks
   C. Overtime pay
   D. Discharge notice

3. Compliance with what law can help reduce workers' compensation insurance costs?

   A. Fair Labor Standards Act

   B. Pregnancy Discrimination Act

   C. Americans with Disabilities Act

   (D.) Occupational Safety and Health Act

4. For how many months must a covered employee have worked for an employer to be eligible for a leave under the Family Medical Leave Act (FMLA)?

   A. 6

   B. 8

   C. 10

   (D.) 12

5. Which factor would determine that an employee should be compensated for injury?

   A. The employee was not at fault.

   B. Training was deemed inadequate.

   C. More than 14 days' work was lost.

   (D.) The accident occurred during work.

6. What factor may prevent successful application for a liquor license?

   (A.) The owner has a narcotics conviction on record.

   B. The manager is charged with a misdemeanor.

   C. The operation attempts to transfer the license.

   D. The operation allows a license to expire.

7. Where are the federal government's recommendations to prevent foodborne illnesses found?

   A. OSHA regulations

   (B.) FDA Food Code

   C. HACCP system

   D. Health codes

8. All 50 states require a minor assisting with alcohol service to

   (A.) be supervised by an employee who is of age.

   B. make application to the state liquor authority.

   C. handle only the customer order and payment.

   D. have an employee who is of age pour the drink.

9. Which situation supports a reasonable care defense against a food-related lawsuit?

   A. Witnesses state that employees took inappropriate action.

   B. The FDA Food Code is posted in the establishment.

   (C.) The operation has standards and training in place.

   D. The operation has all licenses and certifications.

10. Which law prohibits the use of discriminatory work practices against union employees?

   A. Equal Pay Act

   B. Civil Rights Act

   C. Fair Labor Standards Act

   (D.) National Labor Relations Act

9

Employee Compensation and Benefits

INSIDE THIS CHAPTER

- Legal Aspects of Compensation
- Employee Benefit Plans
- Retirement and Health Benefit Laws
- Ensuring Mandatory Benefits
- Ensuring Accurate Compensation
- Controlling Labor Costs

CHAPTER LEARNING OBJECTIVES

After completing this chapter, you should be able to:

- List and describe three federal laws that impact compensation policies and programs.

- Explain the types of voluntary benefits that can be included in a compensation package.

- Identify and describe three retirement and health benefit laws that impact voluntary benefits.

- Describe five employee benefit programs that are mandated by federal laws.

- Explain the procedures that help ensure the correct compensation will be paid to employees.

- Explain the basic procedures that can be used to control labor costs.

KEY TERMS

CASE STUDY

"I am sorry Rhianna has resigned," said Marin, the manager of Lava Flow Grill. Marin was talking to Sedar, the assistant manager. Marin continued, "Rhianna said she was leaving because she accepted a job 15 miles from home that paid 20 cents per hour more. I mentioned that she could almost walk here, but she said the money was more important."

"Well," said Sedar, "she was a good worker. I wonder if our employees know the value of the benefits we provide. I think we are more competitive than other employers in the area, but many employees look only at the dollar amount of their paycheck. If they knew the value of their benefits, maybe they would stay."

1. What role do you think benefits play when entry-level employees make employment decisions?

2. Do you think managers should provide details about benefits to new employees? If so, how might they do this?

LEGAL ASPECTS OF COMPENSATION

Compensation management involves all of the activities related to planning, implementing, and monitoring wages, salaries, and benefits for employees. It also involves addressing the wide range of legal requirements related to employee pay. Large-volume operations may have human resources specialists responsible for compensation activities, while managers in smaller operations may assume many of these tasks. In both cases, compensation programs including a wide variety of possible benefits must be administered legally and fairly.

Managers must understand the laws that govern their workplace and the policies and procedures to comply with them. These laws are numerous and complex, and the consequences of noncompliance can be significant.

Ideally, every manager in an operation would be well trained about employee benefits, company policies and procedures, and workplace laws. Since these areas are so complex and often change, small-volume operations should dedicate at least one management meeting each quarter to reviewing benefit programs. In larger operations, a human resources professional or lawyer may distribute memos or post information to communicate changes as they occur. Carefully read any information from the human resources department, management office, or legal staff.

In operations that do not offer such training or communication, managers may need to keep current with these changes on their own:

- The U.S. Department of Labor and most states provide free or inexpensive resources, and many are available on Web sites.

- The National Restaurant Association and State Restaurant Associations send their members regular updates on legal and other issues.

- Local chambers of commerce often provide information on local, regional, or statewide regulations.

- Various human resources newsletters provide information on regulations affecting businesses.

Managers are responsible for following their operation's policies and for helping employees obtain and use the benefits they are entitled to. It is in everyone's best interest for managers to learn about their operation's compensation programs and the laws that govern them. Managers must continuously update their knowledge about the compensation programs and laws.

Fair Labor Standards Act

The Fair Labor Standards Act (FLSA) serves as the cornerstone of federal employment law. It establishes minimum wage, overtime pay, and record-keeping standards for full- and part-time workers. These regulations help ensure that workers receive a fair wage. The FLSA also has requirements to help protect younger workers (see chapter 8). In addition, many state and local governments have enacted similar laws to ensure fair labor practices and compensation. Some of these laws set a higher minimum wage than federal law requires.

MINIMUM WAGE

The FLSA establishes different types of minimum wages. Most hourly positions in the United States are entitled to the basic minimum wage, but there are exceptions:

- **Tipped employees' minimum wage: Tipped employees** may be paid a lower cash wage when their tips are enough to ensure the basic minimum wage is met. Tipped employees are those who "customarily and regularly" receive more than a certain amount of income in tips each month—more than $30 per month as of March 2011.

- **Youth minimum wage:** Employees younger than 20 years of age may be paid a **youth minimum wage** of not less than $4.25 an hour, which is lower than the basic minimum wage, during their first 90 consecutive days of employment. However, where state or local law requires a higher wage, that higher wage must be paid. The law contains certain protections for employees that prohibit employers from displacing any employee in order to hire someone at the youth minimum wage.

- **Subminimum wage:** Employers may pay certain people a lower minimum wage, or **subminimum wage**. Examples include students placed in a job as part of a vocational or other educational program and individuals with a reduced capacity to be productive because of a physical or mental disability.

The minimum wages for tipped employees and youth are common in the restaurant and foodservice industry. The subminimum wage is less common. Many schools with student-learner programs do not allow participating employers to pay a subminimum wage.

Minimum wage exceptions are allowed only under specific circumstances. For example, to pay a subminimum wage, an employer needs a certificate from the Wage and Hour Division of the Department of Labor and must display a special minimum wage poster. Professional legal advice is useful when considering the use of special minimum wages.

TIP CREDITS

The **tip credit** provision of the FLSA allows operations that employ tipped employees a choice. They may pay the basic minimum wage or pay a reduced cash wage and use a tip credit. This option may be considered only for employees defined by the Department of Labor as tipped employees.

Exhibit 9.1

The basic idea of the tip credit provision is to reduce the payroll burden on some employers while ensuring that tipped employees receive at least the basic minimum wage after their tips are included (*Exhibit 9.1*). If the cash wage for tipped employees is $2.13 and the basic minimum wage is $7.25 per hour (the federal rate in March 2012), tipped employees must earn an average of at least $5.12 in tips each hour for the employer to use the full tip credit provision ($7.25 − $2.13 = $5.12). If tips do not bring the employee's hourly wage up to the basic minimum wage, the employer must pay the difference.

Employers who use the tip credit provision must notify the employees in advance. Generally, operations include this information in the employment letter or employment contract. They must also be able to show that the employee receives at least the basic minimum wage when the reduced cash wage and the employee's tips are combined. Whether an operation can use the tip credit provision and how wages should be calculated are affected by numerous rules. These relate to service charges, tips paid by credit card, deductions for uniforms or equipment, tip-pooling rules, overtime rules, reimbursements for damages or losses caused by the employee, and state and local laws.

Tipped employees and their employers must report tip income on no less than a monthly basis. They also must report their tip income when they file their personal income tax return. Employers must report the total tip income each employee earns per year, and they must also pay and withhold the applicable taxes on tip income.

OVERTIME

In many operations, full-time employees are expected to work 40 hours each week. If an employee works more than 40 hours, the excess hours are known as overtime. Under the FLSA, **exempt employees** are not required to receive extra pay for overtime. However, the FLSA requires that covered hourly paid employees, or **nonexempt employees**, who work more than 40 hours in a workweek be paid overtime wages. The rate for overtime wages is one-and-one-half times their normal hourly rate. For example, if an hourly paid employee earns $10 an hour in normal wages, his or her overtime rate would be $15 for the number of hours worked in excess of 40 hours.

With few exceptions, an exempt employee must be paid at least a specified amount, or $23,600 per year in March 2012, be paid on a salaried basis, and perform exempt job duties. Most employees must meet all three tests to be exempt. Examples of exempt duties include regular supervision or management as the primary duty, and also genuine input into the job status of other employees such as hiring, firing, and promoting. Decisions about exempt and nonexempt status and overtime provisions are complicated. Managers can review information at *www.flsa.gov* for more details.

COMPLIANCE ACTIONS

Managers must monitor their operation's compliance with wage and hour requirements. For example, it is important to determine jobs that are classified as nonexempt or exempt. To do so, all job descriptions should be reviewed. If some are not available, they should be created. Managers should use information from this analysis to ensure that all exempt and nonexempt positions have been properly assigned in compliance with FLSA requirements.

If a position is found to be at odds with requirements, corrective action must be taken. For example, if an employee currently thought to be exempt from overtime regulations is found to be nonexempt, then overtime pay owed must be calculated and paid.

Job descriptions for work by minors should also be checked carefully to ensure that all child labor law requirements are met for employees under 16. In addition, the review of job descriptions can confirm that all positions are in compliance with the Americans with Disabilities Act (ADA). Employees eligible under the ADA must receive the same pay as others working in that position.

It is also important to correctly classify all employee relationships. For example, is each person an employee of the company, or are there any independent contractors who are self-employed? Those who are independent contractors, such as musicians and deep-cleaning workers, along with workers obtained from a temporary agency, will have different compliance requirements.

A salary grade and range should be assigned for each job held by company employees. Salaries should be in line with standards found in a compensation survey. These may be purchased online from various vendors and are often specific to the industry and region.

Compensation should also consider the operation's philosophy. For example, should employee pay be in the middle of the market or above average? The hiring manager and those with budgeting responsibilities should assist with salary planning decisions.

Consumer Credit Protection Act

The Consumer Credit Protection Act (CCPA) is administered by the Wage and Hour Division of the Department of Labor. It prohibits employers from terminating or disciplining employees in some cases when a court or a government mandates that their wages be paid in part to a third party. This situation occurs when a creditor obtains a court order to receive payments directly from an employee's earnings or when a government tax agency, such as the IRS, seizes wages to pay for back taxes, fines, or penalties. Payments taken by a government agency are called **levies**, and payments ordered by a court are called **garnishments**. The law also restricts the amounts of these levies and garnishments based on the employee's income.

Equal Pay Act

The Equal Pay Act (EPA) is administered by the Equal Employment Opportunity Commission (EEOC). This act makes it illegal to pay different wages to men and women if they perform equal work in the same workplace. If there is an inequality in wages between men and women, employers may not reduce the wages of either sex to equalize their pay. However, if the employer can show that the wage difference has a legitimate basis, such as when the higher earner has more seniority or experience, a claim against the operation will likely be rejected.

If two employees actually do the same work, it does not matter if the titles or job descriptions differ. In general, two jobs are equal under the Equal Pay Act when both require equal levels of skill, effort, and responsibility and are performed under similar conditions. Small differences in skill, effort, or responsibility do not make two jobs unequal. Problems can arise where two jobs are basically the same but one includes a few extra duties. This is typically legal except when the higher-paying job with extra duties is consistently reserved for workers of one gender.

An individual alleging a violation of the act may go directly to court without previously filing an EEOC charge. The time limit for filing a charge with the EEOC and the time limit for going to court are the same: within two years of the alleged unlawful compensation practice or, if it was a willful violation, within three years.

Exhibit 9.2

EMPLOYEE BENEFIT PLANS

An **employee benefit plan** is a program of nonwage compensation that an employee is eligible for and the situations under which the employee will receive the benefits. For example, a retirement plan provides a certain monetary benefit to an employee in exchange for a certain number of years at work.

Overview of Employee Benefit Plans

When an employee signs up for a benefit plan, this is called **enrollment**. Employees often are entitled to enroll in benefit plans as soon as they are hired (*Exhibit 9.2*). After that, the plan provider, which is the company offering the benefit such as an insurance company, limits the times when employees can change their plan or coverage. This limited time is known as an **open enrollment period**. It varies by provider, plan, and employer. During open enrollment, employees are typically able to change plans and coverage and add or remove family members. Federal law requires that healthcare plan providers allow people to make changes when certain life events occur that change a family, such as birth, adoption, marriage, divorce, or death.

Depending on the benefit and plan, the person who receives the benefit may be an employee, a former employee, or someone else. For example, an employee may receive healthcare benefits, a former employee will receive a retirement benefit, and, if he or she dies, the spouse or another person may continue to receive retirement benefits.

In general, a **participant** is someone who is a member of a plan and a **beneficiary** is someone who is entitled to receive a benefit under a plan because of his or her relationship with the participant. For example, an employee may be a participant in a healthcare plan, while his or her child may be a beneficiary. With many plans the beneficiary receives the money that the participant is entitled to if the participant dies before receiving the entire benefit.

Most employee and union benefit plans are **group plans**. A group plan provides essentially the same benefit to multiple people, such as a life insurance plan offered to all employees. In contrast, an **individual plan** provides a benefit for one person or family. Most plans purchased outside the workplace are individual plans.

Federal law requires a designated person, department, or company to be responsible for handling administrative tasks for group plans. This person or group is known as the **plan administrator**. In some operations, the human resources department or specific employees are the plan administrators. In other operations, the insurance company that provides the plan or a third-party firm is the plan administrator. This arrangement is the most common situation in small operations.

Types of Benefits

All employers who meet certain conditions are required by federal and state governments to provide certain benefits. Three examples are Social Security, workers' compensation, and unemployment insurance. **Social Security** is a federal government program that provides retirement and disability income and other financial benefits to those who qualify. These mandatory benefits are discussed at length later in the chapter.

Many employers also voluntarily offer other benefits, which can vary widely from operation to operation. Even within the same operation, the benefits voluntarily given to employees can vary based on whether the employee is exempt or nonexempt, part-time or full-time, or other factors. *Exhibit 9.3* on the next page lists benefits that companies may offer and indicates with an asterisk (*) the benefits that are mandated by federal and state governments.

Exhibit 9.3

DESCRIPTIONS OF EMPLOYEE BENEFITS

Type of Benefit	Description
Bonuses	This benefit is extra pay given to employees in a lump sum, usually awarded annually or periodically. Bonuses are often tied to incentive programs and given for good individual or company performance.
Child and dependent care	These benefits can include daycare facilities or flexible spending accounts (see below) for child or dependent care costs.
Death benefits	These benefits include life insurance and payments to help with funeral costs for an employee, or other compensation for the employees' beneficiaries.
Dental insurance	This benefit includes payments for the cost of some types of dental care, usually with annual limits.
Disability benefits	These benefits provide some income when the employee cannot work because of a medical condition, and are also called short- or long-term disability.
Educational and professional development support	These benefits may include tuition and training reimbursement, apprenticeship programs, and professional organization membership dues. Some companies require that employees obtain a specified grade to be eligible for this benefit.
Employee assistance programs (EAPs)	These benefits are designed to help employees deal with mental health issues and personal problems including substance abuse, emotional difficulties, and financial problems. Large companies may have an in-house staff for this assistance, while smaller companies may contract with outside services or provide referrals.
Family and medical leave*	This benefit involves unpaid leave of absence returning to the same or similar job if the leave is taken for certain medical reasons or family situations. Requirements are specified in the Family and Medical Leave Act (FMLA).
Flexible spending accounts (FSAs)	These benefits are special savings accounts set up by employers and owned by employees who contribute pretax income. FSAs are used for healthcare costs not covered by health insurance or for child or dependent care, depending on the type of FSA established.
Funeral leave	This benefit includes unpaid time off to make funeral arrangements for an immediate family member or to attend the funeral.
Health savings accounts (HSAs)	This benefit includes special savings accounts set up by employers and owned by employees who have healthcare plans with large deductibles. A **deductible** is the amount of money an insured party must pay before the insurance company's coverage plan begins. Employees contribute pretax income to these accounts, which are used to pay healthcare costs not covered by a health plan.
Healthcare coverage after termination*	The Consolidated Omnibus Budget Reconciliation Act (COBRA) requires optional healthcare coverage to be offered to some employees after employment ends.
Healthcare plans	Typically, employers pay some of the monthly cost for this benefit, and employees pay the rest. Healthcare plans and the situations they cover vary widely.
Life insurance	This benefit provides money to a deceased employee's beneficiaries to help replace the income the employee earned. Claim amounts are often based on the employee's earnings; for example, a life insurance policy with a claim worth two years of earnings.

Exhibit 9.3

(CONTINUED)

Type of Benefit	Description
Long-term care insurance	This benefit pays for long-term nursing care or at-home healthcare when former employees cannot take care of themselves.
Meals	This benefit includes free or discounted meals provided to employees.
Mental health insurance	This benefit covers the costs of psychotherapy, psychiatric treatment, family and couples counseling, and other mental healthcare costs.
Military leave*	This benefit includes unpaid leave of absence, with the participant returning to the same or similar job, including benefits and anticipated promotions, to fulfill military service obligations. Requirements are defined under the Uniformed Services Employment and Reemployment Rights Act (USERRA).
Paid holidays	This benefit includes pay for workdays that fall on holidays during which the operation is closed. Some operations pay higher wages for working on holidays.
Paid vacation	Vacation time usually accumulates based on how long an employee has worked for the company. Often, after working a certain number of years, employees are given additional vacation time.
Pension and retirement plans	Pension and retirement plans ensure that an employee has income other than Social Security when he or she retires because of old age or a permanent disability. These plans are discussed in detail later in the chapter.
Personal time off, also called personal days	Personal days are often based on how long an employee has worked for a company. This benefit is becoming more common and may replace other specific types of paid time off.
Profit-sharing plans	This benefit includes programs that provide special payments to an employee's profit-sharing account. The employer contributes a set amount to each employee's account, usually a percentage of the company's annual profits. The money is typically distributed to an employee at retirement, year-end, or termination.
Religious holidays	This benefit includes days off to observe a religious holiday, if employees do not need to use vacation or personal days for this purpose.
Social Security*	This benefit is a federal pension program designed to ensure a minimum level of income for retirees and people with disabilities, which is funded through payroll taxes.
Stock option plans	This benefit includes offers made by an employer to sell company stock to employees at a certain price in the future. This offer often gives employees the chance to buy company stock at a reduced rate if the value increases.
Unemployment insurance*	This benefit is a federal requirement to ensure that employees who lose their job under certain circumstances still receive some income.
Uniforms	Operations with uniforms or dress code requirements often provide uniforms or reimburse employees in part or in full for this cost.
Vision care	This benefit includes vision or eye care that is either included in healthcare coverage or chosen by the employee at extra cost.
Workers' compensation*	This benefit pays a set benefit and medical expenses to an employee who becomes injured or disabled while working. This insurance varies by state, and most states also require workers' compensation to cover any diseases an employee develops because of a work environment.

*Government-mandated benefit

Exhibit 9.4

Common Voluntary Benefits

Operations commonly provide a number of voluntary benefits. These include uniforms, meals, healthcare plans, employee assistance programs, and retirement benefits.

UNIFORM BENEFITS

Many establishments provide full or partial uniforms for their employees or reimburse them for purchasing their own uniforms (see *Exhibit 9.4*). Some operations supply their cooks with jackets, but the cooks buy their own pants and shoes. In other cases, the operation provides the shoes or shares the cost with employees. Front-of-the-house employees often are expected to supply their own pants, skirts, or other appropriate wear while the operation may provide the shirts, ties, vests, coats, or polo shirts, depending on the concept. To ensure a clean, crisp, and consistent look, some operations also provide laundry service for uniforms.

Managers must understand their company's dress code and uniform benefit policies. They should be able to explain the dress code and uniform benefits, tell employees why the dress code and uniforms are important, and identify when employee dress is not in compliance.

While uniform benefits can be costly, the positive customer impression they provide can far outweigh the cost. In addition, uniforms may provide some measure of personal protection. In the back of the house, closed-toe shoes protect feet from dropped knives, hot liquids, and other dangers. Shortened jacket sleeves without cuffs help protect cooks from setting their sleeves on fire, snagging them on hot cookware and moving equipment, or trapping hot spills next to their skin.

Exhibit 9.5

It may be less costly to provide uniforms than to pay for the consequences of even one serious workplace accident. When an employee is seriously injured at work, the employer not only loses valuable labor but also may have to pay a workers' compensation claim, including medical costs, and report the accident to the government. There is also the possibility that an injured employee could sue the employer.

MEAL BENEFITS

Meal benefits are provided to many restaurant and foodservice employees (*Exhibit 9.5*). Some operations provide meals as part of the job and others charge, often at a subsidized rate. In some establishments only some positions receive meal benefits, and union contracts determine meal policies in others.

Managers must enforce meal policies and explain them to employees because this helps control costs. There are other ways to control meal benefit costs:

- Set a budget for the meals. For example, perhaps a specified food cost limit is set if there are special employee meals (employee cafeteria). If employees order off the menu, there may be a maximum retail price.

- Provide a meal allowance for employees.

- Manage the schedule to ensure the proper number of employees receive meals.

HEALTHCARE PLANS

Healthcare plans are offered by many employers to attract and keep employees, and the plans can vary greatly. They may include routine exams, medical tests, radiological services, surgery, hospital and emergency care, physical therapy, preventive care, vision care, mental healthcare, dental care, and prescriptions.

Employers may offer two or more group healthcare plans from which their employees can choose. Both employers and employees share the cost of the premiums, or monthly insurance fees. The plans offered usually cost different amounts and provide different types of coverage. In addition, employees often can add family members at extra cost. An employee's portion of the healthcare costs varies based on the plan, coverage options, location, and employer's contribution.

There are several types of healthcare plans:

- Fee-for-service plans: Fee-for-service plans are administered by insurance companies that directly pay service providers, including physicians and hospitals, or reimburse plan participants. Participants choose their own providers, and the plan pays for any covered services performed by any qualified provider. Participants usually pay more when they use these types of plans.

- Preferred provider organizations (PPOs): With these plans service providers discount their charges in exchange for more patients and timely payments. As long as providers are part of the network, participants' costs are usually lower than with fee-for-service plans.

- Health maintenance organizations (HMOs): Healthcare costs through an HMO are almost entirely prepaid through premiums, and service providers are part of the HMO. Participants must usually choose HMO providers or pay all or most service costs themselves. Before seeing a specialist such as an allergist, HMOs usually require that participants visit a general practitioner to obtain a referral. Services provided by HMO providers are often fully covered, so participants usually have minimal expenses they must pay themselves.

Manager's Memo

Some companies offer optional savings plans, such as flexible spending accounts (FSAs) or health savings accounts (HSAs), to help employees cover their costs and encourage them to use their benefits wisely. These special accounts allow employees to contribute a certain amount of income before taxes to their account, which can be used only to pay for certain medical expenses not covered by the healthcare plan. Sometimes employers also contribute to these accounts. With an FSA, any money not used by the end of the year is lost. With an HSA, money not used carries forward, but an HSA can be used only with plans that have high deductibles: maximum out-of-pocket expenses.

THINK ABOUT IT . . .

Do you think operations should offer EAP benefits for employees to seek help with personal problems? Why or why not?

With these plans, employers pay a fee to the insurance company, PPO, or HMO and share the healthcare costs covered under the plan with the plan provider. However, some very large employers are **self-insured** and pay all covered healthcare costs with their own funds.

EMPLOYEE ASSISTANCE PROGRAMS

Managers can often help employees with employees' personal problems. Sometimes providing support can help, but at other times, employees need professional help. **Employee assistance programs (EAPs)** provide counseling and other services to help employees deal with a wide range of problems that hinder their ability to function effectively at work:

- Dependency or abuse, such as alcohol, chemical, gambling, and tobacco
- Domestic violence
- Emotional issues such as depression, low self-esteem, and personal problems
- Financial problems
- Legal problems
- Literacy issues
- Marital, family, or relationship problems
- Stress from any source

Many managers post signs about EAPs with telephone numbers and reminders that calling and obtaining help is always confidential. They may mention these programs in meetings, attach notices to paychecks, send out periodic notices in newsletters, hand out cards, or distribute other reminders. This information also should be provided in the employee handbook.

RETIREMENT BENEFITS

Retirement benefits vary widely between operations. They provide regular payments to employees who resign because of age. Some plans offer regular payments that continue until the retiree dies, and others provide payments that continue for a specified period of time. There are two basic types of retirement benefits: defined benefit and defined contribution.

A **defined benefit (DB)** plan is a retirement benefit in which the employee is guaranteed certain payments on retirement. The payout, or final value of the benefit, is defined. These are traditional pension plans completely paid for by the employer, and are less commonly used today.

Multiple defined benefit retirement plans offer different programs for exempt and nonexempt employees and union and nonunion employees. If an employee's position changes, for example, when an employee is promoted from a nonexempt to an exempt position, the pension plan is changed for the employee as well.

Generally, the employer contributes funds for all eligible employees into a common trust, one or more accounts owned by the employer or plan administrator. When an employee is ready to receive retirement payments, the employee gives notice so the final benefit can be calculated and required paperwork processed.

A **defined contribution (DC)** plan is an increasingly popular retirement program that guarantees certain payments will be made into an account owned by an employee. Perhaps the best-known DC retirement plan is the 401(k) plan. However, there are many other types such as Keogh plans, individual retirement accounts (IRAs), and 403(b) plans. The terms *401(k)* and *403(b)* come from the Internal Revenue Code. Small employers may offer contributions to an IRA or Keogh plan instead of a 401(k) account.

Employees typically contribute a percentage of their pretax income to their own account, and employers match a portion or all of the contribution. For example, an employee might contribute 10 percent of income, and the employer might match one-half of that contribution. The total contributions to the account would be 15 percent of pretax income. When income before taxes is contributed, the employee does not pay any tax until the money is withdrawn. The amount that can be contributed is limited by the Internal Revenue Service (IRS) and can vary widely based on the type of account, the employee's income and age, and other factors.

Normally, contributions to defined contribution retirement accounts are invested in securities, such as stocks and bonds, so the account's value ultimately depends on how well these investments perform. Unlike defined benefit plans, the value of these benefits at retirement is not guaranteed, and accounts can gain or lose value.

Although the IRS imposes stiff penalties if money is withdrawn before retirement, it allows exceptions for certain withdrawals, such as buying a first home or paying major medical expenses. In general, when money is withdrawn, the employee pays the tax due on the amount withdrawn.

RETIREMENT AND HEALTH BENEFIT LAWS

When an operation offers retirement and healthcare benefits, it must follow all laws that govern the plans. Although plan administrators are ultimately responsible for ensuring these laws are followed, managers must also do their part. In some cases, managers may need to communicate certain information to employees and the plan administrator. For example, they may need to provide documents to employees and notify the plan administrator when an employee leaves. Company policy and procedures generally specify these responsibilities, but it is still important to understand the basics of three federal laws that affect retirement and health benefits.

Manager's Memo

Defined benefit and defined contribution retirement plans have certain things in common. First, both have eligibility rules. Usually an employee must work a certain number of hours or days per year for a certain number of years to become entitled to the benefit. To determine the value of the benefit, both types of plans use a formula that is usually based on the employee's salary and how long the employee has worked for the company.

Once an employee is entitled, the benefit belongs to the employee and cannot be revoked, even if the employee leaves the company before retirement. For example, a person worked 10 years at a company, became eligible for its retirement plan, and then left. When he or she retires, the employee will still receive the benefit earned. This guarantee and many other elements of these plans are legislated by federal laws.

The Employee Retirement Income Security Act

The Employee Retirement Income Security Act (ERISA) of 1974 protects employee pensions and healthcare plans from incompetent, unethical, and unfair administration. ERISA was enacted to ensure that the benefits promised would actually be there when employees need them. ERISA requires a designated plan administrator who must provide employees with certain documents.

When an employee is first enrolled in a retirement or healthcare plan, the plan administrator must provide the participant with a **summary plan description (SPD)**. (See *Exhibit 9.6*.) The SPD explains the plan's benefits and describes participants' rights and responsibilities.

Many operations provide SPDs before the employee's first day of work or during orientation. In addition, if a participant requests an SPD at any time, the plan administrator must provide it. The plan administrator is also required to distribute copies of the plan's summary annual report.

Depending on the operation's policies and procedures, the manager may be responsible for distributing the initial SPD document, especially to new hires. Since there are legal requirements for doing this, use of an orientation checklist that indicates the SPD was distributed is a good way to show compliance.

The Consolidated Omnibus Budget Reconciliation Act

The Consolidated Omnibus Budget Reconciliation Act (COBRA) extends healthcare coverage at group rates for people who would otherwise lose their healthcare insurance if, for example, they resigned. COBRA generally requires employers with 20 or more employees and a group healthcare plan to offer this continued coverage to eligible plan participants if they were covered by a group healthcare plan on the day before the event that causes a loss of coverage. *Exhibit 9.7* shows situations that allow coverage to be continued.

Exhibit 9.7

QUALIFYING EVENTS FOR CONTINUATION OF COVERAGE UNDER COBRA

Qualifying events for a covered employee if they cause the employee to lose coverage

- Termination of the covered employee's employment for any reason other than gross misconduct
- Reduction in the covered employee's hours of employment

Qualifying events for a spouse and dependent child of a covered employee if they cause the spouse or child to lose coverage

- Termination of the covered employee's employment for any reason other than gross misconduct
- Reduction in hours worked by the covered employee
- Covered employee becomes entitled to Medicare
- Divorce or legal separation of the spouse from the covered employee
- Death of the covered employee

Qualifying event for a dependent child of a covered employee if it causes the child to lose coverage

- Loss of dependent child status under the plan rules

COBRA enables previous employees to continue their healthcare through the employer's group plan for a limited period. However, they must pay both their own and the employer's share of the costs, and the employer can charge an additional 2 percent as an administration fee. Even though the employer no longer pays for the healthcare, this option enables most eligible people to purchase healthcare coverage for a lower price than they would receive through an individual plan with similar coverage. Generally, adults can continue coverage for 18 months, and dependent children can continue for 36 months. However, if an adult becomes disabled, coverage can be extended to 29 months. Certain qualifying events, or a second qualifying event during the initial period of coverage, may permit a beneficiary to receive a maximum of 36 months of coverage.

A plan administrator must notify eligible persons about COBRA coverage and related information and events, such as open enrollment and cancellation procedures. Managers should be aware of these requirements because some of them involve information that should be distributed during hiring and orientation and posted in the workplace. Managers may also be responsible for notifying the plan administrator when an employee leaves the operation or loses healthcare coverage to ensure that plan participants receive all notices in a timely manner.

The employer must notify the plan administrator within 30 days when a covered employee:

- Terminates employment
- Loses coverage because of a reduction in hours
- Dies
- Becomes eligible for **Medicare**, a federally insured healthcare plan for people age 65 or older

The participant must notify the plan administrator for other qualifying life events, such as divorce, legal separation, or loss of dependent status. In some cases, the participant may notify the manager, who will notify the plan administrator.

Exhibit 9.8

The Health Insurance Portability and Accountability Act

The Health Insurance Portability and Accountability Act (HIPAA) helps ensure that people do not lose access to healthcare because of limits on plan enrollment periods, preexisting conditions, or other health status factors. HIPAA limits exclusions for preexisting health conditions. (See *Exhibit 9.8.*) A **preexisting condition** is a medical condition for which a person has sought medical treatment before applying to join a healthcare plan. HIPAA offers protection both for people who have access to group healthcare plans, such as those commonly offered by employers, and for people who purchase or apply for individual plans, which is usually done outside the workplace.

HIPAA has three main functions:

- To give people the right to add family members to their group healthcare plan at times other than open enrollment, under certain circumstances
- To protect people from being excluded from healthcare plans or denied coverage because of preexisting conditions
- To protect people from discriminatory pricing or treatment under a plan because of preexisting conditions or other health status factors (see *Exhibit 9.9*)

In the past, people with a preexisting condition were denied full or even partial coverage under many healthcare plans for that condition. For example, if a person had been treated for colon polyps, a plan

Exhibit 9.9

HIPAA HEALTH STATUS FACTORS

Health status

Medical conditions (both physical and mental illnesses)

Claims experience

Receipt of healthcare

Medical history

Genetic information

Evidence of insurability

Disability

might stipulate that any future treatment related to colon polyps and colon cancer would not be covered, or it might deny the person any type of coverage. If the plan accepted someone with a preexisting condition, the premiums for that person generally would be much higher.

Sometimes plans also excluded coverage for preexisting conditions for a certain time after enrollment, known as an **exclusion period**. Exclusion periods are still allowed as long as they are applied equally to all plan participants. However, HIPAA limits or eliminates some of these exclusions and provides some protection against higher premiums due to preexisting conditions and other health factors.

Another requirement of HIPAA is to allow people who otherwise might not be able to obtain coverage to enroll in group healthcare plans at certain times other than open enrollment:

- When a person loses other healthcare coverage
- When a person marries someone who has coverage
- When a child is born to someone with coverage
- When a dependent child is adopted or placed for adoption with someone who has coverage

In any of these cases, the person without coverage can enroll in the plan of the family member who is covered under a group plan. To be eligible for special enrollment, the employee must notify the plan administrator within 30 days of losing other coverage or of a qualifying event, such as the birth of a child.

ENSURING MANDATORY BENEFITS

Even though healthcare and retirement benefits are heavily legislated, employers are not required to offer them. However, federal and state governments require most employers to provide or pay for other benefits. These include Social Security, workers' compensation insurance, unemployment compensation insurance, and, in certain situations, unpaid leaves of absence. Since these programs are mandated and must generally be provided, many people do not consider them benefits. However, employers must administer and pay for these programs just as they do for many voluntarily provided benefits.

Managers should be familiar with these programs to help employees understand them and how they relate to any voluntary benefits provided by the operation. They also need to understand their operation's legal responsibilities for providing and administering these mandated benefits.

Social Security

Social Security is a federal program in which most nongovernmental employers and employees must participate. It has evolved to include a broad range of benefits:

- **Retirement benefits:** A pension for eligible workers who have retired, their spouses, and their dependents

- **Survivor benefits:** A pension for the spouses and dependent children of eligible workers who die before they retire

- **Disability benefits:** A pension for workers with disabilities who are younger than full retirement age

- **Medicare:** A federally insured healthcare plan for people age 65 or older

Employers and employees pay for Social Security benefits through a payroll tax. Employers must pay both the employer's and employee's share of this tax to the Social Security trust and deduct the correct amount from each employee's paycheck.

To be eligible for Social Security benefits, a person must have worked for a certain length of time and earned a minimum income or be the spouse or dependent child of someone who meets these work requirements. Persons applying for Social Security disability benefits must meet additional eligibility requirements.

The value of a Social Security benefit depends in large part on how much income the employee earned and when the benefit payments begin. If an employee retires and applies to receive Social Security benefits before full retirement age, the retirement benefit amount is reduced. If the employee applies after full retirement age, the amount is increased.

Unemployment Compensation

Unemployment compensation, also called unemployment insurance, is a program that provides benefits and income to workers who become unemployed through no fault of their own. It provides a reduced level of income to employees who meet specific eligibility requirements. It is intended to help people during short periods of unemployment while they are looking for a new job.

Unemployment compensation is based on federal law, but administered by each state under the state law. Each state has its own rules for the amount of benefits to be paid and for how long. Unemployment benefits are required to be paid for a minimum time as long as the employee remains eligible.

In general, to be eligible for unemployment compensation, a former employee must have worked for an employer for a certain period of time and must be out of work for a certain period of time. Most states also require former employees to be able and available to work and to be actively looking for work. They also specify certain conditions that can disqualify an employee from receiving benefits:

- Being fired because of misconduct
- Turning down a job offer of suitable work
- Going on strike or not working due to a labor dispute
- Receiving certain types of income including workers' compensation, a retirement or Social Security pension, or Social Security payments

Although there are similarities among states' unemployment programs, there are also differences. The examples that follow apply to most, but not all, states. Current information specific to a location can be found by entering "unemployment compensation in [specific state name]" into a search engine:

- Benefits are based on a percentage of earnings over a 52-week period, up to a maximum amount determined by the state.
- Benefits are paid for a maximum of 26 weeks in most states. However, the time has ranged up to 99 weeks in many states during difficult economic times.
- Recipients must be unemployed through no fault of their own and meet the eligibility requirement as determined by state law (see previous text).
- Recipients can appeal if they are denied benefits.
- Employers have an assigned tax rate based on their average annual taxable payroll, unemployment claims against their account, and taxes previously paid.
- If an employer has been at the maximum rate for a specified time, a surcharge can be added to the rate.

Unemployment insurance is funded through payroll taxes paid by employers. The amount of tax varies by state and by employer. If an employer has terminated or laid off many employees who filed for unemployment benefits, that employer's tax rate will be higher compared to employers without as many claims.

When an employee files for unemployment compensation, the state agency gathers information from the employee and the employer and determines whether the employee is entitled to compensation. Employees who are denied unemployment are eligible to appeal the decision.

To best protect their operations, managers must know about the definition of eligibility and the assigned tax rates specified in their state's unemployment compensation laws. Every action taken by management regarding an employee who does not meet the company's performance or other standards should be put in writing and signed by both the employee and a manager. When presenting or appealing a case, the manager can then use the written documents to reinforce the operation's position. Either side can appeal the decision.

Documentation is also important for assigning a tax rate because, in most states, the rate is based on the number of claims a business has against its account: the more claims, the higher the rate. By working with employees and coaching them, there will be fewer terminations. By documenting everything in writing, there will be fewer claims against the business.

As with other aspects of unemployment compensation, laws for communicating unemployment insurance information to employees vary by state. Some states may require that employers notify employees of their rights to unemployment insurance. In addition, the federal Worker Adjustment and Retraining Notification Act (WARN) requires covered employers who are planning mass layoffs to provide those employees with information about unemployment insurance.

Workers' Compensation

Workers' compensation, or workers' comp, is a system for providing financial compensation to employees or their survivors when an employee is injured at work, becomes sick because of the workplace environment, or dies as a result of a workplace situation. Workers' compensation programs are controlled by state laws and differ from state to state.

Generally, employers are responsible for paying for an employee's medical costs and providing a reduced income while the employee is recovering or disabled. State laws specify the amount of these costs and income, along with any limits. Restaurant and foodservice companies typically purchase workers' compensation insurance to pay any claims. The cost of these insurance policies is calculated based on the nature of the employees' work, the operation's safety record, the operation's history of previous claims, and the operation's provision of healthcare benefits. Most State Restaurant Associations provide operations with some assistance, often by offering large group plans. However, very large companies may choose to insure themselves instead.

Family and Medical Leaves of Absence

Exhibit 9.10

Sometimes employees want or need to stop working temporarily and then return to work. When a period of time cannot be covered by paid time-off days such as vacation time, personal days, or sick days (*Exhibit 9.10*), it is called a leave of absence. A leave of absence, or leave, may be short or long. Depending on the employer and the reason for the leave, employees on leave may or may not be paid their normal wages. While employers today often voluntarily accommodate employee requests for unpaid leave, the federal government mandates unpaid leaves of absence in certain situations. Many state laws also apply to certain employers and employees and, in many cases, provide more extensive coverage than the Family and Medical Leave Act (FMLA).

Chapter 8 explained that FMLA gives qualified employees the right to take up to 12 weeks of continuous or intermittent unpaid leave in a rolling 12-month period for certain medical or family care situations. Employers also must provide certain benefits and reemployment to employees who take leaves under FMLA.

One of these situations is for a serious medical condition, which FMLA defines as "an illness, injury, impairment, or physical or mental condition that involves inpatient care . . . [or] continuing treatment by a healthcare provider." The continuing treatment may be for a condition that incapacitates the employee or for which the employee must receive multiple treatments.

If the employee has health insurance through the employer, the employer must continue to provide this benefit during the leave. However, the employee must pay for any benefits he or she normally would pay, such as the employee share of healthcare insurance premiums. When employees return from family or medical leave, they are entitled to the same benefits and essentially the same positions they had before taking the leave.

FMLA requires employers to communicate certain information at certain times. Employers must communicate employees' rights under this act by posting information about it. The Department of Labor provides posters that employers can use to satisfy this requirement.

Employers must also provide information on FMLA or any applicable state law in the employee handbook or through handouts when requested by the employee. This information includes instructions on how to take leave under

FMLA or any applicable state law and contact information for the person or department that administers this benefit.

Family and medical leave laws are complex, and many organizations designate certain people as administrators for this benefit. These persons may be human resources staff in large operations, but they may be people at outside agencies or even managers in smaller establishments. However, to help ensure confidentiality and impartiality, some companies do not use managers as designated contacts.

Sometimes when employees are considering taking leave under FMLA, they first approach their immediate supervisor. Managers should be able to direct their employees to the FMLA contact for their operation. If an employee is willing to discuss his or her need for a leave with a manager, the manager should be able to explain the company's policies for paid and unpaid time off. Managers who know their operation's policies and applicable laws will be able to ensure that the employee's rights are respected while protecting the operation's interests.

Manager's Memo

If employees have been honorably discharged and they return to work within a predetermined time period, they must retain their USERRA coverage. That predetermined time period is based on the service time of the individual.

Service Time	Time Period for Returning to Work
Up to 30 days	Within 1 business day of returning home
Between 31 and 90 days	Within 14 business days after returning home
More than 90 days	Up to 181 days to return to work after returning home from service

Military Leaves

Chapter 8 explained that the federal government protects people who need a leave of absence to serve in any U.S. military service. The Uniformed Services Employment and Reemployment Rights Act (USERRA) protects employees from workplace discrimination based on their obligation to, application for, or interest in military service. However, the main purpose of USERRA is to ensure that military personnel are not penalized in the workplace when they return from duty. USERRA provides similar protections to the FMLA and COBRA, but it provides more extensive protection and applies to all employers regardless of size.

While the employee is on leave, USERRA requires the employer to continue all benefits as if the employee were not on leave. If an eligible employee serves longer than 31 days, the employee can opt to continue healthcare coverage, similar to COBRA, or can use the military's healthcare plan.

Eligible employees are entitled to return to the same job or an equivalent one when their service is finished if they meet certain conditions shown in the USERRA poster in *Exhibit 9.11*. If the employee would have been promoted had he or she continued working, the employer must provide that promotion and any accompanying benefits.

For more information about USERRA, search for "USERRA" on the U.S. Department of Labor's Web site.

Exhibit 9.11

USERRA POSTER

YOUR RIGHTS UNDER USERRA
THE UNIFORMED SERVICES EMPLOYMENT AND REEMPLOYMENT RIGHTS ACT

USERRA protects the job rights of individuals who voluntarily or involuntarily leave employment positions to undertake military service or certain types of service in the National Disaster Medical System. USERRA also prohibits employers from discriminating against past and present members of the uniformed services, and applicants to the uniformed services.

REEMPLOYMENT RIGHTS

You have the right to be reemployed in your civilian job if you leave that job to perform service in the uniformed service and:

☆ you ensure that your employer receives advance written or verbal notice of your service;
☆ you have five years or less of cumulative service in the uniformed services while with that particular employer;
☆ you return to work or apply for reemployment in a timely manner after conclusion of service; and
☆ you have not been separated from service with a disqualifying discharge or under other than honorable conditions.

If you are eligible to be reemployed, you must be restored to the job and benefits you would have attained if you had not been absent due to military service or, in some cases, a comparable job.

RIGHT TO BE FREE FROM DISCRIMINATION AND RETALIATION

If you:

☆ are a past or present member of the uniformed service;
☆ have applied for membership in the uniformed service; or
☆ are obligated to serve in the uniformed service;

then an employer may not deny you:

☆ initial employment;
☆ reemployment;
☆ retention in employment;
☆ promotion; or
☆ any benefit of employment

because of this status.

In addition, an employer may not retaliate against anyone assisting in the enforcement of USERRA rights, including testifying or making a statement in connection with a proceeding under USERRA, even if that person has no service connection.

HEALTH INSURANCE PROTECTION

☆ If you leave your job to perform military service, you have the right to elect to continue your existing employer-based health plan coverage for you and your dependents for up to 24 months while in the military.

☆ Even if you don't elect to continue coverage during your military service, you have the right to be reinstated in your employer's health plan when you are reemployed, generally without any waiting periods or exclusions (e.g., pre-existing condition exclusions) except for service-connected illnesses or injuries.

ENFORCEMENT

☆ The U.S. Department of Labor, Veterans Employment and Training Service (VETS) is authorized to investigate and resolve complaints of USERRA violations.

☆ For assistance in filing a complaint, or for any other information on USERRA, contact VETS at **1-866-4-USA-DOL** or visit its **website at http://www.dol.gov/vets**. An interactive online USERRA Advisor can be viewed at **http://www.dol.gov/elaws/userra.htm**.

☆ If you file a complaint with VETS and VETS is unable to resolve it, you may request that your case be referred to the Department of Justice or the Office of Special Counsel, as applicable, for representation.

☆ You may also bypass the VETS process and bring a civil action against an employer for violations of USERRA.

The rights listed here may vary depending on the circumstances. The text of this notice was prepared by VETS, and may be viewed on the internet at this address: http://www.dol.gov/vets/programs/userra/poster.htm. Federal law requires employers to notify employees of their rights under USERRA, and employers may meet this requirement by displaying the text of this notice where they customarily place notices for employees.

U.S. Department of Labor
1-866-487-2365

U.S. Department of Justice

Office of Special Counsel

1-800-336-4590

Publication Date—July 2008

ENSURING ACCURATE COMPENSATION

Managers must follow their operation's policies and procedures for monitoring employee time reports. They must also follow procedures for working with the **payroll administrator**: the person, department, or external company that ensures paychecks are issued.

Payroll Administrators

Payroll administrators must deliver accurate paychecks on time. They must ensure that the correct taxes, health insurance premiums, benefit contributions, and other applicable items are deducted from each employee's wages. These items must be forwarded to the appropriate agency, company, or account. They also must ensure that any bonuses, expense reimbursements, advances, or special payments owed to an employee are added to paychecks.

In many organizations, payroll administrators also ensure that employees receive accurate credits and debits for any benefits based on length of service. For example, in operations that provide paid vacation, this time may be based on the number of days an employee has worked. This time must be accurately tracked. When vacation days are used, they must be deducted from the number of accumulated vacation days.

Tracking the time and the dates an employee works is also important to determine service requirements for retirement benefits. This information must be communicated to benefit plan administrators. The degree and method of communication and the accuracy of the hours reported depend in part on the operation's payroll system.

Payroll Systems

A payroll system records and tracks employee work times and issues paychecks. It can include time cards, card readers, computers, paperwork, reports, and other resources. It may involve various people and procedures. Employers may use a manual or automated time card process, or employees may sign in and out through the POS system, among other alternatives. Typically, supervisors review and sign employee time records at the end of the week and forward them to the payroll administrator.

Managers must ensure that employees are reporting the correct number of hours and assigning those hours to the correct category, such as workdays versus personal days. Although some managers think they must monitor the hours of only nonexempt workers, they should also review the hours

RESTAURANT TECHNOLOGY

OPEN FOR BUSINESS

Increasingly, operations use computerized payroll systems that are linked to larger systems to automate certain tasks. These tasks include communication among the payroll and plan administrators and human resources staff. When a new employee is hired, his or her start date, salary, personal information, and benefit selections can be entered into the system. When time reports are submitted, the system will issue an accurate paycheck and begin tracking employee service based on the reported hours. When the employee is eligible for benefits that have service requirements, the system will notify the plan administrator. The plan administrator may also generate reports to identify those who will become eligible for certain plans.

worked by salaried employees, although tracking such time is not required. Reasons for this review are noted in *Exhibit 9.12*.

Every payroll system must incorporate methods for keeping records as required by law. For example, the FLSA requires employers to keep certain records for each hourly paid employee. It also requires that other records be kept that show how wages were calculated. Still other required records relate to payroll, collective bargaining agreements, and sales and purchase records.

Exhibit 9.12

REASONS TO VERIFY TIME OF SALARIED EMPLOYEES

- Ensure the employee was at work.
- Ensure time records reflect the correct category such as work, personal leave, or sick days.
- Ensure the employee works a fair number of hours.
- Determine whether the employee is working at the expected times.
- Determine whether the employee is misusing paid time off.

Payroll Administration Options

Many operations outsource payroll administration because outside services specialize in this business. These services handle payroll, tax withholding, tax payments, tax reporting, and other payroll processing details. However, managers must still review their employees' time records before submitting information to the payroll service.

In smaller operations a part-time bookkeeper may handle these tasks. Alternatively, some small operations use bookkeeping software designed especially to help with payroll administration for small businesses.

Selecting the right payroll system is critical. This requires determining what the system must record and report:

- Dates and hours worked, regular hours at different pay rates, and overtime rates and hours
- Federal, state, and local taxes
- Vacation, personal time, and sick day accrual and use
- Employees' healthcare and other insurance premiums
- Dollar value of all the benefits each employee receives
- Employee contributions to defined contribution plans such as a 401(k), and also employer's matching contributions
- Quarterly and annual payroll reports to various government agencies
- Garnishments and levies, pay advances and paybacks of these advances
- Merit- or performance-determined pay and bonuses
- Expense reimbursements and other special payments

CONTROLLING LABOR COSTS

Labor costs account for a large part of most operations' total costs. There are numerous strategies that can help to control labor costs, and two of them are of primary importance.

Set Pay Rates

Managers must offer wages and benefits that will encourage people to apply to and remain with the operation, while keeping labor costs as low as practical. It is important to balance these needs while complying with all applicable laws.

Establishing competitive pay rates is a responsibility of human resources professionals in large organizations. Owners or managers may determine pay rates in smaller operations. The first step is to analyze the operation's total labor needs.

ANALYZE TOTAL LABOR NEEDS

It is important to analyze total labor needs before considering how much to pay. How many labor hours are needed each day and for which positions and times? How many people are needed, and should they be full- or part-time employees? What are the total compensation costs, including benefits, for each full-time and part-time employee?

These are the types of questions that are answered, in part, when employees are scheduled according to estimated business volumes (see chapter 6). Managers must understand their operation, the labor market, and the operation's staffing challenges.

RESEARCH WAGE RATES

The wages offered should reflect what other local operations are offering. To be competitive, it is important to consider other employers who seek persons in the same labor pool. Remember that competitors may include businesses in other industries, and compensation includes employee benefits.

The use of compensation surveys was discussed earlier in this chapter. These surveys typically summarize different measures of compensation for various jobs and types of establishments. For example, they may list the average wage earned by prep cooks in a casual fullservice restaurant. Several government, nonprofit, and business organizations publish wage and salary surveys. For example, the National Restaurant Association and State Restaurant Associations provide information on salary surveys, as do many career or human resources Web sites.

DETERMINE MARKET POSITION

After information about the pay ranges of competitors is known, managers can decide if they want to position the operation as a low-pay, high-pay, or competitive-pay organization. From that decision, the pay ranges for each position can be determined. However, when setting rates, managers must consider minimum wage laws and other laws that prohibit discrimination in compensation.

Control Overtime

The process of controlling overtime costs involves careful planning, clear policies, and a system for planning schedules according to expected business volumes. One common way is to develop a policy that requires advance approval for overtime. This reminds supervisors who schedule employees that overtime is not automatic and should be used sparingly. It also reinforces the importance of good advance planning and an awareness of the impact of overtime payments on labor costs.

Managers can also review employee time records at the end of each shift to ensure no employee's hours could lead to overtime later in the week. Schedules for employees who are getting close to 40 hours might then be rearranged to control overtime.

Reducing overtime can be achieved with careful planning, but there are times when overtime is needed:

- There are unforeseen needs for extra staff due to emergencies or unplanned business.
- Employees must be trained.
- Coverage is needed for vacations and time off.

Paying employees to work overtime can result in higher productivity than possible with new hires or temporary workers. However, this approach should be used carefully because excessive overtime can result in reduced productivity, poor morale, and increased turnover. In short-term situations, overtime can be cost-effective for the operation, and it also can be a "perk" for employees willing to work extra hours.

SUMMARY

1. **List and describe three federal laws that impact compensation policies and programs.**

   The Fair Labor Standards Act (FLSA) establishes minimum wage and overtime pay standards. Most hourly positions are entitled to the basic minimum wage, but state and local laws may set a higher minimum, and tipped employees can be paid less when tips bring their wages up to the minimum. Overtime, 1.5 times the normal hourly rate, must be paid when nonexempt employees work more than 40 hours in a week. Managers must monitor compliance with wage and hour requirements.

The Consumer Credit Protection Act (CCPA) prohibits employers from terminating or disciplining employees when wages must be paid to a third party via levy or garnishment.

The Equal Pay Act (EPA) makes it illegal to pay different wages to men and women for equal work in the same workplace. Equal jobs require equal levels of skill, effort, and responsibility under similar conditions.

2. **Explain the types of voluntary benefits that can be included in a compensation package.**

Managers can offer numerous voluntary benefits to employees who meet requirements that they establish. Examples include bonuses, dependent care, death benefits, dental insurance, disability benefits, and educational and professional development support. Other voluntary benefits may include employee assistance programs, flexible spending accounts, funeral leave, health savings accounts, healthcare plans, and life insurance. Long-term care insurance, meals, mental health insurance, paid holidays and vacation, and pension and retirement plans may also be available. Still other benefits may include personal time off, profit-sharing plans, religious holiday time off, stock option plans, uniforms, and vision care.

3. **Identify and describe three retirement and health benefit laws that impact voluntary benefits.**

The Employee Retirement Income Security Act (ERISA) protects employee pensions and healthcare plans from incompetent, unethical, and unfair administration. The Consolidated Omnibus Budget Reconciliation Act (COBRA) extends healthcare coverage for people who would otherwise lose it. The Health Insurance Portability and Accountability Act (HIPAA) helps ensure people do not lose access to healthcare because of limits on plan enrollment periods, preexisting conditions, or other health status factors.

4. **Describe five employee benefit programs that are mandated by federal laws.**

Social Security is a federal program that includes benefits for retirement, survivors, disabilities, and Medicare insurance. Employers and employees pay for benefits through a payroll tax, and the value of the benefit depends, in part, on how much the employee earned and when the payment begins.

Unemployment compensation temporarily provides a reduced income to employees who lose their job involuntarily. Each state has its own rules for the amount of benefits to be paid and for how long.

Workers' compensation is a system for providing financial compensation to employees or their survivors when an employee is injured, becomes sick, or dies as a result of a workplace situation. These programs differ from state to state.

The Family and Medical Leave Act (FMLA) gives qualified employees the right to take up to 12 weeks of continuous or intermittent unpaid leave in a rolling 12-month period for certain medical or family care situations.

The Uniformed Services Employment and Reemployment Rights Act (USERRA) protects employees from workplace discrimination based on military service. It ensures that military personnel are not penalized when they return from duty.

5. **Explain the procedures that help ensure the correct compensation will be paid to employees.**

   Payroll administrators must deliver accurate employee paychecks on time. A payroll system tracks work times and issues paychecks. These systems may be manual or automated but require that supervisors review and sign employee time records to confirm that they are correct.

   Many managers outsource payroll administration. In smaller operations, a part-time bookkeeper may handle these tasks. Software is also available.

6. **Explain the basic procedures that can be used to control labor costs.**

   A four-step process can be used to establish pay levels. First, establish pay rates and, second, analyze total labor needs. Third, research competitors' wage rates. This will enable managers to determine market position so pay ranges can be determined, which is the fourth step.

   Overtime cost control requires a policy of approval before overtime is incurred. It is also important to review time records at the end of each shift to reduce the likelihood that employee's hours could lead to overtime.

APPLICATION EXERCISE

Many activities are involved in calculating and writing employees' checks. The knowledge and time required may encourage use of an external payroll service.

Enter "business payroll services" into a search engine and review the Web sites of several organizations. Then answer the following questions:

1. What types of payroll services are offered?

2. What are potential advantages of using an external payroll service?

3. What responsibilities will remain for managers?

4. What are the associated costs?

5. What main concerns would managers want to address before deciding whether to use a business payroll service?

REVIEW YOUR LEARNING

Select the best answer for each question.

1. **What type of retirement benefit plan guarantees an employee a certain amount of payment on retirement?**

   A. Defined contribution

   B. Defined benefit

   C. Keogh

   D. IRA

2. **Which mandatory federal program provides retirement and survivor benefits for covered workers?**

   A. Social Security

   B. Unemployment insurance

   C. Workers' compensation

   D. Family and Medical Leave Act

3. Why must managers review hours worked by salaried employees?

   A. To ensure length of service is accurate

   B. To ensure use of hourly workers is minimized

   C. To ensure correct work categories are reflected

   D. To ensure taxes and contributions are deducted

4. What is the purpose of compensation surveys?

   A. To determine compensation of employees at a specific property

   B. To compare compensation for jobs in different establishments

   C. To determine estimated labor costs for budget purposes

   D. To develop total labor costs for employee schedules

5. Which employees may be paid a lower minimum wage during their first 90 consecutive days of employment?

   A. Tipped employees

   B. Exempt employees

   C. Employees under 20

   D. Nonexempt employees

6. Under which circumstances may a server be paid less than minimum wage?

   A. Receiving at least $30 in tips in a typical month

   B. Receiving a tip that exceeds 30% of the check

   C. Receiving tips that average at least 8% of sales

   D. Receiving a tip average that exceeds tips of other servers

7. What must a manager do to help comply with the Consolidated Omnibus Budget Reconciliation Act (COBRA)?

   A. Notify the plan administrator when an employee is promoted

   B. Notify the plan administrator when an employee leaves

   C. Notify employees when they are eligible for Medicare

   D. Notify employees of eligibility and enrollment period

8. What action helps a plan administrator comply with the Health Insurance Portability and Accountability Act (HIPAA)?

   A. Allow persons unable to obtain coverage to enroll in group healthcare plans at times besides open enrollment

   B. Provide a summary plan description to employees on enrollment in the group healthcare plan

   C. Notify employees when a preexisting condition changes their coverage premiums

   D. Post a notice about military leave protections in a prominent place

9. How much leave within a year can be taken for certain medical or family care situations under the Family and Medical Leave Act?

   A. 12 weeks

   B. 16 weeks

   C. 20 weeks

   D. 24 weeks

10. What is one of a manager's key responsibilities when an outsourced payroll provider is used?

    A. Generating all of the employees' paychecks on time

    B. Ensuring employees report the correct number of hours

    C. Computing the amount of payroll tax payments

    D. Submitting quarterly reports to government agencies

FIELD PROJECT

A. Develop a list of several questions you will ask restaurant or foodservice managers about employee benefits at their operation. Examples of questions include:

- What voluntary benefits are offered to entry-level employees at your operation?

- What is the approximate cost of mandatory and voluntary benefits per entry-level employee?

- Is there a difference between the types of benefits preferred by the younger and older employees? If so, what are the differences?

Note: *Save the questions you have developed. Your team will conduct interviews with the managers of restaurant or foodservice operations selected by the team. These interviews will include the questions you have developed in this chapter, as well as questions from previous chapters. You may want to use the interview form (template) in the Field Project Information Handbook at the end of this book, or develop an interview form of your own to list your interview questions. This form can then be used to record the managers' responses when you conduct your interview.*

B. Use the Internet to learn more about employee benefits by entering the following or other search terms into your favorite search engine:

- Administering benefits

- Communicating employee benefit information

- Keeping current with benefit laws

Make a list of several suggestions for managing employee benefits and record them in Part II (Internet Resources) for Chapter 9 in the Field Project Information Handbook at the end of this book.

Information about conducting interviews with managers of the two restaurant or foodservice operations your team has selected is found in the "Instructions" material at the beginning of the Field Project Information Handbook. Your team's interviews can now be scheduled because the complete list of questions to be asked has been developed.

10

Managing a Safe and Healthy Workplace

INSIDE THIS CHAPTER

- The Need for a Safe and Healthy Workplace
- Sexual Harassment
- Other Forms of Harassment
- Ensuring Employees' Rights
- Occupational Safety and Health Administration (OSHA)
- Preventing Workplace Violence
- Emergency Management Programs
- Balancing Food Safety, Employee Rights, and the Law
- Employee Assistance and Wellness Programs

CHAPTER LEARNING OBJECTIVES

After completing this chapter, you should be able to:

- Explain what managers can do to maintain a zero-tolerance sexual harassment policy and explain responsibilities regarding nonsexual types of harassment in the workplace.

- Review the procedures for ensuring the rights of employees who are pregnant or disabled, and younger workers.

- Indicate how the Occupational Safety and Health Administration (OSHA) impacts restaurant and foodservice operations, and explain procedures for establishing and maintaining OSHA-mandated programs and participating in OSHA investigations.

- Identify the compliance posters that operations are required to post.

- Describe the procedures for preventing workplace violence.

- Describe the procedures for developing emergency management programs.

- Explain the basic procedures for balancing food safety, employee rights, and the law.

- Provide an overview of employee assistance and employee wellness programs.

KEY TERMS

bloodborne pathogens
standard, p. 308

cardiopulmonary
resuscitation (CPR), p. 309

designated first-aid
provider, p. 308

employee wellness
program, p. 322

Hazard Communication
Standard (HCS), p. 309

material safety data sheet
(MSDS), p. 310

quid pro quo, p. 300

workplace violence, p. 314

CASE STUDY

"It's tough," said Elias, the manager of McNichol's Green Plate Restaurant, as he met with Gabriel, the assistant manager.

"Myla is an excellent employee," Elias continued, "and she's told me about her financial difficulty. I think I just made matters worse. She had a terrible red rash all over her face, hands, and arms, and she couldn't stop coughing. I had no idea what the problem was—and she didn't either. I just didn't think she should be serving food to customers. I said she couldn't work today and suggested she visit a doctor."

"Wow, it is hard for Myla to lose hours and tips," Gabriel said. "She may have something that isn't contagious. Are you sure you did the right thing?"

1. Do you think Elias did the right thing to tell Myla she couldn't work? Why or why not?

2. How would you word a policy to govern this type of situation?

THE NEED FOR A SAFE AND HEALTHY WORKPLACE

Restaurant and foodservice managers have a legal and professional obligation to provide a safe and healthy workplace for their employees. Staff members have many important responsibilities that require their full attention and commitment. They cannot be endangered or distracted by environmental issues in the workplace that their managers have a responsibility to control. For example, concerns about customers, quality, and costs, among other standards, cannot receive the proper attention if employees are confronted with stress created by sexual or other types of harassment.

Likewise, the potential for and fear of physical harm created by bloodborne pathogens and workplace hazards, violence, and crises is not conducive to an environment in which work performance can receive a priority. Issues in the employees' personal lives relating to health and wellness concerns are also among the challenges managers will need to confront as they facilitate the work of their staff members.

SEXUAL HARASSMENT

Harassment is unwelcome conduct based on race, color, religion, sex (including pregnancy), national origin, age (40 or older), disability, or genetic information. Sexual harassment is a form of sex discrimination and is an issue of particular concern in the restaurant and foodservice industry. Title VII of the Civil Rights Act requires employers to protect their employees from sexual harassment by other staff members and anyone in the workplace, including customers and vendors.

Protecting employees from sexual harassment creates a welcoming environment in which employees feel valued. Ensuring that people can work free from harassment and know that any problems will be resolved fairly builds an environment in which morale is good and turnover is low. Managers must understand what sexual harassment is, how to prevent it, and how to respond when it is reported.

Two Types of Sexual Harassment

Managers must understand two types of sexual harassment:

- **Quid pro quo:** From the Latin phrase meaning "this for that," **quid pro quo** harassment occurs when one person asks for either expressly or implied sexual favors from another person as a condition of that person's employment or advancement or to prevent a tangible employment detriment. Such conditions include hirings, firings, raises, scheduling, or promotions. For example, a supervisor promises a raise in return for a sexual favor. It requires the perpetrator to be in a position of power over the victim such as a supervisor.

THINK ABOUT IT . . .

The victim, not the accused, determines whether behavior is "offensive." What one person regards as simple teasing might be considered harassment by another.

Do you agree that the victim should decide? Why or why not?

- **Hostile environment:** This is an atmosphere that is characterized by unwanted sexually demeaning or intimidating behaviors in which a person is treated poorly or feels uncomfortable (*Exhibit 10.1*). For example, people tell offensive jokes of a sexual nature, display sexually offensive pictures, or otherwise behave in threatening or offensive ways. The conduct may be physical, verbal, or nonverbal in nature.

Exhibit 10.1

Sexual harassment includes men harassing women, women harassing men, men harassing men, and women harassing women. The best managers want to encourage normal, friendly interactions and other social behaviors that create a welcoming workplace environment. Therefore, it is helpful to understand what is not considered sexual harassment:

- Normal, friendly interactions
- Nonoffensive joking
- Being polite or nice
- Socializing and being friendly
- Any behavior that would not offend a reasonable person

Sexual Harassment Policies

Most operations have a zero-tolerance policy against sexual harassment that includes several types of statements. Company policies need to adopt a prevention approach that acknowledges mutual respect as the goal for all who work in the environment:

- The operation does not tolerate harassment in any form by any person.
- All persons are responsible for stopping harassment whenever it occurs.
- Harassment should be reported immediately.

Preventing a Hostile Environment

Managers must follow and enforce their company's policies on sexual harassment. In addition, they must do several other things:

- Help employees understand what sexual harassment is, how to avoid it, and how to deal with it. Educate employees and train them to follow company policies and procedures. Ensure that the training teaches people how to say no and communicate their discomfort, so that others can understand when behavior is unwanted or offensive.

- Encourage open communication. Help employees feel comfortable bringing issues to a manager's attention. Listen to what they say and take their concerns seriously.

- Set a good example by following company policies and demonstrating appropriate behavior. A manager's words and actions should consistently convey that harassment is not acceptable, and reflect positive ways to interact with people.

301

- Look for signs of harassment in the operation. Eliminate anything on bulletin boards or elsewhere that might offend people, such as cartoons or pictures of a sexual nature. Observe how people interact, and stop inappropriate behavior.

- If harassment is observed, promptly enforce policies in a fair and equitable manner. If this is not done, confusion and resentment will be created, and the operation will be at risk for claims of discrimination. Conversely, when sexual harassment policies are enforced, this confirms that the manager and the establishment are serious about protecting employees' rights, and most people will behave accordingly.

Addressing Harassment Claims

Despite a manager's best efforts, sexual harassment may occur. If an employee harasses another employee, managers should address the issue promptly and follow these guidelines unless they conflict with company policy:

- An alleged victim should report the complaint initially to his or her direct supervisor unless that person is the subject of the complaint. If so, the next level of management or a human resources representative should receive the complaint. Assure the person reporting the harassment that everything will be kept as confidential as possible and that there will be no retaliation for reporting the situation. The manager receiving the complaint should inform his or her own supervisor or human resources staff.

- Complaints should be investigated thoroughly by the alleged victim's direct supervisor, unless that person is the subject of the complaint. If so, the next management level or human resources representative should conduct the investigation. In all cases, investigations must be done in confidence to the extent possible.

- The complaint should be processed in accordance with any local or state law, and following company policy. Discuss the complaint with the person who reported it to learn more about the situation. Collect any evidence, such as notes, text messages, or emails. Find out if there were any witnesses and, if so, interview them.

- Employees should not discuss the situation with other employees. Managers should only discuss the situation with appropriate parties.

- If necessary, change the work schedule for either party so that the parties do not work together while the harassment claim is being investigated.

- Always include a third person, such as a manager or supervisor, to witness the interview. Explain the accusation, and ask the accused what he or she believes happened. After this discussion, it may be necessary to talk to the complaining party or witnesses again to clarify the situation.

When the investigation is complete, consult with the manager, human resources department, or legal counsel, and take whatever action is reasonable based on what was discovered. Each case is different, so if harassment is found, the action taken should be reasonably related to the severity of the situation. If the investigation reveals that an employee has harassed another, the offender must be subject to appropriate disciplinary procedures including the possibility of termination.

If an employee mentions harassment by a nonemployee, the manager should promptly explain the establishment's harassment policy to the accused and indicate that everyone who comes to the establishment must follow it. Remain professional and do not get personally involved. Remember to focus on the behavior and not the personalities of the people involved. Further investigation will be required to ensure harassment is prevented or stopped.

OTHER FORMS OF HARASSMENT

While sexual harassment is the most commonly reported type of harassment in restaurant and foodservice operations, other forms of harassment also occur. These include harassment due to race, religion, pregnancy, age, disability, and sexual orientation. Federal laws address all of these except sexual orientation, and some state or local laws address that.

Many of the basic strategies used to manage sexual harassment apply to other forms of harassment. In all cases, conduct becomes unlawful when an employee must endure the offensive conduct as a condition of continued employment, or when the conduct is severe or pervasive enough to create a work environment that a reasonable person would consider intimidating, hostile, or abusive. Antidiscrimination laws prohibit harassment in retaliation for filing a discrimination charge, testifying, or participating in any way in an investigation, proceeding, or lawsuit under these laws. They also protect those who oppose employment practices that they reasonably believe discriminate against individuals in violation of these laws.

Offensive conduct includes name calling, physical assaults or threats, intimidation, ridicule or mockery, insults or put-downs, and interference with work performance. Harassment can occur in numerous ways:

- The harasser can be the victim's manager, supervisor, a supervisor in another area, an agent of the employer, a coworker, or even a nonemployee.
- The victim does not have to be the person harassed; he or she can be anyone affected by the offensive conduct.
- Unlawful harassment may occur without economic injury to, or discharge of, the victim.

THINK ABOUT IT . . .

With a harassment complaint, the best defense against possible legal claims is most often to address the issue promptly, thoroughly, and professionally.

What are examples of things a manager can do that fit this description?

Manager's Memo

Prevention is the best tool for eliminating workplace harassment. Employers should clearly communicate to employees that harassing conduct will not be tolerated. Managers should establish an effective complaint or grievance process, provide antiharassment training to managers and employees, and take immediate and appropriate action when an employee complains. Employers should create an environment in which employees feel free to raise concerns and are confident that their concerns will be addressed.

Employees should inform the harasser directly that the conduct is unwelcome and must stop, although this is not required. They should also report harassment to a manager when it first occurs to prevent its continuance or escalation. If the employee feels eminently threatened, he or she can call the police. If the harasser is the manager, the manager's boss should be contacted. If the manager is the owner, information found on required compliance posters will provide contact information for Equal Employment Opportunity or other regulatory agencies.

An employer is automatically liable for harassment by a supervisor that results in a negative employment action, such as termination, failure to promote or hire, or loss of wages. If the supervisor's harassment results in a hostile work environment, the employer can avoid liability if two conditions are met:

- He or she can prove that a reasonable effort was made to prevent and promptly correct the harassing behavior.
- The employee unreasonably failed to take advantage of any preventive or corrective opportunities provided.

The employer can also be liable for harassment by nonsupervisory employees or nonemployees over whom it has control, such as vendors or customers on the premises. The employer is liable if management knew or should have known about the harassment and failed to take prompt and appropriate corrective action. When investigating allegations of harassment, the EEOC studies the entire record including the nature of the conduct and the context in which the alleged incidents occurred. A determination of whether harassment is severe or pervasive enough to be illegal is made on a case-by-case basis.

ENSURING EMPLOYEES' RIGHTS

This section explores how managers can ensure the employment rights of specific groups. These include employees who are pregnant or disabled, and younger workers.

Rights of Employees Who Are Pregnant

The Pregnancy Discrimination Act prohibits employers from discriminating against women on the basis of pregnancy, childbirth, or related medical conditions. Women affected by these conditions should be treated the same for all employment-related purposes, and they should receive the same benefits as other persons with similar abilities or work limitations.

This law means that managers cannot do the following:

- Refuse to hire a woman because of a pregnancy-related condition while she is able to perform the major functions of the job
- Identify pregnancy-related conditions for special procedures to determine an employee's ability to work
- Require an employee who is pregnant to go on leave or remain on leave until the baby's birth
- Prohibit an employee from returning to work for a predetermined length of time after childbirth

Managers must treat an employee who is temporarily unable to perform her job due to pregnancy the same as any other employee who is temporarily disabled. At this point, the pregnant employee may also be eligible for time off under the Family and Medical Leave Act. Managers must allow pregnant employees to work as long as they are able to do their job. In addition, the Pregnancy Discrimination Act affects the healthcare coverage employers must provide. Healthcare plans must cover the expenses for pregnancy-related conditions on the same basis as the costs for other medical conditions and should offer the same level of coverage to the spouses of both female and male employees. Any pregnancy-related benefits must be given to all pregnant employees, whether or not they are married.

Rights of Employees Who Are Disabled

The Americans with Disabilities Act (ADA) forbids discrimination against anyone in the workplace because of a disability. When a job applicant or employee with disabilities can perform the essential functions of a job with or without reasonable accommodation, the ADA prohibits discrimination. This applies to screening, selection, hiring, training, compensation, promotion, termination, and other terms, conditions, and privileges of employment.

The ADA prohibits discrimination against persons who are disabled in other ways. For example, it requires persons with disabilities, including customers, to have equal access to buildings, spaces within them, and public services. Building codes will require wide restroom stalls for people in wheelchairs. Managers should make braille menus available or train staff to suggest that the menu can be read to customers who are visually impaired. "Talking" menus are also available that provide information to persons with sight disabilities. Note that these menus are also useful for persons who speak and read in a language other than that in which the menu is printed.

Operations with 15 or more employees on each workday during 20 or more weeks in the current or preceding year must comply with the ADA. Employees are considered disabled and are covered by the law if certain conditions are met:

1. They have a physical or mental impairment that substantially limits one or more of the major life activities. (See *Exhibit 10.2*.) Conditions such as epilepsy, paralysis, HIV infection, AIDS, a substantial hearing or visual impairment, mental retardation, or a specific learning disability qualify as an impairment. However, an individual with a minor condition of short duration such as a sprain, a broken limb, or the flu generally would not be covered.

2. They have a record of an impairment, such as cancer or heart disease, but have recovered from it.

3. They may be regarded as having an impairment. This covers people who do not have an impairment but may be discriminated against as if they are impaired. For example, a person with a facial disfigurement is denied a front-of-the-house position because the employer fears negative reactions.

Exhibit 10.2

MAJOR LIFE ACTIVITIES UNDER THE ADA

- Walking
- Seeing
- Hearing
- Breathing
- Sitting
- Standing
- Lifting
- Learning
- Thinking
- Caring for oneself
- Performing manual tasks
- Interacting with others
- Eating
- Sleeping
- Bending
- Speaking
- Reading
- Concentrating
- Communicating
- Working

An employee must meet only one of these conditions to be considered disabled. Temporary impairments caused by alcoholism and illegal drug use are not covered under the ADA. However, permanent impairments such as liver damage that limit a person's ability to work are covered as long as the person is in treatment or has stopped drinking or using drugs.

Exhibit 10.3

Rights of Younger Workers

Minors younger than 18 are more likely than older workers to be injured in the workplace. The Fair Labor Standards Act (FLSA), as amended, has established provisions for child labor (see chapter 8). Also, various state and local laws were built on this federal law to offer further protections.

Minors cannot be employed in jobs or use equipment deemed hazardous by the Department of Labor. While the restaurant and foodservice industry is not considered hazardous, the FLSA restricts the tasks that minors can perform.

Generally, according to the Department of Labor, persons who are 16 and 17 years old can work in front-of-the-house positions (*Exhibit 10.3*) but are restricted in the back of the house. For example, they cannot operate, feed, set up, adjust, repair, or clean any equipment declared hazardous:

- Power-driven meat processing machines, including meat slicers (even if used to slice cheese or vegetables), meat saws, patty-forming machines, meat grinders, and meat choppers
- Commercial mixers, such as vertical dough and batter mixers, including most countertop models
- Certain power-driven bakery machines, such as dough rollers and dough sheeters

Federal law also prohibits minors from most driving jobs. No employee under 18 is allowed to drive on public roads unless it is only incidental to the job. Sixteen-year-olds cannot drive on the job at all, and 17-year-olds with a valid driver's license may drive occasionally with restrictions:

- They cannot make time-sensitive deliveries.
- They cannot drive at night.
- They cannot ride on a motor vehicle outside the cab.

Although 14- and 15-year-olds can work in front-of-the-house positions, the work they are allowed to do in other areas is more restricted. In addition to the restrictions for 16- and 17-year-olds, 14- and 15-year-olds are prohibited from certain tasks:

- Performing any baking tasks, including weighing ingredients
- Operating broilers, fryolators, rotisseries, or pressure cookers
- Operating, setting up, adjusting, cleaning, oiling, or repairing power-driven food slicers and grinders, food choppers and cutters, and bakery-type mixers
- Working in freezers or meat coolers

Minors who are 14 and 15 years old are allowed to perform certain food-preparation tasks:

- Cook with electric and gas grills that do not involve open flames
- Use deep-fat fryers equipped with devices that automatically raise and lower baskets
- Perform kitchen work and other work involved in preparing and serving food and beverages
- Use equipment including dishwashers, toasters, dumbwaiters, popcorn poppers, milkshake blenders, coffee grinders, warmers, steam tables, heat lamps, and microwave ovens—if used only to warm prepared food to temperatures at or below 140°F (60°C)
- Clean kitchen surfaces and non–power-driven kitchen equipment when the surfaces and equipment temperatures are not hotter than 100°F (38°C)
- Filter, transport, and dispose of oil and grease when the oil or grease temperature is not hotter than 100°F (38°C)

Generally, child labor laws prohibit children younger than 14 from any type of work, with some exceptions. State laws may further restrict the tasks that minors can do or the equipment they can use. However, once a person turns 18, child labor laws no longer apply.

The FLSA and many state laws also restrict the hours that minors can work, and violations of time restrictions account for many compliance problems. Fourteen- and 15-year-olds may work outside school hours for only limited time periods. The federal government does not limit the hours of 16- and 17-year-olds. They may even work overtime, and employers must pay them overtime wages. However, state and local laws may apply instead of the FLSA. Therefore, it is always important to check with state and local departments of labor or seek professional advice.

There may be other state or local regulations or restrictions that affect the employment of minors. For example, most states require that minors provide employers with a work permit or age certificate as a condition of employment. Depending on the state, these documents may be issued by the local school district or a government labor department.

OCCUPATIONAL SAFETY AND HEALTH ADMINISTRATION (OSHA)

The Occupational Safety and Health Administration (OSHA) is an agency within the U.S. Department of Labor that enforces the Occupational Safety and Health Act (OSH Act). The purpose of the OSH Act is to ensure safe working conditions and prevent workplace injuries. Many states have created their own occupational safety and health laws and agencies.

Federal and state regulations affect many aspects of running a restaurant or foodservice operation. They cover nearly every potential danger an employee might encounter, and they require preventive and protective measures. Managers should know that safety for employees and customers is a key priority. Failure to provide a safe environment can result in fines, penalties, lawsuits, and imprisonment.

Bloodborne Pathogens Standard

Many restaurant and foodservice employees work in kitchens with sharp knives and equipment (*Exhibit 10.4*), and sometimes they cut themselves. Numerous diseases can be caused by bloodborne pathogens. These include, but are not limited to, hepatitis B (from the hepatitis B virus [HBV]); hepatitis C (from the hepatitis C virus [HCV]); acquired immunodeficiency syndrome (AIDS) (from the human immunodeficiency virus [HIV]); HTLV-I-associated myelopathy (from the human T-lymphotrophic virus Type 1 [HTLV-I]); diseases associated with HTLV-II; and malaria, syphilis, babesiosis, brucellosis, leptospirosis, arboviral infections, relapsing fever, Creutzfeldt-Jakob (known as mad-cow) disease, and viral hemorrhagic fever.

In response, OSHA has developed a process called the **bloodborne pathogens standard**. Its requirements state what employers must do to protect workers who can reasonably be anticipated to come into contact with blood or other potentially infectious materials (OPIM) as a result of doing their job. While this standard is intended primarily for people who work in healthcare, other organizations must also comply if they have a designated first-aid provider.

A **designated first-aid provider** is an employee trained and appointed to provide first aid. This responsibility should be included in the job description but is not part of the employee's main work. For example, a *sous chef* could be a designated first aider, but a company nurse could not be. A designated first aider is sometimes required by local law or if certain severe injuries or illnesses can be anticipated. If an establishment is required to have a designated first-aid provider, the establishment must follow the bloodborne pathogens standard. However, even if the operation is not required to follow

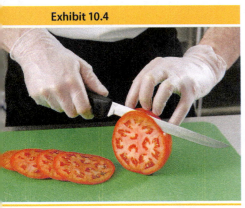

Exhibit 10.4

this standard, doing so can help reduce exposure, create goodwill, and reduce liability risks. The bloodborne pathogens standard requires several preventive measures:

- **Exposure control plan:** Documented operating procedures to eliminate or minimize employees' exposure to another's blood or other potentially infectious materials are required. This plan must include provisions for training, annual reviews, and updates.

- **Vaccinations:** Per OSHA, managers must make hepatitis B vaccinations available to all employees who may have exposure to the disease. The operation must offer the vaccination after the required training and within ten days of the start of the assignment.

- **Training:** Designated first-aid providers should be taught how to safely handle this responsibility. Possible training topics include first-aid techniques and certification; ways to avoid or minimize exposure; handling and removal of gloves, clothing, bandages, and laundry; handwashing; emergency phone numbers; cleaning procedures; ways bloodborne diseases are transmitted; and how to report an exposure incident.

- **Personal protective equipment (PPE):** Gloves, waterproof aprons, eye protection, and disposable CPR devices should be given to the designated first-aid provider. CPR is short for **cardiopulmonary resuscitation**, which involves breathing into the mouth and pressing on the chest to help a person who has stopped breathing, and whose heart may have stopped beating, stay alive.

If an employee is exposed to another employee's blood in the workplace, the bloodborne pathogens standard requires the following actions:

- **Hepatitis B vaccination:** Within 24 hours after an employee is exposed, he or she should be offered a free postexposure vaccination against hepatitis B. Although this action is required only for designated first-aid providers, any exposed employee can be offered the vaccination.

- **Medical evaluation:** Arrange for the employee to have a confidential medical evaluation.

- **Record keeping:** Maintain a record of each occupational exposure to blood.

Hazard Communication Standard

All operations must comply with OSHA's standard for communicating information about workplace hazards. The **Hazard Communication Standard (HCS)**, also known as Right-to-Know or HAZCOM, is designed to protect employees from physical hazards such as explosions and health hazards such as medical conditions caused by exposure to chemicals. HAZCOM is short for "Hazard Communication." A violation of the HCS is the most common problem cited by OSHA for eating and drinking establishments. (See *Exhibit 10.5*.)

Exhibit 10.5

TOP 10 OSHA VIOLATIONS AT EATING AND DRINKING PLACES (2011)

Failure to follow OSHA requirements relating to the following concerns are the most frequently cited problems in restaurant and foodservice related establishments:

1. Hazard Communication
2. General Personal Protective Equipment Requirements
3. General Electrical Requirements
4. Wiring Methods, Components, and Equipment for General Use
5. General Walking/Working Surface Requirements
6. Medical Services and First Aid
7. Exit Route Maintenance and Safeguards
8. Hand Protection
9. Portable Fire Extinguishers
10. Eye and Face Protection

Source: *http://www.osha.gov/SLTC/restaurant/index.html*

To comply with the HCS, employers must communicate information about any potential chemical hazards to employees. This requirement involves use of **material safety data sheets (MSDSs)**. As the example in *Exhibit 10.6* shows, MSDSs are documents that provide information about the chemical content of a material, as well as the following:

- Instructions about safe use and handling
- Physical, health, fire, and reactivity hazards
- Precautions
- Appropriate personal protective equipment (PPE) to wear when using the chemical
- First-aid information and steps to take in an emergency
- Manufacturer's name, address, and phone number
- Preparation date of MSDS
- Hazardous ingredients and identity information

Exhibit 10.6

SAMPLE MATERIAL SAFETY DATA SHEET

Material Safety Data Sheet — ECOLAB
OASIS 146 MULTI-QUAT SANITIZER

Section 1. Chemical product and company identification

Trade name : OASIS 146 MULTI-QUAT SANITIZER
Product use : Sanitizer.
Supplier : Ecolab Inc. Institutional Division
370 N. Wabasha Street
St. Paul, MN 55102
1-800-352-5326

Code : 910787
Date of issue : 30-March-2005
EPA Registraion No. : 1677-198

EMERGENCY HEALTH INFORMATION: 1-800-328-0026
Outside United States and Canada CALL 1-651-222-5352

Section 2. Composition, Information on Ingredients

Name	CAS number	% by weight
quaternary ammonium compounds, di-c8-10-alkyldimethyl, chlorides	68424-95-3	1 - 5
quaternary ammonium compounds, benzyl-c12-c16-alkyldimethyl, chlorides	68424-85-1	1 - 5
Ethanol	64-17-5	1 - 5

Section 3. Hazards identification

Physical state : Liquid. (Liquid.)
Emergency overview : Danger!

CAUSES RESPIRATORY TRACT, EYE AND SKIN BURNS.
MAY BE HARMFUL IF SWALLOWED.
Do not ingest. Do not get in eyes, on skin or clothing. Do not breathe vapor or mist. Keep container closed. Use only with adequate ventilation. Wash thoroughly after handling.

Potential acute health effects

Eyes : Corrosive to eyes.
Skin : Corrosive to the skin.
Inhalation : Corrosive to the respiratory system.
Ingestion : Harmful if swallowed. May cause burns to mouth, throat and stomach.
See toxicological information (section 11)

Section 4. First aid measures

Eye contact : In case of contact, immediately flush eyes with cool running water. Remove contact lenses and continue flushing with plenty of water for at least 15 minutes. Get medical attention immediately.
Skin contact : In case of contact, immediately flush skin with plenty of water for at least 15 minutes while removing contaminated clothing and shoes. Wash clothing before reuse. Thoroughly clean shoes before reuse. Get medical attention immediately.
Inhalation : If inhaled, remove to fresh air. If not breathing, give artificial respiration. If breathing is difficult, give oxygen. Get medical attention immediately.
Ingestion : Rinse mouth; then drink one or two large glasses of water. Do NOT induce vomiting unless directed to do so by medical personnel. Never give anything by mouth to an unconscious person. Get medical attention immediately.

---

6 MULTI-QUAT SANITIZER — Page: 2/4

Section 5. Fire fighting measures

: > 100°C
: Use an extinguishing agent suitable for surrounding fires.

Dike area of fire to prevent product run-off.
No specific hazard.
Fire fighters should wear appropriate protective equipment and self-contained breathing apparatus (SCBA) with a full facepiece operated in positive pressure mode.

Section 6. Accidental release measures

: Ventilate area of leak or spill. Do not touch damaged containers or spilled material unless wearing appropriate protective equipment (Section 8). Stop leak if without risk. Prevent entry into sewers, water courses, basements or confined areas.
: Avoid dispersal of spilled material and runoff and contact with soil, waterways, drains and sewers.
: If emergency personnel are unavailable, contain spilled material. For small spills add absorbent (soil may be used in the absence of other suitable materials) scoop up material and place in a sealed, liquid-proof container for disposal. For large spills dike spilled material or otherwise contain material to ensure runoff does not reach a waterway. Place spilled material in an appropriate container for disposal.

Section 7. Handling and storage

: Do not ingest. Avoid contact with eyes, skin and clothing. Wash thoroughly after handling.
: Keep out of the reach of children. Keep container tightly closed. Keep container in a cool, well-ventilated area.
Do not store below 0°C

Section 8. Exposure Controls, Personal Protection

: Provide exhaust ventilation or other engineering controls to keep the airborne concentrations of vapors below their respective occupational exposure limits. Ensure that eyewash stations and safety showers are proximal to the work-station location.

Use chemical splash goggles. For continued or severe exposure wear a face shield over the goggles.
Use chemical resistant, impervious gloves.
Wear suitable protective clothing.
Use a properly fitted, air-purifying or air-fed respirator complying with an approved standard if a risk assessment indicates this is necessary. Respirator selection must be based on known or anticipated exposure levels, the hazards of the product and the safe working limits of the selected respirator.

Exposure limits
ACGIH TLV (United States, 5/2004). Notes: 1996 Adoption
Refers to Appendix A -- Carcinogens.
TWA: 1880 mg/m³ 8 hour(s). Form: All forms
TWA: 1000 ppm 8 hour(s). Form: All forms
OSHA PEL (United States, 6/1993).
TWA: 1900 mg/m³ 8 hour(s). Form: All forms
TWA: 1000 ppm 8 hour(s). Form: All forms

Courtesy of Ecolab, Inc.

Manufacturers of potentially hazardous materials must provide MSDSs to their customers, who must make them available to employees. Managers must ensure that their vendors provide MSDSs when appropriate. They must ensure that employees know where these documents are located, that they have free access to them, and that staff are trained in how to use any hazardous materials safely.

Not all chemicals used in a restaurant or foodservice operation are considered hazardous materials. OSHA excludes most consumer products, such as window or toilet bowl cleaners, if the material is used as intended and employees are not exposed more frequently than a user in a home environment. Managers who are not sure whether MSDSs are needed for a product should ask the product's vendor.

Managers must ensure that several steps are undertaken to adhere to OSHA requirements. The discussion that follows relates to the management of MSDS records. However, other OSHA-mandated programs including those relating to bloodborne pathogens, personal protective equipment, emergency action plans, and lockout/tagout require similar steps. There may also be state-mandated programs for reporting injuries and preventing illness that require use of a formal process to ensure compliance.

The first step in maintaining OSHA-mandated records is to determine who will be the HAZCOM coordinator for the establishment. This should be a management-level person who has knowledge of OSHA requirements and some knowledge of the chemicals used in the establishment. He or she should also have a good personal safety track record.

OSHA requires employers to develop a written plan describing how they will meet OSHA regulations of the HCS in their establishment. OSHA'S Web site, *www.OSHA.gov*, provides program requirements that are downloadable. The requirements should be reviewed annually. Automatic updates are available from OSHA.

A list of chemicals that require MSDSs, such as soaps, cleaners, sanitizers, degreasers, paints, and printer toner, should be identified. Any chemical used in excess of normal household use within a year could be included. Chemicals shipped with MSDSs must be tracked.

The HAZCOM coordinator, working with other members of the management team, should determine whether the MSDS program will be managed in-house or outsourced. If it is outsourced, the coordinator must maintain MSDSs through the third-party company. If MSDSs are to be maintained in-house, all required sheets should be collected from manufacturers or suppliers. All chemical containers should be properly labeled in compliance with OSHA regulations.

Employees should be trained during orientation and on an ongoing basis about how to properly use all chemicals required on the job. Retraining is needed annually, or whenever a new chemical is introduced for use in the establishment. Training should be documented, a record should be signed by trainee and trainer, and this record should be maintained.

The HAZCOM coordinator should ensure that MSDSs are current for all chemicals, and they should be available in the languages spoken by employees. They can be maintained in a book, and this information should be readily available to all employees. Also, it is helpful to check MSDSs against the inventory of chemicals on a periodic basis such as every three months. A system should be created to keep MSDSs for a required time, such as a specified number of years from time of use, and these records must be organized and searchable.

OSHA Investigations

Someone in the establishment may need to participate in OSHA investigations conducted by an OSHA compliance officer at the property. This manager should be familiar with OSHA regulations and investigation procedures and should have communications access to all interested parties.

He or she must be able to understand the appropriate OSHA documents to prepare and have knowledge of possible causes of investigation and reporting requirements. Another part of his or her responsibility may be to identify instances in which the operation must contact OSHA. For example, when there is a death or serious injury, an immediate report to an OSHA-based or local regulatory authority will be required.

The manager should contact the OSHA area office to confirm that the claim about the investigation is accurate and to review appropriate documents beforehand. The OSHA contact list must be reviewed regularly to maintain accurate information. It will also be important to immediately contact all necessary parties, including corporate superiors, the owner, and the establishment's risk management team, if there is one. A risk management team is composed of managers and others who work cooperatively to identify, assess, and prioritize risks. Once identified, the risk management team creates a plan to reduce or eliminate the impact of the negative events they have identified.

While the manager must cooperate with the OSHA compliance officer, it is appropriate to first check his or her identification to confirm that the individual is authorized. Appropriate meeting space, such as an office or a quiet booth or table, should be provided for the OSHA compliance officer to perform required activities.

The authorized manager should provide any requested documents to the OSHA compliance officer and provide access to any employee for interviews. The manager should accompany the OSHA compliance officer at all times. However, if an OSHA compliance officer wishes to interview an employee, this may be done in private.

The manager should record or photocopy any information provided to the OSHA compliance officer. Also, notes should be kept of all interactions. The manager should ask the OSHA compliance officer to clarify anything about which he or she is uncertain, and a list should be kept of all employees on-site at the time of the investigation.

It is important to provide all information requested and to take corrective action required by OSHA within the required time period. If possible, take action immediately while the OSHA compliance officer is present. Examples of immediate corrective action may include equipment maintenance, changes to procedures, and training.

The manager should also cooperate with the OSHA compliance officer during any follow-up visit to confirm that all requested actions have been taken. A copy should be retained of all information provided to OSHA that describes corrective actions in response to the investigation. Retain all subsequent documentation provided by OSHA. This documentation should be maintained in a secure location.

Exhibit 10.7

Compliance Posters

OSHA requires that compliance posters be posted in accordance with federal, state, and local law. Some procedures are helpful to ensure that this requirement is implemented correctly. Other federal and state mandates may also require posters, and some municipalities may require posters dealing with smoking and handwashing. The steps that follow for OSHA compliance will be useful guidelines for these programs as well.

Managers should determine which posters must be posted in accordance with federal, state, and local laws. Some operations retain a service to determine and update posters as necessary. Penalties for not posting these posters or not providing the correct languages can be severe. Specific information can be found at the Web site for each law.

The required posters are available from the applicable government agency. Alternatively, private organizations will print combination posters that include all necessary information in a single poster. These organizations can also be contracted to provide updated posters as requirements change.

Posters should be posted appropriately in accordance with all legal requirements. They must be posted in common areas where employees can have easy access, such as bulletin boards in break rooms (*Exhibit 10.7*).

It is important to maintain current posters, and requirements can change, so this is an ongoing process. If an outside vendor has been contracted, it will perform this task. Any updated poster should be obtained and posted immediately.

PREVENTING WORKPLACE VIOLENCE

Workplace violence is violence or the threat of violence against workers.[1] It can occur at or outside the workplace and can range from threats and verbal abuse to physical assaults and homicide, one of the leading causes of job-related deaths. However it manifests itself, workplace violence is a growing concern for employers and employees nationwide.

Approximately two million American workers are victims of workplace violence annually. It can occur anywhere, and no one is immune. Some workers, however, are at increased risk, including those who exchange money with the public; deliver products or services; or work alone or in small groups during late night or early morning hours, in high-crime areas, or in community settings. These risk factors apply to many restaurant and foodservice operations.

[1] Adapted from *www.osha.gov/OshDoc/data_General_Facts/factsheet-workplace-violence.pdf*

A workplace violence prevention program can be developed or information can be included in an existing accident prevention program, employee handbook, or standard operating procedures manual. All employees should know the policy and understand that all claims of workplace violence will be investigated and remedied promptly.

Managers can also provide some additional protections:

- Provide safety education for employees so they know what conduct is not acceptable, what to do if they witness or are subjected to workplace violence, and how to protect themselves from it.

- Secure the workplace. Where appropriate, install video surveillance, extra lighting, and alarm systems and minimize access by outsiders through identification badges, electronic keys, and guards.

- Provide drop safes to limit the amount of cash on hand. Keep a minimal amount of cash in registers during evenings and late night hours.

- Instruct employees not to enter any location where they feel unsafe. Introduce a "buddy system" or provide an escort or police assistance in potentially dangerous situations or at night.

Nothing can guarantee that an employee will not become a victim of workplace violence, but some steps can help reduce the odds. First, learn how to recognize, avoid, or defuse potentially violent situations by attending personal safety training programs. Also, alert supervisors to any concerns about safety or security and report all incidents immediately in writing.

Managers should encourage employees to report and record all incidents and threats of workplace violence. They should also report violent incidents to the local police promptly and provide prompt medical evaluation and treatment.

Managers should inform victims of their legal right to prosecute offenders. They should also discuss the circumstances of the incident with staff members and encourage employees to share information about ways to avoid similar situations in the future.

Other important strategies include investigating all violent incidents and threats, monitoring trends by type or situation, and instituting corrective actions. Managers should also discuss changes in procedures during regular employee meetings. Managers may choose to offer stress debriefing sessions and posttraumatic counseling services to help workers recover from a violent incident.

Manager's Memo

The number and types of mandatory and voluntary posters that employers may post are large. For example, here is a list of posters available from the U.S. Department of Labor. Note that not all posters will be required for every operation:

- Job Safety and Health: It's the Law

- Equal Employment Opportunity Is the Law

- Employee Rights Under the Fair Labor Standards Act

- Employee Rights for Workers with Disabilities Paid at Special Minimum Wages

- Your Rights and Responsibilities Under the Family and Medical Leave Act

- Your Rights Under USERRA

- Notice to All Employees Working on Federal or Federally Financed Construction Projects

- Employee Rights on Government Contracts

- Employee Polygraph Protection Act Notice

- Migrant and Seasonal Agricultural Worker Protection Act Notice

- Notification of Employee Rights Under Federal Labor Laws

EMERGENCY MANAGEMENT PROGRAMS

Managers should recognize that emergencies can occur and develop plans to address them. Ideally, these plans will never be needed. However, dangers to employees, customers, and property will be reduced if plans are developed and employees know their roles in implementing them.

Basics of Emergency Management Plans

OSHA requirements provide a framework for the components of an emergency plan:

- A written or oral plan is needed. A plan should be in writing, kept in the workplace, and available to employees for review. Employers with 10 or fewer employees may communicate the plan orally.

- The elements of a plan must include, at a minimum: procedures for reporting a fire or other emergency; procedures for emergency evacuation, including type of evacuation and exit route assignments; and procedures for employees who remain to perform critical operations before they evacuate. Other procedures are required to account for all employees after evacuation and for employees performing rescue or medical duties. Also needed is the name or job title of every employee who may be contacted by employees who need more information or an explanation of their duties.

- An employer must have and maintain an alarm system that alerts all employees to the emergency, and the system must use a distinctive signal for each emergency.

- An employer must designate and train employees to assist in a safe and orderly evacuation of other employees and customers.

- An employer must review the emergency action plan with each employee covered when the plan is developed or the employee is assigned initially to a job, when the employee's responsibilities change, and when the plan is changed.

Fires

Small fires can become large and dangerous very quickly. Employees are exposed to fire hazards from heat-producing equipment such as range ovens, grills, broilers, and deep fryers (*Exhibit 10.8*). These hazards can be caused by working around open flames, poor housekeeping, grease fires, dirty ventilation ducts, improper storage of flammable items, and faulty or frayed electrical cords.

Exhibit 10.8

Several strategies can be used to prevent or address fires in food-production areas:

- Do not carry or move oil containers when the oil is hot or on fire.

- Do not throw water on a grease fire.

- Empty grease traps frequently.

- Keep cooking surfaces clean and free from grease buildup that might cause a fire.

- Do not use defective electrical cords or equipment.

- Do not store flammable items near heat-producing equipment or open flames.

- Extinguish oil or grease fires by sliding a lid over the container's top or using an appropriate fire extinguisher.

Portable fire extinguishers of the proper type can control or extinguish small fires. They also can protect evacuation routes that a fire may block with smoke or burning materials.

There are several types of fire extinguishers:

- A water type is used to extinguish wood, paper, and trash fires.

- A foam type can extinguish fires involving wood, paper, and trash, and also flammable liquids, gasoline, oil, paints, and grease.

- A carbon dioxide extinguisher can extinguish fires caused by flammable liquids, gasoline, oil paints, and grease and electrical equipment fires.

- A sodium or potassium bicarbonate extinguisher can extinguish fires caused by flammable liquids, gasoline, oil, paints, grease, and electrical equipment fires.

- A multipurpose extinguisher can extinguish all the previously listed types of fires.

To use a portable fire extinguisher, the employee must have immediate access to it, know how to activate it, and know how to apply its contents effectively. Risk is involved because fires can increase in size and intensity very quickly. Fire can block the exit path of the employee and in the process create a hazardous environment. Portable fire extinguishers contain very limited contents, which can be discharged in just a few seconds. Before using a portable fire extinguisher, a very quick risk assessment must be made to address several questions. The answers help determine the likelihood that a trained employee can safely put out a fire:

- Is the fire too big to be extinguished by a portable fire extinguisher?

- Is the air safe to breathe?

- Is the environment hot or smoky?

- Is there a safe evacuation path?

REAL MANAGER

CRISIS MANAGEMENT

Crisis management is critical. This is an area where HR professionals can and should champion because people are the first concern—employees and guests. A good plan is comprehensive and involves every function in the business.

I've had experience with developing a crisis plan as well as simply facing a crisis and not having a plan. I remember 9/11 as if it were yesterday. I was in Washington, DC, at the time. Ironically, I was with my team that morning literally about to tee off at a golf course; we were there taking a much needed break from all the opening chaos we had been through. I got a call from my best friend. He just kept shouting at me, "where are you, where are you!" It was eerie, and as I looked around people just started walking toward the clubhouse. Then we got word about the Pentagon. At that point, we had to spring into action, realizing this tragedy wasn't limited to New York.

Frankly, we were ill-prepared for what followed. Fortunately, our management team was together. We put together an action plan to account for all of our people, provide information, and deal with operational challenges, and then we split up. Having spoken to other people in the industry, it's clear that whether it was 9/11 or Hurricane Katrina, their first concern was the same—the safety and well-being of their people. These two events have helped shape the future responses of many in our industry.

Exhibit 10.9

LISTENING TO A TELEPHONE BOMB THREAT

While the listener will experience stress and pressure during a telephone bomb threat, local authorities will ideally want to know the following about the caller:

- Gender
- Adult or young person
- Voice (loud or soft; fast or slow; pitch; hoarse; nasal; slur)
- Did the caller stutter or appear sober?
- English language fluency
- Accent
- Composure (serious or angry)
- Background noises

BOMB SCARES

The proper response to a bomb threat may be part of an establishment's safety training program. Some important points should be included in that training:

- The employee answering the phone call should ask the caller if the manager can take the message. If the caller agrees, the employee should alert the manager. If the caller does not agree, the employee should listen carefully and try to obtain the information shown in *Exhibit 10.9*.

- As soon as the caller hangs up, the local police should be contacted. Their advice regarding a building evacuation, if any, should be followed.

- Any bomb search should be done by qualified local authorities. No staff, including managers, should be involved except at the request of the authorities.

OTHER EMERGENCIES

Managers may be confronted with other types of emergencies:

- **Severe winds:** Hurricanes and tornadoes can affect many areas. Weather service professionals can often provide warnings and information about watches, which are alerts that severe weather may occur within a specified general area. Evacuation plans should be predetermined and, when necessary, followed. If there is no time for evacuation, everyone should seek protection next to the inside wall of the building but away from windows or, preferably, in a basement or cellar. After the storm has passed, managers should check the exterior and grounds for safety hazards.

- **Floods:** Many operations are located in areas where flooding from melting snow, heavy rains, water surges (water pushed ahead of high winds), or other causes can occur. These emergencies often occur with little warning. While there will not likely be employees or customers in buildings after flood alerts have been sounded, fire is a serious threat from live electrical circuits and electrical equipment exposed to water. Debris can create structural problems that must be addressed before the building can be reoccupied, and certificates of occupancy will likely be required.

- **Earthquakes:** Earthquakes cannot be predicted, and there is little that can be done to protect a building structurally after it is constructed. If an earthquake occurs, the best advice is to drop to the ground, take cover by getting under a sturdy table or other piece of furniture, and hold on until the shaking stops. If there is no nearby protection, cover your face and head with your arms and crouch in an inside corner of the building. Stay away from glass, windows, outside doors and walls, and anything that could fall, such as lighting fixtures or furniture. Do not get in a doorway unless it is a strongly supported, load-bearing doorway and is close to you. Stay inside until the shaking stops and it is safe to go outside. Do not exit a building during the shaking. Do not use the elevators. Be aware that the electricity may go out or the sprinkler systems or fire alarms may turn on. Building inspections by qualified professionals will likely be required before buildings can be reoccupied after an earthquake.

BALANCING FOOD SAFETY, EMPLOYEE RIGHTS, AND THE LAW

When an employee appears to be sick or discloses an illness or disability, managers must balance the rights of the employee, the responsibilities to provide safe food and comply with applicable laws, and the rights of the operation to protect its own interests. Depending on the illness, symptoms, or employee disclosure, the FDA Food Code or local health codes might apply, or the ADA could apply. In rare cases where an illness covered by a health code develops into a disability, both could apply. Therefore, managers must know their responsibilities under these regulations and their company's policies for handling these situations.

Guidelines

Although managers may be restricted from asking certain questions in certain situations, it is still legal and appropriate to express concern when an employee first indicates that he or she is ill or has a disability. *Exhibit 10.10* on the next page provides guidelines for responding to various situations.

Communicable Diseases

In recent years, the public has expressed concern over communicable diseases such as human immunodeficiency virus (HIV), acquired immune deficiency syndrome (AIDS), hepatitis B and C, and tuberculosis. These diseases can be spread through intimate contact, bodily fluids, or exposure to blood and blood products. When an employee is ill or disabled because of such a disease, it can be especially challenging to balance the rights, responsibilities, and

OPEN FOR BUSINESS

KEEPING IT SAFE

Electricity can be lost in the aftermath of numerous emergency situations, and this can create a significant potential food safety problem for products held in refrigerated and frozen storage. What should managers do?

If the electricity is off for only a few hours, refrigerated and frozen foods should remain safe, especially if doors to the units are not opened during the outage. As time passes, however, there is increased potential for food contamination. Even though the inventory value can approach thousands of dollars, or more, it is always advisable to discard food when there is the slightest concern about its safety. Doing so is much preferred to taking a chance that products have remained safe for consumption. Professional managers always have a highest priority concern for the safety of their customers and employees.

Exhibit 10.10

GUIDELINES FOR RESPONDING TO AN EMPLOYEE ILLNESS OR DISABILITY

Situation	Response	Applicable Law
Employee appears to be sick but has not said anything about his or her health.	• Do *not* ask about symptoms that are not related to safe food-handling (see below) or specific diseases.	ADA
Food handler has a sore throat with fever.	• If your operation primarily serves a high-risk population (people susceptible to illness because of age or a medical condition), exclude the employee from the establishment. • If your operation does not primarily serve a high-risk population, restrict the employee from working with or around food.	FDA Food Code
Food handler has one or more of the following symptoms: • Vomiting • Diarrhea • Jaundice	• Exclude the employee from the establishment. • For vomiting and diarrhea, do not allow the person to return to work until he or she has been symptom-free for 24 hours or has obtained a written release from a medical practitioner.	FDA Food Code
Food handler has been diagnosed with a foodborne illness caused by one of these pathogens: • *Salmonella* typhi • *Shigella* spp. • Enterohemorrhagic and shiga toxin–producing *E. coli* • Hepatitis A virus • Norovirus	• Exclude the employee from the establishment and notify the local regulatory agency. • Work with the food handler's medical practitioner and local regulatory agency to determine when the employee can safely return to work.	FDA Food Code
Employee discloses that he or she has a disability (as defined by the ADA).	• Keep this information confidential only disclosing it to those with a business need to know. • Do ask questions about work restrictions to determine what, if any, accommodations are needed. • Do *not* ask for a diagnosis or condition. • Document any accommodations made, any accommodations denied and why, or that there were none requested at all.	ADA
Employee (or job applicant) requests reasonable accommodation under the ADA.	• Document the request, the process used to consider it, and your operation's response and reasoning. • Keep this information confidential only disclosing it to those with a business need to know.	ADA

This chart is a guide only. Work with your local regulatory authority to determine the best course of action.

needs of everyone involved. If an employee has a communicable disease, follow applicable policies and procedures and keep certain points in mind:

- Always maintain the confidentiality of employees who disclose health information, even if an employee reports a foodborne illness. Managers can notify other employees that they have been exposed to the illness and may need to be tested. Additionally, the incident should be reported to the local health department.

- HIV, AIDS, hepatitis B and C, and tuberculosis are considered disabilities under the ADA. Consequently, it may be necessary to provide reasonable accommodation and comply with other aspects of this law. The establishment does have a right to obtain medical information relating to the employee's capability.

- HIV, AIDS, hepatitis B and C, and tuberculosis cannot be spread through food or casual contact. Therefore, an employee should not be removed from a food handling position on this basis alone. Normal precautions for safe foodhandling, sanitation, and first aid should protect employees, customers, and other visitors from the possible transmission of these diseases.

EMPLOYEE ASSISTANCE AND WELLNESS PROGRAMS

Employee assistance and employee wellness programs are two examples of organized efforts that employers can make to help provide a safe and healthy workplace. Relatively few operations currently offer formal programs, but that number may increase. Also, there are some aspects of the programs that can be implemented informally.

Employee Assistance Programs

Employee assistance programs (EAPs) are worksite-based programs or resources that can benefit employers and employees. EAPs address productivity issues by helping employees identify and resolve personal concerns. By prevention, identification, and resolution of these issues, EAPs enhance employee effectiveness. They are an important tool for maintaining and improving worker health and productivity, retaining valued employees, and returning employees to work after illnesses or injuries.

Managers in operations offering an EAP may recommend it to an employee who, for example, cannot control anger, has a substance abuse problem, or is having a tough time dealing with some personal issues. Alternatively, if an employee decides to seek help, he or she can simply contact an EAP representative and make an appointment. If an employee must change his or her behavior as a condition of employment, EAP staff typically confirms that the employee attended meetings.

Manager's Memo

EAP services to individuals include mental health-, drug-, and alcohol-related services and referrals, and others related to personal issues such as divorce and parenting. Services may also relate to work and life supports including caring for elderly parents and financial planning. Wellness and health promotion services including smoking cessation and weight reduction, and work-related supports like career counseling may also be provided.

EAP services may address handling mental health, stress, and addictions in the workplace; addressing workplace violence; and safety and emergency preparedness. EAPs also assist businesses by communicating with employees about difficult situations such as mergers, layoffs, or deaths in the workplace. Other programs may relate to absence management and meeting needs of specific workers, such as returning veterans. Many employers actively integrate resources for physical and mental health and expand EAP services to include disease management and preventive health.

However, since information shared within an EAP is confidential, the employee can choose whether to share attendance information. In any case, recommendations to the employee are not shared with the employer.

Employee Wellness Programs

The goal of an **employee wellness program** involves improving employee health and productivity and reducing medical expenses for the employer and employee. These programs have evolved from an emphasis on fitness to health promotion to comprehensive wellness programs. They may address nutrition, mental health, chronic disease prevention, workplace environment, and other concerns.

An effective planning process is required to implement a well-received program. Activities include selecting a planning committee, identifying goals and objectives, assessing needs of employees and the establishment, and selecting program and activity providers.

PLANNING WELLNESS PROGRAMS

Representatives from all levels and functional areas of the establishment should be represented on the planning committee for wellness programs, and someone with human resources or employee benefits responsibilities is especially important. This committee will likely address numerous tasks that include conducting a needs assessment with several objectives:

- To identify employees' interests and needs
- To learn about common health problems in the workplace
- To discover how the workplace environment supports or hinders a healthy lifestyle
- To consider the goals to be attained by the program

One tool that can be used for a needs assessment is an employee survey. It can enable committee members to learn employees' ideas about what should be included in the program. It can also reveal managers' ideas about health-related issues important for company strategies, such as policy changes or medical cost containment.

Here are some suggestions for a well-designed survey:

- Ask a representative group of employees to review the survey before it is distributed to ensure the questions will be understood and are appropriate.
- Include a brief cover letter signed by the manager and a statement about confidentiality and anonymity.
- Invite comments, suggestions, and recommendations, or ask open-ended questions at the end of the survey.
- Request demographic information at the beginning or end, such as gender, shift, and age, to help analyze the responses.

It will also be helpful to evaluate the policies and physical environment of the workplace to learn its impact on employee wellness. Among the factors that can be evaluated are the availability of nutritious foods in employee meals and access to smoke-free areas.

Once employee needs and interests are identified, the wellness committee can identify the program's goals. This will help in selecting the program's activities and the framework for evaluating the program. Goals are broad-based statements about what the program is expected to do, and they will relate to improving the health of employees and the financial health of the company.

Some goals may relate to measures of implementation, such as the number of employees who have participated and the number of promotional activities. Outcome objectives measure what is accomplished, such as the number of participants who quit smoking or lower their cholesterol level.

IMPLEMENTING WELLNESS PROGRAMS

Large-volume employers often use the services of their health insurance provider or another agency to implement a wellness program, or they may hire a staff person to serve as a coordinator. Small-volume organizations typically contract with an outside provider. There are several issues that should be considered when determining how to manage an employee wellness program:

- Do those being considered have the range of health backgrounds and the experience needed for the program to be implemented?
- Will the staff include people from the racial and ethnic backgrounds of the employees and can they effectively communicate with them?
- Do the potential program staff have a professional counseling style when interacting with employees?

The program vendor selected should have acceptable policy statements related to issues such as health data confidentiality and referral of at-risk participants. Other policies should address follow-up with referred participants and those at risk, program evaluation on process and outcomes, and organization of the worksite for wellness promotion.

Decisions are needed about the types of programs and activities and how the program will be structured. The goals determined should be helpful in answering these concerns, as should the resources available to implement the program.

Many employee wellness programs offer health risk screening programs to help participants make the best use of the activities offered. These programs

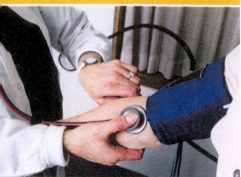

Exhibit 10.11

also typically include suggestions about activities based on screening results. There are several common types of screening programs:

- Blood pressure and blood cholesterol measurements and assessments of treatment status (*Exhibit 10.11*)
- Obesity and physical activity assessments and identification of smoking status
- Diabetes testing
- Heart disease assessments and family history of cardiovascular disease
- Stress assessment
- Referral of participants for treatment

In addition to screening programs, four types of programming are routinely offered: classes, mini-groups, guided self-help, and individual counseling. Offering a combination of these types of programs and activities is useful and allows employees to best meet their wellness needs.

Ideally, a large number of employees will participate, and planning activities will yield some excitement about the program. The program can be publicized in numerous ways including bulletin boards, pamphlets, payroll inserts, voicemail messages, and electronic billboards. A creative program name and logo can also help create a positive image.

Owners and managers who participate in the program will encourage others by their example. Activities should be easy to sign up for and be conveniently located and scheduled. It is helpful to routinely measure participants' satisfaction with content, instructors, and other program elements. A simple ongoing evaluation system such as use of comment cards can determine participant likes and dislikes and generate suggestions for program improvement.

THINK ABOUT IT . . .

If your employer offered a wellness program as a no-cost employee benefit, would you participate? Why or why not?

EVALUATING WELLNESS PROGRAMS

The evaluation of an employee wellness program is important to learn whether and how it is helping employees and to discover any changes that can improve it. As explained earlier, the evaluation should consider both process and outcome measures.

Process measures can answer questions about the basic operation of the program:

- Were activities implemented as planned? If not, why not?
- Who are frequent program users?
- Which activities are most popular?
- Does the program meet participants' needs?
- Are instructors and materials acceptable?

Outcome measures assess the extent to which specific program goals have been achieved. These might include measures of reduced absenteeism, fewer employees smoking, or lower medical claims costs. Outcome information that indicates success can help secure continued managerial support. If goals are not being met, changes may be needed in the program.

SUMMARY

1. **Explain what managers can do to maintain a zero-tolerance sexual harassment policy and explain responsibilities regarding nonsexual types of harassment in the workplace.**

   Managers must protect employees from sexual harassment. Quid pro quo harassment occurs when someone expects a sexual action as a condition of employment, continued employment, or advancement. Hostile environment harassment occurs when the work atmosphere is sexually demeaning or intimidating. Operations should have a zero-tolerance policy against sexual harassment. Managers should help employees understand what sexual harassment is. They should also encourage open communication, set a good example, and address signs of harassment. An alleged victim should report the complaint initially to his or her direct supervisor unless that person is the subject of the complaint. All claims should be thoroughly investigated in accordance with any laws and company policy. Employees should not discuss the situation with others and, if possible, the manager should change the work schedule so the parties do not work together. A third person should always witness discussions between the manager and the accused employee.

   Nonsexual harassment involves unwelcomed conduct based on race, color, religion, pregnancy, national origin, age, disability, or genetic information. An employer will be liable for harassment by a supervisor unless he or she can prove that reasonable effort was made to prevent and promptly correct the behavior or the employee unreasonably failed to take advantage of preventive or corrective opportunities provided.

2. **Review the procedures for ensuring the rights of employees who are pregnant or disabled, and younger workers.**

   The Pregnancy Discrimination Act prohibits employers from discriminating against women on the basis of pregnancy, childbirth, or related conditions. Managers must treat an employee who is temporarily unable to perform her job due to pregnancy the same as any other employee with a temporary disability. The employee may be eligible for time off under the Family and Medical Leave Act.

   The Americans with Disabilities Act forbids discrimination against anyone in the workplace because of a disability. Employees are considered disabled if they have a physical or mental impairment that limits one or more major life activities, if they have a record of impairment, or if they may be regarded as having an impairment.

   Minors younger than 18 are more likely than older workers to be injured on the job. There are specific requirements about work tasks that can be performed by 16- and 17-year-old workers, and requirements are even stricter for employees who are 14 and 15.

3. **Indicate how the Occupational Safety and Health Administration (OSHA) impacts restaurant and foodservice operations, and explain procedures for establishing and maintaining OSHA-mandated programs and participating in OSHA investigations.**

OSHA's role is to ensure safe working conditions and prevent injuries. The bloodborne pathogens standard states what employers must do to protect workers who come in contact with potentially infectious materials. It requires an exposure plan, training, and the use of personal protective equipment. OSHA's hazard communication standard protects employees from physical hazards and health hazards from exposure to chemicals. Employers must communicate information found on material safety data sheets (MSDSs). Managers must maintain records based on detailed guidelines to remain in compliance. The first step is to determine the manager who will be the HAZCOM coordinator. Then a written plan must be developed to implement the OSHA regulations. A list of chemicals used should be identified, and a decision should be made about whether the MSDS program will be managed in-house or outsourced. Employees should be trained about the safe use of chemicals, and MSDSs should be kept current for the chemicals used.

Managers must participate in investigations by OSHA compliance officers. Doing so involves document review and knowledge of what should and should not be done during the investigation. The manager should check the OSHA compliance officer's identification, provide meeting space and requested documents, and offer access to employees for interviews. He or she should also retain copies of all information provided and cooperate with any follow-up visits.

4. **Identify the compliance posters that operations are required to post.**

Managers should determine which posters are required. Some operations retain a service to determine and update posters as necessary. The required posters are available from the applicable government agency. Alternatively, private organizations print combination posters that include all necessary information in a single poster. Posters should be posted in accordance with legal requirements in common areas such as on bulletin boards and in break rooms.

5. **Describe the procedures for preventing workplace violence.**

Managers should establish a zero-tolerance policy toward violence or threats. This policy should be known by all employees, and claims should be investigated and remedied promptly. Managers should learn how to recognize, avoid, and defuse potentially violent situations. They can do so by attending personal safety training programs, encouraging employees to report all incidents, and offering debriefing sessions including counseling for a violent incident.

6. **Describe the procedures for developing emergency management programs.**

Managers and teams must plan and prepare for emergencies. A written plan is preferred and elements should include procedures for reporting, for evacuation, and for employees who remain to complete critical operations before they evacuate. Employers must maintain an employee alarm system, designate and train employees to assist in evacuation, and review emergency action plans. Common emergencies include fires, bomb scares, severe winds, floods, and earthquakes. Employees should be trained about the procedures for each to help protect themselves and customers.

7. **Explain the basic procedures for balancing food safety, employee rights, and the law.**

   It is legal and appropriate to express concern when an employee indicates he or she is ill or has a disability. Managers should develop policies that can be applied consistently to all staff members. They should maintain the confidentiality of employees who disclose health information. They should also understand and apply requirements of the Americans with Disabilities Act (ADA) when making decisions about HIV, AIDS, hepatitis B and C, and tuberculosis.

8. **Provide an overview of employee assistance and employee wellness programs.**

   Employee assistance programs may be recommended to an employee if problems with anger, drugs, drinking, or something else impacts their job performance. Employees in operations with organized programs can seek help through an employee assistance program (EAP). Managers in other operations can refer employees to an external counseling service.

   Employee wellness programs are designed to improve employee health and productivity and reduce medical expenses. These programs may address nutrition, mental health, chronic disease prevention, workplace environment, and other concerns.

   An employee committee can conduct a needs assessment to identify interest and needs, learn about common health problems, discover how the workplace environment affects healthy lifestyles, and consider program goals. Large employers often use their health insurance provider or another agency, or they may hire a staff coordinator. Small organizations typically contract with an outside provider. Wellness programs should be evaluated to learn how they can be improved and whether goals have been achieved.

APPLICATION EXERCISE

You are a new manager and have discovered that your establishment has no formal policy or procedures for common emergencies. You have scheduled a meeting with your department heads to explain why emergencies need to be considered before they happen. You also want to have each department head develop a draft of procedures for certain emergencies. To help them, develop a list of approximately 10 concerns that should be included in the procedures for each emergency.

Select three of the following types of emergencies to learn more about. Enter the terms in a search engine to iden-

tify Web sites that address each type of emergency. If you prefer, you may select one or more emergency types not listed. Then develop a list of sample emergency procedures that you will give to each department head to help them get started.

- Fire safety management plans
- Robbery prevention
- Bomb threats in the workplace
- Tornado safety in the workplace
- Earthquake safety

REVIEW YOUR LEARNING

Select the best answer for each question.

1. **What is an example of hostile environment sexual harassment?**
   A. A male employee opening a door for a female employee
   B. Use of gender-specific terms such as *waiter* and *waitress*
   C. Pornography being circulated around the workplace
   D. A male employee smiling while talking to a female

2. **What is the minimum age addressed by federal laws relating to harassment on the basis of age?**
   A. 35
   B. 40
   C. 45
   D. 50

3. **What element is required for conduct to be offensive?**
   A. The harassment must affect an employee's work.
   B. The harasser must be in a supervisory position.
   C. The victim must be the person harassed.
   D. The victim must have lost his or her job.

4. **What can prevent an operation from being liable for harassment by a supervisor?**
   A. The employee ignored harassment by another employee.
   B. The operation has never had a previous harassment complaint.
   C. The operation has trained all employees about harassment policies.
   D. The employee failed to act on opportunities to correct the harassment.

5. **What is an example of a condition judged to limit one or more major life activities under the Americans with Disabilities Act?**
   A. Broken arm
   B. Injured ankle
   C. Visual impairment
   D. Foodborne illness

6. **What is the minimum age for an employee to drive unrestricted while working?**
   A. 16 years old
   B. 17 years old
   C. 18 years old
   D. 21 years old

7. **What is required to implement OSHA HAZCOM requirements?**
   A. Label hazardous kitchen equipment.
   B. Ensure that MSDSs for chemicals are current.
   C. Document procedures for minimizing blood exposure.
   D. Provide a meeting place for the OSHA compliance officer.

8. **A manager must contact OSHA when**
   A. potentially dangerous equipment such as a meat slicer is purchased.
   B. the manager doesn't know where to obtain an MSDS.
   C. the manager wants to start providing an EAP.
   D. there is a serious employee injury.

9. **What is the minimum number of employees above which OSHA requires written emergency plans?**
   A. 5
   B. 10
   C. 15
   D. 20

10. **Where may a manager obtain compliance posters?**
   A. From the applicable government agency
   B. From the local chamber of commerce
   C. From the local restaurant association
   D. From applicable employee unions

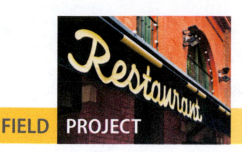

FIELD PROJECT   INFORMATION HANDBOOK

Instructions:

About Your Interviews:

As you will recall from the Field Project found at the end of Chapter 2, the completion of the field project exercises in chapters 2, 3, 5, 7, and 9 of this book will enable you and a team of your colleagues to develop a handbook of human resources management and supervision information.

Throughout this course you and your team have developed lists of questions for your interviews with the managers of two foodservice operations.

Your team may have inserted the questions to be asked on the template for the Interview Questions and Response Sheet on the following page. If not, this should be done (or design your own sheet) before the interviews are conducted.

Blank copies of the sheet should be taken to each of the interviews and can be used to ask each question and record each response.

When the interviews are completed, you and your team can summarize responses to each question and record them in Part I of the Field Project Information Handbook. For example, recruitment and selection suggestions provided by the manager for the first operation visited can be recorded in Part I (Field Interview Suggestions) for operation #1. Responses for the manager of the second operation can be placed in the next box for operation #2.

Hopefully, the team has recorded information learned for Part II (Internet Resources) as the course evolved. If not, the team's internet search results should be recorded in Part II for each of the Chapters.

Part III of the Handbook allows team members to record other suggestions about each chapter's topic. To complete Part III, review the information in Part I (from interviews) and Part II (from Internet searches). Then review the applicable text chapter to identify other suggestions that were not identified in the interviews or Internet searches to round out the lists of suggestions for each topic.

HUMAN RESOURCES MANAGEMENT AND SUPERVISION
Interview Questions and Response Sheet (Template)

Instructions: Please complete a separate Interview Questions and Response Sheet for each of the two restaurant or foodservice operations your team visits.

Date: _____   Team members attending interview: _____

Name of restaurant or foodservice operation: Name of restaurant or foodservice manager:

_____   _____

Part I: Recruiting and Selecting (Chapter 2) *Questions*	*Responses*
Part II: Orientation and Training (Chapter 3) *Questions*	*Responses*
Part III: Managing Change and Conducting Performance Reviews (Chapter 5) *Questions*	*Responses*
Part IV: Professional Development Strategies (Chapter 7) *Questions*	*Responses*
Part V: Employee Benefits (Chapter 9) *Questions*	*Responses*

Topic: Recruiting the Best Employees (Chapter 2)

Part I: Field Interview Suggestions

Operation #1: _____
                        (Name)

Recruitment:	Selection:

Operation #2: _____
                        (Name)

Recruitment:	Selection:

Part II: Internet Resources

Recruitment:	Selection:

Part III: Textbook (Chapter 2) Additional Suggestions

Recruitment:	Selection:

Topic: Employee Orientation and Training (Chapter 3)

Part I: Field Interview Suggestions

Operation #1: _____
  (Name)

Orientation:	Training:

Operation #2: _____
  (Name)

Orientation:	Training:

Part II: Internet Resources

Orientation:	Training:

Part III: Textbook (Chapter 3) Additional Suggestions

Orientation:	Training:

Topic: Facilitating Employees' Work Performance (Chapter 5)

PART I: Field Interview Suggestions

Operation #1: _____
(Name)

Managing Change:	Performance Reviews:

Operation #2: _____
(Name)

Managing Change:	Performance Reviews:

PART II: Internet Resources

Orientation:	Training:

PART III: Textbook (Chapter 5) Additional Suggestions

Orientation:	Training:

Topic: Employee Professional Development Programs (Chapter 7)

PART I: Field Interview Suggestions

Operation #1: _____
(Name)

Professional Development:

Operation #2: _____
(Name)

Professional Development:

PART II: Internet Resources

Professional Development:

PART III: Textbook (Chapter 7) Additional Suggestions

Professional Development:

Topic: Employee Benefits (Chapter 9)

PART I: Field Interview Suggestions

Operation #1: _____
                         (Name)

Employee Benefits:

Operation #2: _____
                         (Name)

Employee Benefits:

PART II: Internet Resources

Employee Benefits:

PART III: Textbook (Chapter 9) Additional Suggestions

Employee Benefits:

GLOSSARY

Affirmative action plan (AAP) A plan that establishes guidelines for recruiting, hiring, and promoting women, qualified minorities, persons with disabilities, and covered veterans to eliminate the present effects of past employment discrimination.

Americans with Disabilities Act (ADA) A law that protects qualified individuals with disabilities from discrimination in the job application and hiring process as well as other terms, conditions, and privileges of employment.

Arbitration A process in which a neutral third party listens and reviews facts and makes a decision to settle a conflict.

Arbitrator An impartial person who hears each party's side of a case, weighs the evidence, applies the law, and makes a decision that is usually binding.

Authority The power to direct the work of employees.

Autocratic (leadership style) A leadership style in which the manager generally makes decisions and resolves problems without input from employees.

Background check Verification of information provided by a job applicant, in order to learn more about the applicant's character and possibly uncover information the applicant has withheld.

Bargain in good faith A duty to approach negotiations with a sincere resolve to reach a collective-bargaining agreement.

Benchmark Any activity that helps identify and analyze best practices to discover ways to improve performance.

Beneficiary Someone who is entitled to receive a benefit under an insurance or retirement plan because of his or her relationship with the plan's participant.

Benefits Compensation other than wages or salary, which may include meals, uniforms, educational assistance, health care, vacation, and sick leave.

Bloodborne pathogens standard A requirement of what employers must do to protect workers who can reasonably be anticipated to come into contact with blood or other potentially infectious materials (OPIM) as a result of doing their jobs.

Bona fide occupational qualification (BFOQ) An employment practice that would normally constitute discrimination toward certain individuals but is permissible because it is related to an essential job function and reasonably necessary for the normal operation of a business.

Bureaucratic (leadership style) A leadership style that relies on rules, regulations, policies, and procedures.

Cardiopulmonary resuscitation (CPR) A technique that involves breathing into the mouth and pressing on the chest to help a person who has stopped breathing, and whose heart may have stopped beating, to stay alive.

Career ladder A plan that explains how job advancement may occur.

Certification The process through which an organization grants recognition to an individual who meets certain established criteria.

Chamber of commerce A voluntary group of business leaders and others who promote businesses within a community.

Change agent A person who leads change in an organization.

Code of ethics A formal statement developed by an operation that explains how its employees should relate to each other and to the persons and groups with whom they interact.

Collective bargaining The negotiation of the terms of a contract between representatives of a union and management.

Communication log Documents used by managers to record information about what has happened during a shift, to be shared with the managers of future shifts.

Compensation All of the financial and nonfinancial rewards given to employees for their work.

Competitive advantage A strategy, tactic, or process that is not offered by a competitor of an establishment.

Conflict resolution A process that encourages finding solutions to problems before more formal grievance procedures are needed.

Consolidated Omnibus Budget Reconciliation Act (COBRA) A law that extends healthcare coverage for a limited time at group rates for people who would otherwise lose their insurance.

Continuous quality improvement (CQI) A management philosophy that emphasizes that most work processes can be improved.

Controlling Keeping an establishment on track to achieve goals.

Corporate culture The shared beliefs, experiences, and standards that characterize a company.

Cover letter A letter used to express interest in a position and offer to provide additional information about the job applicant.

Crew schedule A chart that informs employees who receive wages about the days and hours they are expected to work during a specific time period, usually a week.

Cross-functional team A special type of problem-solving team, composed of members representing different departments who work together.

Cross-training Training in which an employee learns how to do work normally done by someone in a different position.

Deductible The amount of money an insured party must pay before the insurance company's coverage plan begins.

Defined benefit (DB; retirement) A retirement benefit in which an employee is guaranteed certain payments on retirement.

Defined contribution (DC; retirement) A retirement program that guarantees certain payments will be made into an account owned by an employee, such as a 401(k) plan.

Delegation A process of working with and through others to complete a task or project; it shares authority and entrusts employees to accomplish the tasks assigned to them.

Democratic (leadership style) A leadership approach that encourages employees to participate in the decision-making process.

Designated first-aid provider An employee who is trained and appointed to provide first aid but whose main work does not already include this responsibility.

Developmental goal A description of the knowledge and skills that need to be gained or improved on to eliminate or reduce an employee's knowledge and skills gap.

Discrimination The act of treating persons unequally for reasons that do not relate to their abilities, including race, color, religion, gender, national origin, age, and mental or physical abilities.

Diversity The concept that people are unique with individual differences and variations in race, ethnicity, gender, socioeconomic status, age, and physical abilities, among others.

Dram shop laws Regulations that hold a server and an establishment responsible for the actions of those they have served, also called *third-party liability laws.*

Employee assistance program (EAP) A program that provides counseling and other services to help employees deal with a wide range of problems that hinder their ability to function effectively at work.

Employee benefit plan A program of nonwage compensation that an employee is eligible for and the situations under which the employee will receive the benefits.

Employee handbook A description of job requirements and an establishment's policies that is given to new employees.

Employee incentive program A program designed to encourage employees to meet specified goals by offering some kind of reward.

Employee recognition program A program that provides a way for establishments to publicly express appreciation for employees, or to acknowledge and celebrate them as individuals.

Employee wellness program A program that involves improving employee health and productivity and reducing medical expenses for the employer and employee.

Employer of choice A company that is a desired place of employment because employees are treated with dignity and respect.

Employment at will The idea that an employee or an employer can end the relationship at any time for any reason.

Employment contract A legally binding agreement that includes terms of employment such as termination provisions; also called an *employment agreement*.

Employment letter A document that conveys the job details and starting information to the potential employee.

Enrollment The signing up of an employee for a benefit plan.

Entry-level employee An employee who works in a position that requires little experience and has no supervisory duties.

Environmental noise Any sound, such as loud talking or blaring radios, that interferes with communication.

Equal Employment Opportunity Commission (EEOC) The federal agency that enforces employment discrimination laws related to age, sex, race, national origin, disability, creed, and religion.

Essential function A key duty that an individual must be able to perform with or without reasonable accommodation.

Esteem needs Needs that focus on how people feel about themselves and how they think others feel about them.

Ethics The rules or principles that help define what is right and what is wrong.

Evaluating Assessing the extent to which plans are attained, and identifying issues or problems.

Exclusion period The exclusion of coverage for preexisting conditions for a certain time after enrollment in an insurance plan; it is allowable as long as it is applied equally to all plan participants.

Executive order (EO) A proclamation issued by the president of the United States, with implementing regulations issued by federal agencies such as the U.S. Department of Labor.

Exempt employee An employee who is not required to receive extra pay for overtime.

Exit interview A meeting between an employee who is leaving and a manager or someone from the operation's human resources department.

Fair Labor Standards Act (FLSA) A federal law that establishes minimum wage, overtime pay, and record-keeping standards for full- and part-time workers.

Family and Medical Leave Act (FMLA) A federal law that allows eligible employees to take off an extended amount of time for medical and other personal reasons; FMLA applies to businesses employing 50 or more persons.

Fast-track employee An employee who meets work requirements in his or her present position and participates in a professional development program that allows the employee to advance quickly in the operation.

Floater An employee who can perform all tasks in more than one position.

Foodborne illness A disease that is carried or transmitted to people by food.

Food Code The federal government's recommendations for foodservice regulations to prevent foodborne illnesses.

Food safety management system A group of programs and procedures designed to control hazards throughout the flow of food.

Form I-9 A document stating that an employee is legally able to work in the United States, to be completed before beginning work and being placed on the payroll.

Form W-4 (Employee's Withholding Allowance Certificate) A federal tax form that every employee fills out, which is used for payroll and tax withholding purposes.

Four-step training method A training method that consists of the following steps: preparation, presentation, practice, and performance.

Fringe benefit Money paid indirectly in support of employees for purposes such as vacation, holiday pay, sick leave, and health insurance.

Garnishment Payments ordered by a court that are directly deducted from an employee's earnings.

Grapevine An informal channel of communication that relies on word of mouth to transmit information.

Grievance A complaint filed against an employer for breaking the terms of a labor contract.

Group plan (benefits) A plan that provides essentially the same benefit to multiple people, such as a life insurance plan offered to all employees.

Group training A method used to teach the same job-related information to more than one trainee at the same time.

Harassment Unwanted and annoying actions by one or more persons, including threats or demands.

Hazard Analysis Critical Control Point (HACCP) A system that focuses on identifying specific points within the flow of food that are essential for preventing, eliminating, or reducing a biological, chemical, or physical hazard to safe levels.

Hazard Communication Standard (HCS) A standard designed to protect employees from physical hazards such as explosions and health hazards such as medical conditions caused by exposure to chemicals, also known as *Right-to-Know* or *HAZCOM*.

Health code Local laws designed to ensure food safety.

Hiring Tasks relating to employment and benefits documents.

Hostile work environment An atmosphere characterized by unwanted sexually demeaning or intimidating behaviors in which a person is treated poorly or feels uncomfortable.

Income statement A summary of an operation's profitability that shows revenues generated, expenses incurred, and profits or losses realized during a specific accounting period.

Individual plan (benefits) A plan that provides a benefit for one person or family.

Insubordination The failure to follow reasonable instructions.

Integrative practice A training strategy in which a trainee combines and demonstrates several steps in a job task that has already been learned.

Intoxicated Having a blood alcohol concentration (BAC) above the limit specified by the state in which the alcoholic beverage is sold or served.

Involuntary termination A situation in which managers terminate an employee for one or more of these four reasons: lack of work for the employee, lack of

funding, unsatisfactory performance, or violation of a company policy.

Jargon Technical language specific to an occupation or field of study.

Job description A description of the tasks a person in a position must be able to perform.

Job offer A formal invitation to become an employee of an establishment on a certain date to perform a described range of duties for a specific salary or wage, including identified benefits.

Job specification A listing of the personal requirements such as skills and abilities needed to successfully perform tasks in a position.

Knowledge or skill gap A difference between the knowledge or skills a manager or employee already has and those that are needed to do the job.

Labor contract The terms of employment that a union negotiates for its members with an employer, also known as an *employment agreement.*

Labor cost The money and benefit expenses paid to employees for their work.

Labor union An organization designated by employees to negotiate their employment terms such as wages, benefits, discipline, and job security.

Laissez-faire (leadership style) A leadership style in which the manager does not direct work but instead delegates most decisions.

Lawsuit A claim or dispute brought in a court of law for adjudication.

Levy Payments taken by a government agency such as the IRS from an employee's earnings.

Maslow's hierarchy of needs A theory that people have five basic needs that typically arise in a certain order; when one need is fulfilled to the extent desired by the person, he or she is motivated to fulfill the next need.

Material safety data sheet (MSDS) A document that provides information about the chemical content of a material, instructions for its safe use and handling, and other safety-related matters.

Mediation A process in which a neutral third party facilitates a discussion of difficult issues and makes suggestions about an agreement.

Mediator An independent third party who helps those involved in a dispute talk to each other and allows them to resolve the dispute.

Medicare A federally insured healthcare plan for people aged 65 or older.

Mentoring A process in which an experienced employee provides advice to less-experienced employees about concerns relating to the job, establishment, and profession.

Morale The feelings that employees have about their employer, their workplace, and other aspects of the operation.

Multiple-choice question A question with a set number of answer choices.

Negligent hiring The failure to ensure, through background checks, that the applicant is a safe and competent person for the position.

Negotiation A discussion between involved persons with the goal of reaching an acceptable agreement.

Networking The practice of building and maintaining ongoing communication with individuals who can provide potential assistance.

New hire checklist A checklist that is useful for ensuring that all hiring documents are produced or completed.

New hire packet A kit that contains copies of documents that are needed and will be discussed during orientation sessions.

Nonexempt employee An employee paid an hourly wage who is entitled to overtime pay when working more than 40 hours in a week.

Nonverbal communication A speaker's expressions and movements that tell additional information about the message.

Occupational Safety and Health Administration (OSHA) A federal agency with the mission to help businesses protect their workers by reducing deaths, injuries, and illnesses in the workplace.

Off-the-shelf Ready-made training materials that have been developed by associations and other external organizations.

On-the-job training (OJT) A one-on-one approach to training conducted at the work site.

Open-ended question A question that encourages a response that exhibits a person's knowledge or feelings.

Open enrollment period (benefits) A limited time period during which employees are typically able to change benefit plans and coverage and add or remove family members.

Orientation Tasks related to introducing the new employee to the establishment and the job.

Orientation buddy A person who serves as an adviser during orientation.

Orientation checklist A list of the activities to be addressed during orientation, used to ensure that each new employee has the same orientation experience and a chance to learn about the same topics.

Orientation program A formal plan for welcoming new employees and teaching them general information that all staff members must know.

Participant Someone who is a member of a benefit plan.

Participative management A leadership method that increases the quality of decision making by involving employees.

Payroll administrator The person, department, or external company that ensures paychecks are issued.

Performance standard A specification of the required *quality* and *quantity* outputs that define the correct way to perform a task.

Personnel file A confidential file that contains documents related to hiring, training, evaluating, promoting, and, if necessary, disciplining an individual.

Physiological needs The most basic physical needs, such as food, water, air, and sleep.

Plan administrator (benefits) A designated person, department, or company that is responsible for handling administrative tasks for group plans.

Position analysis The process used to identify each task an employee must do and to explain how it should be done.

Preexisting condition A medical condition for which a person has sought medical treatment before applying to join a healthcare plan.

Prejudice A general attitude toward a person, group, or organization based on judgments unrelated to abilities or reality, also called *bias*.

Premium (healthcare) The monthly insurance fee; in most cases both employers and employees share its cost.

Pre-shift meeting A short employee meeting held before the work shift begins to discuss plans and details and sometimes present brief training information.

Probation A specific time period during which an employee must consistently meet job standards or other reasonable conditions imposed by the manager as a condition for continued employment.

Probationary period The time used by the manager to assess whether a new employee can successfully perform the job's tasks.

Professional development Any experience, training, and education provided to help employees do their current jobs better and prepare them for other positions.

Pro forma budget An estimate of revenues, expenses, and profit developed before a business opens.

Progressive discipline A series of corrective actions that become more serious as unacceptable performance continues.

Protected class A group that lawmakers specifically protect from discrimination.

Quality The consistent production and delivery of products and services according to expected standards.

Quid pro quo Harassment that occurs when one person asks for, either expressly or implied, sexual favors from another person as a condition of that person's employment or advancement or to prevent a tangible employment detriment.

Reasonable accommodation Adjustments or modifications to facilities, job duties, equipment, policies, or practices provided by the employer to enable people with disabilities to perform the essential functions of the job.

Reasonable-care defense A defense showing proof that an establishment did everything that could be reasonably expected to ensure the food served was safe.

Recruiting A series of activities designed to influence the largest number of qualified persons to apply for a job.

Resume A written overview of an applicant's background, including education and work experience.

Role model A person who performs in a way that meets the standards expected for employees' behavior.

Safety needs The needs for people to feel safe and secure, such as having a safe work environment.

Salary A fixed amount of money for a certain time period that does not vary based on the number of hours worked.

Scheduling A process that determines which employees will be needed to serve the expected number of customers during specific times.

Screening The process of reviewing the skills, experience, attitudes, and backgrounds of applicants to make a selection.

Self-actualization The drive to do the very best that one can do.

Self-insured A situation in which some very large employers pay all covered healthcare costs with their own funds.

Separation checklist A list of activities to be completed for employees who are leaving the organization.

Sexual harassment Unwelcome sexual advances, sexual favor requests, and other verbal or physical conduct that is sexual in nature and may create an offensive, intimidating, or hostile work environment.

Social needs The needs of people to interact with others.

Social Security A federal government program that provides retirement and disability income and other financial benefits to those who qualify.

Span of control The number of employees that can be supervised by one person.

Staffing The process of finding the right people for the job.

Stakeholder Someone who can impact or be affected by the actions of the work team.

Standard A requirement of the level of quality, speed, food safety, or hospitality that employees should demonstrate.

Standard operating procedures (SOPs) Work procedures that explain what employees must know and do when they perform the work specified in their job descriptions.

Stereotype A belief about particular groups that assumes all members of that group are the same.

Strike An order to all union members at one or more locations to stop working.

Structured interview An interview in which the manager asks a set of specific questions.

Subcontractor A business or person who does work for a company (the contractor) as part of a larger project.

Subminimum wage A wage below the minimum wage that employers may pay certain people, such as students placed in a job as part of a vocational or other educational program.

Succession planning A process used by many organizations to ensure that employees will be recruited for and prepared to fill key positions when they become vacant.

Summary plan description (SPD) An explanation of a retirement or healthcare plan's benefits and participants' rights and responsibilities.

Supervising Planning for and facilitating the work of employees, also called *directing*.

Task breakdown An explanation of exactly how each task in a task list should be done.

Terminable act An action by an employee that typically causes immediate termination.

Third-party administrator (TPA) An insurance claims adjuster or an organization that manages insurance claims for a self-insured organization.

Tip credit (FLSA) The choice given to operations that employ tipped employees to pay the basic minimum wage or to pay a reduced cash wage and use a tip credit.

Tipped employee An employee who may be paid a lower cash wage when his or her tips are enough to ensure that the basic minimum wage is met.

Training lesson The information and methods used to present one session in a training plan.

Training objective The skills and knowledge that trainees should learn as a result of the training.

Training plan A plan that shows how individual training lessons should be sequenced so trainees can learn the required information.

Turnover The rate at which employees leave an operation and are replaced with new employees.

Undue hardship An action causing significant difficulty or expense when considered in light of factors such as an employer's size, financial resources, and the nature and structure of its operation.

Unemployment insurance A program that provides benefits to workers who are unemployed through no fault of their own as determined by state law.

Union dues Fees to help pay for the administration of the union.

Union shop An operation in which all employees are required to join a union and pay dues as a condition of employment.

Union steward An employee who is elected by his or her coworkers to represent them to their employer.

Unstructured interview An interview in which the manager conducts a conversation with the potential employee without prepared questions.

Validation The comparison of training content and evaluation methods to the actual job of an employee who can do the work.

Vision An idea about what an organization would be like if it were ideal.

Voluntary termination A situation in which an employee decides to leave the organization for personal reasons.

W-2 income tax form An information form completed by employers and sent to the federal taxing authorities, used to report wages and salaries paid to employees and taxes withheld.

Wages The money earned by employees who are paid based on the number of hours they work.

Whistleblower A person who exposes wrongdoing within an organization in the hope of stopping it.

Workers' compensation A system that states use to compensate employees when they are injured at work.

Workplace violence Violence or the threat of violence against workers.

Work team A group of employees who cooperate on the job to attain objectives and who hold themselves accountable for their success.

Wrongful discharge A legal action taken by a former employee against a previous employer, alleging that the discharge was in violation of state or federal antidiscrimination laws, public policy, or an implied contract, agreement, or written promise.

Youth minimum wage A wage that employees younger than 20 years of age may be paid, of not less than $4.25 an hour, which is lower than the basic minimum wage, during their first 90 consecutive days of employment.

Zero tolerance A policy that allows no amount or type of harassing behavior.

Zoning ordinance A legal declaration of land-use policies for a city, district, or county that indicates for what purposes specific land areas can be used.

INDEX

N

O

P

physiological needs, 103
plan administrator, with benefits, 273
planning (*see also* employee benefit plans)
  as basic management activity, 4
  employee incentive programs, 116–119
  employment interviews, 53
  orientation programs, 76–79
  with professional development strategies, 212–214
  for success, 106–107
  training program development, 86–88
planning meetings, 215–217, 231
point-of-sale (POS) systems, 118, 183
policies
  employees and absence, 188
  sexual harassment, 301
position analysis, 32, 60
position manager, 36–37
position requirements, 36–37
POS systems (*see* point-of-sale systems)
posters
  compliance, 314, 326
  federal agencies, 258, 313
  U.S. Department of Labor, 313
  USERRA, 289
power, loss of, 319
PPE (*see* personal protective equipment)
pre-employment questions, 238
preexisting condition, 282
pregnancy
  discrimination act, 237, 325
  employee rights with, 304–305
prejudices, 18–19
premiums, with healthcare, 277
pre-shift checklists, 199
pre-shift meeting, 108
probationary period, 78, 151–152
problem-solving teams, 112
production goals, 184
professional development
  for managers, 217–221, 231
  methods, 221–228, 231

overview, 208–209, 230
  planning meetings, 215–217, 231
  programs, 206–233
  responsibilities for, 209
  strategies, 210–215, 230
  with succession plans, 228–230, 231
professional workforce, 105
pro forma budget, 177
progressive discipline procedures, 134, 148–153, 165
promotions, sales forecasts, 181
protected classes, 237
publication information, 37–38
publications, industry, 220

Q

QSR Magazine, 220
quality
  checklists to monitor, 198–201, 203
  communication logs to monitor, 201–202, 203
  CQI, 110, 141
  definition, 11
  goals, 184
  with SOPs, 170–173
questions
  exit interview, 159
  human resources interview, 330–336
  interview, 52–55
  multiple-choice, 158
  open-ended, 115
  pre-employment inquiries and, 238
quid pro quo, 300

R

reasonable accommodations, 38
reasonable care defense, 257
recipes, standardized, 33
recognition program (*see* employee incentive programs)
recruiting
  definition, 40, 60
  for diversity, 19

with job descriptions, 34, 61
  with technology, 11
recruitment
  of employees, 6, 30–63
  job descriptions and tools for, 34–39, 60–61
  job offers with, 58–59
  with job tasks and position analysis, 32–34
  screening and selection for, 48–58
recruitment procedures
  communication with, 45–46
  discrimination with, 46–47, 238
  external, 42–45, 60
  internal, 42
  staff needs forecasted with, 40–41
reference checks, 56–58
relationships
  with managers, 209
  stages in long-term mentoring, 225
  with supervisors and employees, 102
relay teams, 111
repetitive tasks, 222
resistance, to change, 140
responsibilities
  with alcoholic beverage service, 254–257, 263
  for professional development, 209
  scheduling with individual, 185
  of unions, 261–262
restaurant and foodservice operations
  diversity in, 16–21
  ethical concerns with, 22–26
  with human resources management, 4–8
  as labor-intensive, 2–29
  managers facilitating employees' work in, 9–16, 27
Restaurant Business, 220
resume, 50, 59, 69
retention decisions, 15
retirement benefits, 278–279
retirement laws
  Employee Retirement Income Security Act, 280
  health benefits and, 279–283

Index

WARN (*see* Worker Adjustment and
Retraining Notification Act)
warnings
oral, 149–151
probation with, 151–152
written, 151
Web-based training programs, 92–93
wellness programs (*see* employee
wellness programs)
WFF (*see* Women's Foodservice
Forum)
whistleblowers, 258
winds, 318, 326
Women's Foodservice Forum (WFF),
220
Worker Adjustment and Retraining
Notification Act (WARN), 243,
286
workers' compensation, 286
with injury and illness incident
report, 247
legislation, 246–248
work experience, 58
workforce, professional, 105
work location, 46
Work Opportunity Tax Credit
(WOTC), 67
work performance
change managed with, 137–143
coaching with, 133–135, 164
communication with, 124–133
conflict managed with, 135–137
employee performance appraisals
with, 143–148, 164

employees and facilitation of,
124–167
employee termination with,
153–163, 165
progressive discipline procedures
with, 134, 148–153, 165
workplace
alcoholic beverages served
responsibly in, 254–257, 263
federal laws in, 237–245, 262, 325
hostile, 240, 301–302
lawful, 234–265
with laws and impact on
operations, 236–237, 262
operations protected from legal
action in, 257–259, 263
positive, 17
safe food provided in, 251–254,
263
with state and local employment
laws, 245–250, 263
union interaction and, 260–262,
264
workplace safety
emergency management programs
and, 316–319, 326
employee assistance programs
with, 321–322, 327
employee rights ensured with,
304–307
with food safety, employee rights
and legislation, 319–321
management of, 298–336
need for, 300

OSHA and, 241–242, 308–314
other forms of harassment with,
303–304
sexual harassment and, 21,
300–303, 325
violence prevention and, 314–315,
326
wellness program with, 322–325,
327
workplace violence, 314–315, 326
workshift standards
employee scheduling with,
174–198
meeting, 168–205
with operating standards, 170–174
with quality monitored with
checklists, 198–201, 203
with quality monitored with
communication logs, 201–202,
203
work teams, 111–112
WOTC (*see* Work Opportunity Tax
Credit)
writing process, 128–130
written warnings, 151
wrongful discharge, 155

Y

youth minimum wage, 269

Z

zero tolerance, 105, 325, 326
zoning ordinance, 249–250

354